ACTION AND INACTION IN A S(

This book explains how actions and inactions arise
contexts, including social media and face-to-face communication. Its
multidisciplinary perspective covers research from psychology, communication, public health, business studies, and environmental sciences.
The reader can use this cutting-edge approach to design and interpret
effects of behavioral change interventions as well as replicate the materials
and methods implemented to study them. The author provides an
organized set of principles that take the reader from the formation of
attitudes and goals, to the structure of action and inaction. The book also
reflects on how cognitive processes explain excesses of action while
inaction persists elsewhere. This practical guide summarizes the best
practices persuasion and behavioral interventions to promote changes
in health, consumer, and social behaviors.

DOLORES ALBARRACÍN is Professor of Psychology at the University
of Illinois at Urbana–Champaign, USA, and a leading scholar of
attitudes, communication, and behavioral change.

ACTION AND INACTION IN A SOCIAL WORLD

Predicting and Changing Attitudes and Behavior

DOLORES ALBARRACÍN

University of Illinois at Urbana–Champaign

CAMBRIDGE UNIVERSITY PRESS

Shaftesbury Road, Cambridge CB2 8EA, United Kingdom

One Liberty Plaza, 20th Floor, New York, NY 10006, USA

477 Williamstown Road, Port Melbourne, VIC 3207, Australia

314–321, 3rd Floor, Plot 3, Splendor Forum, Jasola District Centre, New Delhi – 110025, India

103 Penang Road, #05–06/07, Visioncrest Commercial, Singapore 238467

Cambridge University Press is part of Cambridge University Press & Assessment, a department of the University of Cambridge.

We share the University's mission to contribute to society through the pursuit of education, learning and research at the highest international levels of excellence.

www.cambridge.org
Information on this title: www.cambridge.org/9781108813945

DOI: 10.1017/9781108878357

First published 2021
First paperback edition 2022

A catalogue record for this publication is available from the British Library

ISBN   978-1-108-84000-2   Hardback
ISBN   978-1-108-81394-5   Paperback

Additional resources for this publication at www.cambridge.org/albarracin

Este libro está dedicado a mis padres. A mi Padre, quien me ayudaba a escribir monografías cuando yo estaba en la escuela primaria y me alentó siempre. A mi Madre, quien fue mi modelo de pensamiento psicológico desde mi infancia.

Contents

There is an online appendix of research materials (meta-analytic coding sheets, experimental materials, and measurement instruments) available of this book

Figures

Tables

Preface

First and foremost, this book concerns my conceptualization of the cognitive processes underlying action and inaction dispositions and the implications of these dispositions for attitudes, persuasion, and behavior initiation and change. The theory encompasses the cognitive and motivational processes that arise from action and inaction goals as well as various information sources, including persuasive communications, past behavioral practice, experience, and other people. On the theoretical side, I propose action and inaction dispositions reflected in goals and mental representations, their contributions to attitudes and behaviors, and the mechanisms underlying the impact of persuasion and behavioral interventions. On the empirical side, I apply my theoretical principles to real-world problems and field interventions to change attitudes and behaviors. Up to this point, I have not had an opportunity to interweave these streams within my work. This book is motivated by this objective.

The book has other objectives as well:

1. The book analyzes the way in which general attitudes and general goals develop and their implications for future behavior and the success of persuasive messages and behavioral interventions. This research has not been covered in any previous volume.
2. The book describes different sequences of processes that are dependent on the type of information available at a time as well as the person's processing ability and motivation to think about a behavior. My research has been important in elucidating these sequences, and this book integrates them and expands coverage to various other phenomena.
3. The book covers laboratory experiments, real-world research, surveys, and meta-analyses. This integration is a departure from the traditional social psychology monograph.

4. Fishbein and Ajzen's (1975, 1980, 2010) analysis of behavior prediction and change provided fundamental insights for our fields. However, in their approach, attitudes are a precursor of behavior. In contrast, this book incorporates reciprocal influences of behavior on key psychological variables (i.e., attitudes, intentions, and social norms) while also characterizing action/inaction goals, the influence of affect, and the involvement of behavioral procedures.

5. The book differentiates the initiation and change of attitudes and behavioral patterns, thus integrating proceduralization, goal activation, and the impact of prior attitudes on processing sequences.

6. The book presents my unique understanding, review, and research concerning how to interpret automatic effects of behavior, their conditions, and the varied psychological nature of intentionality.

7. The book covers the neglected role of language in attitudes, intentions, and behaviors in ways that are new and not previously researched in the field of attitudes.

8. The book connects my theoretical analysis to my own and others' work on virtual experience, messaging, and the use of digital technology for behavioral change.

9. The book facilitates a deeper understanding of how my research has been conducted by tying the research hypotheses and findings to the methods through an extensive appendix of research materials, including questionnaires, messages, videos, meta-analytic coding sheets, messages developed in my laboratory, and individual difference measures created by my collaborators and me. I regularly receive emails asking for details and advice on how to design messages, develop measures, or conduct a meta-analysis. This book centralizes this methodological background in relation to my research findings.

My goal is to present an original conceptualization that integrates and defines interrelated issues from my own perspective. It follows the tradition of a monograph, which presents a point of view and draws connections to existing literatures. It is probably most similar to the following volumes:

Fishbein, M., & Ajzen, I. (1975). *Belief, attitude, and behavior: An introduction to theory and research.* Reading, MA: Addison Wesley.

Fishbein, M., & Ajzen, I. (2010). *Predicting and changing behavior: The reasoned action approach.* New York, NY: Routledge/Psychology Press.

Wyer, R. S. J. (1974). *Cognitive organization and change: An information-processing approach.* Hillsdale, NJ: Erlbaum.

Bandura, A. (1986). *Social foundations of thought and action: A social cognitive theory* (Prentice Hall Series in Social Learning Theory, Vol. 1). Englewood Cliffs, NJ: Prentice Hall.

These books present the authors' perspectives and yet are broad. Monographs are key to (a) draw attention to connections between literatures that run in parallel; (b) reach general conclusions; and, in this case, (c) provide an overarching framework. With these goals, monographs can move a field forward and stimulate new research.

My wish is that this book will be available for researchers who want to learn about the conceptualization I present. I read the above books many times, beginning in graduate school, and believe that other graduate students and researchers studying these issues will be interested in reading my volume. Applied researchers who typically cite and request my publications, including earlier ones, may also appreciate this original synthesis and organizing framework.

Secondarily, the book may also be used for instructional purposes in courses offered in psychology as well as applied disciplines like marketing, political psychology, public policy, health behavior, communication, and sports psychology, which are all fields with a high level of interest in attitudinal and behavioral change. At the undergraduate level, it may be appropriate for classes in the area of attitudes, persuasion, and behavior change. At the graduate level, this monograph could be included in specialized courses on attitudes and behaviors, probably supplemented with journal articles that present other perspectives in more detail. In addition, authors have often used their own volumes to train their research groups and teach specialized seminars. The 1975 and 2010 books by Ajzen and Fishbein are two such cases. I can see my volume serving the same goals in the future.

This volume has been inspired by a class I regularly teach on how attitudes and attitude theory can allow us to change behavior in the real world. This angle is reflected in the book's connections between the framework I propose and my research on substantive social and health problems and interventions to mitigate them. There are 10 chapters, which, supplemented with readings, will be well suited for classes in universities with a quarter system (10 weeks) or in universities with a regular system that want to treat a particular topic in greater depth by adding journal articles. Three possible models are as follows:

Chapter no.	Course length		
	10 weeks	12 weeks	16 weeks
1	Week 1	Week 1	Week 1
2	Week 2	Weeks 2 and 3	Weeks 2 and 3 (plus two research articles)
3	Week 3	Week 3	Weeks 3 and 4 (plus two research articles)
4	Week 4	Week 4	Week 5
5	Week 5	Week 5	Weeks 6 and 7 (plus two research articles)
6	Week 6	Week 6	Weeks 8 and 9 (plus two research articles)
7	Week 7	Weeks 8 and 9 (plus two research articles)	Week 11
8	Week 8	Week 10	Weeks 12 and 13
9	Week 9	Week 11	Weeks 14 and 15
10	Week 10	Week 12	Week 16
Midterm		Week 7	Week 10

More than 40 years have passed since Martin Fishbein and Icek Ajzen published *Belief, Attitude, Intention, and Behavior*. Their 1975 volume was an outstanding presentation of a coherent framework about attitudes, how they are measured, how they change, how they predict behavior, and how they must be distinguished from beliefs, intentions, and behaviors. As the title of my book suggests, these concepts are as key today as they were back then. In addition, this book is inspired by contemporary problems with action excesses and the need to identify solutions to social and health problems.

Acknowledgments

I owe a debt of gratitude first and foremost to my graduate school advisors, Bob S. Wyer Jr. and Martin Fishbein. I was also greatly inspired by doctoral candidates and postdoctoral researchers who have worked with me over the years, in particular, G. Tarcan Kumkale, Laura R. Glasman, Allison N. Earl, Will Hart, Casey McCulloch, Ian Handley, Kenji Noguchi, Hong Li, Sally Chan, Justin Hepler, Melanie Tannenbaum, Duo Jiang, Jing Xu, Evan Weingarten, Jiaying Liu, Mina Kwon, Christopher Jones, Aashna Sunderrajan, Sophie Lohmann, Benjamin White, Wenhao Dai, Ozan Kuru, and Dom Stecula. I am also indebted to a number of collaborators, including Kathleen Hall-Jamieson, Joel B. Cohen, Blair T. Johnson, Alice Eagly, Sharon Shavitt, Joseph Cappella, Bob Hornik, and Icek Ajzen, as well as the many colleagues who have contributed to my interests and my thinking over the years. Of these people, Alice Eagly, Kathleen Hall-Jamieson, and Joel Cohen have been generous mentors who offered their time and advice in a selfless fashion. I am deeply grateful.

I also attribute much of my work to the education I received. My research interests have always been broad, which is probably connected to my training in linguistics and the classics at the National University of La Plata (Argentina), my studies of psychology at the Catholic University of La Plata (Argentina), and my doctoral work in social and clinical psychology at the University of Illinois and University of Belgrano (Argentina), respectively. However, of all the educational institutions I attended, none was as foundational as the Liceo Víctor Mercante, a high school for girls at the National University of La Plata. The university's faculty have inspired many generations of girls, including my own.

PART I

Introduction

CHAPTER I

Definitions, Overview, Goals, and Principles of Cognitive Processing

People's attitudes are important. They organize social structures, shape perceptions of the social and physical world, and influence behavior. Social psychologists have studied attitudes largely to predict behaviors that have an impact on society (Glasman & Scott-Sheldon, 2019; Hagger, 2019; Mata, Dallacker, Vogel, & Hertwig, 2019; Sweeny & Rankin, 2019). Attitudes promote philanthropic enterprises such as ambitious campaigns to end poverty in the world. Attitudes also promote voting behaviors that can steer the course of a nation and the lives of its citizens in a positive direction (Stern & Ondish, 2019). But negative consequences of human behavior are at least as frequent. Attitudes are at the heart of many violent attacks, including random crimes against individuals and master-minded crimes against humanity (e.g., the Holocaust and the terrorist attacks in New York City on September 11, 2001; see Blankenship, Allen, Kane, & Anderson, 2019; Dovidio, Schellhaas, & Pearson, 2019; Esses, Hamilton, & Gaucher, 2019). Attitudes are also at the heart of suburban sprawling and misuse of natural resources (Garling, Bamberg, & Friman, 2019; Milfont & Schultz, 2019), both of which may one day threaten life on our planet.

Beliefs are equally important. They are the reason why Petersburg, Kentucky, has a Museum of Creation. The museum's website (https://cr eationmuseum.org/) advertises "Creation Science: Learn how the Bible, the history book of the universe, provides the starting point for science," and the museum's slogan is "Prepare to Believe." The museum aims to promote religious *beliefs* about creation as *factual knowledge* (i.e., know-ledge defined as a belief with a probability of 1; Wyer & Albarracín, 2005). But misinformation is not the only consequence of beliefs. For example, the states of Alabama, Arkansas, Florida, Indiana, Iowa, Oklahoma, and South Dakota, among others, have all considered laws to teach "creation science" in public schools. Moreover, Americans who are more (vs. less) religious and align with Christianity, Islam, and Judaism are less likely to

approve of vaccines, in part because the technology is perceived as conflicting with a world in which God controls our health and other natural events
(Stecula, Kuru, Jamieson, & Albarracin, in press).

The literature on attitudes, beliefs, and behavior spans decades and
continues to accumulate. Over five decades, attitude research has comprised between 11 percent and 32 percent of the articles in the flagship
Journal of Personality and Social Psychology (Albarracín & Shavitt, 2018).
Despite its popularity, there is an incomplete understanding of attitudes,
beliefs, and behaviors in relation to the goals and processes through which
they unfold. I attempt to address this limitation with this book. Another
gap this book is intended to fill is the lack of consideration of the
mechanisms leading from persuasive communications to behavior. For
example, other persuasion approaches (see, e.g., Chaiken, 1980; Johnson,
Wolf, Maio, & Smith-McLallen, 2019; Petty & Cacioppo, 1986) have
implicitly or explicitly conceptualized behavior change as a natural by-
product of attitude change. However, there are many instances in which
behavior change depends on factors other than attitudes (Ajzen, Fishbein,

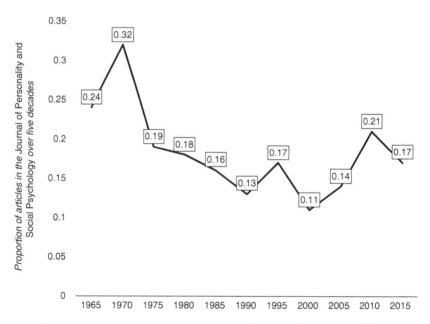

Figure 1.1 Proportion of attitude articles in the *Journal of Personality and Social
Psychology* over time. (Adapted from Albarracín & Shavitt, 2018)

Lohmann, & Albarracín, 2019). For this reason, behavioral interventions and behavior change are central to this book.

One assumption in this book is that goals of action (i.e., effortful behavior) and inaction (i.e., rest) often control beliefs, attitudes, and behaviors as well as our responses to persuasive communications and interventions to change behaviors. But beliefs, attitudes, and behaviors have other functions as well. Beliefs, attitudes, and behaviors inform and guide interactions with the world. Furthermore, beliefs, attitudes, and behaviors enable people to connect with others and organize their social world accordingly. The framework I present in this volume begins an analysis of the psychology of beliefs, attitudes, and behaviors in relation to goals and, particularly, goals of action and inaction. It also characterizes the cognitive and motivational processes that mediate the impact of (a) personal experience and practice with a behavior, (b) other people, as well as (c) persuasive communications (i.e., verbal and visual messages delivered in a standard format to all members of an audience) and behavioral interventions (i.e., more complex programs that involve role-playing, client-centered counseling, or other strategies in which the audience is active). I present an original perspective along with data that are either unpublished or scattered across many chapters, reviews, and empirical papers published over the last two decades. The framework that serves as the starting point for this book is graphically depicted in Figure 1.2.

The book is also unique because I reflect on some of the challenges with action excess (e.g., consumerism, environmental practices associated with climate change) and people's difficulties forming goals of inactions (e.g., conservation). Based on my interdisciplinary work, the book blends a traditional monograph with topics of contemporary interest and an analysis of attitude and behavior change in real and virtual contexts. To the best of my knowledge, there has not been a similar volume; our current time of unprecedented social and health problems is ripe for this contribution.

The Action, Knowledge, and Social Integration Goals

Life is sustained by actions. Living beings respond to their environment and survive by deploying processes of organization (i.e., development of cells, organs, systems), homeostasis (i.e., equilibrium fostered by positive and negative feedback mechanisms), metabolism (i.e., transformation of energy into matter and dissolution of matter), growth (i.e., increase in

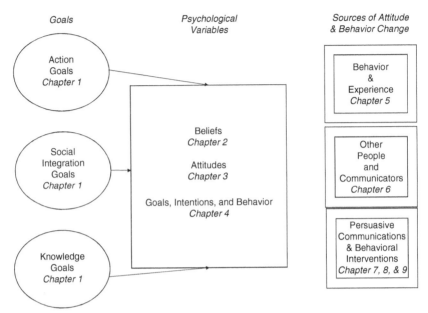

Figure 1.2 Overview of framework.

size), and adaptation (i.e., exchange with and change in response to the environment). A simple organism like the Euglena has two flagella that allow it to swim and grow. We, humans, have limbs and brains to act and transform our surroundings.

Adaptation and responses to the environment bring up an important requirement for life: a system that facilitates knowledge of the environment. Knowledge is as much of a life imperative as is action. In the case of the Euglena, the flagella facilitate light transmission into a redeye spot that receives environmental information that affects the flagella's surfaces through osmotic chemical exchange. In the case of humans, the senses of sight, hearing, audition, smell, taste, proprioception, and touch (i.e., haptics) provide regular perceptual updates of changes in our environments.

Action and knowledge goals concern making sense of our environment. However, for all organisms, but particularly for humans, the environment is experienced subjectively. Both our actions and our knowledge and beliefs about reality bring aspects of the world into focus while leaving out many other aspects. The framework I introduce in this book (see Figure 1.2) starts with the assumption that the action and knowledge goals help to create behaviors, beliefs, and attitudes. In addition, behaviors, beliefs, and attitudes influence how we experience the world.

In addition to action and knowledge imperatives, humans have goals of social integration. We are interdependent and thus must coordinate action and knowledge with other people who both influence us and receive influence from us. The perspective in Figure 1.2 must thus recognize that people reconcile their behaviors, beliefs, and experiences with others through processes of social influence. In sum, this book examines processes that start with action and experience; create functional behaviors, beliefs, and attitudes; modify the experience through behavior; and incorporate the perspectives of other people, often via persuasive communications and behavioral interventions.

Definition of Goals

Goals are aims, much like the circumscribed physical space toward which a ball or dart is directed (i.e., the bull's-eye). They imply a future that currently does not exist. In terms of content, goals fit with the needs of action (i.e., behavioral goals), knowledge (i.e., knowledge goals), and social integration (i.e., social goals or mimicry; see Dalton, Chartrand, & Finkel, 2010; Dunning, Anderson, Schlösser, & Ehlebracht, 2014). Examples of behavioral goals are aiming to increase exercise and aiming to begin a new hobby. Examples of knowledge goals are aiming to learn about architecture and aiming to stay current with the news. Examples of social goals are aiming to meet people and aiming to organize a party. In addition, many goals are simply affective, as people strive to feel pleasure and avoid pain (Higgins, 1997). As described by cognitive dissonance theory (Festinger, 1957), for example, smokers may notice an inconsistency between their smoking and their knowledge of the health risks of smoking (Festinger, 1957). Concluding that smoking is healthier than eating is an effective way of reducing anxiety and the associated discomfort (Festinger, 1957).

The Operation of State and Process Goals

Goals entail either states or processes. Being busy, being informed, and having friends are *states* of being (e.g., being active) or of possessing a concrete or symbolic object (e.g., having a friend and having a good income) at particular points in time. In contrast, increasing exercise, learning about architecture, remembering the details of a past event, and meeting people are *processes* that unfold over time, with a beginning and an end.

Naturally, states and processes are connected, because states are achieved through processes that have been set as goals and thus act as means to meet the goal. For example, the process of reading the newspaper can be a means to the more distant, state goal of "being informed." Likewise, the process of meeting new people is an intermediate goal on the way to the more distant, state goal of "having friends." Furthermore, processes can be aims and means to realizing other process aims. As an example of a stand-alone process goal, the process of "reading the newspaper" can be a goal of action while a patient waits for a medical appointment at a clinic's waiting room. As an example of processes to achieve concatenated process goals, the process of "meeting new people" can be a means to the process goal of "playing tennis with them." This notion is summarized in the following principle:

> **Principle 1. Type of goal objects.** The objects of goals are either states or processes, and both can be behavioral, cognitive, social, or affective. Process goals can be means in and of themselves, means to meet state goals, and means to meet other process goals.

General and Specific Goals

Like any concept, goals can be set at different levels of generality, and different research traditions have emphasized goals that are more specific or more general. Cognitive psychologists have typically studied specific, molecular goals. For example, researchers may ask participants to make coffee (Cooper & Shallice, 2006; Humphreys & Forde, 2001). One can then observe the processes set in motion by the goal of making coffee, which, being highly specific, constrains the means participants can use. Participants may pour the water before the coffee grounds or pour the coffee grounds before the water, but such a simple task greatly limits the ways of achieving the goal.

Behavioral goals can also be classified in relation to different semantic concepts. The concepts of *work* and *leisure*, for example, separate domains of human activity. In addition to these and many other ways of classifying behaviors, my colleagues and I have studied action and inaction concepts (Albarracín, Sunderrajan, Dai, & White, 2019; Albarracín & Handley, 2011; Albarracín et al., 2008; Albarracín, Sunderrajan, & Dai, 2018). The action or inaction nature of a behavior is a judgment, a subjective construal an actor or an observer makes based on concepts of action and inaction. People define action as more intentional and effortful than inaction. In our research

(McCulloch, Li, Hong, & Albarracín, 2012), participants generated a list of words related to "action" or "inaction." As examples of "action," participants wrote *select*, *walk*, and *run*. As examples of "inaction," they wrote "sleep," "calm," and "freeze." The concepts of action and inaction, it turns out, have implications for our goals and can guide processes of behavior initiation and inhibition. For example, although some scholars (Shah, Kruglanski, & Friedman, 2003) define goals as solely related to action, we have shown that goals of *inaction* are possible and healthy under the right conditions. After all, humans survive because they are intentional about where and when to sleep, which allows them to avoid environmental threats and to recover when they are fatigued or injured.

I argue that a *general* disposition toward action is essential for behavioral, cognitive, and social processes. For example, research on the cognitive control of action suggests that indiscriminate movement precedes movement oriented toward specific outcomes. Hommel and colleagues (Camus et al., 2018; Elsner & Hommel, 2001, 2004; Pfister, Janczyk, & Kunde, 2013) proposed a two-stage model to explain how people develop intentional control of their action. Stage 1 of this model involves random movement. Random movement is contingent on internal or external stimulation and allows people to observe the relation between their movements and the effects of the movements. The temporal overlap of the random movement and the observed effects is presumably sufficient to create a mnemonic link between a pattern of activation in the motor system and a cognitive representation of behavioral outcomes.

During Stage 2, people perform goal-directed movement, which requires the specification of an outcome as a goal as well as the selection of the appropriate movements to reach that goal. The selection of what is appropriate is possible because the representation of an outcome is associated with a corresponding motor code. Thus, the selection is also largely automatic, although it may be controlled by additional intentional processes.

Of course, specific action goals can influence action once motor–cognitive associations have been formed (Hommel, 1997). That is, actions are represented in terms of their features, leading to the possibility that single features of the behavior might activate the behavior, including the motor code that precipitates it. Hence, in terms of Elsner and Hommel's (2001, 2004) treatment of action–effects associations, the activation of a single effect might ultimately recruit the corresponding action.

Because Elsner and Hommel specifically discuss the link between actions and *outcomes* of that action, the essential formulation of Fishbein and Ajzen's (1980) model can account for the role of outcomes as specific goals. Thinking about a particular outcome might trigger global evaluations of an action as desirable and, subsequently, the intended overt actions. However, in addition to intentional behavior executed to pursue an outcome, any incidental thoughts about the outcome might automatically give way to behaviors that produced those outcomes at an earlier time.

Motivational and Cognitive Effects of General Action and Inaction Goals as well as Other Behavioral Goals

Even though behavioral goals are not the only goals motivating behavior, they are central to behavior. First, people seek information and form beliefs about and attitudes toward behaviors when they are motivated to act or disengage from action. Thus, the types of beliefs and attitudes that we form when considering action are different from the types of beliefs and attitudes that we form when we adopt the goal of contemplating reality or achieving knowledge for the sake of knowledge.

This volume presents an analysis of the psychology of beliefs, attitudes, and behaviors that emerge from a *preoccupation with behavior*. I characterize cognitive and motivational processes involving (a) goals, (b) behavioral beliefs (including norms and control beliefs), (c) affect, (d) personal experience and practice with a behavior, (e) behavioral procedures, (f) other actors, as well as (g) persuasive communications (i.e., verbal and visual messages delivered in a standard format to all members of an audience) and behavioral interventions (i.e., more complex programs that involve role-playing, client-centered counseling, or other strategies in which the audience is active). Behavioral beliefs, behavioral practice, intentions, and behavioral procedures would not exist if people did not think about behavior. To this extent, action and inaction goals drive the cognitions we need and the cognitive maps we draw.

> **Principle 2. Effects of action goals on other psychological variables.** Goals of action stimulate the formation and use of behavioral beliefs, behavioral procedures, and intentions, which are themselves informed by personal experience and practice with a behavior, behavioral procedures, other people, as well as persuasive communications (i.e., verbal and visual messages delivered in a standard format to all members of an audience) and behavioral interventions (i.e., more complex programs that involve role-playing, client-centered counseling, or other strategies in which the audience is active).

The Psychological Variables at Play

Beliefs comprise judgments (Albarracín, Sunderrajan et al., 2019; Eagly & Chaiken, 1993; Wyer & Albarracín, 2005) about (a) the probability that an object has an attribute (Fishbein, 1963): "Lake Michigan is frozen today," (b) the probability that a behavior has an outcome: "Exercise will improve my fitness" (Ajzen & Fishbein, 1980; Fishbein & Ajzen, 2011b), or the probability that an object or event is real: "I believe in Santa Claus". When beliefs concern the future, they are called "expectations."

Attitudes are evaluations (see also Albarracín, Zanna, Johnson, & Kumkale, 2005), mental links between an attitude object and an evaluative category like "good" or "bad." The attitude object can be a concrete target, a behavior, an abstract entity, a person, or an event (e.g., Albarracín et al., 2005; Eagly & Chaiken, 1993; Fishbein & Ajzen, 1975). For example, we form evaluations of social groups (e.g., prejudice), abstract entities (i.e., values), our own behaviors (attitude toward the behavior; Fishbein & Ajzen, 1975, 2010), ourselves (e.g., self-esteem), and other people (e.g., person impressions) (Eagly & Chaiken, 1993).

Intentions are the mental representation of one's willingness to perform a behavior. These representations can be full-fledged propositions, as in the thought "I will go on vacation next month." They can also be fragmentary thoughts that themselves cue behavioral procedures. For example, people ask subtle questions like "Will I do it?" which is how intentions are often represented in the moment (Lohmann, Jones, & Albarracín, 2019). Finally, intentions can be feelings, including what I call "volitional feelings," which are feelings of determination, motor feelings, and visualization of a behavior before it is executed (Lohmann & Albarracín, 2019).

Behavioral procedures are motor routines and behavioral skills that allow people to implement behaviors. They are formed when sequences of behaviors proceduralize, that is they become efficient and sometimes difficult to stop (Anderson, 2013; Smith, 1989). Motor procedures are a prerequisite to motor behavior. There are also cognitive procedures (e.g., deduction) and affective procedures (e.g., suppressing one's feelings).

Goals are *aims* not realized in the present. They assume a discrepancy between the present and a *future* and thus require a way of reducing the discrepancy (for the notion of discrepancy, see Wiener, 2011). Goals may be affective (the goal to be happy), cognitive (the goal to know), or behavioral (the goal to perform a behavior). Behavioral goals are particularly important in this book.

Behaviors are typically defined as the overt actions of an individual (Albarracín, Zanna et al., 2005). Although many of the behaviors I discuss are overt actions, overt and imagined behaviors can involve similar processes and effects (Albarracín, Handley et al., 2008; Smith, 1989).

Past behavior comprises overt actions or inactions at a time before the present. They provide practice and promote repetition of a behavior in the future (Ouellette & Wood, 1998).

Experience is the direct interaction with objects and behavior. It leaves memories of the sensorial and motor feelings associated with those interactions (Fazio, Zanna, & Cooper, 1978; Glasman & Albarracín, 2006; Handley, Albarracín, Brown, Li, Kumkale, & Kumkale, 2009; Sheeran, Godin, Conner, & Germain, 2017; Wyer, 2019).

Message arguments include the verbal information contained in a message. They often allude to the consequences of behaviors or unique positive aspects of an object (Albarracín & Wyer, 2001; Albarracín, 2002). They can also try to undercut the negatives of an object or behavior.

Other people include close and distant others, as well as communicators, who can also exert influences on our beliefs, attitudes, intentions, and behavior. This important influence has been covered in diverse literatures such as social influence (Ledgerwood et al., 2019; Prislin & Wood, 2005), behavioral skills training (Albarracín et al., 2005; Burchell, Rettie, & Patel, 2013; Casadio et al., 2011; Gist, Rosen, & Schwoerer, 1988; Liu, Huang, & Wang, 2014), and persuasion (Albarracín, Sunderrajan, Lohmann, Chan, & Jiang, 2019; Albarracín, Kumkale, & Poyner-Del Vento, 2017; Albarracín, McNatt et al., 2003; Johnson et al., 2019; Wegener, Clark, & Petty, 2019).

Affective feelings include mood (i.e., feelings of positive and negative affect without a clear source; Clore & Schnall, 2005), as well as emotions (i.e., visceral reactions to an object or behavior; e.g., feelings of fear, happiness, sadness; Clore & Schnall, 2005).

Psychological Measurement

Beliefs

Beliefs are relatively easy to measure with **self-report scales**. For example, Etter, Humair, Bergman, and Perneger (2000) asked a large sample of smokers to answer open-ended questions about the positive and negative aspects of smoking. The most prevalent positive aspects were the pleasurable and relaxing effects of smoking; the most prevalent negative aspects were the health detriments and the unpleasant odor of smoking. Although Etter et al. (2000) intended to measure attitudes, contemporary attitude researchers would consider this scale to be a measure of beliefs. Likewise, Thurstone scales are currently considered to be belief scales. In Thurstone's approach, a collection of statements like "Smoking is enjoyable" and "There is no health benefit to smoking" is rated by a group of participants who act as judges and indicate the degree to which each statement represents a positive attitude toward smoking using a scale from 1 (e.g., *not at all*) to 9 (e.g., *extremely*). Each item with low rating variance receives a value based on the item's mean calculated over participants. Items with high variance are excluded because they do not reflect a clear evaluative meaning. A different group of respondents indicates whether or not they agree with each item, and the median of the checked items becomes the respondent's attitude score.

Expectancy-value models were the first to explicitly distinguish attitude as an evaluation of an object from its underlying beliefs and evaluations (Ajzen et al., 2019; Fishbein, 1963; Fishbein & Ajzen, 2010; Rosenberg, 1960b). In their approach, the belief that smoking makes people feel alert is multiplied by the perceived favorability of feeling alert, and a summary attitude is computed from each belief times evaluation pair (Ajzen & Fishbein, 1972).

Consider a questionnaire developed by Fishbein, Ajzen, and Hanson (1999), which measures the perceived outcomes of smoking. The specific items appearing in Table 1.1 and responses to them are provided on the following scales for evaluations and beliefs, respectively.

bad ____: ____: ____: ____: ____: ____: ____: good
extremely quite slightly neither slightly quite extremely

Unlikely ____: ____: ____: ____: ____: ____: ____: likely
extremely quite slightly neither slightly quite extremely

These responses can be used to derive an expectancy-value measure of attitudes toward smoking. The process requires scoring both beliefs and evaluations from −3 to +3, then multiplying each evaluation (e_i) by its

Table 1.1 *Outcome beliefs and evaluation measures*

Outcome belief measures (unlikely–likely)	Outcome evaluation measures (unlikely–likely)
1. If I smoke cigarettes, it will help me relax:	1. If I do things that help me relax, that is:
2. If I smoke cigarettes, it will make me feel good:	2. If I do things that make me feel good, that is:
3. If I smoke cigarettes, I will get cancer:	3. If I get cancer, that is:
4. If I smoke cigarettes, it will make me smell bad:	4. If I get along with my friends, that is:
5. If I smoke cigarettes, it will be bad for my health:	5. If I get heart disease, that is:
6. If I smoke cigarettes, it will help me control my weight:	6. If I smell bad, that is:
7. If I smoke cigarettes, it will help me get along with my friends:	7. If I do things that increase my chances for health problems, that is:
8. If I smoke cigarettes, I will get heart disease:	8. If I control my weight, that is:
9. If I smoke cigarettes, it will make my teeth yellow:	9. If I have yellow teeth, that is:
10. If I smoke cigarettes, it will be harder for me to breathe:	10. If it is harder for me to breathe, that is:
11. If I smoke cigarettes, it will cost me a lot of money:	11. If I spend a lot of money, that is:
12. If I smoke cigarettes, it will be enjoyable:	12. If I do things that I enjoy, that is:

Source: Adapted from White et al. (2019).

corresponding belief (b_i), and finally summing each $b_i \times e_i$ over the 12 outcomes to compute a summary score, $\Sigma_{i=1}^{12} \ b_i \times e_i$. The main advantage of having these outcome measures is understanding the belief bases of the attitude and potentially targeting them in behavioral interventions or persuasive communications.

Another common way of gauging attitudes through beliefs is to use "expectancy" measures. For example, Brandon and Baker's Short Smoking Consequences Questionnaire appears below, and shows a combination of beliefs about the object (e.g., "cigarettes taste good") and beliefs about smoking outcomes (e.g., "cigarettes help me deal with anxiety and worry"):

Item	0 Completely Unlikely	1 Extremely Unlikely	2 Very Unlikely	3 Somewhat Unlikely	4 A Little Unlikely	5 A Little Likely	6 Somewhat Likely	7 Very Likely	8 Extremely Likely	9 Completely Likely
1. Cigarettes taste good.										
2. Smoking controls my appetite.										
3. Cigarettes help me deal with anxiety or worry.										
4. I enjoy the taste sensations while smoking.										
5. Smoking helps me deal with depression.										
6. Cigarettes keep me from overeating.										
7. Cigarettes help me deal with anger.										
8. When I smoke the taste is pleasant.										
9. I will enjoy the flavor of a cigarette.										
10. I will enjoy feeling a cigarette on my tongue and lips.										
11. By smoking I risk heart disease and lung cancer.										
12. Cigarettes help me reduce or handle tension.										
13. Smoking helps me control my weight.										
14. When I'm upset with someone, a cigarette helps me cope.										
15. The more I smoke, the more I risk my health.										
16. Cigarettes keep me from eating more than I should.										
17. Smoking keeps my weight down.										
18. Smoking is hazardous to my health.										
19. Smoking calms me down when I feel nervous.										
20. When I'm angry a cigarette can calm me down.										
21. Smoking is taking years off my life.										

Importantly, beliefs can also refer to norms and perceived behavioral control, both of which influence behavior and are frequently leveraged in behavioral interventions (Fishbein & Ajzen, 2010). Measures of beliefs about what others want and motivation to comply with the desires of other people are respectively illustrated by the examples (Ajzen, 2019) below.

> Most of my friends who have undergone major heart surgery have exercised for at least 20 min, three times per week for the three months following surgery.

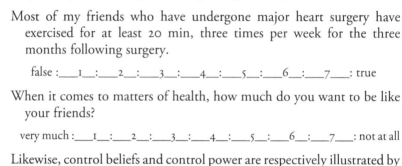

> When it comes to matters of health, how much do you want to be like your friends?

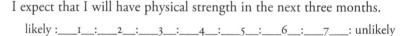

Likewise, control beliefs and control power are respectively illustrated by the examples (Ajzen, 2019) below.

> I expect that I will have physical strength in the next three months.

> likely :___I__:___2__:___3__:___4__:___5__:___6__:___7___: unlikely

> Having physical strength would enable me to exercise for at least 20 min, three times per week for the next three months.

> disagree :___I__:___2__:___3__:___4__:___5__:___6__:___7___: agree

My collaborators and I have used **social media measures** of beliefs using natural language processing. These methods have been in development since the 1960s and aim to extract meaningful representations from text messages (i.e., words, phrases, and sentences) as inputs for machine learning models. One can use these methods to analyze structured text passages in formal written language, such as news articles, academic journal articles, records, and archives, as well as more informal ones, such as tweets, Facebook comments, or text messages.

An important technique applied to measure beliefs has been "topic modeling," which is used to infer latent variables from words that co-occur within a set of words (i.e., a document). Researchers can organize documents by region, by time period, or by individual, to extract a set of latent variables and then obtain probabilities for different emergent topics across regions, time periods, or individuals. The most popular methods are probabilistic latent semantic indexing and latent Dirichlet allocation (LDA) (Blei et al., 2003; Hofmann, 1999). Both of these methods use hierarchical Bayesian networks to identify topics (i.e., latent semantic features) in an unsupervised fashion. LDA assumes that the documents contain a mixture of topics and that each topic includes a list of words that tend to appear together. For a detailed review of these and many other methods, see Chan et al., 2019)

Topic modeling has typically been used to predict outcomes in different domains (e.g., in the stock market), as well as personality (Chan et al., 2018; Ireland et al., 2015, 2016; Kosinski, Stillwell, & Graepel, 2013; Morales et al., 2019; Schwartz et al., 2013). However, my collaborators and I have used it to obtain proxy measures of beliefs across regions. While studying the Zika epidemic of 2016, we created a Zika corpus by searching for a set of Zika-related keywords ("Zika," "dengue," "yellow fever," "Zika virus," "Zika fever," "flaviviridae," "brain shrink," "fetal brain disruption sequence," "mosquitoes," "birth defects," "insect bites," "mosquito bites," "insect-borne virus," "mosquito-borne virus," "microcephaly," and "Guillain-Barre syndrome") using the Twitter streaming API (Application Programming Interface). The resulting data set contained 3.8 million tweets between February 1, 2016, and August 30, 2016, from which we geolocated tweets corresponding to 2,695 different US counties. Table 1.2 presents the topics we obtained.

We validated the topics' meaning by correlating them with survey measures of beliefs in US counties. The survey contained 33,193 nationally representative respondents collected over 33 weeks. We aggregated tweets between the weeks

Table 1.2 *Twitter topics that correlated with survey measures*

Topic name	Words in topic
Zika	*mosquito*, many, *zika*, amp, *virus*, wish, *summer*, full, look, leg
Congress funding 1	*congress*, *funding*, *act*, *emergency*, tell, via2026, *approve*, add, lirikoph, zika2014fast
Microcephaly	mosquito, virus, zika, *microcephaly*, bill, *repellent*, *mosquito*, *summer*, amp, natural
Blood transfusion tech	zika, virus, *tech*, *blood*, mosquito, outbreak, *threat*, *pregnancy*, *government*, brazil
Zika protection and travel	virus, *zika*, mosquito, around, like, *protect*, money, suspected, *health*, *travel*
Insect repellent	zika, virus, *insect*, *abortion*, virus, *repellent*, *prevent*, rubio, mosquito, pregnant
Zika in Miami	mosquito, virus, *zika*, *miami*, state, *dengue*, national, need, *fever*, month
Congress funding 2	virus, zika, *rico*, *puerto*, *congress*, *funding*, obamacare, zika, emergency, scott

Table 1.3 *Belief measures and correlations with Twitter topics (see Table 1.2)*

Survey question	Twitter topic (r)		
	Zika protection and travel	Congress funding 1	Microcephaly
Transmission by sitting next to a carrier: How do scientists think someone can get the Zika virus? By sitting next to someone who has the Zika virus (on a scale 1 = *not likely at all* to 4 = *very likely*).	—	—	—
Transmission by mosquito bite: How do scientists think someone can get the Zika virus? By being bitten by a mosquito that has already bitten someone who has the Zika virus (on a scale 1 = *not likely at all* to 4 = *very likely*).	—	—	—
Microcephaly: How accurate is it to say that a pregnant woman who is infected with the Zika virus is more likely to have a baby with an unusually small head and brain (on a scale 1 = *not accurate at all* to 4 = *very accurate*)?	0.52***	0.51***	0.43***

— indicates that the belief did not correlate with the topic. ***p < 0.001.

of February 16, 2016, and August 18, 2016, to match our survey data. After training the models on the tweets that could not be geolocated, we modeled each document containing all tweets from each of the 2,695 counties. We obtained a number of topics, some of which are presented in Table 1.2.

Our specific objective was to correlate the probability of each of the topics in a particular county with the average responses to belief questions in the same county. Table 1.3 presents correlations between the county topics in Table 1.2 and the county averages of our belief measures. As shown, one out of three beliefs could be meaningfully measured with topics.

Attitude Measures

Researchers have also developed a variety of scales to assess people's attitudes (Fishbein & Ajzen, 1975; Krosnick et al., 2005; Tesser, Whitaker, Martin, & Ward, 1998). Interestingly, of more than 100 studies of social psychological and political attitudes, 37 used 2-point scales, 7 used 3-point scales, 10 used 4-point scales, 27 used 5-point scales, 6 used 6-point scales, 21 used 7-point scales (Robinson, Shaver, & Wrightsman, 1999). A large number of implicit measures are now available for use as well.

Explicit measures. Semantic differential scales are flexible, bipolar, 7-point scales that require simply identifying an object or behavior to be rated and selecting rating scales among a set of commonly used adjectives such as *good/bad, pleasant/unpleasant,* or *harmful/beneficial.* Selecting anchors such as *unwise/wise* and *good/bad* may be done easily by consulting the classic study of meaning by Osgood (1962). After selecting adjectives, measures can be easily assembled and administered, and what is left is to verify if the scales have adequate internal consistency after the questionnaires have been conducted. I will present examples of attitude measures in the area smoking, one that I have reviewed (White et al., 2019). A semantic differential measure used by Hanson and Laffrey (1999) included the following items:

For me, to smoke cigarettes during the next month would be:

nice _____ : _____ : _____ : _____ : _____ : _____ : _____ : awful
     extremely quite   slightly   neither slightly quite   extremely

For me, to smoke cigarettes during the next month would be:

pleasant _____ : _____ : _____ : _____ : _____ : _____ : _____ : not pleasant
     extremely quite   slightly   neither slightly quite   extremely

For me, to smoke cigarettes during the next month would be:

not fun _____ : _____ : _____ : _____ : _____ : _____ : _____ : a lot
at all   of fun
     extremely quite   slightly neither slightly quite   extremely

---

As they generally do, these items have acceptable internal consistencies, as shown by Cronbach's alphas greater than 0.68 for different populations in Hanson and Laffrey's (1999) study.

Likert and Likert-type scales comprise another flexible method that allows researchers to present any statement and ask participants to express their agreement on the following scale:

1	2	3	4	5	
Strongly disagree	Moderately disagree	Neither agree nor disagree	Agree	Moderately agree	Strongly agree

Like Xu and colleagues (2015) did, one may present a statement such as "Smoking is pleasurable" and use agreement as an indication of a favorable attitude. Likert-like scales are equally easy to implement but deviate in the selection of the scale anchors. For example, instead of using a scale going from *Strongly Disagree* to *Strongly Agree*, Lund (2016) used a 1 to 5 scale from *no support* to *full support* to gauge Norwegians' attitudes toward policies designed to reduce cigarette availability. A list of policies presented to participants included "remove duty-free quota on cigarettes completely when entering Norway," "increase cigarette taxes," and "decrease the number of cigarette outlets." The scale was used as an indication of attitudes toward antismoking policies.

Despite the popularity of polichotomous scales such as those from –3 to +3, dichotomous-response options appear to have advantages when it comes to comprehension (Krosnick, Judd, & Wittenbrink, 2005) and may best match the nature of evaluation representations in memory. It seems unlikely that people have –3 to +3 scales stored in memory. To begin, with the exception of specific external requests for a respondent to use a complex scale, or the need to compare similar objects, most explicit judgments probably entail *good* versus *bad* options and are not likely to require finer distinctions. However, dichotomous scales are rarely used, probably because researchers prefer to rely on parametric methods of data analysis.

Implicit measures. Implicit measures of attitudes are covered in detail elsewhere (Krosnick et al., 2005; White et al., 2018). The implicit association test (IAT; Greenwald, McGhee, & Schwartz, 1998), for example, measures associations between an object and "good" or "bad" by gauging whether the associations of the target object with *good* are faster than corresponding associations with *bad*. For example, Czyzewska and Ginsburg (2007) presented 20 words (10 with negative connotations and 10 with positive connotations), in addition to 20 substance-relevant images (e.g., cannabis leaves, bongs or cigarettes, ashtray with cigarette butts) and 20 neutral images (i.e., common objects such as pencils and cups). The implicit attitude index consists of the difference between the average reaction time for the test block linking the target object to positive words and the test block linking the target object to negative words. In this calculation, lower scores suggest a more negative attitude (i.e., faster reaction time to a negative word/substance image combination than to positive word/substance image combination). However, the reliability of the measure is often low and precludes the measure's ability to predict behaviors and outcomes of interest (Ajzen et al., 2019; Krosnick et al., 2005; White et al., 2018).

Other forms of the IAT include approach/avoidance, personalized, and single-target IATs. Approach/avoidance IATs aim to assess preferences for moving toward or away from an attitude object (Rinck & Becker, 2007). The personalized IAT assesses the self-relevance of evaluations and combines evaluative labels such as "I like" and "I dislike" (Olson & Fazio, 2004; White & Albarracín, 2018). The single-target IAT (Wigboldus, Holland, & van Knippenberg, 2004) allows researchers to measure evaluative associations without having to present a countercategory such as cigarettes versus pencils, or men versus women. This test first maps target stimuli and positive items onto one response key and negative items onto the other, and then inverts the response key assignment to map target stimuli and negative items onto one response key and positive items onto the other. Thus, this mapping allows comparing the speed of combining the target stimuli with either positive or negative without relying on a comparison stimulus. Importantly, the reliability of this measure has been shown to be high (e.g., Cronbach's alpha = 0.69; Bluemke & Friese, 2008).

Another measure that is reliable in addition to being brief is the affect misattribution paradigm (Payne, Cheng, Govorun, & Stewart, 2005). Respondents view the attitude object (acting as a prime), followed by a Chinese pictograph for 100 ms, and then a visual mask of a black and white pattern. Participants judge the degree to which the Chinese pictograph is pleasant or unpleasant, a judgment that is presumably affected by the presence of the prime. For example, judging the pictograph as more pleasant after seeing alcohol photos as opposed to water photos can be interpreted as an indication of a positive implicit attitude toward alcohol. The internal consistency of the scale is high (α = 0.76).

Digital measures of attitudes. Social media postings also reflect attitudes. Sentiment analysis is perhaps the more popular social media analysis, and, from the point of view of social psychology, it measures attitudes. The most frequent method is a close-vocabulary approach to gauge the valence of text fragments (Hatzivassiloglou et al., 2001; Hatzivassiloglou & McKeown, 1997; Hatzivassiloglou & Wiebe, 2000; Wiebe, 2000). Close-vocabulary methods rely simply on a list of words (preidentified terms) connected to positive or negative attitudes (i.e., the sentiments). More advanced methods use unsupervised techniques. For example, Turney (2002) developed an unsupervised technique that examines the number of occurrence and co-occurrences between preidentified valenced words and words found via a web search engine. Terms that frequently co-occur with the preidentified positive word "excellent" are considered positive; terms that frequently co-occur with the negative term "poor" are considered negative.

An example of sentiment analysis using a predetermined vocabulary is a study of attitudes toward brands conducted by Mostafa (2013). Specifically, Mostafa developed a corpus of around 6,800 seed adjectives with known orientation (2006 positive-valenced words and 4,783 negative-valenced words). The lexicon was updated by adding words based on a thorough search in the WordNet. Examples of the tweets for attitudes toward Air India appear below, with an indication of whether each is positive or negative according to a manual classification:

1. "#Air India is so fab. Maybe I under rated it all these years. Maybe it is gonna b my fav Indian airline now. Maybe my life is about to change" Positive
2. "Irrespective of what people say, I still like #Air India, far better than snooty staff on most of these so-called low-cost carriers" Positive
3. "Horrible experience with #Air India – bag misplaced on AI101, no updates for two days. Is anyone there? Hello? Anyone with similar experience?" Negative
4. "Don't fly AI then! RT @Terrell_Raupp @ikaveri Air India gives the worst flight experience to its customer http://t.co/NMoabRNc #Air India" Negative

As shown by the tweets above, the challenges of these postings are brevity and informality. However, the close-vocabulary sentiment analyses were able to measure attitudes as judged by the finding that the positivity of the obtained scores ebbed and flowed as a function of a company's marketing strategies. For example, Nokia had a positive spike with the introduction of the then-new "Lumia" phone.

A similar approach has been used to measure well-being, which, although not an "attitude," likely involves aspects of attitudes like self-esteem and life satisfaction. Research conducted by Schwartz (2016) has demonstrated that topics can predict judgments of Twitter postings in relation to positive emotions, engagement, relationships, meaning, and accomplishment (PERMA; Seligman, 2018).

Another measure of attitudes has involved analyzing the "likes" of social media platforms in relation to known attitudes about the users. This method has been used primarily with broad traits (Kosinski, Stillwell, & Graepel, 2013; Youyou, Kosinski, & Stillwell, 2015), although some attitudes are predicted from "likes" as well. For example, a large sample of Facebook users who had completed scales measuring the Big 5 and a couple of fairly broad attitudes (political attitudes and life satisfaction; Youyou et al., 2015) provided access to their Facebook postings. The "likes"-based measure of political attitudes correlated $r = 0.33$ (AUC to r transformation) with self-reported political attitudes, and the "likes"-based measure of life satisfaction correlated $r = 0.52$ with the self-reported measures.

Topic modeling is also popular for "sentiment" analysis, which I prefer to call "attitude" analyses. In the case of sentiment analysis, when individuals talk about an attribute of an object, they are likely to use different terms. So, if terms like "excellent," "fabulous," and "good" appear with running and tennis, a researcher might conclude that the person or, in the case of a county, the county population has a positive attitude toward tennis. We have used topic modeling in a slightly different way, which is to develop topics across counties and then correlate the probability of particular topics being present in a county with the average attitude for that county. The topics were the ones obtained in our Zika study (see Table 1.2; Farhadloo, Winneg, Chan, HQLL-Jamieson, & Albarracín, 2018); the wording of the policy attitudes appears in Table 1.4. As shown in this table, some of the topics were an excellent proxy for attitudes concerning ground spraying and aerial spraying, and, overall, the social media proxies performed better in this case than they did with beliefs (see Table 1.3).

Measures of Goals, Intentions, and Behavior

Goals are typically measured via **self-report**. For example, goals are measured as traits, which are defined as a collection of feelings, behaviors, and thoughts. For example, Lockwood, Jordan, and Kunda's (2002) prevention-promotion scale contains items about frequent thoughts, such as "I often imagine myself experiencing bad things and fear what might happen to me," and "I often think about the person I am afraid I might become in the future." This scale includes other items that specifically tap goals, such as

Table 1.4 *Policy attitude measures and correlations with topics*

Survey question	Twitter topic (*r*)		
	Congress funding 2	Zika protection and travel	Zika in Miami
Support for ground spraying: If there were cases of people getting infected with Zika virus in your city or town, would you approve or disapprove of special spraying at the ground level against mosquitoes to prevent the spread of the Zika virus (on a scale 1 = *strongly disapprove* to 5 = *strongly approve*)?	0.88***	0.68**	—
Support for aerial spraying: If there were cases of people getting infected with the Zika virus in your city or town, would you approve or disapprove of special spraying from the air against mosquitoes to prevent the spread of the Zika virus (on a scale 1 = *strongly disapprove* to 5 = *strongly approve*)?	0.92***	—	0.67***

Note: For the words in the topics, see Table 1.2.
***$p < 0.001$.

"I typically focus on the success I hope to achieve in the future," and "In general, I am focused on achieving positive outcomes in my life."

Goals can also be measured in the moment, as is the case in the *Questionnaire of Current Motivation* (short form; Freund, Kuhn, & Holling, 2011). Its items gauge thoughts about ability, such as "I think I am up to the difficulty of this task," and "I probably won't manage to do this task." The scale also includes an item about interest, namely, "After having read the instruction, the task seems to be very interesting." Finally, the scale also contains an item that more strictly measures a goal ("I am eager to see how I will perform in the task"), although it concerns the goal to find out how well one can do instead of the more critical goal to do well.

Another scale that measures goals in the moment is our action/inaction goal scale (see, e.g., Jiang & Albarracín, 2019). This scale includes the following items: (a) *During this study, I was feeling energetic*; (b) *If I could, I would take a nap after this session* (reverse-scored); (c) *If I could, I would go work out after this session*; (d) *During this study, I wanted to get some rest* (reverse-scored); (e) *Today I am motivated to get a lot of work done*; (f) *My goal for today is to relax as much as possible* (reverse-scored); these are scored on an 11-point scale (from 0 = *Not at all* to 10 = *Very much*). This measure has the advantage of measuring broad goals of action and reflects the impact of manipulations, thus being sensitive to within-participant goal variations. In addition to direct measures of goals, our scale has two feeling items (e.g., *During this study, I was feeling energetic*). The internal consistency of the scale is acceptable (α = 0.69).

Specific goals may also be measured with an item such as "I would like to get an A in the psychology midterm." At first sight, this item might appear to measure intention. However, as indicated by Fishbein and Ajzen (2010), receiving an A on a test is partially outside of our control, as situational factors are also important in achieving this goal. A measure of intention refers to a behavior rather than an outcome, and is typically written as "I intend to study for my psychology midterm."

Measures of behavior come in many forms, including a variety of self-reports of frequency, intensity, and precise counts of occasions of a particular behavior. For example, researchers may measure condom use with an item such as the following:

		I use condoms		
Always	Frequently	Sometimes	Seldom	Never

Researchers may also request a more specific report, such as the number of times a person had sex during the last month. After that, they may ask on how many of those instances a condom was used. These kinds of measures are a good approximation to actual behavior but their validity varies. For example, a study of adherence to an HIV-medication regimen in children included Medication Event Monitoring Systems (MEMS, MWV/ AARDEX Ltd., Switzerland; Vreeman et al., 2019). The system involves a microcircuit that records the time and date of bottle opening and correlates highly with virologic outcomes of treatment. Findings showed that the sensitivity of child self-reported adherence (0.56 to 0.62) was higher than the sensitivity of the caregiver report (0.54 to 0.64). In addition, the association between the child reports and MEMS was much higher in Kenya (0.84 to 0.85) than in South Africa (0.39 to 0.48) or Thailand (0.46 to 0.54).

Social media measures of goals, intentions, and behaviors are increasingly important and allow for flexibility and low-cost measures at the level of individuals, regions, or time points. My team has obtained Twitter-based measures of intentions and behaviors in the aforementioned study about Zika in 2016 (Farhadloo et al., 2018). When we correlated these measures, which appear in Table 1.5, with the topics shown in Table 1.2, we found moderate to high correlations between the topics and the behavioral measures. In addition, there was a strong negative correlation between the intention measure and the "Blood Transfusion Technology" topic. This topic may reflect fear of medical technology and science in general, which might translate into rejection of vaccines in general.

Table 1.5 *Intention and behavior measures and correlations with topics*

Survey question	Twitter topics (r)				
	Blood transfusion tech	Zika	Insect repellent	Congress funding	Zika protection and travel
Intention to Get Zika vaccine: If there were a vaccine that protected you from getting Zika how likely, if at all, is it that you would get the vaccine (on a scale 1 = *not likely at all* to 4 = *very likely*)?	−0.68***	—	—	—	—
Practicing any preventive behavior to avoid Zika: In the past 3 months, have you done anything to protect yourself from getting Zika (on a scale 0 to 1)?	—	0.65***	0.59***	—	—
Discussing Zika with family/ friends: In the past week, how many days, if any, did you discuss the effects of the Zika virus with family or friends (on a scale 0 to 7)?	—	0.47***	0.45***	0.44***	0.30***

Note: For the topics, see Table 1.2.
***p < XX.

My collaborators and I have also obtained social media proxies for general action dispositions. Specifically, in research predicting HIV prevalence at the county level, we used a closed-vocabulary approach (Tausczik & Pennebaker, 2010) to develop a measure of action disposition (Ireland et al., 2016). We created an "action" vocabulary by including LIWC's (linguistic inquiry and word count) existing motion and verb categories and additional synonyms of core action words (work, go, plan, and think) using the Corpus of Contemporary American English (COCA; Davies, 2008). Trained researchers then flagged ambiguous words (e.g., "beat" can be an action such as striking or circularly moving a liquid, the main rhythm unit in music, or an adjective implying exhaustion, among others). These ambiguous words were then removed from our vocabulary when COCA indicated that they were used as an action 50 percent of the time or less. The resulting action dictionary contained 854 words and stems related to general motor (e.g., fly, gaming, gym) and cognitive activity (e.g., plan, deduce, realize). This action dictionary was then used to predict HIV prevalence across US counties (nested within state are presented in Figure 1.3).

Finally, behavior can also be predicted from nonsemantic features. One example has been the use of "likes" to predict the substance use behavior of a Facebook user. For example, Youyou et al. (2015) found an $r = 0.16$, which is not high but is still suggestive, given the private nature of condom use.

Principles of Cognitive Processing, Mental Representations, and Impact of Situational Factors

This book relies on several principles of cognitive functioning that have implications for much of the research reported in this book.

First, for reasons of efficiency, people use a subset of the information available in their environments or accessible at a particular time (Fiske & Taylor, 1991; Wyer et al., 1989).

> **Principle 3. Salience, accessibility, and nature of information used as a basis for attitudes, beliefs, and behaviors.** People form and change attitudes and beliefs, as well as initiate and change behavior, on the basis of whatever is salient and accessible at a particular time.

In addition, the information must be "diagnostic" or relevant for a judgment (Higgins, 1996; Wyer et al., 1989). Furthermore, consciously retrieving, finding, and analyzing the relevance of information require cognitive capacity and motivation (Albarracín & Kumkale, 2003; Chaiken, 1980; Higgins, 1996; Wyer et al., 1989). Hence the following principle:

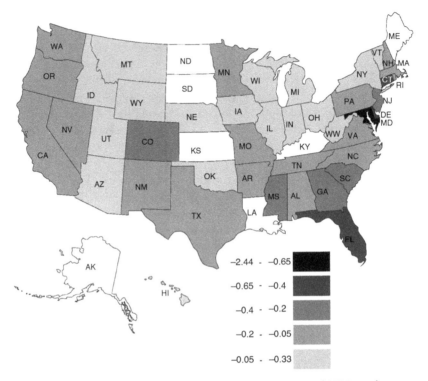

Figure 1.3 Associations between action words within a county and HIV prevalence. Numbers are random effects from a hierarchical linear model in which slopes and intercepts varied randomly between states, controlling for major socioeconomic determinants of HIV (see Ireland et al., 2016).

Principle 4. Selection of salient and accessible information depends on processing ability and motivation, as well as relevance criteria. People consciously select salient and accessible information on the basis of their ability and motivation to think about the information.

Like many others, I assume that people have no control over their cognitive processes underlying behavior and judgment (Bargh, 1994; Dulany, 2006; Wyer et al., 1989). This aspect is important and requires understanding how intention is experienced and the conditions that lead to using inputs that one would not have selected consciously but are present in one's working memory at the time.

Principle 5. Intentionality and awareness of cognitive and behavioral processes. People are generally unintentional about and unaware of the cognitive processes that underlie judgments and behavior.

Finally, people form judgments, attitudes, and intentions by directing their awareness to a stimulus in the environment or a concept in their minds. Also, they pay more attention when they have a specific information-processing goal and when they seek information with a goal in mind. Thus, concepts or issues that receive attention are more likely to be clearly represented and to be associated with a high number of representations (e.g., beliefs or goals) than are concepts or issues that receive no attention. As I will discuss, this general principle has implications for the representations of action and inaction.

> **Principle 6. Formation of representations and judgments.** People form better-defined, richer, and more consequential representations when they pay attention to a stimulus, concept, or behavior. Representations include beliefs, attitudes, and intentions, as well as memories.

Model of Attitudes and Behaviors (MAP)

The disposition toward action motivates the kinds of beliefs and attitudes people form (Principle 1). It also leads to deploying behavioral procedures and forming intentions we would not have if we did not think about action (Principle 1). However, how these psychological variables relate to each other is a question of relevance and informational influence: What are the implications of beliefs about the antecedents of a given behavior for the attitudes toward this behavior? What does my intention to buy milk say about my attitudes toward buying milk? Is my intention to solve a problem sufficient to solve it, or do I need specific behavioral procedures?

The relations among beliefs, attitudes, intentions, and behavioral procedures have been analyzed in many streams of research coming from prolific areas of social psychology and the broader social sciences (Albarracín, 2002; Nolder & Blankenship, 2019). My Model of Attitudes and Behavioral Practices (MAP) appears in Figure 1.4 and summarizes a variety of relations and possible processing sequences that lead to attitudes and behavior, often moderated by the ability and motivation to think about a behavior. These psychological variables are themselves informed by message arguments, past behavior and experience, other people (e.g., friends and teachers), and affective feelings, all of which provide content and direction for beliefs and attitudes.

I view the MAP as a tool to describe relations among psychological variables as they unfold in different processing sequences. Message arguments, other people, and past behavior and experience can influence beliefs

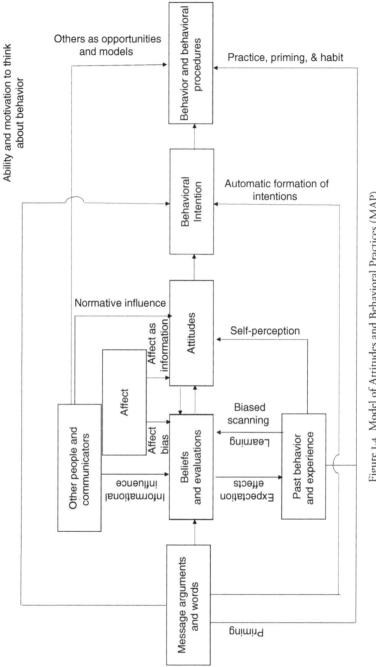

Figure 1.4 Model of Attitudes and Behavioral Practices (MAP).

and attitudes. For example, if other people express pain during a particular circumstance, we may form the belief that the circumstance is painful, and experience it as painful ourselves (see Chapter 5). Past behavior and experience can also influence our attitudes via self-perception (i.e., inferences about what we like to do; see Chapter 4) and our beliefs via learning, biased scanning (i.e., retrieval of memories in support of one's behavior; see Chapter 4), or cognitive dissonance (i.e., conflict between the behavior and other cognitions leading to changes in attitudes and beliefs; see Chapter 4). Furthermore, persuasive messages (e.g., Handley et al., 2009; see Chapter 2) influence our beliefs and ultimately our experiences, and affective feelings influence beliefs (Forgas, 1995; but see Wyer, Clore, & Isbell, 1999).

Attitudes toward the behavior are likely to influence behavioral intentions, which are themselves also influenced by behavioral goals (Gollwitzer, 1996; Jiang & Albarracín, 2019). Goals influence attitudes by activating evaluative procedures (Ferguson & Bargh, 2004; Kunda, 1987), which sometimes occur outside of awareness (Wyer, 2015). For most behaviors of interest in this book, however, the influence of goals on the recruitment of procedures is mediated by intention. Intention implies a degree of awareness that one wants to execute the behavior, but the process is frequently implicit, in the form of visualization of the behavior or brief questions inspired by the environment or haphazard mental associations (Lohmann & Albarracín, 2019; Lohmann, Jones, & Albarracín, 2019).

Behavioral procedures are indispensable for behavior to be executed. Yet, they have been typically neglected in the literatures of attitude change and prediction. Procedures are formed on the basis of our personal practice with past behavior as well as when others train us and when we observe models perform a particular skill (e.g., kicking a ball). Procedures and intentions can also be primed by the individual words in a message (Ireland, Schwartz et al., 2015; Ireland et al., 2016), much like in behavioral priming with specific words presented in controlled conditions (Bargh, 2016; Weingarten et al., 2016b; Wyer, 2015; Xu & Wyer, 2009).

All in all, most relations in MAP can be reciprocal under the right conditions. If attitudes typically guide my intentions, I can infer that a present intention was based on an attitude and *derive* the attitude that perhaps did not exist. For example, expressing the intention to vote may lead to drawing new conclusions about positive aspects of voting. Furthermore, calling attention to the intention to vote may lead to retrieving memories about positive voting experiences. The reciprocity notion illustrated by these examples is expressed in the following principle:

Principle 7. Reciprocity in the relations among beliefs, attitudes, intentions, goals, behavioral procedures, and behavior. Most relations among psychological variables involved in the understanding and change of attitudes and behavior (beliefs, attitudes, intentions, goals, behavioral procedures, and behavior) are reciprocal in nature, so that, if a first variable influences a second variable, the second variable influences the first given the right inferential and retrieval mechanisms.

Different Sequences of Processing

The processes introduced in Figure 1.4 occur in the context of processing ability and motivation, that is the resources and desire to spend effort for a particular evaluation or behavioral decision. This context is presented by the figure's dotted background and determines which processes will ultimately take place. That is, the figure summarizes all, or at least most, possible sequences, many of which I "trace" in later chapters. For example, Figure 1.5 shows the processing sequences obtained in response to a persuasive communication under conditions of either high, moderate, or low elaboration (Albarracín & Wyer, 2001; Albarracín, 2002; Albarracín et al., 2019). It shows sequences of processing among message recipients who both experience a positive or negative mood and read a strong or weak persuasive message. To examine the consequences of ability and motivation, we independently varied both the personal relevance of the message and the distraction participants experienced at the time they read it (Albarracín & Wyer, 2001; Albarracín, 2002). We found that, when ability and motivation allowed for high levels of elaboration, participants used message arguments as a basis for beliefs, attitudes, and intentions, and ultimately behaved accordingly. In these conditions, their high ability to elaborate allowed them to both identify their feelings and realize that the feelings were unrelated to the message. As the combination of either low ability and/or motivation created a moderate amount of elaboration, however, participants based the attitudes on affect, and these attitudes then influenced beliefs and evaluations, as a way of rationalizing the influence of affect. In these conditions, their moderate level of elaboration allowed them to identify their feelings but was insufficient to detect that the feelings were irrelevant (Albarracín & Kumkale, 2003). Last, when the level of thinking was low, participants were unable to identify affect, and only arguments influenced their beliefs and evaluations, and, ultimately, their attitudes and intentions. Thus, even when the influence of arguments decreased, some going from high to moderate, to low elaboration, the influence of affect decreased more.

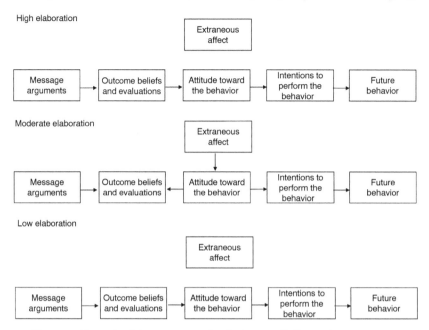

Figure 1.5 Example of three sequences for the impact of affect and message arguments obtained in my research.

I investigated another set of sequences in the context of research on the impact of past behavior. We (Albarracín & Wyer, 2000) gave a group of participants feedback on their ostensible past behavior. The feedback was presented as a measure of unconscious voting behavior. According to the cover story, unconscious behavior was gauged from participants' earlier responses to a subliminal task presenting a number of issues including a new university policy. This cover story allowed us to give participants feedback on whether their past behavior favored or opposed the policy. After the feedback, participants reported their attitudes and intentions to vote in favor of the referendum in the future, as well as their beliefs in and evaluations of outcomes of such behavior. At the end of the experiment, participants also cast an ostensibly anonymous ballot that either favored or opposed the institution of comprehensive exams.

Figure 1.6 summarized the results from this research. As hypothesized, participants reported more favorable attitudes toward comprehensive examinations when they thought that they had voted in favor of the exams than when they thought they had voted against them. Intentions and behaviors were affected similarly. Key to the study, however, was that distraction during the task was manipulated to be either high or low and the type of processing that occurred depended on distraction. As shown in the bottom panel of Figure 1.6, past behavior affected attitudes regardless of distraction, but the effect was mediated by beliefs and evaluations only when distraction was low (see top panel of Figure 1.6). In one case, the sequence was past behavior, behavioral beliefs/evaluations, attitudes, intentions, and behavior; in another, it was past behavior, attitudes, behavioral beliefs/evaluations, intentions, and behavior.

Another example about the sequences that can be traced in Figure 1.4 involves the impact of behavioral goals on intentions. In research I conducted with Duo Jiang (Jiang & Albarracín, 2019; Jiang, Albarracín, & Jiang, 2014), we tested whether active movement (e.g., walking versus standing) could lead to intentions to act quickly in response to an offer to purchase a vaccine (for other interesting effects of motor processes on

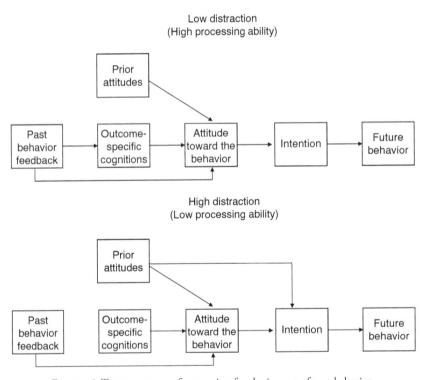

Figure 1.6 Two sequences of processing for the impact of past behavior.

persuasion, see Sherman et al., 2010; Streicher & Estes, 2016). We assigned participants to either walking or standing and then presented an ad promoting a flu shot with either a close deadline (e.g., 1 day) or a control ad (i.e., no time limits or a more distant deadline). The deadline could increase or decrease people's motivation to get the flu shot depending on how active they feel. Participants who had moved felt more active and reported stronger general action goals (i.e., the goal to engage in active behavior regardless of what the behavior is) than did participants who had not moved. Also, participants who had moved and had a close deadline reported stronger intentions to get the flu shot than did participants who had not moved.

The movement-based intentions we observed only occurred with a tight deadline, probably because the action goals and feelings arising from movement were most relevant under those conditions. These intentions were clearly based on a subtle criterion of which participants were not aware. This finding again brings up the notion that intentions can have other subtle origins, based on what I call "conative feelings," and other automatic forms of intention formation on the basis of strings of words (Lohmann & Albarracín, 2019; Lohmann, Jones, & Albarracín, 2019).

Intentions can, of course, be mentally represented as self-referential statements that combine commitment verbs ("will," "intend") with another verb (e.g., to drive) to form propositions like "I will perform X" or "I intend to drive" (Albarracín, Noguchi, & Earl, 2006). In this case, intentions probably guide behavior in a fairly algorithmic fashion, as when following a cooking recipe ("I will first pour two cups of sugar"; "then, I will add the eggs"). However, I argue that intentions may also be formed and experienced in subtle ways (Haggard & Clark, 2003; Lohmann & Albarracín, 2019; Pacherie, 2008; Tsakiris & Haggard, 2005). To understand the feelings of intention (Lohmann & Albarracín, 2019), we asked a group of participants to describe the feelings and words that go through their mind when they form intentions. As we expected, most participants described their intentions as feelings instead of words. Specifically, the phenomenology of intention included feeling "determined" and visualizing the action before executing their behavior.

Another way in which intentions develop is through internal questions people ask themselves. While standing in the aisle of the supermarket, the internal question "What should I buy?" appears important to elicit the behaviors we routinely perform. To test this hypothesis, we (Lohmann, Jones, & Albarracín, 2019) primed questions when people made free decisions after being trained to always choose their favorites in that same task.

Specifically, participants were presented with no question, an affirmative question (e.g., "Which one should I choose?"), a negative question (e.g., "Which one should I not choose?"), or an irrelevant question (e.g., "What should I have for dinner?"). We found that the affirmative question produced a higher level of repetition than did the negative question. Also, the effects were stronger with questions than with statements and persisted in the presence of distraction, thus suggesting that the questions and answers operated efficiently. This research thus illustrates a sequence in which words can help people to form intentions they can report as such even though they may not be aware of what contributed to the intentions (for a discussion of the difference between efficiency and awareness, see Bargh, 1994).

Action Goals in Initiation and Change of Attitudes and Behaviors

A handful of prior conceptualizations have emphasized the importance of prior attitudes for understanding the outcomes of persuasive messages and behavioral interventions. For example, Fazio et al. (1995) described attitude representations in permanent memory as a concept node (e.g., flower) linked to an evaluative node (e.g., pleasant). When this link is strong, the prior evaluation is easily *accessible* in memory. Thus, the evaluation is more likely to be activated whenever one encounters or recalls the attitude object. Importantly, these accessible attitudes are consequential. They influence future evaluative judgments, the processing of information about the attitude object, and the behaviors people perform (e.g., Fazio, 1990). For example, having a prior attitude can blind people to changes in the real object (Fazio, Ledbetter, & Towles-Schwen, 2000). All things considered, for Fazio, evaluative judgments based on existing attitudes are different from judgments based on novel evaluations (see also Albarracín et al., 2004)

Despite a recognition that attitude formation and change differ, there has not been a precise explication of the theoretical differences between attitude formation and change. In an attempt to fill this critical gap, this book addresses this point. Figure 1.7 depicts how the impact of persuasive messages is contingent on the presence of prior attitudes. First, prior attitudes and associated beliefs guide decisions about exposure to messages and behavioral interventions (see sequence A in Figure 1.7). Second, prior attitudes guide processing of new information and, in doing so, can make the impact of messages about prior attitudes dramatically smaller than the impact of messages concerning new issues (see sequence B in Figure 1.7). Whereas persuasive messages about new topics often reach sizable effects

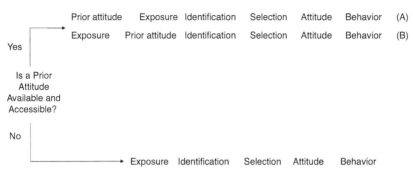

Figure 1.7 Initiation and change of attitudes and behaviors.

(d = 3.08; Chan et al., 2017; Chan, Jones, & Albarracín, 2017), persuasive messages changing those newly formed attitudes have much less success (d = 0.97). Even more disappointing is the size of the impact of persuasion in attempts to change important attitudes. Prior meta-analysis of messages or interventions to change attitudes (Tannenbaum et al., 2015), behaviors (Steinmetz et al., 2016; Tyson, Covey, & Rosenthal, 2014), and intergroup relationships (Lemmer & Wagner, 2015; Miles, Miles, & Crisp, 2013) have shown effects from a d = 0.20 to a d = 0.36. Figure 1.8 shows the specific results.

Another important assumption is that goals of action control the formation and change of many attitudes and behaviors and, in so doing, have opposing influences on the impact of persuasive communications and behavioral interventions. When people lack a prior attitude, the goal to act may lead them to form an attitude that can be used in the service of the goal. Thus, action goals can energize people to form attitudes and behavioral patterns using the information provided by the intervention. In contrast, when people have a prior attitude, the goal to act may lead people to use a prior attitude without having to pay attention to the new information.

Implications for Persuasion and Interventions

My conceptualization has implications for the social promotion of certain attitudes and behaviors. In particular, it suggests the need to instill an appropriate motivational state among recipients to ensure that they will go along with the recommendations. For example, Freud (1912) required clients to abstain from making significant life decisions while undergoing

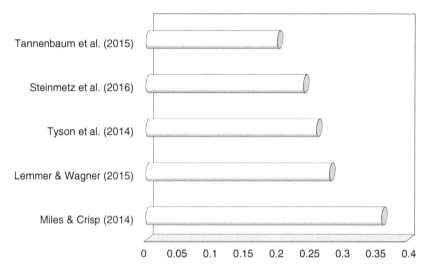

Figure 1.8 Meta-analyses of attempts at changing attitudes in important domains.

analysis (cf. an inaction goal). This practice was intended to reduce potentially detrimental effects of illusory perceptions or defense mechanisms that may arise as part of the analytic process. Albeit for different reasons, my model would also lead to the conclusion that inaction goals at the time of a behavioral intervention facilitate change. Even the title of an intervention might inadvertently prime action goals. An exception may be when the intervention itself allows clients to satisfy an action goal and thus precludes the tendency to retrieve an attitude that leads to repetition of past patterns.

Also, consider a consumer example in which people go to the grocery store because they are hungry. The specific goal to eat is likely to bring about associated attitudes toward the foods or brands they usually consume, thus decreasing their sensitivity to information about new products or brands. For these conditions, marketers who want audiences to switch from a preferred brand to another would do well if they allowed the hungry shoppers to sample the target food. First, the sampling behavior might satisfy the goal to eat while providing important product information. In addition, satisfying the goal to eat may decrease access to prior consumer attitudes and increase receptivity to ads, attractive packages, or coupons.

Let's consider a health intervention example, specifically the case of trying to change the attitudes and behaviors among teenagers who are sexually active. At first sight, one could propose to make this audience think about sexual activities, which would in turn make the message personally more relevant and increase message processing (Petty & Cacioppo, 1986a). However, thinking about a sexual activity may lead recipients to recall past behaviors and attitudes, which would in turn make the message less effective. In contrast, "disconnecting" the audience from the idea of sexual activity may lead recipients to "stay in the present" and process the persuasive message at hand.

Another way of decoupling past attitudes from the present experience may be mindful meditation, which has become popular in substance misuse. Mindfulness focuses on not trying to control thoughts and emotions and abandon all active agendas (Hayes et al., 2004). It includes (a) awareness of immediate experience and (b) a nonjudgmental, accepting attitude toward the experience without any attempts to change the experience or think about the past or the future (Kabat-Zinn, 1990). One of the forms of mindful meditation is Vipassana meditation, which follows the Buddhist tradition of simply paying attention to sensation, such as one's breathing. Vipassana training is typically group based and involves meditating for 10–11 hours per day for 10 days. Mindfulness-based stress reduction is a form of meditation used in medical contexts (Kabat-Zinn, 1990), and involves paying attention to the internal and external experiences occurring in the present moment. In theory, an "observe and accept" approach, which is central to meditation, involves being fully present and aware of current experience without being preoccupied by it. Such an observational, detached approach can decouple the present experience and impulsive responses, and consequently avoid being on "autopilot" or interested in acting quickly to get a "fix" (Ostafin, Bauer, & Myxter, 2012).

I was interested in the evidence of mindful meditation efficacy for substance use outcomes (for the domain of exercise, see Chatzisarantis & Hagger, 2007). A 2003 review (Baer, 2003) showed promising results. Likewise, a 2009 review (Zgierska et al., 2009) suggested potential benefits but recommended further research with randomized controlled trials and larger samples (see also Galante, Galante, Bekkers, & Gallacher, 2014; Maglione et al., 2017). Even with variable evidence, the possibility that meditation can induce attitude and behavior change is intriguing, particularly in light of the mechanisms I propose.

If mindfulness moderates acting on habitual impulses, my model would suggest that it should decrease activation of prior attitudes and behavioral procedures and also increase openness to new information. A prior study examined the association between alcohol attitudes and heavy drinking in a sample of college subjects who regularly drank alcohol (Ostafin & Marlatt, 2008). As the authors predicted, the relation between automatic alcohol attitudes (i.e., in this case, attitudes measured with the implicit association test [IAT]) and heavy drinking was weaker among participants with higher (vs. lower) levels of mindful acceptance. Furthermore, an experiment (Ostafin et al., 2012; for similar results in the domain of exercise, see Chatzisarantis & Hagger, 2007) manipulated mindful meditation and observed its effect on heavy drinking as a function of implicit attitudes. The results from this study appear in Figure 1.9. As shown, meditation reduced heavy drinking among participants with more positive (vs. more negative) implicit attitudes toward alcohol. All in all, this finding supports that an inaction disposition decreases the activation of prior attitudes.

There is also support for the hypothesis that meditation could increase attention to messages. One of the reasons is the control of emotional responses that are distracting while one processes an emotional persuasive

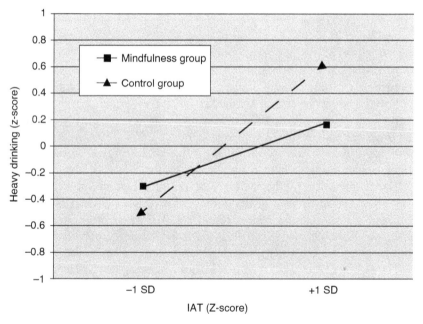

Figure 1.9 Effects of mindful meditation as a function of implicit attitudes.
(Reprinted with permission of Guilford Press)

message. In a study by Takahashi and Earl (2019), participants did or did not meditate before receiving a series of health messages. Participants in the mindfulness condition reported paying more attention to the messages than did participants in the control condition (Cohen's d = 0.67). Overall, although the authors found evidence that these effects were mediated by less fear among participants in the meditation (vs. control) condition, it is also possible that participants in the meditation condition were less prone to activating prior attitudes about health topics like flu, cancer, HIV, herpes, and gonorrhea. In particular, this possibility makes sense for messages that make recommendations like "One of the simplest ways to prevent cancer is to receive regular medical care, avoid tobacco, limit alcohol use, avoid exposure to ultraviolet rays from the sun and tanning beds, eating a healthy diet of fruits and vegetables, preserving a healthy weight, and being physically active." Greater attention to such a message could make college student recipients retrieve prior attitudes and behaviors (not liking fruits and vegetables, drinking habits) that support all of the behaviors the message tries to counter (Albarracín, Handley et al., 2011).

Finally, cultural factors can be expected to facilitate general action and inaction goals, as shown by research studies (Albarracín et al., 2017; Zell et al., 2013) and the news (Rampell, 2011). For example, US adults are supposed to exercise every day while working full-time and commuting to the workplace. They may also be expected to be good parents, to participate in their children's schools, and to thrive in their careers. Even more problematic, children are expected to exercise, perform well in school, and help their parents with household chores. Moreover, children are often expected to learn to play the piano, speak a foreign language, excel in sports, and make friends. All these activities may thrust parents and children into a general action pursuit that is appropriate for the formation of new attitudes and the initiation of behaviors. However, this mindset is likely inappropriate for change in attitudes and behaviors, making attempts at eating less, drinking less, or driving more safely potentially ineffective.

Organization of the Book

This book begins with chapters on the psychological and external variables in Figure 1.4, which indicates what aspects are addressed in particular chapters. Chapter 2 is about beliefs and their influence on attitudes; Chapter 3 is about attitudes; Chapter 4 is about behaviors, goals, and intentions. Each of these chapters outlines basic principles. Chapter 5 is about the influence of past behavior and experience, and Chapter 6 is about the influence of other people. Beyond that point, the book concentrates on the processes of initiation versus change of attitudes and behaviors (Figure 1.7). Chapter 7 describes the model, as well as the contribution of message arguments, the message source, and the affect recipients may experience while processing the message. Then, Chapter 8 discusses persuasion in attitude and behavior change situations, whereas Chapter 9 discusses the behavioral impact of persuasive messages and behavioral interventions and the concept of actionability. Chapter 10 summarizes the principles of the book and suggests future directions.

PART II

Beliefs, Attitudes, and Behaviors

CHAPTER 2

Beliefs

Earlier this year, I asked a sample of approximately 1,000 US inhabitants to indicate their belief in the following statements: "Lizard aliens hybridized with humans who now occupy positions of power around the globe"; "The observation that water surfaces on earth are flat proves that our planet is flat"; "The United Nations had a secret plan termed 'Agenda 21' to force Americans from suburbs into cities and implement mandatory contraception to curb population growth"; and "The US government has in the past used chemtrails – a toxic cocktail of aluminum, strontium and barium sprayed from planes – to control the weather, the population, and our food supply." Even though none of these statements has been verified empirically and most are debunked by all the available scientific evidence, on a scale of 1 (*definitely false*) to 5 (*definitely true*), the average truth ratings were approximately 2, with the rating of "chemtrails" being highest at 2.46 (SD = 1.35). Even more notably, these patently false facts were only slightly less believable than true facts, including "The current human genome reveals a hybridization of modern humans with other species of humans such as Neanderthals"; "The Moon was initially part of the Earth"; "China has a current population growth policy that allows couples to have a maximum of two children"; and "Regional governments in the US have allowed contamination of the water supply with lead." Specifically, these true facts had average truth ratings of between 2.42 (SD = 1.43) and 3.58 (SD = 1.22).

The line between belief and knowledge is blurry. Knowledge is information we can classify as "true" or "false," but a statistical distribution with an M of 2.42 and an SD of 1.43 is hardly a true–false dichotomy. Instead, we move around the world and make social, health, and financial judgments armed with much shakier beliefs. Beliefs are probability judgments (Albarracín et al., 2019; Eagly & Chaiken, 1993; Wyer & Albarracín, 2005). They can describe the probability that an object (i.e., a referent) has an attribute (Fishbein, 1963). "John is smart" and

"The Chicago River is green today" are two such beliefs. They can also describe the probability that a behavior has an outcome (Ajzen & Fishbein, 1980; Fishbein & Ajzen, 2011). "Quitting smoking reduces risk of lung cancer" is one such belief (Ajzen & Fishbein, 1980; Fishbein & Ajzen, 2011). Beliefs can also represent certainty that an object or event is real, as in the case of "I believe in God" and "He believed what she told him." "Expectations" are beliefs that describe what an object or behavior will be like in the future.

According to the expectancy-value formulation (Ajzen et al., 2019; Fishbein & Ajzen, 2011), one's attitude toward an object is a function of both outcome beliefs and evaluations. Presenting vaccination as promoting desirable (vs. undesirable) outcomes will lead people to favor vaccines (Albarracín & Wyer, 2001; Johnson, Smith-McLallen, Killeya, & Levin, 2004). Persuading others that a talc pill will cure a physical disease can reduce symptoms (Geers, Brinol, & Petty, 2019), and the expectation that alcohol makes people social increases sociability among drinkers (Darkes & Goldman, 1998; Davis, Smith, & Briley, 2017). In this chapter, I consider effects of beliefs about objects and experiences and, later, specify the role of beliefs about the antecedents and consequences of behavior. Finally, I turn to the important issue of how to change behavior by changing beliefs and expectations.

Beliefs about Objects and Experiences

Actual experience with an object or behavior is an important belief determinant. For example, experience teaches us what objects are soft, what places are warm, and what behaviors lead to danger. Therefore, we can extract beliefs such as "Florida is warm" and "Wearing leather-sole shoes when it's icy will make you fall." Likewise, seeing miniature deer on Victoria Island in Bariloche, Argentina, will lead to the belief that "Miniature deer exist in some areas of the globe."

Experiences often involve emotional feelings and thus create beliefs about feelings we might experience in the future (i.e., affective expectations). Research in the domain of breastfeeding nicely illustrates the power of affective experiences (DiGirolamo et al., 2005). In this area, a large amount of evidence supports the benefits of breastfeeding for both infants and mothers. This feeding practice boosts the immunological defenses of the infant and accelerates maternal recovery from childbirth (Gartner et al., 2005). Thus, before the child is born, mothers often intend to breastfeed their infants. However, many abandon their attempts to breastfeed, sometimes days after the infant is born. The beliefs based on affective experiences are thus at the basis of breastfeeding discontinuation.

A study on the contribution of the affective beliefs associated with breastfeeding (DiGirolamo et al., 2005) included measures of breastfeeding intentions prior to delivery, emotional comfort during breastfeeding (i.e., affective experience), and frequency and duration of breastfeeding. As one might expect (Albarracín, Johnson, Fishbein, & Muellerleile, 2001), intentions to breastfeed predicted breastfeeding. However, so did the emotional experience of breastfeeding. Among the women who discontinued before 20 weeks, 19 percent reported feeling emotionally uncomfortable. In contrast, less than 1 percent of the women who continued beyond 20 weeks manifested discomfort.

Mere expectations can also drive judgments of affective experience (see also Bruner, 1957; Forgas, 1995). People who expect an object to be pleasant will experience the object as pleasant. Naturally, however, expectations color the experience more when people fail to attend to potential discrepancies between the beliefs and the object (for related issues, see Fazio et al., 2000).

The *placebo effect* is an interesting case of how expectations bias experience and judgments. Beliefs about the effects of substances, drugs, and medical treatments affect reactions to them. People who expect that alcohol will make them more sociable are indeed more sociable when they drink (Lau-Barraco et al., 2012). However, placebo effects are more likely to occur if, in addition to an expectation, an individual has a goal that is compatible with the expectation (Geers et al., 2005). For example, expecting that a drug (actually inert) will make a person feel less nauseous and also having the goal (consciously or nonconsciously) of feeling less nauseous lead to the placebo effect.

A study by Hoegg and Alba (2006) demonstrated the curious influence of beliefs in the domain of taste. Participants in a series of studies were asked to compare the tastes of three samples of orange juice. Pairs could contain either the same juice or a different juice and were presented either numbered from 1 to 4 or differentiated with artificial coloring. Coloring was used as a way of creating the expectation that juices of the same color were the same juice. In all conditions, participants were allowed to taste the samples, and then they rated how different the two samples were. Figure 2.1 presents the results, with higher numbers indicating greater perceived differences across the samples. As can be seen, when the samples were simply numbered (control), participants accurately perceived different types of juice as different. However, when the samples were grouped by

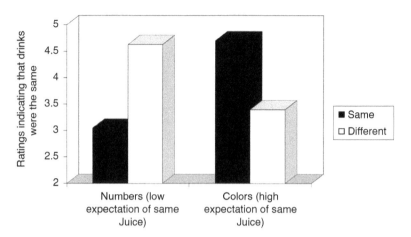

Figure 2.1 Effects of expectations on reported taste.

color, samples with different colors were judged to be more different than samples with different numbers. In other words, the color created expectations that overrode taste perceptions.

Under what conditions do people notice inconsistencies between expectations and reality? Geers, Helfer, Kosbab, Weiland, and Landry (2005) have argued that people who notice inconsistencies between their beliefs and experiences might be negatively influenced by their beliefs (i.e., experience a *contrast* effect). People who are motivated and able to examine an object may judge the experience as less in line with the expectation (Geers & Lassiter, 1999). For example, believing that a movie will induce positive feelings may backfire when the movie actually induces negative feelings.

Importantly, Chang (2004) adopted a more explicit stand on the processes underlying disconfirmation of affective experiences (see also Boulding, Kalra, Staelin, & Zeithaml, 1993; Hoch & Deighton, 1989; Kopalle & Lehmann, 1995, 2001; Olson & Dover, 1979). According to Chang, contradictory experiences reverse the effects of beliefs by producing more careful thinking when people have high knowledge about a product. Participants in this research had either high or low knowledge about fruit juices. They were given an advertisement describing the appealing taste of a new type of juice, which they later sampled. Half of the participants received a good-tasting drink and the other a bad-tasting drink. The findings from this study appear in Figure 2.2. As shown, when participants

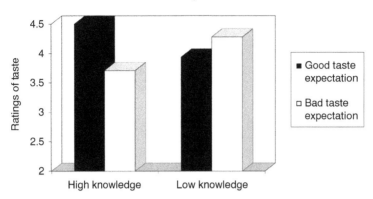

Figure 2.2 Effects of beliefs on taste as a function of knowledge level. Participants were induced beliefs about the good or bad taste of a drink that, in actuality, was bad tasting.

had high knowledge, they reported the product as worse when the taste was bad than when it was good. However, when knowledge was low, the two taste conditions did not differ. If anything, in the low-knowledge conditions, the product was judged as better when its taste was bad than when it was good.

Also within the consumer-behavior domain, research by Oliver (1977) uncovered interesting effects of forming beliefs about positive or negative attributes of a product. Discovering that a product's qualities fall short of expectations (e.g., not enough positive qualities or too many negative qualities) produces dissatisfaction. In contrast, discovering that a product's qualities exceed expectations (e.g., fewer negative or more positive qualities) produces satisfaction. Similarly, Mellers, Schwartz, Ho, and Ritov (1997) propose that consumers engage in counterfactual thinking and compare the actual outcome to the expected outcome. If the outcome and the expectation match, affect is commensurate with the outcome. People feel bad if the outcome is negative but good if the outcome is positive. However, if the outcome is better (worse) than expected (e.g., people win $100 when they expected to win $50 vs. losing $50 when they expected to lose $100), people experience highly positive (negative) affect resulting from a contrast with the expected outcome.

The ironic effects of disconfirming beliefs, however, can be attributed to more than one type of process. According to our research (Handley et al., 2009), there are inferential and perceptual comparative processes, both of which require paying attention to one's affective reactions. That is, people must direct attention or identify their feelings for those feelings to have an influence (Albarracín & Kumkale, 2003). Also, having a naive theory that affective beliefs influence affective experiences calls further attention to affect and leads to correcting attitudes for the presumed effects of the expectation (Handley et al., 2009).

To test this hypothesis, we (Handley et al., 2009) conducted a series of laboratory experiments. In this series, participants first received either a positive or a negative expectation about either a new alcohol-like beverage or a photography book. The results showed that a positive expectation was worse when affect identification was normal or high. Presumably, either normal or high affect identification allows people to infer that the product seemed better because they expected it to be good. However, high affect identification is necessary to elicit the same effect in a perceptual way, that is, in the absence of a theory. In addition, perceptual, belief-consistent effects occurred when affect identification was normal and participants had no naive theory about the influence of affect.

Beliefs about Behavioral Outcomes

Experience both influences beliefs and is influenced by beliefs, but the research I just reviewed is insufficient to understand the critical role of beliefs about the outcomes and antecedents of a behavior. In making behavioral decisions, people wonder whether they would personally *like* to perform the behavior. In doing so, they consider if the consequences of that behavior are desirable (Ajzen & Fishbein, 1980). For example, when purchasing a car, people often form their attitudes toward a car by judging the car's attributes and the desirability of each attribute. They may find out that the car has efficient gas mileage, is compact, and is blue and evaluate each attribute of the car. They may also find out that buying the car will not allow for family trips and will increase their current debt. In this case, the attitude toward the car depends on the evaluations of having efficient gas mileage, being compact, and being blue, combined with the strength of the car-attribute associations. Correspondingly, the attitude toward the behavior depends on the evaluations of "not being able to make family trips" and "increasing one's debt," combined with the probability that buying the car will yield those outcomes.

Fishbein and Ajzen (Ajzen & Fishbein, 1980; Fishbein & Ajzen, 1975, 2010) were the first to introduce the belief–attitude–intention–behavior sequence to social psychology. Their theory, which appears in the top panel of Figure 2.3, posits that a person's overt action is a function of the

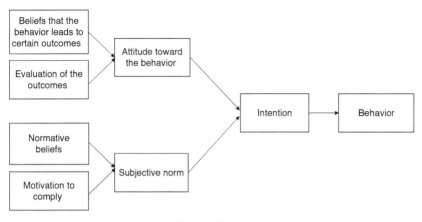

Figure 2.3 Theory of reasoned action.

intention or willingness to perform the behavior. For example, researchers may ask, "How likely is it that, in the next six months, you will [would] use a condom the next time you have vaginal sex with her?" (Albarracín, Johnson, Fishbein, & Muellerleile, 2001). If the theory of reasoned action is correct, respondents should be likely to use condoms when they intend to use them. Intentions, in turn, are influenced by the attitude toward performing the behavior and the subjective norm. Attitude is the degree to which one has a positive versus a negative evaluation of the behavior and is typically measured by a set of semantic differential (e.g., bad/good) scales. The subjective norm is the perception that important others think that one should or should not perform the behavior in question (see Chapter 5 for my discussion of normative influences) and is typically measured by items such as "people who are important to me think I should use condoms" (see, e.g., Fisher, Fisher, & Rye, 1995). In most studies, however, intention is driven by attitudes to a greater extent than by subjective norms (Albarracín, Johnson, Fishbein, & Muellerleile, 2001; Eagly & Chaiken, 1993).

The attitude toward the behavior is assumed to be a function of one's beliefs that performing the behavior in question will lead to various outcomes and the evaluative aspects of those beliefs (i.e., the evaluations of the outcomes). An expectancy-value estimate of attitude is obtained by subjectively weighting each salient belief that the outcome will occur (b_i, $i = 1, \ldots, p$) by the evaluative implications of that outcome (e_i, $i = 1, \ldots, p$). Thus, one is more likely to have a positive attitude toward using condoms if one believes that using a condom will lead to positive outcomes (e.g., "will make sex more fun") and prevent negative outcomes (e.g., "may help prevent HIV"). Formally,

$$A_B = \Sigma\; b_i\; e_i,$$

where A_B is the attitude toward performing behavior B, b_i is the strength of the belief that performing behavior B leads to outcome i, e_i is the evaluation of outcome i, and i is the number of salient outcomes. This component of the model is critical when researchers are interested in modifying attitudes since it assumes that attitudes are formed on the basis of an analysis of behavioral outcomes.

The subjective norm is also influenced by a set of salient beliefs about the normative prescriptions of specific referents, weighted by the motivation to comply with each of those referents. For example, a man may perceive social pressure to use condoms if he believes that his partner thinks that he should use condoms and he is motivated to comply with him or her. Thus,

$$SN_B = \Sigma\; nb_j\; m_j,$$

where SN_B is the subjective norm toward behavior B, nb_j is the normative belief that referent j thinks the respondent should or should not perform the behavior, m_j is the motivation to comply with referent j, and j is the number of referents. Normative beliefs are typically measured by bipolar probability statements about the opinion of a specific referent (e.g., "Does your main partner think that you should or should not get him to use a condom every time you have vaginal sex with him?"; Kamb et al., 1998, p. 12), whereas motivations to comply are measured by means of unipolar items (e.g., "In general, I want to do what my partner wants me to do"). The use of the $\Sigma nb_j m_j$ component to predict subjective norms assumes that people's subjective norms can be changed by changing either the perceived positions of important referents or one's motivation to comply with those referents.

In Fishbein and Ajzen's (1975) model, A_O is the attitude toward the object, b_i is the strength of the belief that the object has attribute i, e_i is the evaluation of attribute i, and the sum is over all salient attributes (Fishbein & Ajzen, 1975). A_O is the attitude toward the object, b_i is the strength of the belief that the behavior will lead to outcome i, e_i is the evaluation of outcome i, and the sum is over all salient outcomes (Fishbein & Ajzen, 1975). The equation for the attitude toward the object is as follows:

$$A_O = \Sigma b_i e_i.$$

Beliefs about Behavioral Antecedents

We (Albarracín et al., 2001) meta-analyzed a large number of empirical studies examining the relation between attitudes toward condom use and the $\Sigma b_i e_i$ concerning condom use. We found that the association between condom use attitudes and $\Sigma b_i e_i$ was positive and strong. However, when people decide whether or not to perform a behavior, they also think about the antecedents to the behavior, that is, the conditions that are necessary for the behavior to take place. Exercise, for example, requires purchasing athletic shoes and finding an appropriate location. In addition, for adults who have not exercised in a long time, exercise requires a medical exam to rule out health risks. If one can estimate the likelihood that these preconditions will be met, one should be equally likely to estimate any person's ability to perform the action in question. Likewise, people who try to gauge their own ability to perform a behavior should go through a similar process of estimating what Ajzen (1991) refers to as "control beliefs." According to him, perceptions of control are contingent on control beliefs and control power, that is, the belief in an antecedent to the behavior (e.g., having condoms available) and the degree to which that event facilitates the behavior. Similar to $A_B = \Sigma b_i e_i$, PBC = $\Sigma cb_k cp_k$, where PBC is perceived behavioral control, cb_k is the control belief concerning event k, and cp_k is the control power of event k to promote or prevent the behavior, all summed over the number of events (k).

Ajzen and colleagues (Ajzen, 1985; Ajzen & Driver, 1990; Ajzen & Madden, 1986; Fishbein & Ajzen, 2010) added the variable of perceived behavioral control in an effort to predict intentions and behaviors that are not completely under volitional control (Figure 2.4). *Perceived behavioral control* refers to one's perception of control over the behavior and is assumed to reflect the obstacles that one encountered in past behavioral performances. With the inclusion of this new factor, Ajzen's theory of planned behavior proposes that perceived behavioral control can influence behavior directly. Thus,

$$B = I + PBC,$$

where B is the behavior, I is intention, and PBC is perceived behavioral control. In addition to contributing to behavioral prediction, perceived behavioral control is assumed to influence a person's intention to use condoms over and above attitudes and norms. That is, people with higher perceived control are more likely to form intentions to perform a particular

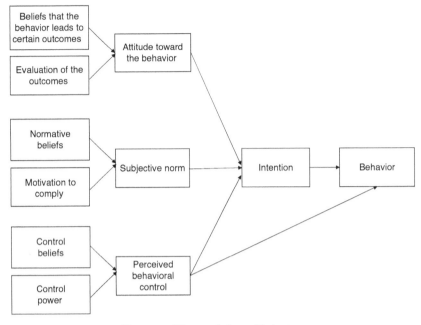

Figure 2.4 Theory of planned behavior.

action than those who perceive that they have little or no control. Formally,

$$I = A_B, + SN_B + PBC,$$

where I, A_B, SN_B, and PBC have been previously defined. Generally, perceived behavioral control is measured as an aggregate of perceptions that (a) one can or cannot perform the behavior if one wants to, (b) performing the behavior is or is not up to oneself, and (c) performing the behavior is easy or difficult (see Ajzen, 1985; Ajzen & Driver, 1990; Ajzen & Madden, 1986; Fishbein & Ajzen, 2010). The theory has performed very well in many domains (Armitage, 1995; Bamberg, Ajzen, & Schmidt, 2003; Davis et al., 2002; De Leeuw et al., 2015; Fishbein, 2008; Fraser et al., 2010; Glasman & Albarracín, 2003; Hagger & Chatzisarantis, 2014; Hassan, Shiu, & Parry, 2016b; Heim et al., 2018; Holtgrave, 2007; Hornik, Ajzen, & Albarracín, 2007; Perkins et al., 2007; Stecker et al., 2010; Zemore & Ajzen, 2014).

What Ajzen's (1991) model does not take into account, however, is that evaluations of the antecedents of the behavior can also contribute to the desirability of the behavior. According to McGuire and McGuire (1991), the desirability of an event's antecedent may affect the overall evaluation of the event. For example, to judge if developing an HIV vaccine is favorable, some people may wish to know how many animals will suffer or die in the process of testing the vaccine (McGuire & McGuire, 1991). Others, however, will focus on the number of lives the vaccine will likely save, as in Fishbein and Ajzen's (1975) model.

The influence of the behavioral antecedents can be conceptualized as the combined influence of the ability of a given event to promote the behavior (i.e., likelihood that a possible antecedent will trigger the behavior) and the perceived desirability of this event. If people believe that performing the behavior involves preparatory actions or events that they find desirable, their attitude is likely to be positive. Moreover, if they believe that performing the behavior does not involve preparatory actions or events that they find desirable, their attitude is likely to be negative (for further details on the double-negative logic, see Ajzen & Fishbein, 1980).

Although both consequences and antecedents are likely to be important, their relative weights may vary. As a case in point, people with little prior experience with a behavior are more likely to first consider how to get to perform it than are people with more experience. Thus, inexperienced ones may think about the likelihood and desirability of the antecedents more than experienced ones may. For example, young adults without sexual experience may evaluate condom use on the basis of not only its outcomes but also its antecedents. In contrast, young adults with sexual experience may evaluate the behavior on the basis solely of the outcomes.

I conducted a study with 438 introductory psychology students to examine the role of antecedents and consequences in attitudes. The questionnaire measured (a) attitudes, (b) beliefs in and evaluations of the antecedents of condom use, (c) beliefs in and evaluations of the outcomes of condom use, and (d) sexual experience. Attitudes were measured with semantic differential scales (*unsafe* vs. *safe*, *something I don't like* vs. *something I like*). Condom use antecedents were elicited in a qualitative questionnaire previously administered to an independent sample of 30 students. Specifically, the earlier participants were asked to describe the "good and bad things that would need to happen for you to use a condom correctly every time you have sex in the next year" and the "events that would facilitate or hinder your correct condom use every time you have sex in the next year." Five events were mentioned by at least 10 percent of the earlier participants: (a) "having condoms available," (b) "being careful," (c) "being in a monogamous relationship," (d) "being sexually excited when a condom is not around," and (e) "having a partner who does not want to use a condom." In the main study, we measured antecedent beliefs by asking participants to "judge the extent to which each of the following events would lead to using condoms correctly every time you have sex during the next year" on a scale of –3 (*unlikely*) to +3 (*likely*). Similarly, we measured antecedent evaluations by asking participants to rate each situation (e.g., "having condoms available") using a scale ranging from –3 (*bad*) to +3 (*good*). As a summary measure of *cognitions about behavioral antecedents*, we multiplied the likelihood that each antecedent would promote condom use by the desirability of the corresponding antecedent and summed over the five antecedents in the scale.

We also measured judgments of the consequences of condom use. These consequences were elicited following Ajzen and Fishbein's (1980) procedures. Specifically, participants reported the "advantages and disadvantages" and "good and bad results" of their using a condom correctly in the next year. Consequences mentioned by at least 10 percent of the participants were considered modally salient and used in the study questionnaire. To measure outcome beliefs, participants were asked to use a scale from –3 (*unlikely*) to +3 (*likely*) to rate the likelihood that "using condoms correctly every time you have sex during the next year will:" (a) "prevent HIV," (b) "prevent sexually transmitted diseases," (c) "prevent pregnancy," (d) "make me feel safe," and (e) "reduce my sexual pleasure." To measure outcome evaluations, participants rated the desirability of the outcomes on a scale from –3 (*bad*) to +3 (*good*). As with antecedent cognitions, we weighted the likelihood that the behavior would lead to each consequence by the perceived desirability of the consequence. Next, we summed the resulting scores as an overall index of *cognitions about outcomes*.

If behavioral experience moderates the implications of behavior antecedents for attitudes toward the behavior, we might observe stronger correlations with antecedent cognitions when participants had no sexual experience. As expected, the attitudes of sexually inexperienced participants correlated with antecedents of condom use more highly than did the attitudes of sexually experienced ones. However, the correlation with outcome perceptions was similar across the two groups.

Changing Cognitions about Outcomes and Antecedents

Changing an attitude toward a behavior often requires changing beliefs and evaluations of outcomes. For example, interventions that discuss the outcomes of implementing condom use (Albarracín et al., 2005; Albarracín, McNatt et al., 2003) increase positive **outcome** beliefs and evaluations of these outcomes. As a result, these interventions are generally more effective than those that do not discuss outcomes (Albarracín et al., 2005; Albarracín, McNatt et al., 2003). Furthermore, programs to change behavior are often successful if they increase the probability of events that causally precede the target behavior. To begin, verbal arguments may teach people to gather resources for and sort obstacles to a behavior like condom use (what we have called *behavioral skills arguments*; Albarracín et al., 2005; Albarracín, McNatt et al., 2003). In addition, a widely accepted behavioral intervention strategy is to have individuals role-play behavioral skills like condom application or negotiation in the case of condom use (i.e., *behavioral skills training*). These two strategies offer an ideal opportunity to examine how to induce critical **antecedents** that facilitate or hinder a behavior.

We investigated the effects of behavioral skills arguments and training in a meta-analysis of the effects of HIV-prevention interventions designed to promote condom use. As part of this project (Albarracín et al., 2003, 2005), we selected over 350 interventions and around 100 control groups comprising a large number of countries, US states, and years. For each of these groups or conditions, we calculated amount of change in behavior over time (e.g., increases in condom use frequency from the pretest to the posttest). We also coded for presence of behavioral skills arguments (e.g., describing how carrying condoms around is beneficial), as well as training in condom use skills (e.g., practice with unwrapping and applying condoms), interpersonal skills (e.g., role-playing interpersonal conflict over condom use and initiation of discussions about protection), and self-management skills (e.g., practice in decision-making while intoxicated, avoidance of risky situations). We also calculated change in various psychological variables including *behavioral skills* (knowing how to obtain and apply condoms and knowing how to negotiate condom use with a partner).

The results of comparing interventions that did and did not include behavioral skills arguments and training appear in Table 2.1. They show that including behavioral skills arguments as well as self-management behavior-skills training in the interventions led to positive change.

Nonetheless, the finding that a behavioral skill strategy influences behavior change is not sufficient to conclude that behavioral skills mediate the effect. To investigate that possibility, we (Albarracín, Gillette et al., 2005) conducted path analyses using a dummy code to signal the use of self-management skills training, a measure of change in perceptions of control or behavioral skills as the mediator, and change in condom use as the outcome. The analyses for perceptions of control and self-management skills training appears in Figure 2.5. As shown, the effect of self-management skills training on behavior change was mediated by changes in perceptions of control and behavioral skills.

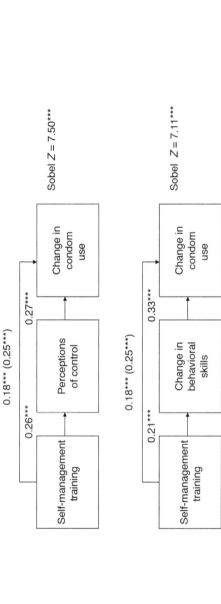

Figure 2.5 Effects of behavioral skills training on condom use change. (Adapted from Albarracín, Gillette, et al., 2005)

Table 2.1 *Effects of behavioral skills arguments and training on change in condom use behavior*

	Was strategy included in intervention?		
	Yes	No	Q_{B_1}
Behavioral skills arguments	0.33	0.16	44.49***
Behavioral skills training			
Condom use skills training	0.31	0.30	0.71
Interpersonal skills training	0.25	0.36	10.14**
Self-management skills training	0.51	0.10	251.08***

Note: All factors were dummy coded (strategy included 1; strategy not included 0). Entries are fixed-effects weighted model means adjusted for all other effects. Control groups (*d.* 0.08, confidence interval 0.06 to 0.10) were excluded. Threat-inducing arguments, normative arguments, attitudinal arguments, informational arguments, counseling and testing, and condom use provision were included in the analysis, as was condom provision. Q_B homogeneity coefficient for the difference across levels of a factor, distributed as a chi-square with degrees of freedom equal to the number of factor levels.
**$p < 0.01$. ***$p < 0.001$.
Source: Adapted from Albarracín, Gillette et al. (2005).

Despite positive effects of self-management skills training, the other two skills training were much less promising. As shown in Table 2.1, including condom use skills training had no effect, and including interpersonal skills training had a negative effect, leading to less change with it than without it. However, we need to consider that each of these training strategies is gender specific. Condom use skills training is geared toward men who can actually apply the male condom, and behavioral skills training is geared toward women who must persuade their partners to use the male condom. Therefore, we analyzed if the impact of behavioral skills strategies was moderated by gender and found partial support for our hypothesis. Condom use skills training was efficacious for predominantly male samples but counterproductive for predominantly female samples, and interpersonal skills training had no effect for predominantly female samples but was counterproductive for predominantly male samples. In addition, even when self-management skills training (e.g., not to drink around sex) was efficacious across genders, its impact was stronger for females than males.

But do behavioral skills strategies, which are designed to increase actual ability to promote antecedents that are preconditions to a behavior, have differential effects as a function of experience with a behavior? Do these strategies work better for people who have less experience with the

Table 2.2 *Effects of behavioral skills training as a function of the audience being predominantly male or female*

	Strategy included in intervention?					
	Males			Females		
	Yes	No	Q_{B_1}	Yes	No	Q_{B_1}
Condom use skills training	0.54	0.36	48.17***	0.27	0.40	9.35**
Interpersonal skills training	0.37	0.53	14.27***	0.33	0.35	0.11
Self-management skills training	0.62	0.28	94.03***	0.62	0.06	196.11***

antecedents of a behavior like condom use? My earlier analyses predicting attitudes toward condom use from beliefs and evaluations about antecedents and outcomes suggested that outcomes mattered regardless of sexual experience, whereas antecedents mattered more for the inexperienced. Thus, behavioral skills arguments and training could also matter more for the inexperienced.

In the meta-analysis of condom use interventions, we (Albarracín et al., 2003, 2005) (see Table 2.2) examined whether intervention efficacy depends on the level of sexual experience. Condom use interventions are generally applied to populations with sexual experience, except for school interventions, which naturally capture adolescents and young adults, who typically have less experience. We also compared recipients over and under 21 years of age. Interestingly, condom use skills, which are essential for somebody without experience to be able to use condoms, were more influential both for school interventions and for samples under 21 in average. In contrast, looking at the effects of attitudinal arguments, which typically describe the *outcomes* of condom use, showed no difference in efficacy across school versus nonschool interventions or younger versus older samples.

In the domain of condom use, sexual experience is probably a proxy for having the most basic skills necessary to begin practicing the behavior. However, another important issue is the degree to which discussions about antecedents and outcomes have different effects depending on the degree to which people have already been practicing the recommended behavior (in this case, condom use). The transtheoretical model (Prochaska, DiClemente, & Norcross, 1992) has described a sequence of stages that go from behavior initiation, to adoption, to maintenance. According to this model (Prochaska et al., 1994), people who are aware that their behavior is problematic but do not intend to change it are in the precontemplation stage. People who consider performing the behavior at some point in their lives but have no actual plans to change it are in the contemplation stage (Prochaska et al., 1994). People who are committed to changing their behavior within the next month and engage in the behavior occasionally are in the preparation stage (Prochaska et al., 1994). People who engage in the behavior on a regular basis for less than 6 months are in the action stage (Prochaska et al., 1994). People who engage in a behavior on a regular basis for 6 months or more are in the maintenance stage (Prochaska et al., 1994). Presumably, earlier stages require motivational interventions and later stages require behavioral skills training.

We analyzed the effects of self-management training and information in combination with the level of past condom use of the audience. According to the transtheoretical model, people who are not yet using condoms may become motivated if they are presented with an attitudinal or informational appeal. Later on, however, a focus on behavioral skills should facilitate movement toward the more consistent implementation of the recommended behavior (Bandura, 1997, 2001; Bandura & Wood, 1989). We found that intervention strategies varied in their effectiveness for people who had lower and higher levels of condom use prior to the intervention. Consistent with Prochaska et al.'s (1992) predictions, the beneficial effects of self-management skills training were greater among higher condom users than lower condom users. However, contrary to Prochaska et al.'s (1994) predictions, the influence of attitudinal arguments was the same across levels of past condom use. If anything, attitudinal arguments had a greater effect among higher than lower condom users, which is opposite to Prochaska et al.'s hypothesis.

All in all, changing beliefs and evaluations concerning both outcomes and antecedents can produce changes in attitudes toward the behavior and ultimately the behavior as well. This is summarized in the following principle:

> **Principle 8. Impact of beliefs on attitudes.** Changing beliefs about the outcomes and antecedents of a behavior generally changes attitudes.

Beliefs about Actions and Inactions

Another important dimension of beliefs is whether they pertain to action or inaction. Movement attracts attention in most living beings, including humans. Likewise, action may attract more attention than inaction even if movement is not involved. One preliminary indication that people are more interested in action than inaction comes from Google searches for action and inaction, as well as the adjectives active, passive, and inactive.

Table 2.3 *Number of associations with action and inaction*

	Action	Inaction	*t*-Test[a]
What are the advantages of action/inaction (in whatever way you understand it)?	6.70	3.45	19.60***
What are the disadvantages of action/inaction (in whatever way you understand it)?	5.33	3.17	13.78***
What does it take (need to happen) for action/inaction (in whatever way you understand it) to be possible?	4.34	2.98	19.60***

[a]$N = 407$.
***$p < .001$

This analysis showed that interest in action is also between 70 and 100 times higher than interest in inaction. Similarly, interest in "active" is about twice as strong as is interest in "passive" and "inactive."

If people pay more attention to action than inaction, they should have more beliefs about action than inaction. For that reason, I asked a group of participants to describe advantages of "action" and "inaction," disadvantaged of "action" and "inaction," and antecedents of "action" and "inaction." As shown in Table 2.3, general action produces more associations than general inaction. In fact, there are between about one and three more associations for action than inaction, representing between 30 percent and 100 percent more beliefs about action than beliefs about inaction. This finding supports the following principle:

Principle 9. Relative numerosity of beliefs about action and inaction. There are more beliefs about general action than about general inaction.

General action and general inaction are both abstract concepts. Naturally, to exert an effect, these concepts need to be applicable to specific behaviors. We argue that general action concepts will shape beliefs about any behavior that can be construed as an action. Correspondingly, general inaction concepts will shape beliefs about any behavior that can be construed as an inaction.

Principle 10. Influence of beliefs about action and inaction on specific beliefs. Beliefs about action and inaction can influence beliefs about any specific behavior that can be construed as action or inaction.

For example, in the same study presented in Table 2.3, I asked participants to describe advantages, disadvantages, and antecedents of two specific behaviors,

Table 2.4 *Number of associations with run and sleep*

	Run	Sleep	*t*-Test[a]
What are the advantages of action/inaction (in whatever way you understand it)?	3.20	2.69	6.36***
What are the disadvantages of action/inaction (in whatever way you understand it)?	2.74	2.27	5.22***
What does it take (need to happen) for action/inaction (in whatever way you understand it) to be possible?	2.74	2.30	6.36***

[a]*N* = 406.
***p < 0.001.

run and sleep. Naturally, these specific concepts map onto the general notion of action and inaction and had the same pattern of numerosity. Table 2.4 shows the number of associations for run and sleep. The pattern of number of associations found for specific concepts was the same as the one found for the general category, although the differences were weaker. Thus, even though the formation of beliefs about specific actions and inaction were likely driven by various factors, the relation to the category remained strong.

Summary

This chapter covered the role of beliefs, including beliefs about objects and behaviors and expectations about experiences or objects not yet encountered. Beliefs exert powerful effects on our attitudes and experiences and combine with experiences in ways that amplify discrepancies. For example, expecting that a drug will have positive (vs. negative) effects can lead to a more negative evaluation if the experience is negative. This chapter also identified two types of cognitions relevant for analyzing attitudes and behaviors. To estimate the desirability of the event, people can refer to the expected value of the event's outcomes. Alternatively, they may refer to the desirability of an event's antecedents. Interestingly, when reflecting about a behavior, people without experience in the domain think about the conditions that will facilitate the behavior more than those with experience. Moreover, verbal arguments and forms of training designed to change perceptions about the behavior's desirability and control have critical effects when the right conditions are met. Finally, this chapter describes beliefs about actions and inactions, how they are represented, and how action and inaction are subjective concepts that serve to organize thoughts at the most general level.

CHAPTER 3

Attitudes

As measured in 2017, approval of President Trump oscillated between 35 percent and 45 percent during his first year in office (*Time*, 2018). As measured in 2018, approval of a policy to ban the sale of all guns to the US public ranges from 8 percent among Americans who voted for Trump during the 2016 election to 45 percent among Americans who voted for Clinton during the 2016 election (*Economist*, 2018). As measured in 2015, prescription drug use is perceived to be a serious problem among a third of the US population (NORC Center for Public Affairs, 2015). Name a topic and you will find a poll that has measured those attitudes in recent years.

I define attitudes as evaluations (Albarracín, Wang et al., 2011; Albarracín, Sunderrajan, Lohmann, Chan, Jiang et al., 2019; Albarracín & Shavitt, 2018; Albarracín, Johnson, & Zanna, 2005), that is, associations between an attitude object and an evaluative category such as *good* or *bad*. Attitudes have memory and judgment components because they can be stored in memory but are also represented in judgments people make in the moment (Albarracín, Johnson et al., 2005; Albarracín & Shavitt, 2018; Albarracín et al., 2019; Albarracín, Wang et al., 2011). The memory component involves representations stored in permanent memory; the judgment component involves online evaluative thoughts generated about an object at a particular time and place.

In this chapter, I first review the structure of attitudes, with particular attention to implicit and explicit attitudes (for an excellent, in-depth review, see Gawronski & Brannon, 2019). Implicit attitudes are spontaneous evaluative associations reflected in the time required to respond to an object-evaluative category pair. Explicit attitudes are overt characterizations of an object as *favorable* or *unfavorable*. This section is followed by an account of how evaluative judgments are structured and formed by means of reasoned, associative, and configural processes. The chapter also discuss general attitudes and attitudes about general action and inaction, the

64

relation between memory structures and evaluative judgments, and the attitude–behavior association.

Attitudes

Learning occurs when one clearly recalls having learned a particular task but also when tasks are acquired in subtle, difficult-to-remember ways (Richardson-Klavehn & Bjork, 1988). Specific memories about learning instances, such as a vivid memory of your grandfather teaching you to ride a bicycle, as opposed to your current, learned ability to ride a bike, are commonly referred to as *explicit* memory and *implicit* memory, respectively. Arguably, then, explicitly thinking "I like ice cream" is different from bringing to mind the texture, sweetness, and positive affective reactions associated with ice cream. Likewise, acute awareness of disliking a political candidate is different than remembering the candidate's rude behaviors when one has not settled on an evaluation of the candidate.

Using the explicit/implicit distinction, automatic or implicit attitudes have been contrasted with deliberate, explicit attitudes. Whereas explicit attitudes are measured with self-reported evaluations ("President Trump is *good* or *bad*"), implicit attitudes are often measured with methods that assess the time required to link the good or bad category with a particular object (e.g., President Bush) (Fazio et al., 1995; Greenwald, McGhee, & Schwartz, 1998; Krosnick, Judd, & Wittenbrink, 2005). Implicit-measurement methods have yielded an impressive amount of evidence about attitudes, as well as considerable speculation about what the measures actually capture. In the upcoming sections, I describe various structural aspects of attitudes.

Valence and arousal. Affect can be understood in terms of the two dimensions of (a) positive versus negative valence and (b) high versus low arousal (Bradley, Codispoti, Cuthbert, & Lang, 2001; Russell, 2003; for reviews, see Albarracín & Vargas, 2010; Clore & Schnall, 2005; Schimmack, 2005). A person may feel sad, angry, content, or excited, and these four emotions vary not only in their negative or positive valence but also in their associated arousal (Russell, 2003). Arousal comprises autonomic activation and can be measured by changes in skin conductance, heart rate, or brain waves (Bradley et al., 2007; Cacioppo, Berntson, & Crites, 1996). Feeling anxious, tense, alert, and excited all involve high autonomic activation or arousal (e.g., high heart and breathing rate),

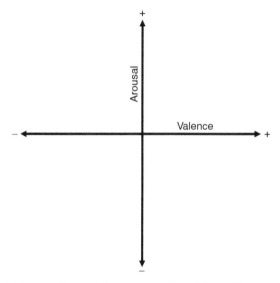

Figure 3.1 Valence and arousal dimensions. (Adapted from Albarracín & Vargas, 2010)

whereas feeling sad and content involve low autonomic activation or arousal (e.g., lower heart and breathing rate; somnolence).

The valence and arousal dimensions also apply to attitudes and are graphically depicted in Figure 3.1. On the horizontal, valence axis, people may dislike or like a presidential candidate, or may dislike or like a particular food. Supporting the existence of this axis, pleasant and unpleasant ratings are bipolar, meaning that people who report experiencing high pleasure also report experiencing low displeasure (Watson & Tellegen, 1985, 1999). More direct evidence, however, comes from work conducted by Judd and Kulik (1980). These researchers proposed that, if attitudes are mentally represented as a bipolar continuum, bipolar questions should facilitate retention and retrieval of consistent and inconsistent information. In line with this hypothesis, bipolar questions were more readily answered than unipolar ones, and information processed with bipolar questions was better recalled at a later point in time (Judd & Kulik, 1980).

On the vertical, arousal axis, people's attitudes may vary in importance, confidence, or the degree to which they elicit strong emotional responses (see Cuthbert et al., 2000; Fabrigar, MacDonald, & Wegener, 2005; Lang, Ohman, & Vaitl, 1988). Highly involving objects such as racial and gender issues often trigger strong attitudes that arouse emotional feelings, connect to the self, and are reported as more extreme and confident (Brauer, Judd, & Gliner, 1995; Eagly & Chaiken, 1993; Fabrigar, MacDonald, & Wegener, 2005). Interestingly, objects with extremely positive and negative valence are often important and generate high autonomic arousal (for a review, see Bradley et al., 2001). As a result, highly positive valence and highly negative valence are both associated with high arousal, whereas neutral valence is associated with low arousal, leading to *U* relation between the two dimensions (Bradley et al., 2001; Remington, Fabrigar, & Visser, 2000). This pattern is represented in Figure 3.2.

Ambivalence. One limitation of bipolar measurement procedures is that they obscure the possibility that negativity and positivity can be experienced simultaneously. In fact, social psychologists have long identified attitudes entailing positive and negative evaluations of an object (for reviews, see Fabrigar et al., 2005). Ambivalence can occur because of conflict between the implications of either the various beliefs associated with an object, or the beliefs and the affect associated with an object (Ajzen, 2001). Whatever the case, the subjective experience of attitudinal

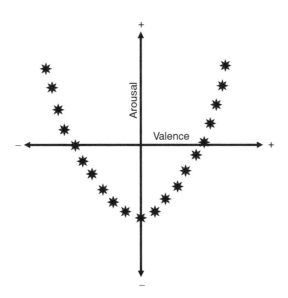

Figure 3.2 Relation between valence and arousal. (Adapted from Albarracín & Vargas, 2010)

ambivalence is stronger when both of the conflicting evaluations are simultaneously accessible (Newby-Clark, McGregor, & Zanna, 2002).

Ambivalence (Gebauer, Maio, & Pakizeh, 2013) has many consequences for attitude formation and change. For example, ambivalence decreases the speed of judgments because ambivalent people need time to integrate evaluatively incongruent attributes into an overall judgment (Van Harreveld et al., 2004). Also, ambivalent individuals are more persuadable than unambivalent ones presumably because the external information can shift the weight of existing positive or negative evaluations (MacDonald & Zanna, 1998). In addition, ambivalent attitudes are associated with more systematic information processing than unambivalent ones (Maio, Bell, & Esses, 1996), and greater motivated processing of persuasive communications (Clark & Wegener, 2008). For this reason, ambivalent (vs. unambivalent) people are easier to influence with compelling information about the advocacy.

Although ambivalence often provokes anxiety, it need not be experienced consciously to exert effects. According to Petty and colleagues (Petty et al., 2006), when an attitude changes, the newly generated attitude does not necessarily replace the old one in memory. As a result, people have more neutral and less confident attitudes as a reflection of the combination of the new and the old information. Clearly then, people's conscious sense that their attitudes have changed does not preclude implicit ambivalence from influencing explicit attitudes.

Implications of negative and positive evaluations. Even in the absence of ambivalence, the negative and positive dimensions of attitudes have an interesting asymmetry. Specifically, compared with positive information, negative information tends to have a greater impact on attitudes and decisions (Cacioppo, Gardner, & Berntson, 1997; Fiske & Taylor, 1991; Matthews & Dietz-Uhler, 1998). People also tend to have a better memory for negative versus positive stimulus words (Ohira, Winton, & Oyama, 1998), and the negative (vs. positive) aspects of an ambivalent attitude can have stronger effects on behavior (Cacioppo, Gardner, & Berntson, 1997; Miller, 1944).

Other lines of research, however, suggest that the impact of negative (vs. positive) information is greater only under certain conditions. For example, messages that are framed negatively, or that contain negative information, are more persuasive than their positive counterparts when the information is difficult to process and when recipients are motivated to make accurate judgments (Ahluwalia, 2002; Block & Keller, 1995; Homer

& Batra, 1994; Meyers-Levy & Maheswaran, 2004; Meyers & Smith, 1995). Moreover, negative information is less effective when people imagine scenarios, presumably because they are free to construct events under the most favorable possible light (Adaval & Wyer, 1998). Consistent with this interpretation, negative information has more impact when people are motivated to process information in an even-handed fashion than when they are motivated to arrive at a positive judgment (Ahluwalia, 2002).

Accessibility. People activate a prior attitude if they retrieve an object-category association that they previously stored in memory (Fazio & Williams, 1986). For instance, one may recall that a particular food is "good" or "bad," an event is "desirable" or "undesirable," or a person is "attractive" or "unattractive" (for the processes underlying categorization, see Bargh, Chaiken, Govender, & Prato, 1992; Markman & Gentner, 2001; Medin & Coley, 1998; Smith, Fazio, & Cejka, 1996; Wyer & Srull, 1989). Attitude retrieval from memory can occur automatically or follow the application of effortful recall strategies (see Lingle & Ostrom, 1981). For example, teachers have less difficulty retrieving their evaluations of a student presently taking their class than they do retrieving their evaluations of a student who took their class 4 years ago (for a discussion of goal-directed recall, see Koriat, 2000).

There is evidence that activation of prior attitudes is important for attitude maintenance. A lot of this evidence comes from studies on the attitude–behavior relation. For instance, Fazio and his colleagues (Fazio et al., 1982; Fazio, Powell, & Williams, 1989; Fazio & Williams, 1986) showed that people are more likely to use a prior attitude when it is accessible. In this research, participants first reported their attitudes toward food products and then were allowed to take products home. The correlation between participants' attitudes and their later selection of products was stronger when attitudes were initially more accessible (i.e., lower response latency). That is, attitudes guided behavioral decisions to a greater extent when, at the time of selecting products, participants could quickly recall how much they liked each product.

Demonstrations that attitudes are activated automatically have come from the use of priming paradigms. Attitude objects (e.g., a "flag") have been used as primes to bias judgments of other objects (e.g., "cat") as *good* or *bad* (Fazio et al., 1986). Imagine that people are told to learn words on a list but are later asked to evaluate the words. When the two words were separated by brief times, presenting the word "flag" facilitates classifying the word "cat" as "good." Similar results have been obtained when the attitude objects are presented subliminally (Greenwald, Draine, & Abrams, 1996). Thus, this finding is typically interpreted as reflecting automatic (unintended) attitude activation in response to the mere presence of an attitude object.

If the facilitation effects of priming are due to personally held attitudes, then stronger associations between a particular object and "good" or "bad" should result in greater priming effects. Fazio et al.'s (1986) studies involved an initial task in which participants were asked to judge objects as "good" or "bad." The latencies of these responses were then used as a proxy for associative strength. Findings revealed that the priming effect was only present when the evaluation of the object used as a prime was highly accessible. Furthermore, another study of the series included a manipulation of associative strength by having some participants express their attitudes multiple times before the priming test. This time, priming was apparent in both the rehearsed and unrehearsed conditions. However, it was stronger when participants had recently expressed their attitudes.

One ambiguity of the automatic activation effect is that associative strength appears to moderate priming effects only when the measures or manipulations of associations have been conducted immediately before the priming procedure. Based on this observation, Bargh, Chen, and Burrows (1996) and Chaiken and Bargh (1993) tested and showed that the moderation was not present if one administered the priming at a later session. Furthermore, Bargh, Chiken, Govender, and Pratto (1992) produced the effect for both weak and strong attitudes. This finding has important implications for understanding what is activated in priming tasks. If attitude strength does not moderate the priming effects, the automatic activation effect likely reflects chronic semantic associations between an object and "good" or "bad." That is, one may not endorse the associations personally, yet the facilitation may occur due to semantic activation or socially shared knowledge about objects. Indeed, as I discuss presently, this very argument has been raised in relation to the IAT (Implicit Association Test).

Relations between Implicit and Explicit Attitudes

We can define and measure explicit and implicit attitudes, but how do they relate to each other? There are several possible models of the relation between implicit and explicit attitudes. We describe a model in which the explicit and the implicit attitudes are separate (Greenwald et al., 2002), a model in which the two attitudinal responses reflect different levels of processing – and censure – but do not exist as separate structures (Fazio, 2007), and a model in which the two attitudes are separate but interact (Gawronski & Bodenhausen, 2007; Petty, Brinol, & DeMarree, 2007).

Dissociated systems. Greenwald and Banaji (1995) defined implicit attitudes as introspectively, and often inaccurately, unidentified traces of past experience that mediate favorable or unfavorable feelings, thoughts, or actions concerning social objects. They initially argued that implicit attitudes reflect unconscious evaluations of an attitude object (Banaji, Lemm, & Carpenter, 2001) and are not subject to conscious editing on the basis of social or personal concerns. Thus, awareness and disapproval of either negative or positive associations can trigger a dissociation in which, similar to the concept of psychoanalytic repression (Bargh, 2014; Freud, 1912), the implicit and explicit attitudes have contradictory implications, or, at least, low correspondence.

This dissociative model is parsimonious and has received some support in domains affected by social desirability. For example, studies of attitudes toward gender (Greenwald & Farnham, 2000), race (Greenwald, McGhee, & Schwartz, 1998; Greenwald et al., 2002), ethnicity (Greenwald, McGhee, & Schwartz, 1998), and age (Mellott & Greenwald, 2000) have found low correspondence between explicit and implicit attitudes. These low associations contrast with the high correspondence sometimes found in studies of political and consumer attitudes (Brunel et al., 1999; Greenwald et al., 2002). Presumably, prejudice, but not consumer attitudes, produce mental dissociations between implicit and explicit attitudes because people try to hide their prejudicial attitudes as a way of appearing egalitarian.

A meta-analysis of this research (Hofmann et al., 2005; Oswald et al., 2013) revealed a mean $r = 0.24$ between IAT measures and self-reported attitudes. However, the correlation was reported to be higher when, as decided by coders, study participants were likely to rely on their "gut feeling" about the attitude object. Correspondingly, the correlation was lower when, as decided by coders, the attitude object likely elicited social desirability concerns.

Separate interacting systems. A second model assumes separate though interacting explicit and implicit attitudes. Gawronski and Bodenhausen (2007), for example, maintain that implicit and explicit attitudes involve distinct associative and propositional processes. Associative evaluations exist in memory and can be activated irrespective of whether or not a person considers them accurate. In contrast, explicit attitudes are evaluative judgments of an attitude object rooted in propositional reasoning and assume that the person identifies with the attitude.

In Gawronski and Bodenhausen's framework (Gawronski & Bodenhausen, 2007; Gawronski & Brannon, 2019; Gawronski, Strack, & Bodenhausen, 2012), even though explicit and implicit attitudes are separate, they exert reciprocal influences on each other. People may use automatic affective reactions (implicit attitudes) toward an object as a basis for evaluative judgments (explicit attitudes) of this object. This influence, however, is supposedly present if and only if the automatic affective reaction is considered valid (e.g., consistent with other propositions). Moreover, people may base their implicit associations on explicit evaluative judgments. For instance, if new propositions link an object with an evaluative category, the new connections should be represented as implicit attitudes.

Continuum. Fazio (2007) has questioned the conceptualization of implicit and explicit responses as *different* attitudes. Instead, implicit and explicit attitudes are conceptualized as the by-product of an original response that underwent more or less editing in light of social desirability concerns. In Fazio's view, participants in studies of implicit attitudes are aware that they have certain attitudes they do not want to express, even though they are not necessarily aware of the goals of the study. In that case, participants who have the ability and motivation to modify their responses may avoid using the initial categorization evoked by the implicit attitude measure. The more sensitive the issue, the greater the likelihood that participants will be motivated to move their explicit response away from their implicit attitude. In a nutshell, the implicit measure captures relatively raw material, whereas the direct measure captures reactions altered by the motivation to conform to a standard (social desirability).

Hypothesizing specific roles for motivation and opportunity (i.e., ability) leads to the hypothesis that, when an issue is sensitive, motivation and opportunity to correct responses should affect the correspondence of implicit and explicit attitudes with behavior. Clearly, when motivation and opportunity are high, explicit measures will predict behavior better because the more desirable associations have been deliberatively selected as a basis for that behavior. Less clearly, however, Fazio (2007) also stated that implicit measures should be more predictive when motivation and opportunity are low. In principle, when people cannot engage in careful selection, disguise, and/or selection of implicit associations, the explicit measures should be direct translations of the implicit ones. Therefore, both implicit and explicit measures should be highly predictive of current responses to an object under low motivation and opportunity conditions.

Although the continuum notion is proposed as a counter to dissociated systems, they make some of the same predictions. Whereas Greenwald, McGhee, and Schwartz (1998) assumed that social desirability concerns trigger a dissociation, Fazio (2007) assumed that the same concerns lead to better response control and selection. Ultimately then, if Greenwald and Banaji are correct, people should have no awareness of their implicit attitudes, nor should they be able to control them intentionally. However, a large literature has shown that attitudes are malleable and that people use different intentional ways of exerting control (Dasgupta, 2013). All in all, the possibility of dissociation is thus out of favor.

Distributed networks. A model by Bassili and Brown (2005) suggests that attitudes emerge from microconceptual networks that are activated by particular context configurations. In this model, microconcepts are molecular elements of knowledge that may yield evaluations in combination with other microconcepts in the network. For example, for a woman who played competitive tennis as an adolescent, tennis is represented as a collection of microconcepts having to do with competition, discipline, pressures, fairness, the joys of winning, the disappointments of losing, traveling to tournaments, and hanging out with other competitors. These prior experiences together comprise the microconcepts by which the woman evaluates the sport of tennis.

The potentiated recruitment framework can easily explain the structure of explicit and implicit attitudes as sharing many of the microconcepts that form the basis for attitudes. The difference is in potentiation, akin to level of activation. Potentiation depends on recent and current information about the attitude object and cognitive attention to an object. Implicit attitudes are activations under the potentiation level, which therefore preclude the involvement of deliberate processes. In contrast, explicit attitudes are activated by deliberative processes that require attention.

Explicit Attitudes and Attitudinal Judgments

Online judgments are formed when one evaluates an object either explicitly or spontaneously. Explicitly, one may open a clothing catalog with the intent of evaluating the designs. Alternatively, one may browse the catalog with the intent of selecting pictures for a child's project and notice attractive designs in passing. That is, the processes that yield these judgments can be either intentional or spontaneous. In the following section, I consider whether the processes are associative, reasoned, meta-cognitive, or configural. Associative processes imply a simple transfer of meaning from one stimulus to the other. Reasoned processes involve formal reasoning and the application of an algorithm leading to an evaluative conclusion. Configural processes entail a specific combination of stimuli that, when processed in connection with each other, leads to liking an object. Meta-cognitive processes involve reasoning about properties of one's attitudes and thoughts, which may lead to changes in attitudes.

Associative processes. Staats and Staats (1957) showed that pairing nonsense syllables with positive or negative words altered the affective response to the nonsense syllables. The evaluation of the words apparently transferred to otherwise neutral stimuli by what is referred to as *evaluative conditioning*. This phenomenon is different from classical conditioning in which a neutral stimulus is *followed* by a reward. Whereas in classical conditioning, the reward signals that the unconditioned stimulus will have a positive outcome, the valenced stimulus in evaluative conditioning can precede, follow, or coincide with the neutral stimulus, suggesting merely associative processes.

Reasoned processes. Judgments can also emerge from the application of formal reasoning. A model formulated by McGuire (1960, 1985) and extended by Wyer (Fong & Wyer, 2003; Wyer, 1974a, 1974b; Wyer & Goldberg, 1970) described how prior beliefs can influence new beliefs via logical reasoning. Two cognitions, A (antecedent) and C (conclusion), relate to each other by means of a syllogism of the form "A; if A, then C; C." In this case, the probability of C (e.g., "an event is good") is a function of the beliefs in the premise or antecedent, and beliefs that "A is true" *and* "if A is true, C is true." For example, "I like ice cream" may be combined with "If I like ice cream, I like summer" to conclude that "I like summer." Although this model approximates actual human judgments quite well, Wyer (1974a; Wyer & Goldberg, 1970) observed that C might be true for reasons other than premise A. Specifically, beliefs in these alternate reasons should also determine the probability of the conclusion ("not A; if not A, then C"). Therefore, $P(C)$ should be a function of the beliefs in these two mutually exclusive premises, or

$$P(C) = P(A)P(C/A) + P(\sim A)P(C/\sim A),$$

where $P(A)$ and $P(\sim A)$ $[= 1 - P(A)]$ are beliefs that A is and is not true, respectively. $P(C/A)$ and $P(C/\sim A)$ are conditional beliefs that C is true if A is and is not true, respectively. The revised equation considers all the reasons I like summer other than the fact that I can eat ice cream. For example, $\sim A$ can include that I like to be outside, not wear a coat, and go on vacation.

A limitation of the conditional inference model is its use of a single premise with all the other criteria (e.g., being outside, not wearing a coat, and going on vacation) being part of $P(C/\sim A)$, that is, the belief that the conclusion is true for reasons other than A. In contrast, Lichtenstein and Slovic (1971) postulated that people who predict an unknown event from a *set* of cues are likely to sum up the cues. Therefore, regression procedures can be used to predict beliefs on the basis of multiple pieces of information. In this case, regression weights can represent the relative importance of being outside, not wearing a coat, and going on vacation.

Multiple-regression approaches can identify between-person differences in the weights given to different types of cues (Wiggins, Hoffman, & Taber, 1969). Nevertheless, these additive assumptions are often incorrect (Anderson, 1974, 1981; Fishbein & Ajzen, 1975c; Wiggins et al., 1969). According to Birnbaum and Stegner (1979), estimates of a car's value is often an *average* rather than the sum of its blue book value and the opinion of another person, with the weight of each piece of information depending on the credibility of its source.

Configural or structural processes. Attitudes are not always the product of careful deliberation. In many instances, neither summative nor averaging models may be applicable. Kahneman and Tversky (1982) provided strong evidence that people's estimates of the conjunction of two features (e.g., the likelihood that a woman is a feminist bank teller) are not predictable from their estimates of each feature (i.e., being a feminist or being a bank teller) considered in isolation. Instead, people appear to process the information in a "gestalt" fashion rather than analyzing each piece of information separately (see Wyer & Albarracín, 2005, for a general discussion of these matters).

Another configural process relates to the organization of information in a *familiar form* (Wyer & Albarracín, 2005). As shown by research on mere exposure, neutral information gains in favorability with its mere presentation. That is, repeated presentations of a neutral stimulus produce a mild pleasant response to the stimulus at a later time (Bornstein, 1989; Zajonc, 1968). Notably, the effect is evident in the lab as well as in naturalistic settings. For example, Law, Schimmack, and Braun (2003) presented brief video sketches containing one of two brands of food products to a group of participants. One week later, despite their lack of recall or recognition of the presentation, participants liked the previously presented brands better than the unpresented ones.

Meta-cognitive processes. Human meta-cognitive capacity allows individuals to first form attitude judgments, then form judgments about those judgments, and last form judgments about their ability to make good judgments (see Jost, Kruglanski, & Nelson, 1998). These types of processes form multilayered structures in which each layer represents a unique logical level. For example, analyses of meta-cognitive principles have been applied to attitude confidence, defined as a subjective sense of certainty or validity regarding one's attitude (Festinger, 1950, 1954). In this case, the object of the judgment is the attitude itself. In other words, attitude confidence implies a judgment about one's attitude, thus constituting a meta-level relative to the attitude. Attitude confidence is higher when one has been repeatedly exposed to the source of the attitude (e.g., an advertisement; Berger & Mitchell, 1989), when one experiences positive affect (Schwarz & Clore, 1983, 2007), and when beliefs and attitudes are univalent rather than complex (Jonas, Diehl, & Brömer, 1997). Attitude confidence has several notable consequences, including using the particular attitude as a basis for later behaviors (Fazio & Zanna, 1978; Albarracín, Wallace, & Glasman, 2004) and making attitudes more resistant to change (Krosnick & Abelson, 1992; Swann, Pelham, & Chidester, 1988).

In addition to studying attitude confidence, researchers have examined confidence in the beliefs or evaluations that underlie a particular attitude toward an object. According to Petty, Brinol, and Tormala (2002), people's confidence in the validity of their thoughts about an object influences attitudes in interaction with the valence of their thoughts. That is, when positive thoughts dominate responses to a communication, increasing confidence in these thoughts makes attitudes toward the message topic more favorable. In contrast, when negative thoughts dominate responses, increasing confidence makes attitudes toward the message topic less favorable.

Another meta-cognitive aspect examined in past research is the perceived strength of the persuasive attack. In research by Tormala and Petty (2002), participants in experimental conditions were asked to resist messages that were described as strong or weak. Findings indicated that participants had equally extreme attitudes regardless of the supposed strength of the message they resisted. However, participants were more certain about their attitudes after resisting an ostensibly strong message than after resisting an ostensibly weak message or resisting arguments of unknown strength. That is, people interpret their personal success in protecting their attitudes from a strong attack as evidence of the correctness of their attitude and increase their attitude certainty for that reason.

Conventional strength, however, is not the only judgment people make about the sources of their attitudes. How intuitive a judgment is, for example, can influence attitude confidence (Simmons & Nelson, 2006). Moreover, judgments based on what is subjectively defined as "intuitive" can last longer than judgments based on what is subjectively defined as "reasoned." Presumably, these intuitions are either not questioned, or cognitive resources are recruited to bolster them. Both of these processes can explain the durability of intuitions.

Relations between Memory Representations and Judgments

Attitudes are represented in memory and also exist as evaluative judgments. Thus, understanding the relation between attitudes in memory and online judgments is important to a complete conceptualization of attitudes. In the following sections, I discuss models that emphasize how attitudes in memory guide responses to objects, models that address how judgments are constructed online, and models that consider the interplay between memory representations and judgments.

Representational Models of Attitudes: Memory as the Primary Basis for Judgments

Attitudes fall on a continuum defined on one end by representations of attitude objects without a summary evaluation (i.e., *nonattitudes*; see Converse & Apter, 1964) and on the other end by representations of attitude objects with a strong link to a summary evaluation.

According to Fazio (Fazio, 1990; Fazio et al., 1995; Fazio & Williams, 1986), summary evaluations associated with an attitude object are stored in permanent memory. Although the object-evaluation associations are supposedly integrated into broader representational networks, this model concentrates on the strength of the association between an evaluation and an attitude object.

As explained previously, attitude accessibility is determined by the strength of the association between an attitude object and its evaluation.

When the object-evaluation link is strong, the attitude is highly accessible and exposure to the attitude object is sufficient to activate the evaluation. This automatic process is important because activated evaluations can guide behavior in response to the sole presence of the attitude object (Ajzen et al., 2019; Fazio, 1990). For example, highly accessible attitudes influence behavior (Fazio, 1990) and judgments of attitude objects (Fazio, Ledbetter, & Towles-Schwen, 2000) automatically.

Although Fazio's model recognizes that existing attitudes often influence the impact of novel information, it does not describe the process by which information available in the moment affects the response. Other models, however, have attempted to explicate those processes. I turn to these next.

Models Emphasizing Online Information

In contrast to traditional representational models of attitudes, in constructionist models, judgments derive from whatever information happens to be salient and accessible at the time they are made. Schwarz and Bohner (2001) argue that evaluative judgments are guided by information present in the external context. For example, people may use momentarily experienced affective reactions (Schwarz & Clore, 1983, 2007) or physiological arousal (Valins, 1966; Wells & Petty, 1980) to determine their evaluations of objects. They may use this information without ever bothering to retrieve a previously stored prior attitude toward an object.

The online use of information as a basis for judgments can be effectively modeled with an inclusion/exclusion model (Schwarz, 1999; Schwarz & Bless, 1992). The IEM (Schwarz & Bless, 1992) assumes that attitudes require two representations: the target and the standard against which it is evaluated. Both the target and the standard are formed based on whatever information is most accessible when people make the judgment. The size of assimilation effects increases with the amount of information in the target that matches the standard. The size of the contrast effect (i.e., subtraction-based contrast effect) increases with the amount and extremity of information in the standard that is not present in the target. In addition, information in the standard that is not present in the target may be used for constructing a representation of a new standard (i.e., comparison-based contrast effect). For example, unmatched positive information in the standard may be used to form an even more positive standard, and this new standard tends to be applied to all targets. Thus, the notion of comparison-based standard implies that a standard becomes more general and extreme over a series of judgments.

Models That Integrate Memory Representations and Online Information

Several models explain attitudes as being a function of both memory-based information and online contents. According to the **social judgment theory** (Sherif & Hovland, 1961; but see Eiser, 1973; Eiser & White, 1973; for an excellent review, see Eagly & Chaiken, 1993), for example, attitude change is analogous to a perceptual process. When the position of the communication is close to the recipient's attitude, people become closer to the position advocated in the communication by "assimilating" their own attitude to the advocacy. In contrast, when the communication is subjectively distant from their prior attitudes, there is a "contrast" effect or perception that one's attitude is more discrepant from the communication than it actually is. In these situations, people change in opposition to the communication.

Several hypotheses from social judgment theory concern the conditions leading to contrast versus assimilation. A chief assumption is that attitude change is a function of the range of positions a person accepts and rejects. When the message position falls within this latitude of acceptance, people assimilate this position to their attitudes. When the position falls within the latitude of rejection, people contrast their attitudes with that position. Furthermore, topics that are highly involving shrink the latitudes of acceptance and expand the latitudes of rejection. As a result, people are more resistant to change (Johnson et al., 1995; Johnson, Maio, & Smith-McLallen, 2005; Maio & Olson, 1995; Petty & Cacioppo, 1990). Although interesting, this prediction has not received consistent support over the years (Eagly & Chaiken, 1993; Johnson et al., 2005).

Another theory that incorporates memory-based and online information is Anderson's information-integration theory (Norman, 1976). According to Anderson, if a person receives n items of information, the response (R) to the set of items ($s, i \ldots n$) is given by

$$R = W_0 S_0 + W_1 S_1 + W_2 S_2 + \ldots + W_n S_n,$$

where w_i are the weights and s_i are the scale values of each item. Because Anderson (1968, 1974) argued that information is normally combined by averaging rather than adding, the sum of the weights is typically set to 1. However, Fishbein and Ajzen (1975) argued that an additive model is more plausible. The main source of controversy between the additive and averaging models is their ability to account for the "set-size" effect, that is increases in extremity as new elements of the same value are incorporated. Whereas additive models naturally account for the set-size effect, the averaging model needs to assume an initial moderate attitude to explain increases in valence when same value elements are added (Anderson, 1981).

Albarracín, Wallace, and Glasman (2004) also conceptualized the role of memory representations and online information in producing evaluative judgments. They proposed an **activation and comparison model** in which attitude change depends on three processes: (a) activating the prior attitude (retrieving it from memory), (b) activating information related to the prior attitude (which can come from memory or an external source), and (c) comparing the prior attitude with the related information. People may activate their prior attitude as well as related information. For example, a man planning to vote in an upcoming political election may recall his prior favorable attitude toward the candidate and also attend to media portrayals of the candidate. Comparison can proceed in a bottom-up fashion or a top-down fashion. For example, alignable objects (two types of fruits) are more likely to elicit comparison than unalignable ones (a fruit and a desk). Alternatively, one may receive direct instructions to reconsider one's prior position on an issue in light of newly available information (e.g., during a judicial trial). When this happens, one must activate the new specific information as well as the prior attitude to perform the comparison. The goal to compare two elements may produce biases in what information is selected. For example, if one compares the new information with the old information, the unique features of the new information will determine the outcome of the comparison. This model receives more attention in Chapter 8.

Models inspired by connectionism (Smith, Fazio, & Cejka, 1996) offer an alternative account of the influences of both enduring attitudes and the evaluative implications of momentarily accessible information. For example, as described before, according to the **potentiated recruitment framework** (Bassili & Brown, 2005), attitudes are represented as molecular elements that have the potential to be recruited in various mixes depending on the eliciting context and chronic potentiating factors. According to Bassili and Brown (2005), evaluations emerge as a result of four primary sources of potentiation. One source is recent cognitive experiences that prime particular microconcepts in memory. Another source is current information about the attitude object and the context in which it appears. Thus, even subtle features of the context can exert considerable influence on the emergent evaluation. The third source of potentiation consists of the flow of activation between linked microconcepts that reflect the influence of general knowledge and culture on attitudes. Finally, cognitive activity in working memory is an important source of potentiation when individuals have the explicit goal of evaluating an object. Therefore, evaluations are as fluid and context dependent as allowed by the combined activation of chronic and temporary information.

Specific and General Attitudes toward Objects and Behaviors

Both attitude objects and behaviors are represented with different degrees of generality. General attitudes are functional because they reduce the need to store specific attitudes in memory (for similar notions about the benefits of abstract construal, see Trope & Liberman, 2010). For example, a person who dislikes seafood does not need to retrieve specific attitudes toward shellfish, white fish, and octopus. She can simply use her general negative attitude on all relevant decisions without the additional time required to consider the specifics of each attitude object. As highlighted by the following principle, these attitudes integrate a multitude of objects and behaviors:

> **Principle 11. Function of general attitudes.** General attitudes are a means to integrating all objects and behaviors, all actions, and all inactions.

Hepler and Albarracín (2013) studied general tendencies to like or dislike stimuli, defined as systematic variation in attitude valence as a function of the person instead of the attitude object. These general attitudes were assessed by having participants evaluate a large number of stimuli and computing the mean attitudes. An initial set of 200 attitude objects yielded a final scale of 16 items about such diverse objects as taxidermy, politics, and soccer. This scale has high internal consistency as well as high test–retest reliability, and exhibits adequate convergent and divergent validity. For example, we correlated general attitudes with relevant traits like optimism, need for cognition, neuroticism, and a number of others. These results appear in Table 3.1. As one might expect, traits associated with positive or negative affect (e.g., extraversion, optimism) correlated with the measure of dispositional attitudes, although all personality measures, including those related to positive and negative affect, accounted for only about 20 percent of the variance in general attitudes.

One of the most general ways of describing behaviors is in terms of action and inaction. Importantly, attitudes toward action and inaction vary: the concept of action is subjectively more favorable than the concept of inaction (Ireland et al., 2015; Zell et al., 2013). In our research (McCulloch et al., 2012, Study 2), participants rated words that went

Table 3.1 *Correlations between general attitudes and relevant personality traits*

Predictor	Dispositional attitude β	Novel object β
1. Dispositional attitude	–	0.21**
2. Openness	0.30**	–0.02
3. Conscientiousness	–0.11	–0.15*
4. Extraversion	–0.01	–0.09
5. Agreeableness	–0.05	0.12
6. Neuroticism	–0.18	0.11
7. Positive affect	0.23**	–0.08
8. Negative affect	–0.02	–0.01
9. Optimism	–0.08	0.01
10. Self-esteem	–0.05	0.00
11. Life satisfaction	–0.05	0.08
12. Behavioral activation	0.04	0.19*
13. Behavioral inhibition	–0.13	–0.13
14. Promotion focus	0.01	0.01
15. Prevention focus	0.04	0.07
16. Social desirability	0.08	0.05
17. Attachment avoidance	–0.04	0.09
18. Attachment anxiety	–0.00	0.11

Source: Adapted from Hepler and Albarracín (2011, Study 2).

from most active (e.g., *run*) to least active (or inactive; e.g., *sleep*) on a scale from negative to positive. Consistent with the hypothesis of differential desirability, words like *active, run,* and *jump* received more positive evaluations than words like *inactive, stationary,* and *still.*

Other research was conducted to further explore attitudes toward action and inaction. In research conducted by Sunderrajan and Albarracín (2017), participants received instructions to imagine themselves eating (or not eating) broccoli, and then rated the behavior on a scale ranging from completely negative/not desirable to completely positive/desirable. In the absence of additional information, participants who imagined themselves eating broccoli (an action) evaluated the behavior more favorably than participants who imagined themselves not eating broccoli (an inaction). In a similar study, participants were asked to imagine themselves eating (or not eating) cake. As in the broccoli study, participants who imagined themselves eating cake (an action) evaluated the behavior more favorably than participants who imagined themselves not eating cake. In yet another study, participants were asked to imagine themselves during the trivial instance of pressing (or not pressing) a button. Of course, knowledge about devastating consequences of a behavior should affect judgments, but for relatively neutral behaviors like pressing a button, people still viewed the action as more positive than the inaction.

Actions are also subjectively more positive than inactions, in part because of the attribution of higher intentionality to actions. Prior evidence indicates that positive attitudes are associated with strong intentions (Ajzen & Fishbein, 2005), both because attitudes cause intentions and because intentions and behaviors can be used as a basis for attitudes (Albarracín & Wyer, 2001; Bem, 1972). Therefore, intentional behaviors may be automatically judged as more positive than unintentional behaviors. To test this notion, in our research (Sunderrajan & Albarracín, 2017, 2020), participants who read behavior scenarios with varying levels of intentionality (high, low, and unspecified) also provided evaluations. As actions are subjectively more favorable to begin, describing them as intentional had no additional effect. However, as inactions are subjectively more negative to begin, describing them as intentional produced more positive evaluations. These results further suggest that positive general attitudes toward action are driven by attributions of intentionality.

Another reason why action may be seen as more desirable than inaction is an overgeneralization of the Protestant work ethic (McCulloch et al., 2012). In Hsee, Yang, and Wang's (2010) research, participants could choose the option to be busy or be idle: After completing a survey, participants had a 15-min break during which they had the option to deliver their completed survey to a nearby location and wait out the remaining time (idle option) or deliver their completed survey to a faraway location (busy option). Participants who chose to occupy themselves reported higher feelings of happiness than participants who chose to be idle. Apparently, people desire busyness and dread idleness (Hsee, Yang, & Wang, 2010) to the extent that being busy increases feelings of happiness.

Liking for action and inaction, however, is malleable. In a series of experiments we conducted (Feldman & Albarracín, 2017), participants were assigned to one of three norm conditions: action, inaction, and control. We adjusted the classic Kahneman and Tversky (1982) scenario of the two stock traders – George switches investments and loses (action), and Paul retains his original investments and loses (inaction). We included an action-norm condition describing the investment company as emphasizing action and evaluating its employees based on their ability to act and actively pursue good investments. A corresponding inaction-norm condition emphasized cautious and responsible decision-making, stating that the company evaluated its employees based on their ability to refrain from bad invest-ments. A control condition did not indicate company preferences. We then measured regret, which allowed us to gauge what the norm was. Participants reported that George (who acted) would experience the highest regret in the inaction-norm condition, followed by the control condition, followed by the action-norm condition (88 percent, 72 percent, and 56 percent, respectively). However, participants reported that Paul (who did not act) would experi-ence the highest regret in the action-norm condition than in the inaction-norm condition. The fact that the company norm affected regret in this fashion suggests that evaluations of action and inaction are malleable.

An important question is how attitudes toward action and inaction are represented. If attitudes toward action are better represented than attitudes toward inaction, people should think of more advantages and disadvan-tages of action than inaction, as well as more antecedents of action than inaction. I conducted a study with participants who answered questions about advantages, disadvantages, and antecedents for action (in whatever way you understand it) and inaction (in whatever way you understand it). As shown in Table 2.3, the underlying structure of attitudes toward behaviors is stronger for action than inaction. This leads to the following principle:

> **Principle 12. Representation of attitudes toward action and attitudes toward inaction.** Attitudes toward action are better represented than atti-tudes toward inaction. As a result, attitudes toward action may have more influence on other judgments and on behavior.

The Impact of Attitudes on Behaviors

People clearly form attitudes toward objects, including liking expensive cars and fashion. However, as pointed out by Ajzen and Fishbein (1980), these positive attitudes do not necessarily predict purchasing those expen-sive items because liking the objects does not necessarily imply that purchasing them is desirable. In fact, a summary of meta-analyses of the attitude–behavior correlation presented in Table 3.2 (Ajzen et al., 2019) suggests considerable variability in the association strength of correlations involving attitudes toward the object. For example, the attitude toward purchasing the object is a much better predictor of purchasing behavior that is the attitude toward the object (Ajzen & Fishbein, 1980; Glasman & Albarracín, 2006). That is, to predict a specific behavior, one must measure the attitude toward that behavior.

Table 3.2 *Meta-analyses of the attitude–behavior relation*

Study	Short description	Effect size type	Effect size	Measure of variance	k	N
M.-S. Kim and Hunter (1993)	Various domains	R	0.47	SD = 0.14	138	90,808
Eckes and Six (1994)	Various domains	R	0.39	SE = 0.04	396	156,598
Kraus (1995)	Various domains	Unweighted r	0.38	SD = 0.21	88	22,106
Wallace, Paulson, Lord, and Bond (2005)	Various domains; behavioral outcome variables only	Unweighted r	0.36		466	–
Glasman and Albarracín (2006)	Newly formed attitudes (toward unfamiliar attitude objects) and behaviors	R	0.51		128	
Greenwald et al. (2009)	IATs about attitudes, belief, self-concept, or self-esteem, correlated with explicit outcome measures (including, but not limited to, observed behavior)	R	0.27		184	
	Explicit attitude, belief, self-concept, or self-esteem measures, correlated with explicit outcome measures (including, but not limited to, observed behavior)	R	0.36		156	
McEachan, Conner, Taylor, and Lawton (2011)	Various health behaviors	r	–	–	209	–
Cameron, Brown-Iannuzzi, and Payne (2012)	Sequential priming tasks, correlated with behavior or intentions	R	0.28		86	–

Table 3.2 (*cont.*)

Study	Short description	Effect size type	Effect size	Measure of variance	k	N
Oswald, Mitchell, Blanton, Jaccard, and Tetlock (2013)	Interracial/-ethnic IATs (includes both attitude IATs, which measure evaluative associations, and stereotype IATs, which measure semantic associations) and interpersonal behavior	R	0.14		11 effects nested within 6 samples	
	Interracial/-ethnic IATs (includes both attitude IATs, which measure evaluative associations, and stereotype IATs, which measure semantic associations) and microbehaviors	R	0.07		96 effects nested within 21 samples	
	Explicit interracial/-ethnic attitude measures and interpersonal behavior	R	0.19		9 effects nested within 3 samples	
	Explicit interracial/-ethnic attitude measures and microbehaviors	R	0.04		92 effects nested within 18 samples	

Note: Except for the Greenwald et al. (2009) and Cameron et al. (2012) meta-analyses, where such a distinction could not be made, only overt behavior was included, and outcomes such as judgments, physiological reactions, or measures of intention were excluded from this table. This table was adapted from Ajzen et al. (2018).

Even though the attitude toward the object is a poor predictor of a specific behavior, attitudes and behaviors with the same level of generality correlate strongly. In a study by Sivacek and Crano (1982), college students completed a scale that assessed their attitudes toward instituting a comprehensive exam at their university as a prerequisite for graduation. The attitude concerned an object, thus being fairly general. In addition, the researchers measured a number of behaviors, including (a) whether or not participants signed a petition opposing the proposed exam, (b) whether or not they volunteered to help distribute petitions, and (c) the number of hours of help they pledged. These behavioral measures were then aggregated. As previously demonstrated by Fishbein and Ajzen (1974), the attitude–behavior correlation ranged from 0.34 to 0.43 for the individual actions but was 0.60 for the behavioral aggregate.

Just like general attitudes toward an object can predict an aggregate of behaviors related to the object, general attitudes measured with a collection of objects are useful to predict unknown attitudes, including attitudes toward completely novel objects (Hepler & Albarracín, 2013; for related concepts, see Albarracín et al., 2008; Albarracín, Hepler, & Tannenbaum, 2011). In addition, these general dispositional attitudes predict behavior broadly as well, a possibility we examined (Hepler & Albarracín, 2014). Participants in two studies reported their general attitudes and the time they spent on a number of daily behaviors, such as personal care, working, education, and traveling. General dispositional attitudes predicted the number of behaviors reported.

Summary

Chapter 2 presented my integration of the concept and key features of attitudes. I define attitudes as evaluations (Albarracín, Wang et al., 2011; Albarracín, Sunderrajan, Lohmann, Chan, Jiang et al., 2019; Albarracín & Shavitt, 2018; Albarracín, Johnson, & Zanna, 2005), that is, associations between an attitude object and an evaluative category such as *good* or *bad*. Attitudes have memory and judgment components (Albarracín, Johnson et al., 2005; Albarracín & Shavitt, 2018; Albarracín et al., 2019; Albarracín, Wang et al., 2011). The memory aspect of attitudes comprises representations stored in permanent memory; the judgment aspect comprises online evaluative thoughts generated about an object at a particular time and place. Although some researchers have suggested that the term *attitudes* should only involve a representation in permanent memory (Bizer et al., 2006; Eagly & Chaiken, 2005, 2007; Fazio, 2007; Petty, Brinol, &

DeMarree, 2007), it is impossible to imagine attitude change without recognizing that these two components are part of attitudes.

In this chapter, I first review the structure of attitudes, discussing its dimensions (valence and arousal), ambivalence, and implicit and explicit attitudes. Implicit attitudes are spontaneous evaluative associations reflected in short times to respond to an object-evaluative category pair, whereas explicit attitudes are overt characterizations of an object as *favorable* or *unfavorable*. I also review the most general attitudes, which include general attitudes toward a collection of objects and predict unknown attitudes and attitudes toward novel objects (Hepler & Albarracín, 2013; for related concepts, see Albarracín et al., 2008; Albarracín, Hepler, & Tannenbaum, 2011). In fact, general dispositional attitudes predict the time people spend on a number of daily behaviors, such as personal care, working, education, and traveling (Hepler & Albarracín, 2014). Finally, the chapter also addresses the status of the attitude–behavior relation.

CHAPTER 4

Goals, Intentions, and Behavior

We begin each year with goals to lose weight, work out more, and be a little healthier, and our days with intentions to complete everything that we failed to complete yesterday. As imperfect as goals are, they allow us to get an education, take care of our children, and provide timely feedback to our students. They also make sure that we don't walk on stage to play the piano when we cannot play the piano. Goals involve behavioral aims (i.e., ride a bicycle), affective aims (e.g., feeling good), cognitive aims (e.g., having more knowledge of music), social aims (e.g., making a new friend), and objective aims (e.g., losing 5 pounds). They may be either general (to get tenure) or specific (to publish a paper), and, when they are behavioral, they may focus on actions or inactions (effortful behavior vs. rest).

Goals have implications for behaviors when they highlight behavioral processes that may lead to realizing the goal. In this case, goals can influence intentions and actual behavioral execution. For example, students who enroll in college do so by previously setting academic goals to complete prerequisites. However, the goals cannot produce behavior in the absence of motor and cognitive procedures. For example, completing prerequisites involves processes that go from selecting appropriate classes to studying for exams and obtaining adequate grades in those classes.

Fortunately, our current knowledge on the behavioral effects of goals and intentions is extensive. For example, the reasoned action approach identified intention as the immediate determinant of behavior (Fishbein & Ajzen, 2010). Social cognitive theory has emphasized the role of goals and how setting realistic and unrealistic goals can affect performance (Bandura, 2001; Bandura & Wood, 1989). Other research has investigated implementation intentions and difficulties in goal pursuit, such as insufficient effort, excessive rumination, and exercise (Bagozzi & Warshaw, 1990; Brown, 1995; Gollwitzer, 1999; Hagger et al., 2016; Kuhl, 1984). However, past research has two limitations that this chapter is intended to address. First, past research on goals and intentions has not fully addressed how these psychological variables fit within a goal hierarchy. Second, the research on goals and intentions has developed relatively separately from the research on less deliberate behavior. Thus, this chapter describes how goals and intentions operate as highly conscious, deliberative, strategic processes, but also in more passive ways that are in between the point of full deliberation and the point of conditioned responses.

Goal Definition and Hierarchy

In this book, a "goal" is defined as an aim, which can involve a state (i.e., a steady situation of being or possessing) or a process (i.e., a process that unfolds over time). In terms of a state, the goal of feeling happy entails a state of happiness, and the state of owning a home entails possession of an object that brings comfort and security to most people. In terms of a process, the goal of achieving happiness entails a sequence of unfolding events, including taking stock of the positive aspects of one's life and deepening relationships.

Goal Generality

Like other authors (Shah, Kruglanski, & Friedman, 2003), I believe that goals are hierarchically organized. Goals like the achievement motivation or the affiliation need (Elliot & Church, 1997; Vallerand, 1997) are fairly general. Others are all encompassing and are often measured as part of personality traits like locomotion/assessment, prevention/promotion, or BIS/BAS. A *locomotion* regulatory mode, for example, entails a behavioral orientation toward quickness and ease of execution (Avnet & Higgins, 2003). An *assessment* regulatory mode entails an orientation toward critical evaluation to determine the best possible option.

Prevention-promotion is a general disposition to seek positive outcomes or avoid negative outcomes and seek safety. In Higgins's (1997) terms, some people are promotion oriented, whereas others are prevention oriented. People who are promotion oriented are likely to prefer products characterized by many positive attributes. They are also less sensitive to negative attributes that heighten the risk of a decision. In contrast, people who are prevention oriented are likely to prefer products with few negative attributes. They are also less sensitive to the presence or absence of positive product attributes.

General Action and Inaction Goals and Hierarchical Relations

General action and inaction goals are as general as locomotion/assessment or prevention/promotion. My colleagues and I (Albarracín, Hepler et al., 2011; Albarracín & Handley, 2011; Albarracín et al., 2008, 2018) have defined them as goals to engage in action irrespective of what the action might be, versus goals to rest or abstain from action irrespective of how this might be achieved. Specifically, the activation of these goals may trigger the pursuit or interruption of *any* particular (overt or covert) behavior that is subjectively relevant to the goal.

I first proposed the notion of general action and inaction goals based on observations of inter- and intraindividual variation in people's level of activity. Some people run 100-mile races, whereas others struggle to get out of bed in the morning (e.g., individuals suffering from depression) (American Psychiatric Association, 2000). The same person may be calm sometimes but hyperactive at other times. For example, during a manic episode, people may purchase objects they would normally not acquire, stay up all night, and rapidly switch from one activity to another. This hyperactivity often ranges from racing thoughts or plans to solve difficult problems, to unusual levels of physical effort.

Personality traits related to action and inaction goals involve extraversion/introversion and impulsivity. Extraversion comprises sociability and risk taking but also optimism; introversion comprises introspection and reservation but also pessimism (Eysenck, 1967; Taub, 1998). Eysenck (1967) dedicated much effort to link extraversion to corresponding responses in a particular arousal system. According to him, deficits in arousal underlie extroverts' search for external stimulation (Eysenck & Eysenck, 1985; Ludvigh & Happ, 1974; Shigehisa & Symons, 1973). Consistent with this hypothesis, extroverts in fact show lesser cerebral blood flow during resting states than do introverts (Mathew, Weinman, & Barr, 1984).

With respect to impulsivity, according to Gray (1991, 2000), behavior is controlled by three regulatory systems: (a) the behavioral approach system (BAS), (b) the behavioral inhibition system (BIS), and (c) the fight-flight-freezing system (FFFS). First, the BAS regulates approach behavior by responding to positively valenced stimuli, rewards, or relief from punishment (Gray & McNaughton, 2000; Gray, 1991). BAS correlates with impulsivity, risk taking, and predisposition for mania (Gray & McNaughton, 2000; Gray, 1991). Second, the BIS responds to conflicting goals by inhibiting one of them (Gray & McNaughton, 2000; Gray, 1991).

This system is sensitive to punishment, absence of rewards, and novelty, and reduces negative or painful outcomes by inhibiting movement toward risky goals (Gray & McNaughton, 2000; Gray, 1991). Correlates of BAS include high anxiety, generalized anxiety disorder, and obsessive-compulsive disorder (Gray & McNaughton, 2000). Third, the FFFS regulates escape/avoidance behavior as responses to aversive stimuli. Correlates include fear, avoidant personality disorder, phobias, and panic attacks (Gray & McNaughton, 2000).

Ontogenetically, action goals emerge early, when infants go from disorganized movement to behavioral control. Moreover, these action goals remain general, as evidenced by children resisting sitting around in a variety of educational and social settings. However, I conceive general action–inaction goals to be at the level of prevention-promotion goals or approach-avoidance goals. Even if action–inaction goals precede other goals during human development, once self-regulation is established, people can set either action–inaction goals or prevention-promotion goals. In fact, these two sets of goals are theoretically orthogonal. A person may promote positive outcomes either by not doing anything that could disrupt a positive event, or by pursuing positive outcomes in an active way. Likewise, a person may prevent negative outcomes either by remaining inactive and not running any risks, or by avoiding out-comes in an active way. In other words, people can pursue active approach, active avoidance, or doing nothing, as described in the following principle:

> **Principle 13. Hierarchical position of general goals of action and inaction.** General goals of action and inaction either begin a motivational process, or become active in the service of other high-level goals such as seeking pleasure. For example, general goals of action or inaction can be met through prevention and promotion, yielding active approach, active avoid-ance, and doing nothing. Likewise, general goals of action and inaction can be met through locomotion and assessment goals, yielding locomotion, assessment, and doing nothing. In addition, general goals of action and inaction can be met through specific goals construed as action or inaction, respectively.

The same considerations apply to promotion and prevention in regula-tory focus theory (Higgins, 2012), approach versus avoidance (Carver & White, 1994), and grasping versus escaping in Buddhist philosophy (Gowans, 2004). For example, a promotion focus is associated with seeking gains, whereas a prevention focus is associated with avoiding losses and seeking safety (Higgins, 1997). Like with BAS and BIS, even though a promotion focus might appear similar to a goal of action, promotion and prevention are orthogonal to action and inaction (Albarracín et al., 2008). People may seek to prevent harm by taking preventive action, as shown by research in which prevention-focused students initiated preventive actions before promotion-focused participants (Freitas & Higgins, 2002). Furthermore, people may seek gains by taking action, as shown by students who engaged in behaviors designed to achieve positive outcomes (Freitas & Higgins, 2002).

As any personality characteristic, prevention and promotion are patterns of behavior that tend to permeate many situations. People who score high in promotion have chronic responses of eagerness and enthusiasm, whereas people who score high in prevention have chronic responses of vigilance. Therefore, manipulating action and inaction goals may moderate the degree to which people respond in a prevention fashion or a promotion fashion.

In a study we conducted (Earl, Hart, Handley, & Albarracín, 2004), participants first received either action or inaction primes, then were asked to either move or rest, and finally read scenarios that described pairs of possible choices (*A* vs. *B*). For example, participants were presented with the option of buying a book that focused on (a) how to avoid instability and anxiety or (b) how to excel and achieve. Also, they were asked to select a snack described as (a) preventing fatigue or (b) increasing energy. Then, participants indicated whether *A* or *B* were preferable for them. We analyzed the degree to which high-promotion participants preferred the promotion-compatible option or high-prevention participants preferred the prevention-compatible option. As expected, chronic behavioral tendencies were more influential when participants had action than inaction goals.

Action and inaction goals could also energize salient or accessible mindsets or behavioral procedures (for a review, see Gollwitzer & Bayer, 1999). A primary difference between the notion of mindset versus goals is that *mindsets* (see Gollwitzer, Heckhausen, & Steller, 1990) are collections of specific behavioral procedures (Smith, 1994). In contrast, goals are desired end states that can promote various behavioral procedures until the goal is satisfied (for excellent reviews on goal properties, see Gollwitzer, 2004; Shah, Kruglanski, & Friedman, 2003). For example, Golwitzer, Heckhausen, and Steller (1990) manipulated mindsets by having participants either deliberate on an unresolved personal problem or plan the implementation of a chosen goal. After this task, participants read unfinished fairy tales and were instructed to write an ending for them. Even though the two tasks were unrelated, having deliberated about and having planned the implementation of a goal each had carry-over effects. When the writers were previously induced to deliberate about a personal problem, the fairy-tale endings included the protagonists' reflections about whether or not to choose a goal. In contrast, when the writers were previously induced to plan a way of meeting a personal goal, the endings were dominated by the protagonists' considerations about how to implement a goal. Presumably, practicing deliberative or implemental procedures as part of the first task increased the likelihood of the respective procedures being applied in the second task.[1]

Because implemental and deliberative mindsets are collections of procedures, both action and inaction goals may be satisfied by either implemental or deliberative activities. Thus, individuals who are motivated to act could think of ways of implementing an action (a cognitive action in Figure 4.1) or perform an overt action (see also Figure 4.1). Alternatively, the same individuals could deliberate about what action course to take (another cognitive action) or try the behavior (e.g., running, folding a paper airplane in Figure 4.1) to assess it. This distinction is also important to understand the relation between action and inaction goals and locomotion-assessment. In a study examining dietary decisions, participants who were either locomotion oriented or assessment oriented read essays about dietary change that espoused benefits for either one outcome or two outcomes and then evaluated their intentions to engage in the behavior (Orehek et al., 2012). Locomotion-oriented participants formed stronger intentions to make the dietary change in the single-outcome condition, presumably because a single outcome appears to be a direct path toward one's goal. In contrast, assessment-oriented participants formed stronger intentions in the multioutcome condition, presumably because they enjoyed evaluating multiple outcomes. All in all, both groups

---

[1] By contrast, a behavioral performance that can satisfy a goal, such as deliberating about a personal problem following a deliberation *goal* (not a mindset), may decrease the likelihood of subsequently applying that same deliberation procedure (see, e.g., Bargh et al., 2001). Consistent with this possibility, goals to maintain a favorable self-image, for example, often trigger rationalization processes in situations of cognitive dissonance. However, self-affirming through other means effectively restores a desirable self-image and thus eliminates the need to reduce cognitive dissonance by changing attitudes (Steele & Liu, 1981). Similarly, past research has demonstrated that priming goals outside of awareness stimulates behaviors consistent with these goals (Bargh et al., 2001; Chartrand & Bargh, 1999). However, when these goals are satisfied by means of an alternate procedure (means substitution or equifinality; see Shah & Kruglanski, 2002), such as receiving positive feedback when the goal is self-enhancement, the goal-directed activity may cease (e.g., Steele & Liu, 1981).

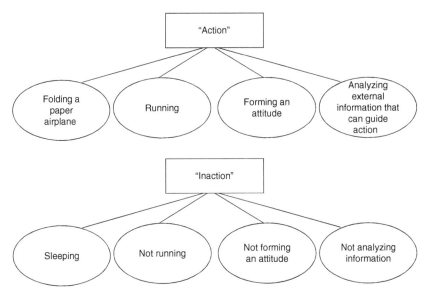

Figure 4.1 Possible means of satisfaction of general action and inaction goals.

developed goals of action, but they responded differently to the information presented to them.

Setting *general* action and inaction goals may be useful for a number of reasons. First, general action goals facilitate doing something about a problem even when one initially does not know what to do. That is, because of their generality, they may elicit novel solutions. Eventually, a useful activity may develop that corrects the problem that triggered the general action goal to begin. Thus, the general action goal may allow for flexibility, exploration, and innovation in ways that more specific action goals may not. When one specific course of action fails, there are advantages to taking a general approach to the problem ("I need to do something, what can I do?").

Second, general action and inaction goals presumably allow individuals to plan their lives according to awake and rest cycles. Humans must be able to sleep at a convenient time and place (e.g., when it is dark, when the place is safe), which makes the capacity for inaction invaluable. Culturally managing these patterns is important to satisfy the biological, psychological, and social needs of people in a community.

There are also potential disadvantages to setting general action and inaction goals. Most notably, merely doing something does not imply doing something useful. Instead, merely striving to do may promote detrimental activity such as overspending or going beyond one's physical limitations. Thus, to be adaptive, general action and inaction goals have to be linked to more specific ones, such as performing healthy behaviors or making smart decisions. When these behaviors are neither salient nor chronically accessible, any general goal can produce detrimental action.

Realizing Goals through Processes: Identifying Processes and Distinguishing State Goals from Active and Inactive Processes

To be realized, all goals, whether state or process goals, require a process. When the goal is a state, this state must be linked to a process that can be expected to yield the state. When the goal is a process, the goal itself specifies behavioral, cognitive, social, or affective steps to carry out.

This sequence of goals and process goals is illustrated in Figure 4.2. For example, the goal may be to learn to play tennis and the process may be signing up for tennis lessons. The process is usually behavioral, such as making a phone call to sign up for a particular lesson. However, the process may also be cognitive. For example, I may have the goal of knowing when to make a trip and mentally search for possible dates, a cognitive process that can be executed intentionally to realize the goal.

The identification of process goals is not trivial and depends on finding a process that can be construed as fitting the state, particularly when the state is broad. For example, people with an inaction goal should look for processes to reach a state of inaction, whereas people with an action goal should look for processes to reach action. First, this identification will depend on finding a behavior that people can construe as an action or an inaction. To study these subjective definitions, I asked participants to rate behaviors on dimensions that may define action and inaction. Specifically, participants were asked to indicate whether behaviors like "sleeping,"

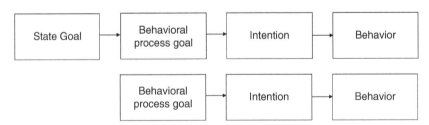

Figure 4.2 State goal, behavioral process goal, intention, and behavior.

"walking," and "solving an intellectual problem" (a) induced change, (b) required effort, (c) consumed energy, (d) were acts of will, (e) were purposeful, (f) required talking, (g) required forming or maintaining an idea in one's mind, (h) required reflection, (i) required logical thinking, and (j) required opinions. Interestingly, a factor analysis revealed three groups of events, including movement and problem solving, relaxation and passive activities (e.g., sleeping), and contemplation (e.g., daydreaming and sitting still). Three of the measured behaviors (one from the relaxation cluster and two from the movement/problem-solving cluster) illustrate how participants defined them and appear in Figure 4.3. As shown, effort and energy demand most strongly differentiated walking and intellectual problem solving from sleeping. Thus, comparing sleeping with other behaviors suggested that energy demand, effort, and will were defining features of both movement and thought. There were also differences between intellectual problem solving and walking/sleeping. Not surprisingly, compared to sleeping and to walking, intellectual problem solving reportedly involved more reflection, idea formation, logical thinking, and talking with oneself.

In experimental settings, the researcher may first try to induce a general action goal or a general inaction goal. For instance, participants may view

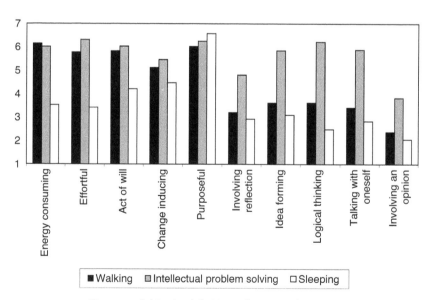

Figure 4.3 Subjective definitions of action and inaction.

icons of runners or sleepers. Then, as part of the study, participants may be offered the option of relaxing or folding a paper airplane. In general, individuals are likely to conceptualize relaxing as inaction and folding a paper airplane as action. Thus, they may choose to respectively relax or fold a piece of paper. The selection of ways of satisfying general goals of action and inaction appear in Figure 4.1.

Although general action and inaction goals can both trigger execution or cessation of specific behaviors, the goals are different from the means. In the case of action goals, the behaviors executed to satisfy the goal can also be a process goal in and of themselves. In contrast, in the case of inaction goals, the aim is not a behavior such as stopping but a state of inaction. The inactive state of the inaction goal may be reached by actively interrupting behavior or by preventing new activities. In this sense, the end of an inaction state is inactive but the process to achieve it may be active. These two possibilities appear in Figure 4.4.

> **Principle 14. General action and inaction goals and active/inactive means.** General action and inaction goals are satisfied through active (e.g., running, or suddenly interrupting a run), or passive processes (e.g., continuing to lie down in bed, or remaining still on a conveyor belt).

Effects of General Action and Inaction Goals

The upcoming sections review a variety of effects of priming action and inaction goals. In addition, these effects are summarized in detail in Table 4.1, which presents the results of a meta-analysis we conducted (Albarracín, Sunderrajan, Dai et al., 2019). The synthesized

Figure 4.4 Action–inaction goals in the goal hierarchy.

Table 4.1 *Meta-analysis of action and inaction manipulations*

Study	Experiment	N	Outcome of interest	Goal manipulation	Action vs. control d	Inaction vs. control d	Action vs. inaction d
Albarracín et al. (2008)	1	98	Choice of active (doodling) vs. passive (resting) task	Word completion			0.91
	2	38	Eating grapes (no. of grapes eaten)	Word completion			0.61
	3	136	Number of times participants freely pressed a keyboard button	Word completion	0.31	−0.13	0.44
	4	37	Memory (proportion of facts correctly recalled from a passage)	Subliminal priming			0.46
	5	36	Number of SAT problems correctly solved	Scrambled sentence task			0.32
	7	49	Number of reported thoughts; active task	Word completion	−0.24	−0.96	0.59
	7	49	Number of reported thoughts; inactive task	Word completion	0.96	0.94	0.14
Albarracín, Wang, and Leeper (2009)	1	53	Eating raisins (kcal consumed)	Exposure to exercise (control) ads	0.54		
	2	51	Eating M&Ms, peanuts, and raisins (kcal consumed)	Subliminal priming	0.34		
Albarracín and Handley (2011a)	1	54	Speed of response in reporting attitude	Word completion	0.80	−0.89	1.69
Albarracín and Hart (2011)	2	70	Willingness to read as part of decision-making task; positive mood	Word completion	0.48		

Table 4.1 (*cont.*)

Study	Experiment	N	Outcome of interest	Goal manipulation	Action vs. control d	Inaction vs. control d	Action vs. inaction d
	2	69	Number of articles selected; negative mood	Word completion	−0.30		
	3	40	Correct rejection of unseen photos; positive mood	Scrambled sentence task		−0.55	
	3	41	Correct rejection of unseen photos; negative mood	Scrambled sentence task		0.63	
Gendolla and Silvestrini (2010)	1	64	Reaction times for a memory task	Subliminal priming	0.41	−0.59	1.00
Hart and Albarracín (2012)	1	160	Selection of consistent vs. inconsistent selective exposure	Word completion	0.37	−0.54	0.91
Hart and Gable (2013)	1	31	Number of correct answers on test; high motivational intensity	Word completion	1.66		
	1	31	Number of correct answers on test; low motivational intensity	Word completion	0.87		
	1	31	Number of correct answers on test; no motivation manipulation	Word completion	0.56		
	2	47	Number of correct answers on test; high motivational intensity	Word completion		−1.43	

Study	k	Dependent variable	Measure			
	2	Number of correct answers on test; low motivational intensity	Word completion	−0.56		0.13
Hepler and Albarracín (2009)	1	Performance on change blindness task (no. of differences noticed)	Subliminal priming	−0.04	0.09	0.06
	2	Performance on visual search task (no. of differences noticed)	Subliminal priming	−0.08	−0.02	
Nosek et al. (2015)	1	Number of SAT problems correctly solved	Scrambled sentence task			−0.06
Noguchi, Handley, and Albarracín (2011)	3	Intention to vote in presidential election	Word completion	−0.24	0.27	0.51
	4	Intention to volunteer time for political cause	Word completion			0.53
Nyhuis (2012)	1	Intention to vote in election	Subliminal priming			0.00
Nyhuis, Gosselt, and Rosema (2016)	1	Attitudes and intentions toward getting involved in election	Subliminal priming			0.51
Seske (2012)	1	Exercise intentions	Movement/relaxing			0.53
Takarada and Nozaki (2014)	1	Motor action responses	Subliminal priming		0.25	
	1	Motor action responses	Supraliminal priming		0.25	
Total weighted average d				−0.327	0.345	0.487

Source: Adapted from Albarracín, Sunderrajan, Dai, and White (2019).

effects support the idea that general goals can lead to initiating specific behaviors and procedures in the service of the activated goals.

Motor behavior. There is evidence that action goals increase performance of a number of behaviors. For example, we primed participants with either action or inaction words inserted in a word completion task (Albarracín, Hepler et al., 2011; Albarracín et al., 2008). After the priming task, participants were told that they would have a break during which they could doodle on or fold a piece of paper, or they could close their eyes and rest. Results indicated that the probability of doodling/folding was greater when the prime was action than when it was inaction. Conversely, the probability of resting was greater when the prime was inaction than when it was action.

In another study, we (Albarracín et al., 2008) used the same priming procedures to investigate the effect of general action and inaction goals on reactions to the behavior of another person. We first presented participants with either action or inaction relevant words to complete. Then, we showed a video of a college student performing a series of daily activities such as checking email and having a drink. The participants' task was to watch the video and to click on the mouse each time they identified a meaningful event (see Lassiter, Geers, & Apple, 2002). In response to these vague instructions, some participants could spontaneously describe the video as "the behavior of a college student in a dorm" (1 behavioral unit = 1 click), whereas others could describe the video as "the drinking" and "the typing" behaviors of a college student in a dorm (2 behavioral units = 2 clicks). Normally, however, greater efforts in pursuing this goal translate into more identified behavioral units (see Lassiter, Geers, & Apple, 2002). Thus, identifying a greater number of units was taken as an indication of a more active behavior than identifying a smaller number of units. Consistent with our hypothesis, participants who received the action prime identified a greater number of behavioral units than participants who received the inaction prime[2].

Learning. In another study investigating action and inaction goals (Albarracín et al., 2008), we primed action and inaction using very brief presentations (50 ms) of action/inaction words. We then asked participants

---

[2] Note that the effects of inaction goals in this case may be interpreted as yielding a more abstract construal of the behavior (Vallacher, 2014; Vallacher & Wegner, 2012). This is an interesting possibility. However, one should be able to construe both action and inaction at more abstract or more concrete levels. For instance, if the different events were getting ready to sleep, getting in bed, and closing one's eyes, an inaction goal may lead to more specific construal than an action goal.

to study a passage about evolutionary psychology. We measured correct recall of the material based on open-ended responses. As expected, we found that the action primes facilitated learning more than did the inaction primes.

Eating. General action and inaction goals can also control overt behaviors with important health implications. We (Albarracín et al., 2008, 2009) reasoned that, if general action goals can be satisfied with any behavior, then subtly telling people to be active may trigger both eating and exercise. To test this possibility, we first primed a group of participants with general action or control words and then introduced two ostensible tasting tasks in counterbalanced order. Specifically, we told participants that we were sampling and rating two new products (i.e., grapes packaged with a new packaging system, and an exercise video). As predicted, participants ate more grapes and exercised longer after being primed with action words than after being primed with control words.

Political participation. Another series of studies provided evidence on the effects of general action and inaction goals on political participation (Noguchi, Handley, & Albarracín, 2011). Participants first completed either action or inaction words and then received a persuasive communication advocating the institution of a new policy. At the end of the study, they were asked whether they were willing to volunteer time to make phone calls related to the policy. Participants could volunteer to make these phone calls and either advocate in favor of or against the policy. Overall, participants volunteered between 10 and 20 min to make phone calls. However, those participants primed with action goals were willing to volunteer more time than those primed with inaction goals.

Ability to execute other behaviors. Requesting actions is more demanding than requesting inactions. We (Albarracín, Wang, & McCulloch, 2018) proposed that people are more likely to spontaneously form action than inaction goals and therefore to experience greater cognitive impairment in response to multiple action demands than in response to multiple inaction demands. Compared to inactions, actions attract more attention and may elicit stronger emotional reactions (Landman, 1987; Zhou, Yu, & Zhou, 2010). Also, action is more informative than inaction. In animal perception and learning, pigeons are better able to associate rewards with video images of other pigeons that are moving than with other pigeons that are standing still (Dittrich & Lea, 1993). In humans, people who signal agreement by enacting a response later agree with a behavior more than people who signal agreement by avoiding a response (Allison & Messick, 1988; Cioffi & Garner, 1996; Fazio, Sherman, & Herr, 1982).

One implication of the attention-capture produced by action goals is that, when multiple behaviors are requested, a greater number of actions is more distracting than a greater number of inactions (Albarracín, Wang et al., 2018). Supporting this hypothesis, a series of experiments using a multiple Go/No-Go task showed that both misses and false alarms were more frequent when participants had to press a key in response to three targets than when they had to not press a key in response to three targets. This pattern of results was attributable to the greater cognitive load posed by the multiple action goals and by people's natural focus on action. However, when participants were encouraged to focus on inaction (Experiment 4), the difference in errors decreased.

Impulsive and deliberate behaviors. We have shown that general action goals can increase impulsivity during delay discounting tasks (Hepler, Albarracín, McCulloch, & Noguchi, 2012). Specifically, participants were presented with a series of choices between two hypothetical rewards. Varying the size and time of the rewards allows researchers to gauge preferences for immediate versus delayed gratification. For instance, participants may be asked *Would you prefer $11 now or $30 in 7 days from now?* A high-impulsivity response is to choose the $11 immediate reward over the $30 reward a week later. Furthermore, these responses allow researchers to analyze the willingness to discount the reward as a function of the delay to receive it. This index is an area under the curve termed *k*-value and is plotted in Figure 4.5. As shown in Figure 4.5A, impulsivity was greater in response to a general action prime, which was also confirmed in a second experiment using a Go/No-Go task (see Figure 4.5). As shown in Figure 4.5B, there were more false alarms in response to action than in response to inaction primes.

Intentions

In my model, goals are *aims* not currently realized. They are a discrepancy between the present and a *future* and thus require a behavior that will reduce the discrepancy (for the notion of discrepancy, see Wiener, 2011). In contrast, intentions are defined as existing in the *present*, comprising a sense of will over the execution of an imminent or ongoing behavior.

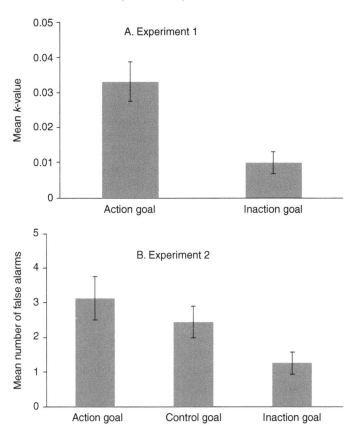

Figure 4.5 Action goal effects on impulsivity. (Adapted from Hepler, Albarracín et al., 2007)

In the past, the theoretical difference between goals and intentions has been murky, in part because different research traditions use different terms. First, Ajzen and Fishbein (Ajzen & Fishbein, 1980; Ajzen et al., 2019; Fishbein & Ajzen, 2010) use the term "intention" and "goal" to describe degree of controllability. In their view, one may have the intention to study but the goal to receive an A on the next exam. Thus, "intention" refers to a behavior, whereas "goal" refers to an expected outcome or event that actors do not control (e.g., in this example, the teacher will assign the grade). Second, Gollwitzer (1999) has described "goal intention" and "implementation intention." "Goal intention" is the intention to pursue the goal, and "implementation intention" is an "if-then" plan that specifies when or under what circumstances a behavior should be executed. Third, Kruglanski (1996) has defined goals as "desired states of affairs that mobilize behavior" and "means" as the subgoals used to meet a goal.

My definition of intention is the same as Ajzen and Fishbein's (Ajzen & Fishbein, 1980; Ajzen et al., 2019; Fishbein & Ajzen, 2010). Furthermore, my definition of intentions can encompass Gollwitzer's "goal intentions" and "implementation intentions." For example, the intention to exercise might be called "goal intention," whereas the "intention to exercise at home after waking up every day" might be called an "implementation intention." Ajzen and Fishbein would describe the first intention as more general than the second because the second specifies a time and a context. I would as well. Ajzen (2002; Ajzen, Czasch, & Flood, 2009) has also pointed out that implementation intentions are only relevant when people have an intention to perform a behavior to begin. For example, whether or not to exercise immediately after waking up is only relevant for those who intend to exercise to begin with.

Kruglanski's (1996) definition of goals is similar to mine except that I do not see mobilizing behavior as a necessary part of the definition of goals. First, goals are not always behavioral, as is the case with cognitive or affective goals. Second, behavioral goals may have no behavioral consequences, as is the case when they are not translated into intentions or when the resulting intentions are not carried out.

A behavior is intentional when there is a willingness to perform it (Ajzen & Fishbein, 1980; Albarracín et al., 2007; Fishbein & Ajzen, 1975, 2010). Arguably, such intentionality ensures that one's goals will translate into behavior at least under some conditions. Consistent with this notion, a large literature has shown that the intention to perform a behavior is an excellent predictor of actual behavior (Ajzen et al., 2019). For example, meta-analyses of specific health behaviors, such as condom use and exercise, have yielded average intention–behavior correlations ranging from 0.44 to 0.56 (Albarracín, Johnson, Fishbein, & Muellerleile, 2001; Godin & Kok, 1996; Hausenblas, Carron, & Mack, 1997).

The degree to which intentions are necessary to elicit behavior is likely variable, and has been a matter of some debate. Figure 4.6 describes behaviors executed with and without intention. Sometimes people form intentions after analyzing the desirability and feasibility of performing a behavior (see, e.g., Albarracín & Wyer, 2001; Fishbein & Ajzen, 2010). They may then implement intentions in a deliberative way.

Other times, however, people engage in fairly automatic behavior (Fazio, 1990; Orbell & Verplanken, 2015; Ouellette & Wood, 1998). For example, people are less deliberate when they do not care about the behavior (see, e.g., Albarracín, 2002; Albarracín & Wyer, 2000; Petty & Cacioppo, 1986). Similarly, frequent performance of a behavior facilitates less deliberate executions (Smith, 1994). That is, with practice, people may move from a deliberate, intentional performance to a more automatic performance. As shall be seen, however, I believe the conditions for unintentional behavior to be uncommon and highly dependent on how intentions are represented in people's minds.

Involvement of Intentions and Goals in Behavioral Enactment

Automatic behavior does exist. Epilepsy and the stereotypic behavior observed in severe forms of mental illness are clear examples of initiating a behavior without awareness or intention to do so. Sleepwalking and unintentional motor adjustments while we walk are other examples. However, it is difficult to imagine that one reads the newspaper or purchases milk completely "inadvertently" or "unintentionally."

Defining automaticity is therefore key. A number of years ago, Bargh (1994) pointed out that "automaticity" is a complex phenomenon that includes awareness (knowing that one is executing the behavior or knowing the reasons for the behavior), intentionality (ability to initiate the behavior), efficiency (speed with which the behavior is executed), and control (ability to stop the behavior). With these four considerations in mind, many behaviors can be considered automatic because they are efficient and difficult to control. However, outside of purely reflexive behavior (e.g., blinking) or stereotypic behavior (e.g., a nervous tic), we are generally aware of what we do and would assert that our behavior is *intentional*. Most behaviors of interest in social psychology, communication, as well as consumer, political, environmental, and health psychology are unlikely to occur without awareness or intentionality.

Intention and awareness in thought processes (for a review, see Bargh, 1994) are not the same as intention and awareness in behavior. Thoughts are largely spontaneous, emergent phenomena we generally do not control. For example, I can try to recall what I did yesterday step by step and review behavior by behavior in the order I want. Even in that case, however, my chain of thought is generally interrupted by seemingly random images, words, and ideas that simply come to mind. In contrast to the automaticity of thoughts, behaviors like eating or shopping often occur with intention and awareness. In the coming sections, I analyze this problem as well as exceptions to this generalization.

My assertion that behaviors typically involve awareness and intentionality does not imply absence of automaticity. Moreover, this assertion needs to be reconciled with prior findings in the area of behavioral priming and low correlations between intention and behavior under some conditions. First, repeated exposure to incidental stimuli (e.g., one's random thoughts, or incidentally presented words and images) that are linked to a behavior have been shown to set behavior in motion (e.g., Bargh et al., 1996; Bargh, Gollwitzer, Lee-Chai, Barndollar, & Trötschel, 2001; Weingarten et al., 2016a). For example, words related to achievement can influence people's performance (e.g., Bargh et al., 1996; Hart & Albarracín, 2009) and elicit goals that in turn affect performance (Bargh et al., 2001; Kruglanski & Higgins, 2007). Furthermore, as judged by direct measures of intentions, incidental movements can affect people's intentions to act in other contexts (Jiang & Albarracín, 2019). Second, intentions have been shown to have low correlations with behavior when the behavior is habitual (Ouellette & Wood, 1998). Presumably, when behavior becomes habitual, automatic stimulus-response sequences produce the behavior and intentionality is less important. My review of awareness and intentionality in the coming sections will discuss these issues.

Involvement of Goals and Intentions in Behavior Performance

Primary direct stimulus-behavior effects (strictly without goal mediation) are possible but likely require a peculiar set of conditions. These possibilities appear in Figure 4.6. First, a stimulus may directly influence a behavior when the behavior was *not* goal mediated in prior instances (see Figure 4.6A). For example, nonverbal mimicry starts very early in life, without intention, and continues without much conscious control throughout one's lifetime. Second, a stimulus may produce a behavior when a stimulus and a given set of spatial features co-occur (see Figure 4.6B). A person who sits on a chair with an inclined backrest may become accustomed to that posture while working on her computer. Later, sitting on a different chair to work on the computer may still elicit the same posture because the computer and the posture have become associated in an incidental way. Of note, however, both mimicry and posture involve a realm of behavior that occurs with little if any awareness and intentionality to begin.

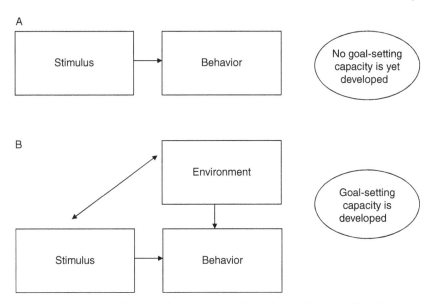

Figure 4.6 Conditions under which a stimulus influences behavior directly.

Second, some behavioral responses may become conditioned even if the sequence of behaviors is initiated intentionally. Starting to drive, for example, initially requires the intention to execute each movement associated with driving. A teenager might intentionally sit in the car, intentionally push the break, turn on the car, and so on. This type of stimulus–goal/intention–behavior sequence appears in Figure 4.7. However, as shown in Figure 4.7B, with training, driving motions may be performed without intention, likely because the behavior has become conditioned, or because, over time, a wholistic structure (i.e., a procedure) integrates the goal or intention into a sequence that is executed automatically (Anderson, 2013; Wyer, 2016). In other words, a behavior that was goal directed and intentional has become automatic secondarily to practice. Even in those situations, the behavioral sequence is initiated intentionally. For example, driving to work requires the intention to get ready to get in the car even for experienced drivers. Overall, this analysis leads to the following principle:

> **Principle 15. Conditions for behavior without goal or intention mediation.** Goals (relatively abstract aims) and intentions to execute the behavior in a particular context are unnecessary only when behaviors are conditioned responses to stimuli.

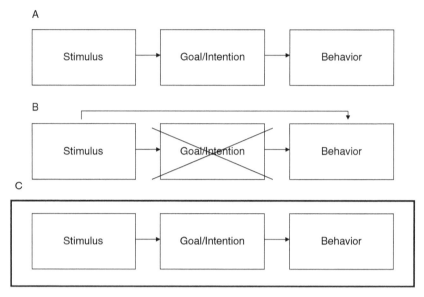

Figure 4.7 Involvement of goals and intentions in behavior: (A) goal mediation; (B) goal no longer necessary; (C) proceduralization.

Efficiency and Proceduralization

As shown in Figure 4.7C, behaviors can automate due to increases in proceduralization, defined as the increasingly faster, more efficient application of a behavioral procedure (i.e., a motor sequence). Much research on proceduralization has been conducted in the domain of social cognitive procedures. For example, in research conducted by Smith and colleagues (Smith, Branscombe, & Bormann, 1988), participants judged whether a series of behaviors (i.e., a verb, e.g., analyze) implied a particular trait (i.e., "intelligent" or "kind"). The trait was constant across the first 150 trials but changed during the last 50 trials (i.e., from "intelligent" to "kind" or from "kind" to "intelligent"). There was a general practice effect by which participants were faster at inferring "intelligence" from a new behavior when they previously practiced making intelligence judgments. In addition, the speed of making trait (intelligence) inferences from past behaviors ("analyze") was greater when the specific behavior had already been evaluated in terms of intelligence (i.e., specific practice effect). Naturally, Smith et al. (1988) concluded that making intelligence judgments makes one quicker at judging novel behaviors in terms of intelligence. In addition, having evaluated the specific behavior brings further efficiency for new judgments of that behavior.

In Smith et al.'s (1988) study, judgment efficiency was partly due to general practice evaluating behaviors in terms of intelligence (different behavior, same trait). However, the specific practice effect (greater efficiency for same behavior/same task conditions) could involve: (a) facilitation of reading the words ("analyze"), (b) storage of a stimulus-response pair in memory (e.g., if "analyze" is presented, respond "yes"), and/or (c) creation of a stimulus-specific judgment task (e.g., "if asked to decide whether 'analyze' implies intellect, say 'yes'"). In research to elucidate these mechanisms (Smith, 1989), some participants first evaluated behaviors in terms of either "intelligence" or "kindness." Other participants first evaluated whether words had long *A* or *E* sounds. Then, the participants were asked to judge either the same or different stimuli on the basis of the same or different targets (e.g., for the trait task, intelligence again, or switch to kindness). In addition to these four conditions, two other conditions involved the unpracticed task with either the same or different behaviors. That is, using either the previous or new behaviors, participants who previously judged sounds were asked to judge traits, whereas participants who previously judged traits were asked to judge sounds.

General practice should be reflected in speedy responses when the same trait judgment is applied to new behaviors. Specific effects may yield different results depending on what drives the effect. If the specific practice effect is due to categorizing a specific behavior, then changes to the behavior should slow down responses. If the specific practice effect is due to judging the same trait (same target), then changes to the trait should slow down responses. If the specific practice effect is due to the facilitation of reading the behavior, then presenting a different behavior should slow down responses.

Smith's (1989) practice results as a function of behavior, task, and target appear in Table 4.2. The first column shows whether the task (i.e., judging traits or sounds) was the same or different; the second shows whether the behavior (e.g., "kiss" or "analyze") was the same or different; and the third shows whether the target (judging "kindness" or "intelligence") was the same or different.

The key measure was how much faster participants were at making judgments during the second task. As shown in Table 4.2, evaluating the same behavior with the same trait yielded the largest time savings (100 ms). Using the same target of judgment (e.g., "intelligent") for a different behavior produced moderate time savings (e.g., 1 ms in savings in the different behavior, same task, and same response). Finally, only practicing the task (trait or sound categorizations; first column) and only reading the behavior each produced very small if any savings.

Table 4.2 *Summary of the effects of practice across same/different behaviors, tasks, and targets*

Task (i.e., trait inference or sound)	Behavior (e.g., kiss or analyze)	Target (e.g., kind or intelligent sound task)	Size of effect	Description
Same	Same	Same	Highest: 100 ms in savings per trial	High specific practice effect: savings when nothing changes
Same	Different	Same	Moderate: 1 ms in savings per trial	Moderate general practice effect: savings for same judgments of new behaviors
Same	Same	Different	Null: no savings	No savings from reading the behavior
Same	Different	Different	Low: 0.5 ms in savings per trial	Small general practice effect, different target trait: savings when the same task (making trait inferences or judging sounds) is applied to new targets and behaviors
Different	Same	–	Low: 0.5 ms in savings per trial	Small savings from reading the behavior
Different	Different	–	Null: no savings	No savings when all aspects are new

Source: Adapted from Smith (1989).

One reason for the large specific practice effect in Table 4.2 is that solving a mathematical problem leaves a memory trace of both the problem and the answer (Logan, 1988). Thus, when people are asked to solve the same problem again, they retrieve the answer and the cognitive procedure used to reach this answer in parallel. Normally, if the previous answer comes to mind before they finish recalculating it, they reuse the previous one. In contrast, if the previous response is slower to come to mind, they use the recalculated response.

At least two other conceptualizations explain proceduralization. First, according to Anderson (1983), frequent use of a procedure leads to compiling several procedural steps into a single one. In addition, neural network models (Rumelhart & McClelland, 1986) assume that declarative knowledge and procedural knowledge are both stored as connection weights in a network. Learning affects connection weights that reflect both the type of input (declarative knowledge) and the processing of the input (procedural knowledge). As a result, the information used to solve a problem, the procedure, and the response are all tightly linked and all contribute to making behaviors more efficient.

Intentionality and the Psychological Representation of Intentions

Figure 4.6 and Figure 4.7 suggest that a behavior that was initially intentional may be proceduralized and lead the intention to be an efficient step in the process. According to Betsch, Fiedler, and Brinkmann (1998), a routine is a behavioral strategy that comes to mind when one is confronted with a problem. Some of the routines are established by environmental rewards and repetition, whereas others can be executed without prior direct experience in the domain (calling the fire department if there is a fire). Moreover, some of these routines are habits. As such, they can be performed automatically (Bryan & Harter, 1899; Ouellette & Wood, 1998), without the intervention of a conscious intention and without considering the rewards or losses of the behavior. Other routines are not habits but decisions selected with the intervention of more controlled processes (Ronis, Yates, & Kirscht, 1989).

Betsch and his colleagues (1998) studied whether time pressure and novelty influence deviations from prior routines. The authors designed a computer game in which participants had to select one of the three possible paths to deliver a truck full of melons to its destination. After each choice, participants received feedback about the gains and losses of taking a particular route. As people gain practice with the game, one of the routes emerges as the best in terms of outcomes. For each of three different goals, participants more frequently selected one route over others. Thus, each choice becomes a routine solution for saving time, reducing costs, or protecting the cargo.

After the training/routinization of solutions, Betsch et al. (1998) changed the pay-offs of each particular route and observed whether participants adhered to or changed their earlier routines. Some participants were given 20 s to make their choices, whereas others had no time pressure. In addition, for one-half of the participants, the display of the options was identical to the one used during the training phase. In contrast, for the other participants, the display of the options contained some initials that were not present during the training phase (novelty condition). Figure 4.8

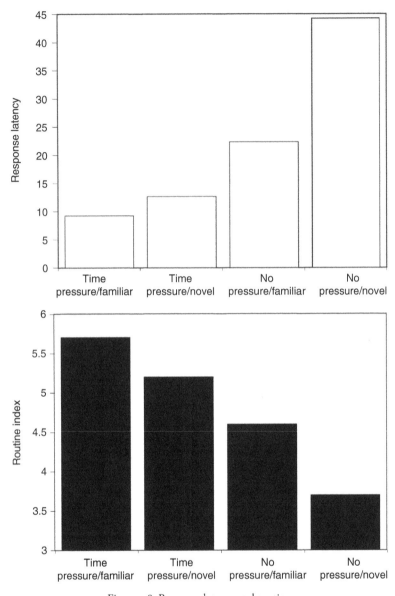

Figure 4.8 Response latency and routine.

presents the data as a function of both manipulations. As shown, these manipulations had additive effects. Participants were faster in the presence of time pressure and a familiar display than in the absence of these conditions. In addition, a routine index calculated by the authors indicated that time pressure and familiarity decreased deviations from the routines established during the learning phase of the study. That is, time pressure and familiarity can make people insensitive to the changes in the outcomes of their choices.

In my view, proceduralization and efficiency do not imply that a behavior is executed without intention, at least not to the point of reporting that one did not intend the behavior. However, researchers (Ouellette & Wood, 1998) have argued that, when a behavior is habitual, the past behavior reflects environmental triggers that consistently elicit the behavior, bypassing intentions. For example, when people always exercise at the same time and in the same place, time and place automatically cue exercise without intentions being necessary. People perform the behavior in an automatic fashion, without even realizing that they do, let alone reflect on the reasons for their intentions. Therefore, intentions predict behavior less when behavior occurs in stable places and times (Ouellette & Wood, 1998).

Behaviors that we repeat become associated with a number of contextual cues. Hence, the presence of the cues facilitates repetition of the behavior. In research on the habitual behaviors of college students, Wood, Tam, and Witt (2005) identified contextual cues that trigger everyday habits. Then, they examined whether changes in these cues triggered a disruption of habits when participants transferred from one university to another. In particular, they measured whether three behaviors (exercising, watching television, and reading the newspaper) were performed (a) usually (vs. rarely) in the same location and (b) usually (vs. rarely) with other people. They also measured the self-reported frequency with which people performed the behavior (e.g., *never* and *just about every day*). As expected when the behavior was frequent to begin (strong habit), changes in the location in which a behavior was performed led to a decrease in exercise. However, when the behavior was less frequent (weaker habit), changes in location had a smaller impact on exercise. Furthermore, intentions influenced behavior more when the habit was weaker than when it was stronger.

Similar data were obtained by Wood et al. (2002) in a diary study. In this research, participants wrote what they were thinking while they were performing various behaviors. Of these behaviors, the authors selected watching TV and driving, mainly because the behaviors were classified as habitual and nonhabitual by similar proportions of people. They then coded the thoughts participants wrote as either corresponding or noncorresponding to the behavior. That is, some participants wrote things like "I'm watching game shows so I am thinking about the answers," whereas others wrote things like "I'm hungry." When the behavior was frequent (habitual), only 36 percent of their thoughts were related to the behavior. In contrast, when the behavior was infrequent (nonhabitual), 51 percent of the thoughts were related to the behavior. This finding suggested that more frequent, habitual behaviors require little behavior-related thought. Presumably, various cues automatically elicit the behavior in a relatively mindless fashion.

I tested the influence of past behavior vis-à-vis intentions through a reanalysis of the condom use prediction literature (Albarracín et al., 2001). The meta-analysis included studies that reported associations among several variables relevant to using condoms, including: (a) behavior (i.e., past, future or both) or intentions, (b) attitudes, (c) subjective norms, and (d) control perceptions (i.e., perceived behavior control and/or self-efficacy). I reanalyzed these data (i.e., 129 data sets) to determine the extent to which the frequency of past condom use influenced the intention–future behavior relation. The results from these analyses appear in Figure 4.9 as a function of frequency of past behavior (A: high frequency; B: moderate frequency; C: low frequency). Reproducing Ouellette and Wood's (1998) findings, the intention–behavior correlation was weaker when the behavior was less frequent. Correspondingly, the correlation between past behavior and future behavior was stronger when the behavior was more frequent.

Despite the findings of my reanalysis, it is difficult to imagine that a person would be having sex, stop to search for a condom, open the wrapper, and apply the condom, all unintentionally. Anybody would report that their behavior was willful and that they were aware of performing it at that time. However, it is possible that the intention is represented differently when people perform the behavior frequently as opposed to only occasionally. For example, intentions to use condoms among frequent users likely involve representations of specific people and circumstances. Furthermore, they may not have a verbal representation like "I will use condoms consistently in the next three months."

In fact, if the environment cues the behavior directly, other measures related to the environment could predict behavior when behavior is more (vs. less) frequent. For example, external circumstances like having condoms available may exert influences over and above the influence of intentions. If so, the influence of perceived behavioral control on future behavior may be greater when people use condoms more (vs. less) frequently. Likewise, individuals who use condoms frequently may be "forced" by either external circumstances, such as the demands of their sexual partners. Therefore, I analyzed the associations of behavior with perceived behavioral control and norms. These relations also appear in Figure 4.9. As shown, however, I found no evidence that either perceived behavioral control or norms had stronger influences on future behavior when the behavior was more (vs. less) frequent. Perceived control had coefficients that hovered around 0, and norms had lower influence when the behavior was more than less frequent (i.e., β = 0.03, *ns*, and 0.12, p < 0.001).

What I did find was evidence that intentions overall perform more poorly for frequent (vs. infrequent) condom users. Whereas Ouellette and Wood restricted their analyses to the relation between intention and future behavior, I also considered the relations of intentions with attitudes, norms, and perceived behavioral control. I found that the correlations between attitudes and intentions, norms and intentions, and perceived control and intentions were all stronger when the frequency of past behavior was lower (vs. higher) (see Figure 4.9). This pattern lends credence to the possibility that, in their natural form, perhaps for frequent behaviors, intentions themselves may be experienced differently, perhaps affectively or via simpler forms of verbal representation. If so, measures that work for less frequent users may be less able to capture intentionality among more frequent users.

The Psychological Nature of Intentions

Gauging the degree of intentionality of a behavior requires understanding the nature of intention. Intentions can stem from beliefs that inform intentions in a syllogistic fashion (Jaccard & King, 1977). Believing that smoking is unhealthy, for example, may lead to the decision and intention to quit. Moreover, intentions can be mentally represented as self-referential statements involving commitment verbs ("will," "intend") in addition to a second verb (e.g., drive) to form propositions like "I will perform X" or "I intend to achieve X" (Albarracín, Noguchi, & Earl, 2006). Intentions may also drive behavior in a fairly algorithmic fashion, as when following a cooking recipe ("I will first pour two cups of flour"; "Now, I will add the milk"). In this case, it makes sense to measure people's intention to take a vacation next summer, their intention to use a condom, and so on.

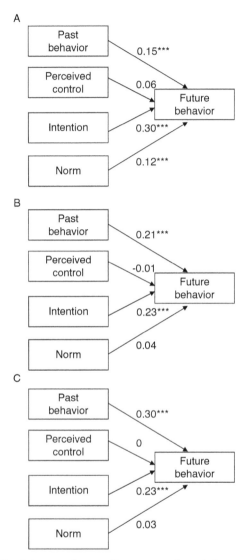

Figure 4.9 Variability in influence of intention and past behavior on behavior:
(A) low frequency; (B) moderate frequency; (C) high frequency.

I argue that intentions may also be formed and experienced in more subtle ways (de la Corte, Kruglanski, de Miguel, Sabucedo, & Diaz, 2007; Haggard & Clark, 2003; Lohmann & Albarracín, 2019; Pacherie, 2008;

Tsakiris & Haggard, 2005). Verbal representations of intentions aside, intention is also an experience or feeling (Albarracín, Hart, & McCulloch, 2006; Albarracín, Noguchi, & Earl, 2006). Measures of commitment, for example, often include conative feelings, such as a feeling of determination (Locke, Latham, & Erez, 1988; Lohmann & Albarracín, 2019; Sevincer & Oettingen, 2009). To characterize the feelings of intention, we (Lohmann & Albarracín, 2019) asked participants to report the feelings and words that go through their mind when they form intentions. Most participants experienced their intentions as feelings instead of words. The feelings included feeling determined and visualizing the action, which actors perceive as the way in which intentions appear phenomenologically.

Could such subtle representations of intention exist for habitual behaviors? Clearly, repeated and relatively mindless behaviors do exist. Past studies have estimated that between 30 percent and 50 percent of our daily behavior is repeated behavior. For example, 48 percent of the annual expenditures of the average US household involve purchasing a product they purchased before (e.g., breakfast cereal), implying consistent choices of brand, flavor, and size over a 1-year period (Hansen & Singh, 2015; Lohmann, Jones, & Albarracín, 2019; Wood, Quinn, & Kashy, 2002). Although such repeated behavior is often referred to as automatic, a closer examination suggests that behaviors assumed to be automatic still involve deliberative processes (Lohmann, Jones, & Albarracín, 2019). For example, while standing in the aisle of the supermarket, we briefly ask ourselves "What should I buy?" even when we know what we chose the last time we were at the store. My colleagues and I (Lohmann, Jones, & Albarracín, 2019) proposed that, instead of automatically reaching for the same products without awareness, repeated choice emerges from the quick internal conversations we hold with ourselves. This process still leads to choosing the same products, but the repeated choice is mediated through subtle inner speech.

Past research on language and behavior has shown that questions play a critical role. Instead of telling ourselves "I will do this task," we often ask ourselves "Will I do this task?" Asking ourselves a question instead of rehearsing a statement has been associated with a higher likelihood of enacting the behavior (Godin et al., 2012). In addition, when the behavior is enacted, questions (vs. statements) increase performance, both through self-talk and through externally presented messages (Müller et al., 2016; Senay, Albarracín, & Noguchi, 2010; Suri et al., 2014). For example, in a series of experiments we conducted (Senay, Albarracín, & Noguchi,

2010), participants were instructed to prepare for an anagram-solving task by spending 1 min thinking either *whether* they would work on anagrams (question condition) or simply *that* they would work on anagrams (assertion condition). Immediately following this thinking task, participants worked on the anagram task. The number of solved anagrams for each condition appears in Figure 4.10. As shown, the deliberate self-posed questions produced better performance. Presumably, the answer to the question in those conditions is affirmative and thus helps the person to invoke a positive attitude and intention toward the task. In addition, however, simply priming the question structure by presenting "will you" as opposed to "you will" led to better performance and stronger intentions to exercise in the future (Senay, Albarracín, & Noguchi, 2010), an effect that was mediated by attitudes. This mediational analysis appears in the bottom panel of Figure 4.10 and is summarized in the following principle:

> **Principle 16. Nature of intentional behavior.** Intentional behavior is rarely executed algorithmically. Hence, intentions are represented as full-fledged mental propositions ("I will climb the wall"), but also as feelings

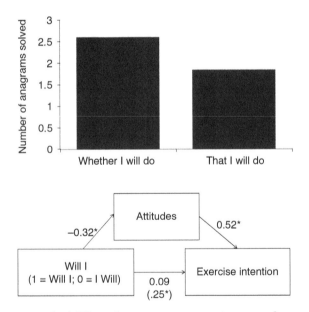

Figure 4.10 (top) Effects of questions versus assertions on performance. (bottom) Mediation of effect of questions versus assertions on word order. (Adapted from Senay et al., 2010)

(conative feelings), or as a haphazard string of fragmentary stimuli or words that imply an intention ("will climbing").

Self-direction via self-talk can also be highly explicit and demanding. For example, our research (Zell, Warriner, & Albarracín, 2012) has found that challenges and preparation for action elicit a more imperative style and more second-person self-talk. We asked participants to write what they would tell themselves in the different situations presented in Table 4.3. We expected that negative (vs. positive) outcomes, internal (vs. external) pressure to control a behavior, and action (vs. preparation for action and evaluation) would produce more self-talk geared toward controlling behavior. Accordingly, results showed that the imperative style was seven times more frequent in response to negative than positive events, 30 percent more frequent in response to internal demands, and twice more frequent during action than during action preparation or evaluation. The use of the second person "you" showed a similar pattern. It was four times as likely in response to negative than positive events and more than twice as likely in response to internally controlled events. Furthermore, in another series of studies, we manipulated the use of the second person and showed that

Table 4.3 *Scenarios manipulating conditions that produce explicit self-talk*

Level	Dimension
Experiment 1	
Negative	Christine attends a party where she is ignored and socially isolated. She feels awkward.
Positive	Brad switches schools and joins a new soccer team. He is treated very warmly by his new teammates and is invited to a party.
Experiment 2	
Internal	Stacey is a first-year college student who, despite being socially awkward in high school, is looking to make a fresh start. She attends a residence party and makes a conscious effort to smile, relax, and look confident.
External	Alice attends a Christmas party with her parents. She is bored and wants to leave, but her parents insist on staying. She is struggling to be polite and maintain her composure.
Experiment 3	
Action	Tyler is chasing a ball during tryouts.
Preparation	Tyler is thinking about whether he should try out for a soccer team.
Evaluation	Tyler just learns that he did not make the team.

participants performed better after preparing for the task using the second than the first person (Dolcos & Albarracín, 2014).

It turns out that similar though more efficient questions can lead to forming intentions in a relatively spontaneous fashion. Figure 4.11 shows a continuum from a top-down form of self-direction (Zell, Warriner, & Albarracín, 2012) to completely automatic, stimulus-response processes. We (Lohmann, Jones, & Albarracín, 2019) proposed a default perspective to explain how intentional behavior in the middle of the continuum combines automatic and propositional processes through efficient forms of self-talk. According to this perspective, when a default option exists, that option represents the most accessible response and is therefore used to answer self-talk questions that ultimate influence behavior. In the case of making a choice such as what to buy, asking a question like *Which one should I choose?* would most likely be answered by the previously chosen, highly accessible option, leading to making the same choice again. This pattern, however, should not be observed when the question is negative or irrelevant. If one asks *Which one should I not choose?* then the default response will be automatically paired with "no," decreasing, instead of increasing, choice repetition.

Table 4.4 presents the results of three experiments in which questions were primed when people made free decisions after being trained to choose their favorites in that same task. Before their free choices, participants were presented with no question, an affirmative question (e.g., Which one should I choose?), a negative question (e.g., Which one should I not choose?), or an irrelevant question (e.g., What should I have for dinner?). As shown in Table 4.4, the affirmative question produced the highest level of repetition, whereas the negative question produced the lowest level of repetition. Importantly, the effects were stronger with questions than with

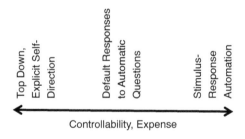

Figure 4.11 Top-down and more automatic self-talk.

Table 4.4 *Effects of questions on mean proportion of choice repetition*

Question	Experiment 1	Experiment 2	Experiment 3	Experiment 4		Experiment 5	
				Questions	Statements	Control	Distraction
None	0.49	0.57	0.47	0.41	0.43	0.52	0.53
Affirmative	0.62	0.68	0.52	0.61	0.51	0.61	0.58
Negative	0.19	0.31	0.32	0.25	0.36	0.39	0.42
Irrelevant	–	0.49	0.39	–	–	0.49	0.51
N	43	47	60	65	56	107	107

Source: Adapted from Lohmann et al. (2019).

statements and persisted in the presence of distraction, thus implying that the questions and answers can operate efficiently.

Furthermore, syntax probably plays a role in how intentions can be subtly formed on the fly by combining incidental words that are "strung together" and are "read" like an intention. Judgments emerge from temporally organized information stored in working memory. As stimuli flow through working memory in a particular sequence, the order of stimuli can determine judgments. Thus, linguistic propositions may emerge when the order of relatively random material in working memory is syntactically compatible with a given proposition (Albarracín, Hart, & McCulloch, 2006). My colleagues and I (Albarracín, Noguchi, & Fischler, 2011) investigated the formation of intentions based on implicit propositions formed by random environmental inputs. We reasoned that people could form intentions on the basis of the mere succession of certain words presented in a given behavioral context. For example, participants who previously played a prisoner's dilemma game (the behavioral context) engaged in a word-detection task. The word-detection task was introduced as an unrelated study while participants waited for the scores of the game. In this task, participants were instructed to press a key when words began with certain letters (e.g., A or N). Over a series of trials, two sets of words comprised the experimental manipulation. The manipulated words were five synonyms of "act" or five synonyms of "nice." In one condition, participants were exposed to the words "act" (or e.g., "play") and "nice" (or e.g., "fair") in this sequence. In the other condition, participants were exposed to the same words in the opposite order ("nice" – "act"). (For other relevant research, see Albarracín, Noguchi, & Fischler, 2011b; Carrera et al., 2014; Carrera, Muñoz, Caballero, Fernández, & Albarracín, 2012; Hart & Albarracín, 2009b.)

After the word-detection manipulation, participants played another prisoner's dilemma game. The prediction was that the implicit proposition "act"-"nice" might motivate participants to cooperate because the word order forms an imperative sentence, much like ones people use when they want to push themselves to do something. In contrast, the implicit proposition "nice"-"act" could be perceived as a compliment. As a result, "nice"-"act" may suggest that participants have already been nice in the prior game. In turn, this assessment may reduce the perceived need to be nice in a future game. Supporting these expectations, the "act"-"nice" sequence increased cooperativeness from the first to the second game. Correspondingly, the "nice"-"act" sequence decreased cooperativeness from the first to the second game. Thus, these findings were produced with the combination or configuration of words, which were mentally parsed as different intentions.

Summary

Goals are desired states or processes and can set behavior in motion. They vary in their object, including action and inaction, and generality. When they are general, they produce broad striving toward action or inaction because they can be linked to any specific behavior relevant in a particular context or for a given person.

State and process goals can lead to intentions that ultimately predict behavior. Behavior can also occur without the intervention of intentions, in response to environmental cues. Direct stimulus-response processes, however, are probably restricted to behaviors that are conditioned responses to stimuli, such as posture and gestures. Goals and intentions are likely involved in most health, consumer, and financial behaviors, although intentionality must be understood in a broad sense. I propose that intention has highly deliberative as well as highly efficient representations, both of which are experienced as intentions. In fact, most of our behavior is likely executed in response to rudimentary thoughts and feelings of determination, without a direct translation into propositional thoughts of the form "I will go to the movies."

As noted in past research (Ajzen & Fishbein, 1980; Ajzen et al., 2019; Fishbein & Ajzen, 2010), the correspondence between goals or intentions and behavior is not perfect. Correspondence between a goal and executing a behavioral process may be low (a) because of lack of personal control over the process, or (b) because the goal is met through a different process. For instance, the goal to solve an equation mentally may not be feasible due to the complexity of the equation. Likewise, the goal to lose weight may not produce changes in eating because of external temptations. In contrast, a woman who wants to lose weight may fall ill and end up losing weight unintentionally. Likewise, a person may have the goal of doing a house chore but another household member may complete it before she gets to it. That is, factors outside of the person's control can satisfy the goals of losing weight and completing a chore without the need to activate a process goal or an intention. In fact, even observing others complete a task that one intended to complete promotes a sense of goal satiation (McCulloch, Fitzsimons, Chua, & Albarracín, 2011).

PART III

Influences of the Past and the Situation

CHAPTER 5

The Impact of Past Experience and Past Behavior on Attitudes and Behavior

It is a commonplace that experiences are ineffable. Mysticism is one such experience. Eating cotton candy is another. One may attempt to describe them with words but the sensations, experience of time, the physical location, and the memories of what is happening at those moments are too idiosyncratic to communicate. Adding to this difficulty, our behaviors often exist only as motor memories that we must reenact to be able to remember.

Experience and past behavior are critical sources of information about the world. People acquire rich information and form attitudes through experiences and behavioral performance. In addition, simply performing a behavior alone increases the probability of repeating the behavior in the future. For example, people who have performed a certain behavior often think about its possible consequences. In turn, these thoughts guide future decisions in the direction of their past behavior. Even when people do not stop to reflect about their behavior in a deep way, their past behavior is often enough information for them to conclude that they like the behavior. These processes are presented in Figure 5.1 and are the focus of this chapter.

The model in Figure 5.1 is useful to conceptualize the influence of past behavior on outcome-related beliefs and evaluations, as well as attitudes. As Janis and King (1954) postulated, after people have engaged in a particular behavior, they often conduct a biased search of memory for previously acquired knowledge that validates their behavior. For example, they may identify probable consequences of the behavior and assess their desirability (Albarracín, 2002; Albarracín & Wyer, 2000). They may then combine these beliefs and evaluations to form a new attitude toward the behavior. This attitude, in turn, might influence both intentions to repeat the behavior and actual behavior when a new occasion arises.

The biased-scanning hypothesis implies that past behavior guides recall of prior knowledge about and judgments of the behavior's consequences (Albarracín, 2002; Albarracín & Wyer, 2000). However,

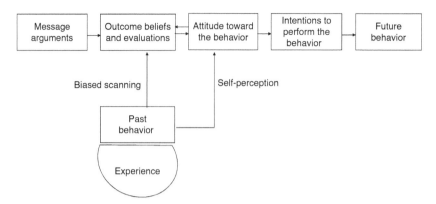

Figure 5.1 Influence of past behavior and experience on attitudes and future behavior.

according to the model in Figure 5.1, this mediating cognitive activity may not be necessary for the effects to occur. According to self-perception theory (Albarracín & Wyer, 2000b; Bem, 1967), when people report an attitude, they often infer this attitude directly from a past behavior that happens to be salient at the time. Moreover, they may engage in this process with little if any conscious deliberation, simply reasoning that, if they have performed the behavior voluntarily, they must consider it to be desirable (Bem & McConnell, 1970). The deliberation that underlies this inference is minimal. Therefore, self-perception should be easier than forming attitudes on the basis of prior knowledge or beliefs about the outcomes of the behavior. Thus, self-perception may occur even when people are unmotivated or unable to think about the reasons for their behavior.

Self-perception theory has generally been applied in conceptualizing the effects of past behavior on attitudes. However, past behavior may have a direct influence on future behavior independently of attitudes. Dissonance theory has been applied in conceptualizing the same effects. Nevertheless, dissonance theory also assumes that people who perform a behavior that contradicts their attitudes experience discomfort and are likely to change their attitude as a result. The chapter first addresses the influence of behavioral experiences obtained in real life and virtually. This section is followed by a discussion of biased scanning, self-perception, and cognitive dissonance, and a description of the conditions under which each of these processes takes place.

Effects of the Behavioral Experience

Chapter 4 described the role of thoughts about the outcomes of the behavior based on prior knowledge. However, in addition to prior knowledge, executing a behavior teaches people concrete information and behavioral routines.

Real-life experience. Regan and Fazio (1977) explored the attitudinal effects of acquiring experience with an object. Some participants were allowed to play with examples of five types of puzzles (direct experience). A second group was presented with examples of the types of puzzles already solved by another person (no direct experience). Next, all participants reported how interesting they found each type of puzzle and were allowed to play with the puzzles freely for up to 15 min. The study revealed that attitudes (the interest ratings) were stronger predictors of actual behavior when they were based on direct experience playing with the puzzles than when they were not.

There are many potential explanations for the effect of past experience on the attitude–behavior relation. According to Fazio, Powell, and Herr (1983), direct experience facilitates rehearsing one's attitudes toward the object in question. Just like reporting one's attitude repeatedly increases its impact on behavior, so does rehearsing one's attitude at the time of the experience. Another explanation is that direct experience provides information about the object. In this case, the boosting effects of direct experience on the attitude–behavior relation should only be observed when the information is homogenous in quality (see Glasman & Albarracín, 2006; Wright & Lynch, 1995). Although both attitude accessibility and information homogeneity improve the attitude–behavior relation (Glasman & Albarracín, 2006), the exact mechanisms of direct experience have not been fully elucidated.

Some people are sensitive to particular modalities of experience. For example, people differ in their need for touch, with some people preferring and even requiring haptic (touch) information to a greater extent than others. To measure this difference, Peck and Childers (2003) wrote items such as "touching products can be fun" and "the only way to make sure that a product is worth buying is touching it." The scale had adequate validity and two practical consequences. First, participants with a high need for touch were faster to identify tactile words as being words than were people with a low need for touch. Second, participants with a high need for touch benefited more from direct, tactile experience with the object than did people with a low need for touch. Specifically, high-need-for-touch participants were more confident in their judgments of the products when they were able to touch them. In contrast, the lower-need-to-touch group was unaffected.

As we already discussed, the formation of attitudes may be more likely if people gain experience with the object. In addition, other factors may increase the influence of experience on future behavior. For example, behavior experiences can sometimes increase attitude confidence (Marks & Kamins, 1988; Smith & Swinyard, 1988; but see Wright & Lynch, 1995). Also, direct experiences may be more affect-inducing and thus provide important emotional and sensorial information (see Peck & Childers, 2003).

Virtual experience. The role of direct experience in learning and attitude formation could imply that indirect experience has weak effects (see, e.g., Praxmarer, 2011). This conclusion, however, would be wrong (see, e.g., Meslot, Gauchet, Allenet, François, & Hagger, 2016).

Currently, people in the United States spend an average of 24 hours a week online, and the internet plays an integral role in social and political life (*Technology Review*, 2019). The information presented via both trad-itional and emerging media is not representative of the world in general because anything "newsworthy" can easily be assumed to be infrequent. Soap operas, for example, often portray individuals with affluent life styles. Even "reality television" concentrates on characters like police and drug dealers, or people who get shot and go to emergency services, or on characters that are more attractive than average (Wyer & Albarracín, 2005). However, direct experience may not be feasible, or it may not be strong enough to falsify media-based impressions. Therefore, our know-ledge is largely affected by fictional and virtual experiences (see Gerbner, Gross, Morgan, & Signorielli, 1980, 1982; Bryant & Oliver, 2009).

With the introduction of the internet, virtual simulations of experiences have become very common. For example, one no longer has to cut one's hair to experience a new hairstyle. Instead, one can purchase a computer program that digitally alters one's image to show what one would look like with the new hair style. These methodologies provide more information about the psychological effects of experience.

In a study of virtual experience (Griffith & Chen, 2004), some products, such as movies, were expected to be easy to experience in a digital fashion. Participants simply saw ads about these products and either did or did not experience the product virtually. Other products like sunglasses are more difficult to experience virtually. Still, the researchers created movie clips of

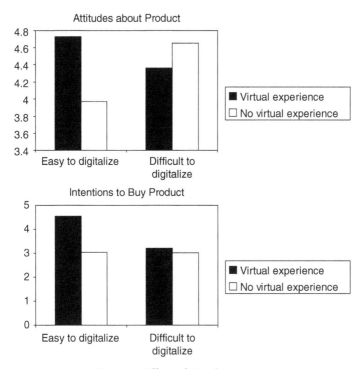

Figure 5.2 Effects of virtual experience.

the actual visual experience to simulate what happens when one wears the sunglasses. Thus, for these difficult-to-digitize products, participants saw ads and either did or did not experience the product virtually.

The effects of the virtual experience appear in Figure 5.2. As shown, when the experience was easy to digitize, there were differences between virtually experiencing and not experiencing the product. Participants had more positive evaluations and stronger intentions to buy the product with virtual viewing than without virtual viewing. However, these effects disappeared when the products were difficult to digitize. In that case, attitudes and purchasing intentions were the same with and without the virtual experience.

Mental simulations and planning. Mental simulation shares commonalities with experience and entails imagining a sequence of events (Taylor & Schneider, 1989). Constructing these hypothetical scenarios improves attitudes toward those actions, behavioral intentions, and actual behavior (e.g., Anderson, 1983; Epstude, Scholl, & Roese, 2016; Matheson, White, & McMullen, 2015; Meugnot, Almecija, & Toussaint, 2014). In particular, mentally rehearsing how to reach a goal is more effective than imagining the outcomes of attaining the goal. Presumably, a step-by-step rehearsal of an action allows people to formulate plans and work out potential approaches to obstacles. In this sense, the goal to act can produce learning even when the action is simulated.

Implementation intentions as anticipation of experience. Asking people when, where, and how they will perform a given behavior increases the likelihood that they will do so. According to Gollwitzer (1999), implementation intentions allow individuals to delegate control of their goal-directed behaviors to the stimulus situation. Presumably, linking one's specific intention to the concrete time and place for the behavior ensures automatic behavior when one gets to that time and that place (see also Aarts, Dijksterhuis, & Midden, 1999; Brandstatter, Lengfelder, & Gollwitzer, 2001; Gollwitzer, 1996).[1] However, formulating these intentions appears to have effects even when the behavior is new to the individual. Thus, the process of simulating the experience is likely to be partially responsible for the effects of implementation intentions. In other words, a behavior simulation can be the basis of attitudes and corresponding behavioral intentions. As an illustration, Ajzen, Czasch, and Flood (2009) asked people to write when, where, and how they would return a brief survey concerning TV newscasts. As expected, this instruction increased the rate at which participants accomplished what they intended (for a review, see Ajzen et al., 2019).

Learning schemas and procedures from experience. Current educational theories assume that the most effective and efficient instruction happens when the learner has experience with a real or model environment (see, e.g., Byrne & Johnson-Laird, 1989). Solving carefully selected and sequenced problems allows the learner to gain new skills through a controlled experience with the environment. The interaction with the

---

[1] According to Ajzen and his colleagues (2002), the effectiveness of implementation intentions is due to a sense of commitment. In fact, in their TV survey study, making a behavioral commitment produced as high rate of return as forming the implementation intention. Signing a public commitment to return the survey increased return rates just as much as indicating how that would be done. There is lots of evidence that making a commitment can greatly increase the likelihood that people will perform the behavior to which they committed (Kiesler, 1971; Mayer, Duval, & Duval, 1980). Nonetheless, commitment and implementation intentions are both instances of an action goal in a specific domain.

model presumably results in a *mental* model (Byrne & Johnson-Laird, 1989; Gentner & Gentner, 1983; Norman, 1983) that governs future behavior in that environment.

Learning through experience should be particularly effective when knowledge is organized schematically or configurally (Rumelhart, 1994, 2018; Wyer, 2019; Wyer & Albarracín, 2005). In psychology, the term "schema" denotes a cluster of features that have become associated with a referent and are stored in memory as a unit (Fiske & Taylor, 1991). The spatial, temporal, or logical rules that guide schemata can be learned through experience (Brewer & Lichtenstein, 1981; Mandler & DeForest, 1979). A spatially organized schema allows individuals in an organization to interpret an organizational chart. This structure suggests degrees of and types of hierarchies; if there is a hierarchy, vertical switching of the people in the chart produces an erroneous understanding of the environment. A temporally organized schema may indicate how one should proceed in school. Kindergarteners are trained to exchange salutations, organize their materials, and proceed with each task in a specific order. As another example of forming a temporal schema, experience using computers should teach users to turn on the computer before keyboarding.

Although experience with an environment is expected to produce schemas, features of the situation may impede this learning. One particularly interesting feature is that having a specific goal appears to distract individuals from acquiring "survey" knowledge. For example, Rossano and Reardon (1999) had participants tour unfamiliar areas of a university campus using a computer model. In one of the conditions, participants were instructed to simply tour the campus (no specific goal). In another, they were asked to keep a specific location of the campus in mind during their virtual tour (specific goal). After gaining experience with the virtual environment, participants were asked to draw a map plotting the location of certain buildings. The researchers computed indexes of angle and distance errors. Then, they compared these errors across conditions with and without a specific goal and also with a control condition that had a secondary task but no specific goal. The results are summarized in Figure 5.3. As shown, having the specific goal of keeping in mind one location led to more errors than did navigating the environment in a more casual, open-minded way. Importantly, this effect appeared due to having a specific goal and not to general distraction, as suggested by no difference between the no-goal condition and the secondary-task condition.

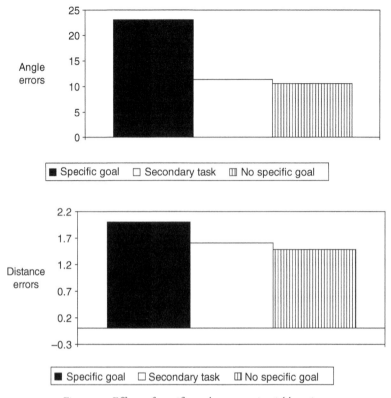

Figure 5.3 Effects of specific goals on experiential learning.

Embodiment in experience. One important consideration concerning the role of experience is embodiment, which can be defined as the relation between bodily states and higher cognitive processes (e.g., learning and understanding the behavior of others). In particular, sensory and motor information influences judgment in a variety of contexts (Suitner, Giacomantonio, & Maass, 2015). For example, visual information, such as whether an object is dark or light, influences categorization. In research conducted by Meier et al. (2004), participants had to categorize words like "justice" and "danger" as positive or negative, and the words appeared in either dark or light colors. Consistent with Western associations between good and light, participants were faster at categorizing good words in light color and bad words in dark colors. Tactile sensations appear to have conceptual effects as well. For example, in research by Ackerman, Nocera, and Bargh (2010), participants who had conducted a task that involved touching sandpaper perceived a person with whom they interacted later as less friendly than those who had not.

Motor information also has interesting effects on judgments. For example, people appear to use their own movements implying discontent as a basis of their attitudes toward other people. In research by Chandler and Schwarz (2009), participants ostensibly worked on a motor task requiring extending their middle finger or their index finger while reading information about a target person. The target person was judged more negatively when participants read the information while extending their middle finger than while extending their index finger.

Biased Processing and Attention to One's Behaviors

There is interesting evidence suggestive of biased scanning in various domains. For instance, research on counterfactuals has elucidated biases in the types of thoughts associated with a past behavior. Also, selective attention to stimuli ultimately biases one's thoughts and thus represents a form of biased scanning.

Effects of format of behavior report on subsequent attitudes. Research on self-reports (see, e.g., Schwarz & Oyserman, 2001) has shown how the scale used to report behavior can influence the behavioral measure. For example, Schwarz and Scheuring (1992) gave 60 patients from a mental health clinic one of two scales to report their symptoms (see Figure 5.4). Patients supposedly assume that the researcher constructed a meaningful scale that has the average frequency of symptoms in the middle. Hence, respondents using the low-frequency scale perceive having symptoms "twice a month" as high. In contrast, respondents using the high-frequency scale perceive having symptoms "twice a month" as low. These perceptions of the meaning of the points of the scale lead to different perceptions of their symptoms. Specifically, users of the low-frequency

Figure 5.4 Experimental scales.

scale believe their symptoms to be more serious than users of the high-frequency scale.

Counterfactuals. Often people imagine what the outcomes of a situation might have been had they acted differently in that situation (i.e., a counterfactual; Gilovich, Medvec, & Kahneman, 1998; Kahneman & Miller, 1986; Roese & Olson, 1997). The degree to which they engage in counterfactuals, however, depends on their cognitive capacity to think about their behavior (Roese, 2004). Furthermore, individuals vary in the type of counterfactuals they generate. In particular, some focus on the acquisition of positive goals, whereas others focus on avoiding negative goals (Higgins, 1997). Thus, people motivated by positive goals (high in promotion) should think about what they could have done but did not. In contrast, people motivated by negative goals (high in prevention) should think about what they did but should not have done. To study this possibility, Roese, Hur, and Pennington (1999) used the following scenario: "Sue was investing in the stock market for the first time. Although she initially enjoyed some solid profits, she tried to be extremely careful about not going in over her head. Soon after, however, the market took a wild turn, and Sue lost a huge amount of money."

Roese, Hur, and Pennington (1999) predicted that people who score high in promotion should think about the things that Sue could have done (additive counterfactuals). Conversely, people who score high in prevention should think about the things Sue could have avoided (subtractive counterfactuals). As shown in Figure 5.5, this was the case.

Although both groups should evaluate their failures negatively, which type of failure matters most should depend on their chronic concerns.

Past actions and inactions. As explained before, an action often attracts more attention than its absence. In animal perception and learning, pigeons are better able to learn from rewards associated with video images of moving pigeons than those associated with video images of still pigeons (Dittrich & Lea, 1993). In humans, people who produce a response to signal agreement with a behavior later agree with and perform the behavior more than people who avoid responding to signal agreement (Allison & Messick, 1988; Cioffi & Garner, 1996; Fazio, Sherman, & Herr, 1982). Thus, other things being equal, self-perception for actions is stronger than self-perception for inactions.

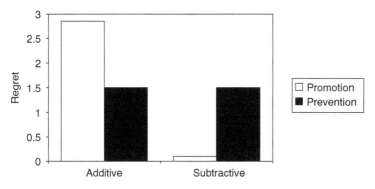

Figure 5.5 Effects of promotion and prevention on numbers of thoughts for additive and subtractive counterfactuals.

Cognitive Dissonance

Festinger (1957) observed that people are not consistent in the way they carry out their lives. For example, smokers are aware of the damage of their behavior to their health. Thus, the only way to continue to smoke is for them to adjust their attitudes and beliefs in ways that justify smoking despite the health threat. Smokers then reason that smoking is enjoyable or that the risks of not smoking (e.g., weight gain) are greater than the risks of smoking. If smokers cannot resolve the inconsistency in this way, they are likely to change their attitude and quit smoking.

The first demonstration of attitude change following a behavior-attitude conflict was provided by Festinger and Carlsmith (1959). In this study, male participants worked for 1 hour on boring tasks such as turning spools on a board. Immediately after this task, participants were told that the experimenter was investigating the effects of expectancies on performance. They were further informed that they were in a control condition that did not receive any information before beginning the tasks. However, they learned, other participants were scheduled to receive information to create a positive attitude toward the task. The positive attitude, they learned, had to be created by telling other students that the task was enjoyable. Importantly, these participants were offered either $1 or $20 for providing a positive evaluation of the task to the other participant. The other participant was actually an experimenter's accomplice, and the focus was the final attitude of the participants who paid either $1 or $20. Thus, at the end of the study, the participants in both conditions reported their attitudes toward the task.

Reports of how enjoyable the task was depended on the amount of money participants received. Participants who were paid $1 for describing the experiment as enjoyable rated the tasks as more enjoyable than did participants who were paid $20. Festinger and Carlsmith (1959) argued that participants who lied experienced dissonance created by the conflicting cognitions "The tasks were boring" and "I told someone the tasks were enjoyable." Those who were paid $20, however, had an important consonant cognition in "I was paid a lot of money to tell someone the tasks were enjoyable." This additional belief was sufficient to reduce the magnitude of their dissonance and, correspondingly, reduce the influence of their behavior on their attitudes.

Dissonance also develops when people compare their effort with their interest in performing a behavior. To determine if attitude change occurs in these conditions, Aronson and Mills (1959) recruited female university students for an ostensible "sexual discussion group." The women were informed that participation required a screening test. In the high-effort condition, the supposed test was administered by a male experimenter and included reading out loud embarrassing words such as "erection" as well as detailed descriptions of sexual behavior. In the low-effort condition, participants simply read sex-related words that were less graphic (e.g., "petting"). After the test, participants were reported how interesting the discussion and the group members were. Participants who went through the embarrassing screening test rated the group and its members as more interesting than did participants who went through the mild screening test.

Performing the behavior despite a severe punishment should produce more cognitive dissonance than performing the behavior despite a light punishment. To test this possibility, Aronson and Carlsmith (1963) asked preschool children to play with and evaluate some toys. One of the most attractive toys was then placed on a table, and the experimenter told the child that playing with this toy was not allowed. Some children were given a strong incentive to follow this direction. Specifically, the experimenter indicated that playing with the forbidden toy would make the experimenter angry and that all of the toys would be taken away. Other children were simply told that the experimenter would be "a little unhappy" if the child played with the forbidden toy. The experimenter then left the room for 10 min. None of the children played with the forbidden toy during this time. When the experimenter returned, the children played with the toys and then evaluated all of the toys again. Interestingly, the children who were threatened with the mild punishment evaluated the toy more negatively than did the children who were threatened with severe punishment. Presumably, the severe threat served as a consonant cognition that reduced dissonance between the cognitive elements "I like this toy" and "I did not play with this toy." By contrast, the mild threat was insufficient to decrease dissonance and led to a less positive attitude toward the toy.

The basic tenet of dissonance theory is that counterattitudinal behavior causes an unpleasant state of arousal or tension. In turn, this state of arousal motivates attitude change or alternate forms of dissonance reduction. This assumption was put to the test by Zanna and Cooper (1974). They proposed that dissonance causes a state of arousal that is attributed to the cognitive conflict. However, if one managed to induce a misattribution to a source other than one's behavior, one would reduce attempts to decrease the arousal by changing attitudes. To test this possibility, participants ingested a placebo pill, allegedly to investigate the effect of the drug on memory later in the session. Some participants were told that the pill would have the "side effect" of making them feel tense. Other participants were told that the pill would have the effect of making them feel relaxed. A control group was told that the pill would have no noticeable effects. While participants ostensibly waited for the substance to be absorbed, they were asked to write a counterattitudinal essay under high- or low-choice conditions and to report their own attitudes toward the issue of concern in the essay.

Experiments that ask participants to write an essay that supports a position inconsistent with their own have uncovered interesting effects of choice. In the typical "free choice" manipulation, participants are told that the experimenter needs essays on both positions and that s/he now needs one on the counterattitudinal position. Other participants are simply assigned the task without allowing them to agree or refuse. Following the logic of dissonance theory, writing an essay favoring a position one does not endorse should create dissonance. The dissonance can be easily reduced if one "has been forced" but is difficult to reduce if one "volunteered." As a result, participants who have a choice change their attitudes in line with the advocated position more than participants who do not.

Zanna and Cooper (1974) used this paradigm in their study. They predicted that the difference between the free- and forced-choice conditions would be greater when participants did not expect the pill to produce anxiety. As expected, when participants did not expect any side effects from the drug, those in the high-choice condition reported more favorable attitudes toward the advocacy than did those in the low-choice condition. In contrast, there was no attitude change when high-choice participants expected the pill to create unpleasant arousal. In these conditions, participants opposed the essay topic irrespective of whether they were in the high- or low-choice conditions. Thus, these findings pointed to arousal as a mediator of attitude change in dissonance studies (Cooper, Zanna, & Taves, 1978; Elkin & Leippe, 1986; Losch & Cacioppo, 1990).

Self-Perception

Bem (1967, 1972; Bem & McConnell, 1970) proposed self-perception as a mechanism that could account for the dissonance findings without the need to invoke arousal. He proposed that participants in Festinger and Carlsmith's (1959) study had knowledge of having told another person that the tasks were enjoyable and also knowledge of the incentive they received ($20 vs. $1). Consequently, the mere observation of their behavior could lead to the explanation that, in the absence of a strong incentive, only internal attitudes could explain the behavior. In contrast, a strong incentive was a sufficient explanation of the behavior regardless of whether the behavior belonged to oneself or to others (see Kelley, 1973).

Given the assumption that self-perception obeys the principles of interpersonal perception, then the inferences of *observers* of dissonance studies should be similar to those by the participants in the studies. To test this reasoning, Bem (1967) asked participants to listen to a tape recording that described the original study in detail. The observers also learned that the focal participant was promised either $1 or $20 to tell a waiting participant that the tasks were fun. Consistent with Bem's hypothesis, the observers estimated that the $1 participant actually enjoyed the tasks more than did the $20 participant.[2]

Self-perception goes beyond explaining cognitive dissonance observations, however. A variety of important phenomena have observation of one's behavior as the primary mechanism of influence. I turn to these phenomena next.

---

[2] Dissonance theorists responded that individuals in Bem's study lacked information about the initial attitude of the participants (e.g., Jones, Linder, Kiesler, Zanna, & Brehm, 1968). Also, they showed that providing this information prevented replication of dissonance findings. Bem (1968; Bem & McConnell, 1970), however, maintained that participants' prior attitudes are rarely salient. Thus, the phenomena reproduced in the study were appropriate.

Foot-in-the-door effect. Compliance with a small request increases compliance with subsequent larger requests. Freedman and Fraser (1966) termed this phenomenon the *foot-in-the-door effect*. They observed that signing a petition to keep one's state beautiful led to higher rates of agreement to place an unattractive "Drive Carefully" yard sign. From the point of view of self-perception (Burger, 1999; Burger & Caldwell, 2003), agreeing to perform a small favor may stimulate the inference that one enjoys being helpful. This inference then guides agreement to the larger request for help.

Intrinsic motivation judgments. According to self-perception theory, inferences that one has a favorable attitude should occur only if there are no strong external justifications for behavior. Thus, being paid for an enjoyable task the first time one performs it should make the attitude toward the task less positive. For example, Lepper, Greene, and Nisbett (1973) asked preschool children to draw pictures using attractive magic marker pens. Before drawing, some children were offered a "Good Player Award" in exchange for the task. A second group unexpectedly received this reward after drawing. A third group of children never received or heard about the reward. Ironically, the reward decreased the children's interest in playing with the markers days or weeks later. Presumably, the rewarded children attributed their drawing with the markers to the reward. In contrast, the nonrewarded children concluded that they drew because they liked the markers.

Emotional perceptions. Self-perception types of mechanisms have also been proposed to explain emotions. This approach relies on the finding that facial muscles can express at least six distinct emotions (happiness, surprise, anger, fear, sadness, disgust; see Ekman, 1973, 1994; Izard, 2005). Thus, the overt expressions themselves might allow individuals to reach conclusions about the subjective meaning of their emotions. Consistent with this possibility, a meta-analysis of these studies concluded that facial feedback has a small to moderate effect on emotional experiences (Matsumoto, 1987). Thus, self-perception likely plays a role in shaping emotions on the basis of overt behavior.

A review of the topic by Schimmack and Crites (Schimmack & Crites, 2005) concluded that facial feedback may be more informative for some emotions than others. Specifically, Kleinke, Peterson, and Rutledge (1998) studied reactions to videos. In this study, intentional smiling increased experiences of pleasure. However, intentionally expressing negative emotions had no effect on feelings (see also Soussignan, 2002), and, in other research, patients with facial paralysis have normal emotional experiences (Keillor et al., 2002). Therefore, self-perception contributes to but is clearly not the only factor involved in emotional experiences.

Attitudes toward a message topic. Just like bodily movements influence emotions, they also influence attitudes. To test this hypothesis, Wells and Petty (1980) asked some participants to move their heads up-and-down (a gesture of "yes") or side-to-side (a gesture of "no") to test their headphones while listening to music and an editorial. Other participants received no instructions and simply listened to the music and the editorial over headphones. As predicted, attitudes were more in line with the position advocated in the message when participants nodded than when they shook their heads. In a conceptual replication of this finding, Tom, Pettersen, Lau, Burton, and Cook (1991) found that nodding increased preference for a previously neutral object, whereas shaking decreased preference for the neutral object (see Förster & Strack, 1996, for another application of this paradigm).

Brinol and Petty (2003) hypothesized that increased confidence in one's thoughts would create more favorable effects if the thoughts were negative but more negative effects if the thoughts were positive. For example, when the thoughts are negative, nodding may reduce persuasion by increasing confidence in one's negative thoughts about the message. Correspondingly, shaking may increase persuasion by undermining confidence in one's negative thoughts.

To examine this hypothesis, Brinol and Petty (2003) instructed participants to nod or shake their heads while attending to a message containing either strong or weak arguments on a topic of interest to their college student participants. As predicted, when participants received a weak message, nodding decreased persuasion relative to shaking. In contrast, when participants received a strong message, nodding increased persuasion relative to shaking. This effect, however, was only present when the likelihood of thinking about the message was high. A similar demonstration was provided by Tormala and Petty (2004) in the domain of resistance to persuasion. In this research, resistance to a recommendation yielded more confident attitudes when the communicator was credible (vs. not credible). Presumably, people conclude that, if a credible communicator fails to persuade them, then they have good reasons not to be swayed.

Ease of retrieval. Self-perception can also explain how the perceived ease of recalling information influences attitudes (Wyer & Albarracín, 2005).

This phenomenon has been labeled *availability heuristic* by Tversky and Kahneman (1973) and *ease-of-retrieval heuristic* by Schwarz et al. (1991). According to Wyer and Albarracín (2005), this heuristic can be viewed as an application of an if-then molecule as follows:

> [*X* occurs frequently (infrequently); Instances of *X* come to mind easily (with difficulty)]

People use this molecule to infer that, if things occur frequently, then they are easy to remember (Wyer & Albarracín, 2005). For example, Norbert Schwarz and his colleagues (for a review, see Schwarz, 1999) asked a group of participants (Schwarz et al., 1991) to generate six instances of recent assertive behavior. They also asked another group of participants to generate 12 instances of recent assertive behavior. As expected, participants reported more instances of assertiveness when they were asked to generate 12 than when they were asked to generate 6. Nonetheless, they judged themselves to be less assertive when they were asked to generate 12 than when they were asked to generate 6. Apparently, the ease with which six instances were retrieved led to the conclusion that assertiveness came easy and thus was natural for them. In contrast, the difficulty of retrieving 12 instances gave participants the impression that they were not assertive. Thus, judgments are influenced by not only the perception of having performed a behavior but also the perception of how easily one recalls that behavior.

Like other judgments, attitudes also appear to depend on meta-cognitive feelings (for a review, see Wyer, 2019; Wyer & Albarracín, 2005). Research by Wanke, Bless, and Biller (1996) supports this possibility. Participants were asked to generate either three or seven arguments that either favored or opposed a specific issue, after which they were asked to report their attitudes. Other participants read the arguments that individuals in the first group had written. The participants in the first group reported more favorable attitudes toward the position when they had generated three arguments than when they had generated seven. In contrast, the participants in the second group reported more favorable attitudes toward the position when they had read seven arguments than when they had read three arguments. Clearly, the arguments generated by the first group were persuasive. However, the greater difficulty of retrieving seven (vs. three) arguments made seven less persuasive than three. In other words, the effects of ease of retrieval overrode the influence of the actual number of generated arguments.

Effects of behavior in the content of behavior-relevant persuasive messages. Self-perception also appears to play an important role when people think about their own behavior in light of a previously received recommendation. Practitioners often present young people with messages that advocate abstinence from alcohol in the hopes that the recipients will form intentions to abstain from alcohol (for work on this problem, see Bensley & Wu, 1991; Brown, Christiansen, & Goldman, 2015; Darkes & Goldman, 1998; Hasking, Lyvers, & Carlopio, 2011; Lau-Barraco et al., 2012). In an ideal world, people who expect to abstain from alcohol in the future will indeed abstain. However, many decades of research on the intention–behavior relation (for reviews, see Ajzen et al., 2019) have shown that the recipients of abstinence messages often use alcohol even when they earlier intended to not use it (Bettes et al., 1990; Kline, Canter, & Robin, 1987). When recipients behave in ways that contradict their earlier, message-based behavioral expectations, they may attempt to explain the reasons why they engaged in the behavior (Albarracín & Wyer, 2000; Bem, 1967). For example, they may reason that, if they performed the behavior even when they previously intended not to (and when the message clearly recommended not to), they must have an irresistible attraction to that behavior. That is, they will attribute their behavior to their attitude toward the behavior, causing their attitude to change in the opposite direction of the communication advocacy (Albarracín, Cohen, & Kumkale, 2003).

Recipients of a message that recommends moderation are more likely to expect to use alcohol at some point than recipients of a message that advocates abstinence from a behavior. On the one hand, a more "permissive" message may be detrimental because participants who intend to try alcohol may in fact try it. When they do, recipients may infer a favorable attitude toward alcohol to explain why they drank despite the abstinence recommendation. On the other hand, the less extreme message is likely more *realistic* because many adolescents and young adults will try alcohol regardless of what they are told. When they do, the moderation message will not conflict with consuming alcohol at a later point in time. To this extent, using a moderation message (e.g., alcohol among young people over 21) may be more appropriate than using an abstinence message.

Research we (Albarracín, Cohen, & Kumkale, 2003) conducted suggested that inducing an unrealistic expectation that is later disconfirmed can increase retroactive resistance to persuasion. In this research, the experimenter informed participants that we were conducting research on an alcohol-substitute product to be marketed to people of all ages. She then explained that participants would see materials from a consumer education program designed to inform the public about products containing the alcohol substitute. She indicated that parts of the program were more informational in content and tone, whereas other parts more closely resembled advertising messages. All participants then received one of two versions (i.e., abstinence vs. moderation) of a booklet that contained four persuasive messages that recommended either abstinence from or moderation in the use of simulated alcohol. For example, one of the abstinence messages presented a picture of a dog and read, "When your dog is looking sexy . . . you know you've had too much to drink. There is a new product coming your way. Even though it is not legally alcohol, it has the same effects. No one needs to drink. Say no!" The moderation version was identical except that the recommendation was "Play it smart. Set limits!"

After reading the consumer education materials, participants either tried the product or performed a filler task. The participants who tried the ostensible simulated alcohol drank a mixture of tonic water and fruit juice (trial conditions). The other participants performed a filler task, consisting of completing individual difference scales (no-trial conditions). At the end of this session, all participants reported their intentions to use the product in the future. Results indicated that participants who received the message but did not undergo trial had moderate intentions to drink once the product came to the market regardless of the message. In contrast, as anticipated, participants in trial conditions had stronger intentions to drink when they previously received the abstinence message than when they previously received the moderation message.

If the effects of Experiment 1 are due to an inference, an interpersonal simulation in which people read about the conditions of Experiment 1 should reproduce the findings. Therefore, in Experiment 2, participants acted as observers of the conditions in Experiment 1. Half of the participants were told that participants in an earlier study received a message advocating abstinence from a simulated-alcohol product. The other half were told that participants in the earlier study received a message advocating moderation in the use of the product. In trial conditions, she further explained that, after reading these consumer education materials, the participants in the earlier study tried the product. Participants in the no-trial conditions were told that participants in the earlier experiment read either the abstinence or the moderation message but were given no information about whether the earlier participants tried the product. After reading the introductory information and the persuasive messages used in Experiment 1, all participants assessed (guessed) the intentions of participants in Experiment 1 regarding the likely use of "simulated alcohol when it hits the market" and regular "use of the product . . . at that time."

We analyzed drinking intentions as a function of message type (abstinence vs. moderation) and trial behavior (trial vs. message only). The overall consistency of the results across the two experiments was confirmed by a nonsignificant interaction between type of message, trial, and experiment (1 vs. 2). Given this finding, Table 5.1 presents the average results from the two experiments combined. As can be seen, participants who did not try the product reported stronger intentions to drink when they received the moderation message than when they received the abstinence message. In contrast, when participants tried the product after receiving the message, recipients of the abstinence message had stronger drinking intentions than recipients of the moderation message. Importantly, the similarity of the effects across actual (Experiment 1) and observed (Experiment 2) experiences supported the interpretation that the effects are driven by self-perception.

As the above research illustrates, communications often induce resistance to their intended message. However, some characteristics of persuasive communications can change this unintended effect. Specifically, inducing an external attribution of the expectancy disconfirmation should decrease attitude change in response to the conflict. For example, people who engage in a behavior that contradicts a prior persuasive communication may conclude that the message and the source were weak. This external attribution should prevent attitude change.

A similar process may be elicited when people believe they acted due to external influences. For example, a persuasive communication that recommends abstinence may assert that the social norm supports drinking. In these situations, the message increases the salience of a potential "excuse" that message recipients can use to discount or reduce the significance of their behavior when they contradict a recommendation. In this way,

Table 5.1 *Intentions to drink the product in Albarracín, Cohen, and Kumkale (2003)*

Condition	Message type	
	Abstinence	Moderation
No trial	2.87	3.78
Trial	5.06	3.90

a strong social norm in favor of the behavior persuaders want to discourage may have protective effects.

Emphasizing that a behavior is controllable may also produce ironic attitude change. For example, assuming that one was in control of the behavior should increase attributions of the behavior to one's attitudes. In contrast, conveying that people do not always control the behavior may allow message recipients to make an external attribution. In those situations, counterproductive effects of abstinence messages should be less likely. For example, stating that people sometimes drink for reasons outside of their control may be more effective at reducing drinking than recommending abstinence.

To examine the effects of norms and perceived control, I conducted a secondary analysis of the data from Project RESPECT (Albarracín et al., 2000). This project consisted of a large-scale intervention to reduce HIV infection, in which recipients of various counseling and testing programs completed measures of attitudes, behavior, perceived norms, and other factors over a period of 12 months. The participants were approximately 5,000 clients of STI clinics who were instructed in consistent condom use by the clinic counselors. I reasoned that people who believe that using condoms is under their personal control would be more likely to infer their attitudes from their behavior (Bem, 1965, 1972) over the course of the 12 months. For example, among participants who decrease their condom use after the intervention, those who think that condom use is "up to them" and "something they can control" may develop more negative attitudes toward condom use than those who think that they cannot control their behavior. Concomitantly, participants who believe that they cannot control condom use may be more likely to conclude that their behavior was pressured by others. I used change in condom use behavior to predict change in attitudes (desirability of using condoms) and change in social norms (other people's opinions that the participant should use condoms or not). Furthermore, I included perceived control (perceiving condom use to be up to the participant and controllable) as a moderator. As predicted, change in behavior predicted change in attitudes to a greater extent when participants thought that condom use was under their personal control than when they did not. Correspondingly, the change in behavior predicted change in norms to a greater extent when participants thought that condom use was not under their personal control than when they did.

The processes of dissonance and self-perception described so far all involve a comparison between the prior attitude and the attitude-inconsistent information (e.g., the behavior). For example, McGregor, Newby-Clark, and Zanna (1999) proposed that dissonance entails a situation in which a person simultaneously holds two highly accessible but inconsistent cognitions. Like a state of ambivalence, McGregor et al. noted, dissonance and attitude change should be more likely when people pay attention to the inconsistent cognitions. In contrast, dissonance and attitude change should be less likely when the inconsistent elements are not accessible or people pay no attention to them.

Furthermore, Stone and Cooper (2001) developed a process model of how beliefs about the self influence dissonance processes. They asserted that behavior may be evaluated on the basis of attitudes, beliefs, or self-knowledge. The actual criterion in a situation, however, depends on what is brought to mind at that particular time. If normative standards of judgment are accessible, then people interpret and evaluate their behavior using the rules and prescriptions of their social group. Alternatively, people may interpret and evaluate their behavior using information related to their own personal, self-concept standards (Aronson, 1968). When personal standards are accessible, then the behavior is compared to one's own, idiosyncratic self-beliefs. Hence, people with high self-esteem, who expect superior behavior from themselves, are more likely to perceive the behavior as a discrepancy and show more attitude change. In contrast, people with low self-esteem, who have much more modest self-expectations, are likely to perceive less of a discrepancy and show less attitude change. Although a more complete presentation of the model is not germane to this chapter, the model identifies different pairs of cognitive elements that can be compared with a behavior.

The Impact of Ability and Motivation of Biased Scanning and Self-Perception

Although self-perception accounts for many phenomena, some effects are likely due to more thoughtful processes. Ease-of-retrieval effects, for example, may sometimes require ability and motivation to think about the issues (e.g., Chen & Chaiken, 1999). Specifically, Petty et al. (2002) asked a group of message recipients to generate either a low or a high number of positive or negative thoughts about the message. When ability and motivation to think about the issue were high, generating more thoughts led to less persuasion in line with the valence of the thoughts than generating fewer thoughts. Surprisingly, however, no ease-of-retrieval effect was observed when ability or motivation was low. In these situations, generating more arguments actually led to greater persuasion.

Decreases in the ease-of-retrieval effect when ability and motivation are low appear due to an inability to engage in the ease-of-retrieval inference. Nonetheless, if people could retain their ability to engage in the inference, decreases in ability and motivation should actually strengthen the effect. That is, generating a large number of thoughts is more difficult when one has low ability and motivation. Consequently, any inference based on this retrieval should accentuate the effect. Possibly, however, the decrease in ability and motivation might have been too extreme for this effect to occur.

The degree to which elaboration is required for different effects of past behavior was examined in my own work (Albarracín & Wyer, 2000). We induced participants to believe that they had performed a behavior outside of awareness and measured the effects of this information on beliefs in and evaluations of the outcomes of the behavior, as well as attitudes, intentions, and overt behavior. In addition, we manipulated the distraction participants experienced. By inducing distraction, we were able to manipulate the extent to which participants were able to form outcome beliefs and evaluations. Moreover, we could distinguish this elaborative attitude process from more direct influences of past behavior on attitudes (see Figure 5.6).

In designing this research, we noted that the lack of prior evidence on these issues reflected the difficulty of separating the informational effects of a person's past behavior per se from the effects of situational and motivational factors that accompany and influence the decision to engage in it (Eagly & Chaiken, 1993). To avoid this ambiguity, we manipulated people's past behavior (or, more specifically, their perception that they performed it) independently of any cognitive activity that could potentially have influenced the behavior. Specifically, participants were induced to believe that, outside of awareness, they had either supported or opposed the institution of comprehensive examinations at their university. They were told that they would be taking part in an investigation of a new technique for assessing their unconscious reactions to social policies that were presented subliminally. After generating each response, participants received feedback that they had unconsciously either supported or opposed the policy in question. Because the feedback was experimentally manipulated, we were able to examine the causal influence of participants' past behavior on both their later behavior and the cognitive processes that mediated this behavior.

We considered two factors that theoretically influence the magnitude of the effects presented in Figure 5.1. First, biased scanning requires the recall and reassessment of prior knowledge about the behavior. To this extent, distracting participants from thinking about their behavior should decrease the effects of the behavioral feedback on their attitudes and, therefore, on their decision to repeat the behavior at some later time. In contrast, self-perception processes, which can proceed without cognitive deliberation, should be less influenced by distraction. Therefore, the effect of the situational distraction on the impact of behavior allowed us to distinguish the alternative processes in Figure 5.1.

After receiving the feedback on their ostensible past behavior, response items were presented on the computer screen. Specifically, participants reported their attitudes and intentions concerning voting in favor of the referendum in the future, as well as their beliefs in and evaluations of outcomes derived from prior knowledge. There were seven belief statements about the outcomes that participants had spontaneously generated in an independent study. These outcomes were all negative. All variables were measured along a scale from 0 (e.g., *not at all likely*) to 9 (e.g., *extremely likely*). To create a composite measure of outcome-related cognitions (Ajzen & Fishbein, 1980), we mapped the evaluation measures onto a scale from -5 to +5 with no neutral point, weighted these measures by the corresponding beliefs, and summed the products over the set of outcomes being considered. At the end of the experiment, participants also cast an ostensibly anonymous ballot that either favored or opposed the institution of comprehensive exams.

As expected, participants reported more favorable attitudes toward comprehensive examinations when they thought that they had voted in favor of the exams than when they thought they had voted against them. Their intentions to repeat the behavior, and their likelihood of actually doing so (votes they cast at the end of the experiment) were affected similarly. These overall effects are compatible with all processes in Figure 4.11. Therefore, the effects of distraction were key.

The plausibility of the cognitive sequences in Figure 5.1 were identified using path analyses. As shown in Figure 5.6, participants' perceptions of their past behavior had a substantial effect on their beliefs and evaluations when distraction was low. However, this effect was reduced to nonsignificance when distraction was high. In other words, distraction prevented participants from engaging in their normal evaluation of the consequences of their behavior.

The path analyses also tested self-perception processes. Specifically, the impact of past behavior on attitudes was independent of the cognitions about specific outcomes. Although this impact was less when distraction

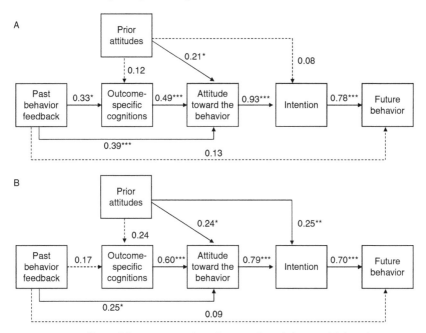

Figure 5.6 Effects of distraction on the influence of past behavior: (A) low distraction; (B) high distraction. (Adapted from Albarracín & Wyer, 2000)

was high than when it was low, it was significant in both cases. This effect suggested that people could form attitudes regardless of distraction.

Further insight into the effects of behavior feedback can be gained by comparing the judgment response times of feedback recipients with those of control participants (with no feedback). First, suppose participants who became aware of their behavior spontaneously assessed its outcomes for use as a basis of behavior. Then, these participants should report the likelihood and desirability of these consequences more quickly than participants who did not receive this feedback. This possibility was assessed under conditions in which outcome beliefs and evaluations were assessed first, before attitudes and intentions. As expected, participants took less time to report these cognitions when they received the behavior feedback than when they did not. However, this difference was similar regardless of whether participants were distracted or not. Presumably, people thought about outcomes even under high distraction, when these outcomes did not influence attitudes.

Path analyses suggested that participants based their attitudes on both outcome beliefs and evaluations and their past behavior. This conclusion was confirmed by differences in the time that participants took to report their attitudes when each criterion (outcome cognitions or past behavior) was or was not salient. Specifically, participants who did not receive the behavior feedback reported their attitudes much more quickly when they had estimated their outcome beliefs and evaluations earlier in the questionnaire than when they had not. Thus, participants who received no feedback appeared to base their attitudes on the implications of the behavior's possible consequences, taking less time to integrate these implications when they had estimated the outcomes' likelihood and desirability earlier in the questionnaire. When participants had received feedback about their behavior, however, they reported their attitudes quickly regardless of whether or not they had considered the behavior's consequences beforehand.

In combination, these data suggest that participants based their attitudes primarily on whatever information happened to be salient at the time they reported these attitudes. That is, if they had formed and reported outcome-specific beliefs and evaluations earlier in the questionnaire, they used these cognitions. In contrast, when they had not focused on outcome-specific cognitions but past behavior was salient, participants based their attitudes on this behavior. All in all, these findings provide further support for the self-perception hypothesis.

The Role of Processing Ability and Motivation in Cognitive Dissonance

There are two points of view with respect to the role of processing ability in cognitive dissonance. On the one hand, dissonance reduction may occur even under cognitive load and in the absence of awareness of one's past behavior. On the other hand, dissonance reduction may rely on propositional reasoning, which is assumed to be slow, effortful, flexible, and logical. From this point of view, dissonance reduction should require high processing ability.

According to cognitive dissonance theory (Festinger, 1957), choosing an alternative makes that alternative more attractive than an initially similar alternative. If dissonance resolution is automatic, this effect should take place irrespective of one's cognitive resources or awareness of the choice. To test this possibility, Lieberman, Ochsner, Gilbert, and Schacter (2001) studied the phenomenon in amnesic patients. Amnesic patients and healthy volunteers ranked and then selected their favorite painting from an array, then were distracted, and last reranked the paintings. Findings indicated that both amnesic patients and healthy volunteers manifested a spread of alternatives similar to nonpatients.

In a second study, Lieberman et al. (2001) examined the effect of cognitive load on the spread-of-alternatives effect in normal volunteers. The cognitive load manipulation involved rehearsing a series of numbers while people made a choice and reassessed the choices. As with the amnesic patients, the spreading of alternatives was present with and without cognitive load. Thus, Lieberman et al. (2001) concluded that dissonance reduction occurs without awareness of the triggering event (Experiment 1) and without high processing ability (Experiment 2).[3]

The notion that dissonance can be reduced automatically, however, has been questioned by Gawronski and colleagues (Gawronski & Bodenhausen, 2006; Gawronski, & Strack, 2004) based on their distinction between propositional and associative reasoning. Propositional reasoning is fast, ability demanding, and logic dependent, whereas associative reasoning is slow, nonability demanding, and logic independent. The products of each type of reasoning can be predominantly observed in explicit and implicit attitudes. Given these premises, if dissonance reduction is a propositional process, its effects should manifest in explicit attitude measures but not in implicit attitude measures.

Gawronski and Strack (2004) conducted two experiments to test their hypothesis. In Experiment 1, participants wrote a counterattitudinal essay advocating prohibition of alcohol in either high- or low-choice conditions, or did not write an essay. In the high-choice conditions, participants were given a chance to refuse; in the low-choice conditions, they were not. At the end of the study, all participants completed explicit measures concerning the prohibition and implicit measures of attitudes toward alcoholic beverages. As expected, the choice manipulation had an effect on explicit attitudes. That is, explicit attitude change was greater when participants had voluntarily written the essay than when they had been forced.

A shortcoming of this experiment was that the implicit and explicit measures assessed different attitudes. The explicit measure assessed attitudes toward the policy, whereas the implicit measure assessed attitudes toward alcoholic beverages. Because these attitudes concerned different

---

[3] Lieberman et al. (2001) also found that a measure of memory for past rankings was negatively correlated with the spreading of alternatives. In other words, the better the recall participants had of their choice (and prior rankings), the less likely they were to spread the alternatives in their ratings. This finding was interpreted as supporting the automaticity hypothesis. Nevertheless, if memory is negatively associated with dissonance resolution, one should expect the amnesic participants to show greater rather than equal dissonance.

objects, the study was replicated using prejudice toward African Americans among European Americans who previously wrote an essay in favor of affirmative action. The results reproduced the findings from the previous study. High (vs. low) choice yielded lower prejudice on the explicit measure of prejudice but had no effect on the implicit measure of prejudice.

The motivation to process information is also likely to affect the comparative processes that underlie cognitive dissonance. For example, in a study by Eisenstadt and Leippe (2005), participants were asked to write a counterattitudinal essay on increasing tuition. To manipulate personal relevance, participants were told that the tuition increase was to occur either in 6 years (low relevance) or the following semester (high relevance). High choice resulted in more attitude change in the direction of the advocacy when participants believed that the tuition increase would occur in 6 years.

Interestingly, high choice did not produce attitude change when the topic was too important to the participants (Eisenstadt & Leippe, 2005). Participants who wrote an essay in favor of raising tuition at the university did not change their attitudes in the direction of a counterattitudinal advocacy when the tuition rise would occur next semester (very high relevance). Under these circumstances, the attitude was presumably too important to change.

Summary

This chapter covered the impact of experience and past behavior on attitude and behavior change. In addition to experience, the influence of past behavior can be due to biased scanning, cognitive dissonance, and self-perception. Biased scanning entails forming attitudes on the basis of thoughts about specific information associated with the behavior. Cognitive dissonance entails a conflict between one's attitude and one's behavior and can lead to changing the attitude to resolve the inconsistency. Self-perception theory entails inferring one's attitude from a past behavior that is salient at the time.

Cognitive dissonance and self-perception processes can also occur when people think about their own behavior vis-à-vis a persuasive communication. To begin, acting in ways that contradict a prior persuasive message can lead to more change against the message advocacy when the message presents an extreme behavior. That is, due to augmentation, acting in ways that contradict an extreme message may induce strong attitudes opposite to the message. Furthermore, perceiving control over one's behavior is typically assumed to have uniformly positive effects on future behavior. However, increasing perceptions of control can yield inferences contrary to the communication objectives when people act in ways opposite to the message. Conversely, inducing low perceptions of control may allow message recipients to attribute their behavior to external factors. For example, recipients may infer that their behavior was due to social influence. From the persuader's standpoint, such external attributions may decrease counterproductive message effects.

CHAPTER 6

The Impact of Others on Attitudes and Behaviors

My son, Martin, believes that the democrats will win the 2020 election if they choose a very liberal candidate. This belief is shared by other redditors, and he is very active on Reddit, which is currently the fifth most visited site on the internet. Reddit ("Reddit," n.d.) is popular because it aggregates news while giving redditors the ability to interact with likeminded others who believe that US voters want a candidate who will not hesitate to implement gun control, increase taxes, and protect human rights in the United States.

The influence of social networks on people's attitudes was the focus of a now-classic study by Newcomb (1943). He assessed the attitudes toward social issues among the entering students of Bennington College, which was at that point an all-women college. The women were from conservative and economically privileged families and were themselves politically conservative when they entered school. By contrast, Bennington College had an unconventional curriculum that rejected many entrenched traditions of academia and included liberally oriented courses on social issues. After 4 years of intense social interaction in this environment, the majority of baccalaureates had substantially less conservative attitudes (Newcomb, 1943). Moreover, they retained these less conservative attitudes throughout their lives (Alwin, Cohen, & Newcomb, 1991; for a review, see Prislin & Wood, 2005).

Clearly then, electronic and real–life networks can shape attitudes (Asch, 1952; Guimond, 1999). A contemporary demonstration of this phenomenon comes from a study of migration from and to the South of the United States. There are important cultural differences between the South and the rest of the country. The South is more conservative (Hurlbert, 1989), has more racist beliefs, and more traditional attitudes toward religion and toward gender roles. Thus, moving to and from the South may produce attitude change among the migrants (Rice & Pepper, 1997). Consistent with this possibility, Rice and

Pepper (1997) found that Southerners who moved outside the South established new networks with non-Southerners. As a result, their attitudes changed relative to those of the Southerners who remained in the South. In contrast, the non-Southerners who moved to the South had many non-Southerner networks available. Correspondingly, their attitudes did not change relative to those of non-Southerners who remained in the South (for other important work on network attitudes, see Levitan & Visser, 2008).

Furthermore, the prescriptions and behaviors of other people have interested researchers for many decades. Ajzen and Fishbein (1980), for example, asserted that the degree to which friends, relatives, and other members of our group want us to engage in a particular behavior affects our behavior. When we believe that close others expect us to perform the behavior, we feel pressure to do so (Ajzen et al., 2019). One curious example comes from a study by Patry and Pelletier (2001), who asked a group of Canadian college students about their intentions to report an abduction by extraterrestrials. In addition, participants stated (a) whether people who were important to them would want them to report these situations to authorities, (b) whether specific people would want them to do so, and (c) whether participants were willing to comply with these specific referents. Reporting an alien abduction was a rather new behavior because only 2 percent of the sample reported being abducted by aliens in the past. Moreover, the behavior was so specific that participants were unlikely to have thought about it in the past. Nevertheless, 49 percent of the sample intended to report an abduction to the authorities should it occur, and intentions were stronger when participants believed that people close to them would support the report.

As another, more serious real-life example, norms guide adolescent behavior more than many other factors (for the processes of norm formation, see Paluck & Shepherd, 2012; Schmidt, Butler, Heinz, & Tomasello, 2016; Shank, Peters, Li, Robins, & Kirley, 2019). For example, in a study of the smoking initiation of 14- to 17-year-olds (Huang et al., 2005), of all factors (demographics, body weight, exercising, smoking in the household, schooling, depression, and smoking among friends), smoking among friends was the single most important predictor of smoking initiation (Gunther et al., 2006; Hong & Cody, 2002; Hong, Rice, & Johnson, 2012; Liu et al., 2017). Estimated susceptibility in the sample was 11 percent when no friend smoked, 28 percent when few to less than half of the friends smoked, and 44 percent when half or more of the friends smoked.

This chapter focuses on how the behavior of and the verbal messages from others instill norms (beliefs that others favor an object or behavior) that then drive conformity (i.e., "normative influence"). Alternatively, the behavior of and the verbal messages from others instill beliefs that then inform attitudes (as in "informational influence"). In addition, others facilitate one's behavior via help, mandates, encouragement, and training. I review these possibilities to provide an understanding of social influences on attitudes and behavior.

Influence of Others on Norms, Attitudes, and Beliefs

Any situation that highlights the opinions of a group can have normative and attitudinal influences. First, hearing the *verbal expressions* of others leads to questions of whether we conform to their expectations and agree with their points of view. Second, witnessing the *behavior* of others leads to thoughts about norms, attitudes, and beliefs. In addition, others serve as sources of help and opportunity, training, and imitation. Figure 6.1 depicts both normative and informational influences. Normative influence is represented as direct effects on norms (Figure 6.1A); informational influence is represented as indirect effects on attitudes, with beliefs and evaluations mediating that influence (Figure 6.1B).

Influence on Norms

The behavior and statements of other people communicate what they think. As a result, agreeable observers can simply adopt a position after seeing others support it, either implicitly, through behaviors, or explicitly, through what they say. Figure 6.1A represents attitudes that line up with a norm without corresponding changes in beliefs about the issues. The surprising extent of such normative influence was first experimentally demonstrated by Asch (1952). Participants were asked to report the relative length of two lines after trained experimental confederates offered incorrect responses. Surprisingly, even when one line was visibly longer than the other, one-third of participants who performed the judgments as part of a group based their response on the incorrect judgments of the confederates. In contrast, participants who performed the judgments individually responded correctly on all occasions. This evidence was important in demonstrating blind compliance with a group despite clear inconsistencies between the factual evidence and the group opinions.

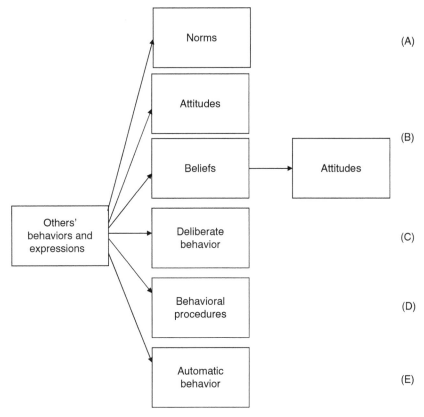

Figure 6.1 Influences of others' expressions and behaviors on norms, attitudes, and beliefs/evaluations.

The strong impact of social influence can be illustrated with the effects of electronic social networking interventions on behavior. A meta-analysis conducted by Laranjo et al. (2014) synthesized interventions to change health behaviors by using social networking sites. Twelve studies were identified. The individual studies included in the meta-analysis appear in Figure 2.5. Laranjo et al. reported an overall positive effect of health behavior outcomes (d = 0.24; 95% CI 0.04 to 0.43). However, the effects are quite variable, and for the ones that had a design comparing a social network intervention with either no intervention (passive control) or a non-social network intervention, the mode of the effect sizes was zero.

Furthermore, an inspection of Table 6.1 revealed three effect sizes that were either moderate or large: Centola (2010, 2011) and Napolitano, Hayes, Bennett, Ives, and Foster (2012). Unfortunately, Centola's experiments are not compared with a control, and Napolitano et al. has a control that shows that a basic Facebook intervention had no effect. Together. though, they reveal two critical preconditions for social influence. First, not all networks are equal; random networks (i.e., each member is connected with all others) and homophilic networks (i.e., high similarity across network members) maximize behavioral change. Furthermore, what the members of a network actually *do* is key to eliciting change. Specifically, goal setting, self-monitoring, and social support communicated via text messaging are largely responsible for the effect of the social networking interventions. In the future, studying the combined effects of these three factors might shed further light on these complex processes.

Influences on Attitudes

The mere presence of others is often enough for observers to shift attitudes. In a study by Lundgren and Prislin (1998, Study 1), participants expected to discuss an attitude issue with a partner. Some were told that the study focused on social agreement and rapport skills; others were told that the study focused on defending attitudes. Participants who believed that the study was about agreement selected information that agreed with the partner's attitude. Also, their thoughts and attitudes supported the partner's. In contrast, participants who believed that the study was an opportunity to defend their own attitudes selected information, generated thoughts, and expressed attitudes congruent with their own point of view. In short, people adjusted their attitudes and brought knowledge to bear in ways that would allow them to meet their social goals at a particular time.

One important finding in Lundgren and Prislin's (1998) study is that the influence of agreement and contention goals were not just temporary. Rather, the attitudes participants expressed persisted later, in conditions of private report. As noted by Prislin and Wood (2005), this persistence finding nicely supplements earlier research showing temporary shifts in response to a social situation (Cialdini, Herman, Levy, Kozlowski, & Petty, 1976; Cialdini, Levy, Herman, & Evenbeck, 1973). As Prislin and Wood (2005) as well as Cialdini and colleagues (1973, 1976) commented, social influences need not be temporary.

People's attitude objects are also defined strategically in relation to other people. Asch (1940; for a review, see Prislin & Wood, 2005) maintained

Table 6.1 *Effect sizes from research on the effects of social network interventions on health behaviors*

	Design	*d*	Comments
Brindal et al. (2012)	3 experimental conditions (informational site, supportive site, and personalized supportive site)	0.016	
Cavallo et al. (2012)	Experiment vs. control	0.150	In this case, *d* is a good representation of the impact of the social networking intervention. Small effect.
Centola (2010)	2 experimental conditions, no control condition	0.348	In this case, *d* is a good representation of the impact homophily in the design of social networking interventions. Moderate effect.
Centola (2011)	2 experimental conditions, no control condition	0.708	In this case, *d* is a good representation of the impact homophily in the design of social networking interventions. Large effect.
Graham et al. (2011)	2 experimental conditions, 1 active control	0.021	Effect reflects a comparison between internet enhanced social support with tailored content, vs. basic internet plus phone vs. basic internet. No effect.
Napolitano et al. (2012)	2 experimental conditions, 1 passive control condition Facebook, plus (i.e., goal setting, self-monitoring, and social support communicated via text messaging), Facebook (private group, polls, invitation to in-person events), and waitlist control	0.827	Although the calculated effect is large, there was no impact of social media when the Facebook only condition was compared with a waitlist control.
Turner-McGrievy and Tate (2011)	2 experimental conditions, 1 with a mobile group and 1 without	0	*d* represents the effect of adding a mobile group to the podcast. No effect.
Valle, Tate, Mayer, Allicock, and Cai (2013)	Facebook condition vs. self-monitoring on Facebook	0.06	*d* represents the effect of adding a group interaction on Facebook to the podcast. No effect.

that social influence affects the definition and meaning of objects and events. For instance, in one of Asch's (1940) experiments, participants were presented with either favorable or unfavorable evaluations of "politicians." As one might expect, participants' own attitudes toward politicians were influenced by others' opinions. The reason, however, was that the interpretation of the meaning of "politician" varied. When others favored politicians, participants interpreted the term to mean "statesmen." In contrast, when others had negative views, participants interpreted the term to mean "Machiavellian."

A similar form of projection happens when people assume that others agree with their positions (Erb & Bohner, 2007, 2010). People project their own attitudes onto others. Hence, they see themselves as members of the majority on a number of issues (Krueger & Clement, 1997). For example, in 1999, Princeton University imposed a shower ban on campus dormitories due to a sudden water shortage (Monin & Norton, 2003). Naturally, perceptions of others' behavior can promote collective compliance with such a regulation, making it important to determine how objective people are in these perceptions. Interestingly, the study revealed a striking false-consensus effect. Participants who took one or more showers estimated that 72 percent of other students were taking showers. In contrast, participants who did not take showers estimated that 44 percent of other students were taking showers.

Influences on Beliefs

Besides people complying with norms, witnessing the behavior and verbal expressions of others can lead to the conclusion that a norm is in place because it is sound (Asch, 1957; Festinger, 1954; Sherif & Sherif, 1936). One way in which this happens is that the behaviors and verbal messages of other people influence our beliefs. An illustration of this influence appears in Figure 6.1B. Consistent with this notion, research has shown that consensus affects subjective judgments (i.e., attitudes) more than it does objective ones (Crano & Hannula-Bral, 1994; Wood et al., 1994). People may use the heuristic that consensus implies correctness, particularly among members of a well-liked group (Wood et al., 1996). However, the effects of consensus are not always heuristic. When people fear social sanctions, or fear making mistakes that might have consequences for how others perceive them, they need to be persuaded of the reasons underlying the consensus. Probably for this reason, consensus often requires in-depth discussion of the problem being examined (Wilder, 1977), which in turn provides a firmer attitudinal basis.

Furthermore, social consensus has an influence when the position is ambiguous or the issue is inherently subjective (Festinger, 1954; Turner, 1985). In addition, maintaining consensual attitudes can yield valuable social approval. In a study by Schachter (1951), groups of around six naive participants and three confederates discussed an issue. One confederate agreed with the modal position of the group. Another confederate shifted from an initial extreme opposition to the modal position. A final confederate consistently advocated an extremely unpopular position. Following an intense group interaction, there was a clear pattern of acceptance of the group's position. Whereas the positions of confederates who agreed with the most frequent group position were accepted, those of the deviates were rejected (Levine & Moreland, 2002; Mannetti et al., 2010; Marques, Abrams, & Serôdio, 2001; Moreland & Levine, 1988).

The dual influences of norms through compliance or through information have been investigated extensively. According to Deutsch and Gerard (1955; for a review, see Prislin & Wood, 2005), social groups influence individuals for normative and informational reasons. Normative influence (Figure 6.1A) implies conforming to the expectations of others (i.e., compliance; Deutsch & Gerard, 1955). Informational influence (i.e., internalization) implies accepting the *information* conveyed by others as valid.

Deutsch and Gerard (1955) used Asch's (1952) paradigm to show how normative and informational influences coexist. Norms should increase conformity when observers want to be liked by others, that is, when they have a high need for social integration (see Chapter 1). They should also increase conformity when observers have had close contact with the group. In contrast, informational processes should increase tendencies to agree when people need information, that is, when they have a high need for knowledge (see Chapter 1). Thus, agreement via information may increase when observers have viewed the lines for a short time, are unsure of what they saw, and can disambiguate their observations by relying on others. Supporting Deutsch and Gerard's predictions, observers showed more agreement in the presence of face-to-face interactions with the group than in the absence of such interactions. In addition, observers showed more agreement when the lines were displayed for only a few seconds than when the lines were displayed throughout the judgment process. Clearly, then, closeness with the group and insufficient factual information both produced agreement, although the processes underlying agreement were normative and informational, respectively.

Awareness of a norm may also increase awareness of certain social outcomes and thus lead to the formation of new beliefs. When people realize that others have expectations about how they should behave, they can think about either social acceptance and rejection or their own identity (Abrams et al., 1990; Abrams & Hogg, 2008; Abrams, Thomas, & Hogg, 1990; Leonardelli, Pickett, & Brewer, 2010). Expecting social acceptance and fearing rejection leads to agreement when the group can surveil its members' behavior. Conversely, concerns about the identity consequences of disagreeing with the group for one's identity leads to agreement when the group does not surveil its members' behavior.

If expectations of acceptance and rejection lead to public attitudes aligning with the group, whereas self-definition leads to private attitudes aligning with the group, the overall effect of surveillance should be null. Supporting this hypothesis, Bond and Smith (1996) meta-analyzed studies using Asch's (1952) line-judging paradigm. Findings indicated no differences between attitude change in public or private settings, thus providing support for different mediating influences on social expectations.

Influences of the behavior of others on beliefs about the intentionality of behavior. One fascinating aspect of social influence is that observing what others do allows us to determine what we ourselves do. According to Wegner and colleagues (Wegner & Sparrow, 2004; Wegner, Sparrow, & Winerman, 2004), people have various sources of information about the authorship of a given behavior. First, proximity between a person and the object of a behavior can indicate that the person performs the behavior. Second, if Person *A* gives instructions and Person *B* listens, *A*'s instruction to perform a behavior may imply that *B* performs the behavior. Third, if a person thought about performing a behavior before observing the behavior, she is likely to feel that she performed the behavior.

Some of the implications of Wegner and Sparrow's (2004) analysis were investigated in a series of experiments with two participants who simultaneously faced a mirror using the physical arrangement shown in Figure 6.2. One of the two participants was designated to be the "participant" and the other to be the "hand helper." The "participant" wore a pair of gloves and a tunic that had a cardboard back extending over her head as well as a set of headphones. The hand helper wore similar gloves and headphones, stood behind the cardboard, and inserted her hands in the sleeves of the tunic. Thus, the body reflected in the mirror belonged to the "participant" and the hands reflected in the mirror were the helper's, while the "participant's" hands remained under the tunic at all times.

The experimental device in Figure 6.2 served to dissociate the actor and the perceiver of behavior to study if features of the spatial and temporal

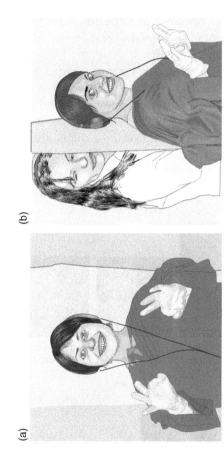

(a)　　　(b)

Figure 6.2 Device to study feelings of performing a behavior. (Reproduced from Wegner, Sparrow, & Winerman, 2004, with authors' permission)

context influenced the participant's perception that the behavior was actually hers. Specifically, "participants" either did or did not hear the instructions to move the hands that the hand helpers received. Furthermore, "participants" heard the instructions, but the instructions came before or after the hand helper executed the movements. For example, in some conditions, the "participant" heard the instruction "wave hello with your hand" right before the hand helper actually "waved hello." In other conditions, "participants" did not hear any instructions. Also, the instructions "participants" heard were either consistent or inconsistent with the hand movements.

The study focused on the effects of the experimental manipulations on the feelings of the "participants" that they controlled and consciously moved their arms. Results for a composite of these two measures appear in Figure 6.3, organized according to (a) whether the participants heard consistent instructions, no instructions, or inconsistent instructions (Experiment 2) and (b) whether the "participants" heard the consistent

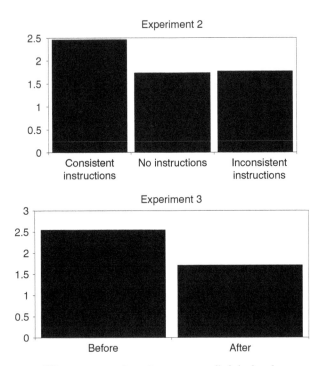

Figure 6.3 Effects on perceptions that one controlled the hand movements.

instructions before or after the hand helper moved her hands (some of the conditions in Experiment 3). As shown, "participants" reported feeling greater control over their behavior when the instructions corresponded to the hand movements (top panel) and when the instructions were presented before the hand movements (bottom panel).

Other research by Wegner and colleagues (Wegner, Fuller, & Sparrow, 2003, Experiment 3) pointed to the conditions that lead people to attribute their own behavior to others. A "facilitated communication" paradigm reproduced the technique in which a person assists sufferers of autism to type on a keyboard. This technique, now discredited, supposedly allowed people who were unable to speak to communicate by having close contact with a "facilitator" who types the intended communication on a keyboard. In the study, the facilitator's hand remained on the keyboard while supporting the hand of the ostensible communicator. The facilitator received a series of questions and believed that the communicator also did. Moreover, the facilitator believed that the communicator could

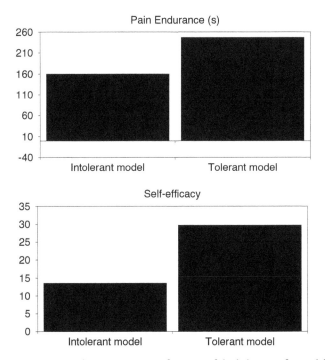

Figure 6.4 Pain tolerance scores as a function of the behavior of a model.

transmit unconscious, subtle movements to his or her hand. In reality, the communicator did not see the answers, and the correct responses came entirely from the facilitator. Nevertheless, once the task was complete, the facilitator estimated that the communicator contributed over 30 percent of the correct answers even when her actual contribution was zero.

Influence of the behavior of others on beliefs about behavioral control. People's perceptions of control over their behavior are also influenced by the overt behaviors of others. Take, for example, research on the expression of pain conducted by Symbaluk, Heth, Cameron, and Pierce (1997). In this research, male participants went to the researchers' laboratory wearing comfortable clothing and were asked to squat above a wooden box containing a pressure plate. They were asked to report their pain at different pressures of the plate while watching a video. Participants viewed a video of a confederate performing the same exercise, who was seemingly either in pain or not in pain. For example, one video showed that the confederate collapsed after 60 s following grimaces, moans, and hand and leg shaking. In contrast, the other video showed that the confederate remained stoic and did not collapse.

The reactions of the participants in Symbaluk et al.'s (1997) experiment conformed to the idea that observers self-attribute the level of control modeled by others. As shown in Figure 6.3, viewers of the stoic confederate endured the pain for over 90 s more than viewers of the sensitive confederate. In addition, viewers of the stoic confederate were more confident in their ability (i.e., had higher self-efficacy) to tolerate the exercise than viewers of the sensitive confederate. These results suggest that the models' behaviors alter observers' actual control over their own behavior as well as their self-efficacy. For other effects of norms, see Sparkman and Walton (2019).

Effects on opportunities for deliberate behaviors. Other people shape our own lives by facilitating behaviors we would not perform without them. This influence appears in Figure 6.4C and is illustrated by peer influences on drinking. In a cohort study in Maryland (Simons-Morton, 2004), for example, teenagers reported their drinking behavior in the last 12 months and in the last 30 days. Peer influence was measured by asking respondents to indicate how many of their five closest friends drank and engaged in forbidden activities (e.g., on a test, bullying, and stealing). Expectancies about the outcomes of drinking alcohol and parental expectations about their child's drinking were also measured. Not surprisingly, peer influence, alcohol expectancies, and parental expectations all predicted drinking initiation way beyond other factors like school engagement, presence of depression, and parental involvement. Interestingly, expectations about the outcomes of drinking (i.e., alcohol expectancies) only mattered when children expected their parents to be permissive. When children expected their parents to be upset if they drank, alcohol expectancies did not matter.

One reason for the effects of peer influence as measured by Simons-Morton (2004) is that friends who already engage in a given behavior provide behavioral opportunities for their peers. In fact, the availability of alcohol and drugs in the social environment is a strong predictor of consumption, even after statistically controlling for environmental norms (White et al., 2019).

Effects on Behavioral Skills

Others can also help us develop new skills, an influence represented in Figure 6.1D. Complex skills require structured forms of training delivered by people who have already acquired those skills. According to Bandura (1986), the most successful forms of training have three components. First, the trainer models the basic rules of behavior and strategies to reach a set of goals. Second, the trainer guides the practice of the trainee under simulated conditions to ensure that the trainee crystallizes the skills. Third, the trainer assists the trainee in effectively applying the skills to real problems.

Not surprisingly, research in the domain of occupational training indicates that programs in which somebody actually demonstrates the skills are more successful than programs that provide either written instructions or feedback based on a computer algorithm. Gist, Rosen, and Schwoerer (1988), for example, compared a computerized tutorial of the use of a spreadsheet with the same information demonstrated by a videotaped model tutorial. The study showed that the videotaped model was superior in eliciting the necessary skills. In addition, the videotaped program instilled a greater sense of self-efficacy regardless of the level of the trainees' self-efficacy prior to the program.

Direct Effects on Automatic Behavior

The human capacity for imitation has ensured that other people can automatically influence our own behavior. Figure 6.1E shows this influence, which is discussed in detail in the coming sections.

The formation of imitative behavior. Humans and other animals develop behavior by imitation, a capacity that appears to be present since infancy. Imitation involves enacting a behavior upon seeing another human, particularly a face, perform the behavior, and appears before the cerebral cortex is fully developed. Subcortical brain structures appear to facilitate imitation even among cortically blind neonates, who, by definition, receive visual information through their eyes but are unable to decode it in the occipital cortex (Jones, 2007).

Imitation allows newborns to establish behaviors they can later attempt to influence in others (i.e., provocation). In a study by Nagy and Molnar (2004), an experimenter protruded her tongue in front of infants for 1 min. After the experimenter made sure the baby saw the movement, she stopped and waited for 2 min for the baby to mimic her. Then, the experimenter protruded her tongue again and again, waiting for a response from the baby. Once the pattern was established, the experimenter changed the intervals to which the baby was accustomed in order to determine if the baby tried to produce the same behavior in the experimenter.

Nagy and Molnar's (2004) results indicated that, out of 35 newborns, all showed imitation and 17 showed provocation. The coding of provocation and imitation behavior was reliable across observers. In addition, imitation and provocation behaviors were associated with different patterns of heart rate. When the behavior was coded as imitation, there was an acceleration in the babies' heart rate. Conversely, when the behavior was coded as provocation, there was a deceleration in the babies' heart rate. Moreover, babies who presumably initiated the observed behavior appeared to do so in an attempt to "provoke" the experimenter. Even more, the babies who exhibited provocation made eye contact and became distressed when the experimenter failed to respond. Thus, the imitation favored a behavior that the infants could actively reproduce later to elicit imitation by the other person. The change in the frequency of the experimenter's behavior led infants to protrude their tongues to stimulate the experimenter to protrude her own tongue.

One important consequence of the human capacity to imitate is that imitation facilitates behaviors beyond infancy. For example, in the domain of helping behavior, children learn to be helpful by imitating others who provide help. Bar Tal, Raviv, and Goldberg (1982) observed 156 children ages 18–76 months in a playground and coded whether they shared with others, gave something to others, aided others, and comforted others. The study indicated that younger kids engaged in helping acts both during a play and in a real interaction that explicitly required help, whereas older kids provided real help in almost every instance. That is, older children had internalized helping others and did not need situational prompts. Furthermore, in the younger group, both witnessing others help and promises of social rewards (e.g., "other children will like you") correlated with helping in the context of a play. In contrast, in the older group, help was either self-initiated or enacted in response to a request from others but did not occur by imitation. That is, imitation (and symbolic social rewards) first allowed for imitation and simulation of the behavior as part of a play. After the behavior was established, children were able to make independent decisions to help others and imitation was no longer necessary.

Mimicry and schemas. One's behavior is influenced by others in part because the mere observation of the behavior can activate similar schemas in oneself. In the domain of aggression, for example, perceiving hostile social behaviors can make observers act in a hostile manner (Carver et al., 1983). In the domain of affiliation, people who interact with strangers tend to mimic them. Thus, they rub their face if the stranger does so, and they shake their foot if the stranger does so (Chartrand & Bargh, 1999, Experiment 1). This mimicry appears to elicit positive feelings about the partner and the interaction quality (Chartrand & Bargh, 1999; Hatfield, Cacioppo, & Rapson, 1994).

However, some individuals are more prone to mimicry than others. People who are good at taking the perspective of others spontaneously mimic social behavior (Chartrand & Bargh, 1999). In addition, some people are more sensitive to the identity of the person with whom they interact. High self-monitors, for example, are more interested in projecting an adequate public image than low self-monitors (Gangestad & Snyder, 2000; Snyder, 1974). In a study performed by Cheng and Chartrand (2003), college students were in the same room with a confederate that was introduced as a peer (another college student) or as a nonpeer (either a graduate student or a high school student). High self-monitors shook their feet in response to the confederate's foot shaking to a greater extent than did low self-monitors. However, this difference was only present when high self-monitors thought that the confederate was another college student like them. High self-monitors did not mimic when they thought that the confederate was not their peer.

Another aspect involved in automatically mirroring the behavior of others is the degree to which people depend on others. In research by van Baaren, Maddux, Chartrand, de Bouter, and van Knippenberg (2003), participants were asked to form sentences that evoked either social inter-dependence (e.g., "together," "group") or independence (e.g., "unique," "alone"). Immediately after these primes, participants had to state their ratings of pieces of music for the experimenter to write them down. The recordings were played by an experimenter who was purposely playing with her pen to elicit mimicry. Even when the participant did not need a pen to complete their ratings, many of the participants mimicked the behavior of the experimenter. The amount of mimicry, however, was greater when participants were primed to be interdependent than when they were primed to be independent.

Mimicry in the formation of attitudes toward people. Adults also synchronize their behavior when they interact with others (Kendon, 1970; LaFrance & Broadbent, 1976). People who interact develop similar accents and speech patterns (Cappella, 1981; Cappella & Planalp, 1981), use similar syntax (Levelt & Kelter, 1982), and adopt similar posture and gestures (Chartrand & Bargh, 1999). Interestingly, this mimicry allows people to form new attitudes, particularly about the people with whom they interact. In fact, mimicking others appears to make people more likable to those others (Chartrand & Bargh, 1999), as shown by actors being friendlier toward those who mimic them (van Baaren, Holland et al., 2003).

An ingenious study investigated the frequency of mimicry when one of the people in the interaction is a virtual agent. In collaborative virtual settings (Blascovich et al., 2002; Slater et al., 2000), people from remote physical locations see the verbal and nonverbal behaviors of an agent using a standardized digital format (Bailenson & Blascovich, 2004). The process of digitalizing the real occurrences allows for exact measures of the behavior of the two people, including moving, smiling, and talking. Thus, these environments follow the same patterns as real-life social interactions (Blascovich et al., 2002; Loomis, Blascovich, & Beall, 1999).

Bailenson and Yee (2005) utilized virtual agents to determine the degree to which mimicry increases liking. They were interested in whether the positive social effects of automatic mimicry would occur when one of the actors is a humanlike digital representation controlled by a computer. Participants entered the virtual environment and listened to an embodied agent read a persuasive message about a new university policy. The virtual agent mimicked the head movements of either the participant interacting with the agent, or a different participant. If attitudes toward the commu-nication source and topic are influenced by mimicry, message recipients should like the agent and be more persuaded about the advocacy when the agent mimics the recipient than when the agent mimics somebody else.

Figure 6.5 shows the study's three-dimensional models, both of which used a standardized male or female body and presented the same message. The study considered the influence of the participant's gender (male or female), the agent's gender (male or female), and the agent's behavior (mimicry present or absent). In the mimicry condition, the pitch, yaw, and roll of the agent's head movements mimicked those of the participant in an exact way. In contrast, in the control condition, the agent's head movements mimicked the movements of a previous participant in an exact way. According to the study results, the agents who mimicked the participants were viewed as more likable and persuasive than the agents who did not. In addition, participants interacting with a mimicking agent looked at the agent more than those interacting with a nonmimicking one, and this greater attention apparently caused positive attitudes toward the agent and greater persuasion.

The Impact of Normative Information Relative to Other Sources of Information

Norms are powerful forces in real life. However, their effects are stronger when the recipients of influence are concerned about how others view them. For instance, Cialdini (for related matters, see Cialdini et al., 1976; Cialdini & Goldstein, 2004; Cialdini & Trost, 1998; Jacobson, Mortensen, & Cialdini, 2011) studied people as they approached their cars in a parking lot. The parking lot was either clean or dirty, and an experimenter's accomplice was either littering or not littering at the time people approached their cars. As expected, what the participants coming into the lot did depended on how clean the lot was to begin and what they observed the accomplice doing. Participants were more likely to throw a flyer left on their windshields when the lot was already dirty. This effect, however, was strongest when the confederates also littered the lot at precisely that time, presumably because their behavior acted as a signal to pay attention to how other people generally behaved in this parking lot. According to Cialdini, increasing sensitivity to the norms of the situation (the littered state of the parking lot) allowed a "descriptive" norm (what the confederate did) to exert more influence. Moreover, this descriptive norm is often highly influential even though people deny being influenced (Schultz et al., 2019).

Figure 6.5 Virtual agents. (From Bailenson & Yee, 2005, reproduced with the authors' permission)

On a related note, many researchers divide cultures into those that emphasize collective versus individual well-being and motivations (Markus & Kitayama, 1991; Triandis, 2005; Triandis & Suh, 2002). By definition, then, social influence should be greater in collectivistic than individualistic cultures. Supporting this principle, Bond and Smith's (1996) meta-analytic synthesis of research using Asch's line-judging paradigm revealed greater confederate influence in collectivistic than individualistic cultures. In a similar way, social consensus has stronger influences in collectivistic than individualistic cultures (Cialdini, Wosinska, Barrett, Butner, & Gornik Durose, 2001). These differences appear to be related to greater affiliation need and group interdependence, which also vary within a cultural group (see Prislin & Wood, 2005).

Teenagers are also more attentive to their peers' opinions and behaviors and better networked than are adults (Kerr et al., 2002; McHale, Dariotis, & Kauh, 2003). In addition, groups that have more social power, such as, for example, men and ethnic majorities, generally have greater access to social networks (see, e.g., Lopez & Stack, 2001). Consequently, existing norms might have a stronger influence among males, people with higher education, and ethnic majorities than among females, people with lower education, and ethnic minorities.

The impact of norms across groups was studied by Albarracín, Kumkale, and Johnson (2004) in the domain of condom use. A meta-analysis included the demographics of each sample as well as the correlations between norms and intentions. If groups with more social networks display greater normative influences, then males, ethnic majorities and teens should have the strongest correlations between intentions and norms. Conversely, groups that are less networked should have the weakest correlations between norms and intentions. As predicted, these hypotheses received support.

The strength of normative influence also depends on the salience of normative considerations. Ybarra and Trafimow (1998) primed the importance of the private and the public selves. They hypothesized that priming the private self would lead participants to shift their intentions to use condoms in the direction of their attitudes. Correspondingly, priming the public self should increase the weight of attitudes as a basis for intentions. The average regression weights from three experiments on this topic are presented in Figure 6.6. As can be seen, norms influenced intentions more when the public self was primed, whereas attitudes influenced intentions more when the private self was primed.

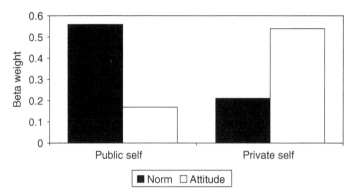

Figure 6.6 Effects of norms and attitudes as a manipulation of private and public selves.

Another body of research on degree of normative change is based on social identity theory (Abrams & Hogg, 2008). According to this model, prior attitudes should not influence behavior when the norm of a group important to the person (social identity is salient) conflicts with the person's attitude. In contrast, prior attitudes should influence behavior when the norm agrees with the person's attitude and when the group is not important to the person's identity. A study on volunteerism tested these hypotheses. Terry, Hogg, and White (1999) manipulated the salience of gender as a social identity. Then they made sure participants had highly accessible attitudes toward a proposal to introduce separate bicycle lanes on roads. Specifically, participants were asked to repeat their attitudes a number of times, and these attitudes became faster to report. Participants then received information that other people of their own gender either supported or opposed the proposal. The results from this experiment revealed that the normative information had more influence when the participants' gender was made salient, that is, when the gender identity was emphasized.

Interestingly, the influence of the group is so prevalent that incorrectly attributing a position to a group can make people behave in opposition to their own attitudes. In research on this phenomenon – termed "pluralistic ignorance" – Prentice and Miller (1993) found that college students were unhappy about their excessive drinking habits but believed that others were not. As a result, all students drank more than they personally wished to, based on erroneously inferred social norms. This normative ignorance, however, can be remedied. In another study on college drinking (Schroeder & Prentice, 1998), a group of students was educated about this phenomenon and asked to share their true attitudes toward alcohol with the other group members. Compared to a condition without this correction for pluralistic ignorance, students in the normative condition drank 40 percent fewer drinks a week. Thus, dispelling the idea that other students were heavy drinkers actually decreased drinking.

Summary

Others can influence norms, beliefs, and attitudes. Normative influence implies fairly direct effects without recipients of the influence becoming persuaded of the merits of a point of view. In contrast, informational influence implies that beliefs and attitudes are formed by internalizing the social norm. Finally, other people provide behavioral opportunities, teach skills, and induce mimicry. The degree of influence of normative information, however, depends on characteristics of the person, including cultural collectivism, group identity, and linkage to existing social networks.

One aspect not mentioned before is that norms can also moderate the impact of persuasive messages. We (Chan & Albarracín, 2019) examined whether a prevailing descriptive norm (i.e., what people actually do) (Cialdini & Goldstein, 2004; J. Liu et al., 2017; Monroe et al., 2018; Reid, Cialdini, & Aiken, 2010) in support of same-sex couples influenced the degree to which HIV-prevention and testing messages were associated with positive behaviors among men who have sex with men in the United States. We measured the norm by obtaining data on the same-sex couple prevalence (i.e., proportions of same-sex couples) within a county, and then determined if the norm affected the ability of Twitter messages to exert an effect across counties. We obtained Twitter topics as a measure of social media messaging and measured behavior at a county level by analyzing a national survey of men who have sex with men.

Twitter postings may be directly associated with county-level HIV testing and prevention, but this may only happen in the right social normative context, that is, a context that allows for open discussions of same-sex relations. In addition, social media may only influence testing and prevention if they manage to promote in-depth discussions with physicians in the region. In short, observing that same-sex couples are common may lead to greater openness discussing HIV, which in turn may influence HIV testing and prevention. Nonetheless, some regions may not reach the necessary threshold level of discussion to ultimately ensure that Twitter messages promote HIV testing and prevention.

We derived reports of HIV testing, condom use, and PrEP use from the American Men Internet Survey (AMIS, 2014–2016). AMIS also measured discussions about HIV and discussions about PrEP with healthcare providers. Results indicated that counties with low prevalence of same-sex couples showed almost no associations between Twitter postings about HIV and the HIV-prevention and testing behavior among men who have sex with men. In contrast, counties with high prevalence of same-sex couples showed associations between Twitter postings about HIV and the HIV-prevention and testing behavior among gay men, and these associations were frequently mediated by discussions with physicians. In sum, real-life others could strengthen the influence of messages posted on social media.

PART IV

*The Impact of Persuasive Communications
and Behavioral Interventions*

CHAPTER 7

The Processing of Persuasive Communications and Behavioral Interventions

Persuasive communications have many objectives. Religious ministers preach to strengthen their audiences' belief in the afterlife, whereas politicians want us to believe that jobs lost to China will return to the United States. Marketing firms promote a brand image and positive attitudes toward new products, and political campaign managers do their best to make their candidates likable. Yet, other communications and all behavioral interventions aim to change behavior. Religious ministers solicit help during religious services, campaign managers promote donations for their candidates, and marketers try to increase purchases.

This chapter is the first of three chapters dedicated to persuasive communications and behavioral interventions. I define *persuasive communications* as messages delivered to a passive audience and *behavioral interventions* as programs with an active audience. Both persuasive communications and behavioral interventions have the intent to persuade. The difference between the two is that behavioral interventions include activities like role-playing and client-centered counseling in addition to persuasive arguments, which are present in both persuasive communications and behavioral interventions. In this chapter, I first discuss classic stage models of persuasion as well as other models, such as the cognitive response model, the elaboration-likelihood model, the heuristic systematic model, and the unimodel. Next, I turn to the proposed differences in processes of attitude formation and change, with special attention to the influence of prior attitudes on the decision to seek out a persuasive message.

Stage Models

Hovland's and McGuire's Stage Models

According to Hovland (1959), the processing of a persuasive message involves three phases: (a) attention, (b) comprehension, and (c) acceptance of the message content. Attention and comprehension involve learning and retaining the message content. Acceptance involves agreeing with the message's conclusion and occurs when agreeing is rewarding. For example, recipients may feel rewarded when they expect that the message source will like them. They may also feel rewarded when they expect that following the message recommendation will bring them benefits.

McGuire (1968a, 1968b) extended Hovland's (1959) theorizing by capitalizing on a cognitive perspective and abandoning consideration of learning and rewards. McGuire argued that the impact of a persuasive communication is the result of a series of information-processing stages. These stages include (a) exposure (i.e., E), (b) attention (A), (c) comprehension (C), (d) yielding (Y), (e) retention (R), and (f) behavior (B). A message can only be effective if it is presented to potential recipients who themselves attend to and comprehend the arguments discussed in the message. Recipients must also agree with the conclusion of the message. Moreover, for the attitude to persist, people must retain this yielding over a period of time. Ultimately, however, recipients may or may not behave in the manner recommended by the communication. As a result, the success of the message can depend on its actual behavioral impact; that is,

$$P_I = P_E \times P_A \times P_C \times P_Y \times P_R \times P_B,$$

where P_I is the probability of influence of the persuasive message and the remaining probabilities are associated with exposure, attention, comprehension, retention, and behavior.

McGuire (1968a, 1968b) later simplified this six-stage model. He noted difficulties in measuring attention and comprehension as separate processes and synthesized these processes along with exposure under the overall label of "reception" (R). With this reduction, the equation became

$$P_I = P_R \times P_Y,$$

where the probability of influence is a multiplicative function of the probability of receiving the message and the probability of yielding to the content one has received. This two-step model has important empirical implications. In particular, when a situational or personal factor has the same influence on both reception and yielding, the factor's influence should be monotonic. For example, a factor that increases both reception and yielding should increase persuasion. In contrast, when a factor has opposite influences on reception and yielding, the factor's influence should be curvilinear.

Curvilinear effects of communication factors have been an important topic in several domains. For example, according to Janis and Milholland (1954), extreme fear appeals increase attention to the message content. Janis and Milholland also proposed that extreme fear appeals induce anxiety and thus rejection of the message content. Consequently, moderate fear appeals are supposedly more effective than either very low or very high levels of fear appeal (but see Tannenbaum et al., 2015). Similarly, McGuire (1968a) observed that intelligence increases reception of the content of the persuasive message because more intelligent recipients can understand the message arguments more easily than can less intelligent recipients. In addition, however, intelligence decreases yielding to the message recommendation because more intelligent recipients can identify flaws in the message more easily than can less intelligent recipients. As a result, recipients of moderate intelligence are more susceptible to the influence of a persuasive communication than are those of either low or high intelligence.

What these initial stage models did not specify was how exposure decisions are made or how receiving and yielding to the content of the persuasive message influence recipients' attitudes and behaviors after exposure to a communication. In contrast, the model I discuss in this chapter explicates exposure, how various cognitions are formed, and how factors other than message arguments (e.g., one's mood) influence behavior (see, e.g., Yan et al., 2010; Ziegler & Diehl, 2011).

Wyer's Stage Model

Wyer (1974) further elaborated McGuire's (1972) model using conditional probabilities. In this revision, the probability of a message's influence is a function of the probability of a person being influenced (I) given that she receives the communication (R) plus the probability of moving in the message's direction even though she has not received (R') the communication; that is,

$$P_I = P_R \, P_{I/R} + P_R \, P_{I/R'}.$$

The probability of being influenced, assuming that one receives the communication, can itself be rewritten as the probability of yielding. Yielding in turn depends on the probability of yielding when one successfully counterargues the communication ($P_{Y/CA}$) as well as the probability of yielding when one fails to refute it ($P_{Y/CA'}$). Then, the full equation predicting influence can be restated as follows:

$$P_I = P_R \, (P_{CA} \, P_{Y/CA} + P_{CA'} \, P_{Y/CA'}) + P_R \, P_{I/R'}.$$

In this new equation, the parenthetical term is a function of the strength of the arguments in the message. Stronger, more compelling arguments should induce less counterarguing and more persuasion. Furthermore, the parenthetical term describes yielding or resistance for reasons *other* than the arguments contained in the message. For example, the affective feelings recipients experience for reasons unrelated to the communication can increase yielding to a given position (see, e.g., Albarracín & Wyer, 2001; Hui et al., 2008). Hence, the message may be persuasive even if recipients counterargue the message content ($P_{Y/CA} = P_{Y/CA'}$).

One deficiency of McGuire's (1968a) and Wyer's (1974) stage models, however, is their inability to explain the construction and integration of judgments. For example, message recipients may or may not believe the scenarios described in a persuasive message. However, how recipients form beliefs and attitudes is important. Moreover, past stage models do not distinguish probabilistic (belief) and evaluative judgments, nor do they explicate how information from multiple sources is ultimately integrated. The model I describe in this chapter contributes to filling this gap.

Cognitive Processing Models

People who are presented with a persuasive message engage in a series of cognitive activities to process its content as well as information concerning the context of the message.

Cognitive Response Model

As McGuire (1968a) proposed, receiving the arguments presented in a persuasive message influences yielding to the conclusion advocated in the message. Yielding comprises agreement with the propositions presented in the message and generating supporting beliefs based on prior knowledge. Thus, proper reception of the propositions can facilitate yielding, a possibility tested by Eagly and others (Carpenter & Boster, 2013; Eagly, 1974) through a manipulation of message comprehensibility. In this research, recall of the message arguments and open-ended answers about these arguments measured reception, and conventional scales concerning evaluations of the message's position measured attitudes. The results from this work indicated that the reception of the message content results in both memory for and yielding to its content.

Despite a relation between reception and yielding, reception is not a precondition for yielding, nor does it always facilitate yielding. In contrast, the correlation between reception (memory) and yielding depends on how much recipients counterargue when they are processing the message. For example, Chaiken and Eagly (1976) found that difficult-to-understand messages were better received when presented in print than when presented on video or audio. Interestingly, the correlation between reception and attitudes was lower when a difficult message was presented in writing than on video or audio. Apparently, message recipients counterargue communications to a greater extent when the communications are presented in writing than when they are presented on video or audio. When communications are presented in writing, attitudes correlate with the counterarguments but not with the recall of the presented arguments.

Once researchers realized that mere comprehension was insufficient to explain persuasion, they turned to studying "cognitive responses" and focused on measuring the arguments people *generate*. According to Greenwald and Albert (1968), people who receive a persuasive message relate the information contained in the message to their existing knowledge about the topic. Consequently, their attitudes may be based on cognitive material that is not part of the communication. When the thoughts based on this material are positive, attitudes are positive. When, in contrast, thoughts based on this material are negative, attitudes are negative.

To test the role of cognitive responses, Greenwald and Cullen (cited in Greenwald, 1968) asked participants to read a message about specialized versus broad education. After reading the persuasive message, participants listed their thoughts "pertinent to forming and expressing an opinion on the issue of general versus specialized education." Afterward, they reported their attitudes and were instructed to code their own thoughts. Specifically, they coded how favorable each thought was in general and with respect to specialized or general education. Moreover, thoughts were classified by either the participants or the researchers as (a) externally generated (message based), (b) recipient modified (message based), and (c) recipient generated (knowledge based). Results showed that 44 percent and 56 percent of the listed thoughts were classified as message and knowledge based. In addition, knowledge-based thoughts correlated more strongly with attitudes than did either category of message-based thoughts. Thus, these findings suggest that knowledge-based thoughts have greater influence than message-based ones (Greenwald, 1968).

The cognitive response model provided valuable insights into the role of prior knowledge in persuasion. There were, however, two deficiencies. First, it is not appropriate to compare correlations based on different metrics. Thus, the relative role of message-based versus knowledge-based cognitions must be determined by comparing the role of each cognition in different situations.

However, the cognitive response model provided a useful demonstration of the important role of knowledge-based cognitions.

Elaboration-Likelihood Model

Reception processes received research attention from the beginning of persuasion research but were systematically addressed starting in the 1970s. For example, Osterhouse and Brock (1970) assigned participants to either monitoring a series of light flashes or doing nothing. Not surprisingly, increases in distraction led to a steady decrease in the retention of the message arguments, as judged by participants recognizing what messages they had received. More importantly, this research provided a key paradigm to understand cognitive processing and how distraction can increase or decrease yielding, depending on the information contained in the message.

In the research initiated by Osterhouse and Brock (1970), the success of a persuasion attempt depends on distraction but also on the *quality* of the arguments presented in the message. For instance, Petty et al. (1976; for a conceptual replication, see Jeong & Hwang, 2012) studied the consequences of distraction on yielding to different types of messages. Participants received either strong, compelling arguments or weak, specious arguments. As predicted, strong arguments were more persuasive when the arguments could be adequately received due to the absence of distraction. In contrast, weak arguments were more persuasive when the arguments could not be adequately received due to high distraction.

The role of situational and personal factors leading to persuasion has been the center of Petty and Cacioppo's (1986a, 1986b) elaboration-likelihood model. According to them, high ability and motivation to think about the information contained in a message lead to reliance on the arguments in the message. That is, when ability and motivation are high, recipients of strong arguments are more persuaded than are recipients of weak arguments. In contrast, low processing ability and motivation lead to a reliance on easier processes. When ability and motivation are low, recipients may be influenced by claims that the source is or is not an expert or by the affect they experience for reasons unrelated to the message (e.g., background music). In other words, high ability and motivation trigger processing of what is "central" to the message. Correspondingly, low ability and motivation trigger processing of "peripheral" information, which includes thoughts about relatively irrelevant material (e.g., extraneous affect), the application of a heuristic (see Petty & Cacioppo, 1986a), and classical conditioning.

The elaboration-likelihood model greatly contributed to understanding when different types of information have an influence. However, the elaboration-likelihood model implies that people's ability and motivation to think about the information exert monotonic effects on persuasion. Briefly, the higher processing ability and motivation are, the higher the attention people pay to the arguments in a persuasive message. Conversely, the higher processing ability and motivation are, the higher is the probability that people will use simpler processes within the peripheral route (e.g., affect as information and classical conditioning). According to the model I propose, however, these assumptions may not always apply. Another limitation of Petty and Cacioppo's (1986a, 1986b) model is lack of specification of the cognitive activities responsible for persuasion and ultimate effects on behavior. By specifying these processes, this book is an attempt to fill this gap.

Heuristic Systematic Model

Other developments in the area of persuasion shifted focus from types of information to how information meets the goals of message recipients. Chaiken (1980) proposed that the impact of the information contained in a message depends first and foremost on the ease of processing the information. This impact also depends on the recipient's actual and desired confidence and the information's potential to increase actual confidence when there is a confidence gap.

Chaiken (1980) maintained that people are cognitive misers who first attempt to use a heuristic to arrive at a conclusion. A heuristic is a simple "if-then" rule that can be applied to make a decision. For example, recipients of a persuasive message may apply an "experts know better" heuristic and base their decisions on the expertise of the communication source. Therefore, they may process the information contained in the arguments only when a heuristic is not available or when the heuristic is unable to provide the confidence they desire. When recipients have a heuristic available and their level of desired confidence can be easily achieved by using the heuristic, they are unlikely to exert themselves to scrutinize the message arguments.

Processing ability and motivation may affect either desired or actual confidence. For example, message recipients may feel more confident while distracted, thus withdrawing efforts to understand the arguments in a message. In addition, recipients may desire to achieve a lower level of confidence while distracted. Whatever the case, how people process information depends on their confidence levels rather than on whether the information comes from the arguments or from other message cues. This line of reasoning was taken further by Kruglanski and Thompson's (1999a, 1999b) "unimodel."

Unimodel

Kruglanski and Thompson (1999a, 1999b) assumed that the use of information depends on its complexity and relevance, as well as the recipients' ability and motivation at a particular time. According to them, because any information is easier to process when presented in simple formats, both arguments and source information can vary in processing ease. In one of their studies, participants were assigned to read either long, detailed arguments advocating a tuition increase at their university, or brief, easy-to-comprehend arguments why the policy should be instituted. As hypothesized, both long arguments or long source descriptions had more influence when ability was high (vs. low). Conversely, both short arguments or short source descriptions had more influence when ability was low (vs. high).

Key to the unimodel is the assumption of a single type of cognitive process. Virtually any information can influence attitudes under both high or low processing ability and motivation. However, more complex information requires high ability and motivation regardless of whether it is arguments or source descriptions. As will be seen, this model shares assumptions with our model. Nonetheless, this model does not describe the processing stages in different situations or the way in which persuasive communications can influence behavior.

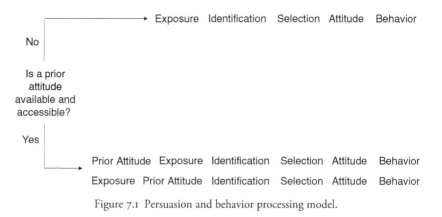

Figure 7.1 Persuasion and behavior processing model.

Persuasion and Change Model

Several decades of persuasion research have made clear that recipients of a communication actively seek and transform the information presented to them. In fact, Hovland (1959), McGuire (1968a, 1985), and Wyer (1974a) all contributed to the current understanding of the sequence of activities at play during the processing of a persuasive message. However, after reception, yielding may involve forming beliefs, attitudes, or intentions, and may depend on the actual information presented in the message and the affective reactions recipients experience for unrelated reasons (e.g., their mood at the time). Furthermore, the order of these processes may vary and affect the likely impact of the message. In this context, the model I describe in this book provides a detailed account of processing going from exposure to a persuasive communication to performing the behaviors recommended to the recipients. Below I describe the stages of processing that explain the impact of persuasive communications and behavioral interventions on attitudes and behavior.

Stages of Processing

Exposure. The exposure stage follows the definition of exposure as encompassing both exposure and comprehension in McGuire's (1968a) reception and yielding model. Exposure to persuasive communications is often de facto, as when the audience cannot avoid messages introduced through its social network or its regular news channel (Freedman & Sears, 1966). Other exposure, however, is intentional. For example, the digital media allow people to seek out specific information and specific points of view. People may select information that is useful, that they wish to learn, and that agrees with their prior attitudes (Hart et al., 2009).

With respect to comprehension, recipients understand messages and interventions that are in the language of the recipients, have a linguistic complexity appropriate for the level of education of the audience, and use language and concepts that are accessible in terms of required expertise. Features that make messages and interventions accessible to audiences include being understandable. Messages should be understandable even when the audience has low literacy and numeracy, which are respectively the ability to read written verbal materials and to execute basic mathematical functions (Sheridan et al., 2011). In research conducted by Peters, Dieckmann, Dixon, Hibbard, and Mertz (2007), low and high literacy recipients of health information about hospital quality had better comprehension when they received only essential information. Furthermore, presenting the essential information first, before other information, improved comprehension among participants with low numeracy (Peters, Dieckmann, Dixon, Hibbard, & Mertz, 2007). Using higher numbers to describe the presence of a characteristic (i.e., hospital quality; Peters et al., 2007), and presenting disease risk and treatment benefit information using the same (versus different) denominators (Garcia-Retamero & Galesic, 2009), also improve comprehension for audiences with limited numeracy. Furthermore, presenting comparative information about the harms and benefits of two drugs using tables rather than text maximizes understanding, particularly for recipients with low literacy (Tait, Voepel-Lewis, Zikmund-Fisher, & Fagerlin, 2010). Finally, pictorial information and graphic symbols can also facilitate comprehension, although some of the findings are conflicting (Sheridan et al., 2011).

Information identification and selection. People scan their environments and their own feelings and may focus on specific aspects, such as the behavioral recommendations and arguments contained in a persuasive message or the feelings they experience in a particular situation. People then select information that they perceive to be relevant to their beliefs, evaluations, or behavioral decisions.

Prior attitude retrieval. Fazio (1989) has shown that highly accessible attitudes are activated by the mere presence of the attitude object. These attitudes are generally activated automatically and can guide the selection of the messages and interventions when recipients make exposure decisions. This topic is covered in Chapter 8.

Attitude computation. Attitudes, and often beliefs, are formed on the basis of the information and feelings elicited at the time people receive a message. These attitudes may either derive from beliefs or influence beliefs, and may also affect intentions when people have behavioral goals. When prior attitudes are activated as well, computing an attitude requires integrating it with and often comparing it with the new information at hand. These processes are covered in Chapter 8.

Behavioral enactment. People may engage in specific behaviors following the recommendations contained in persuasive communications and behavioral interventions. The processes that mediate the impact of a persuasive message on behavior are described in Chapter 9.

A limitation in past research has been ignoring the **distinction between (a) persuasion to induce a new attitude or behavior and (b) persuasion to change attitudes or behaviors.** Prior models have all recognized that actual persuasion is the result of receiving and yielding to a persuasive communication. However, they have neglected to fully conceptualize the influence of prior attitudes on persuasion, even though people make decisions to seek information largely due to their existing attitudes on a topic. After all, merely anticipating what the message is about can bring prior attitudes to mind. These prior attitudes are powerful forces that guide exposure to messages, favoring messages that support the prior point of view.

My model describes different sequences of processes for attitude formation and change. As shown in the top half of Figure 7.1, when people lack a prior attitude, they may choose a message based on their interest in the source or their expectations that the message might be interesting or informative. Alternatively, they may simply encounter a message de facto (Freedman & Sears, 1966). After receiving the message, people select among available sources of information, which include the message content, the communicator or source of the message, and their affective feelings at that time.

How recipients select this information depends on their ability and motivation to think about the issues at the time. For example, we (Albarracín & Kumkale, 2003b) showed that the extraneous affect people experience has little impact on message recipients when their level of processing is high and people recognize that this affect is not relevant to the message. Extraneous affect also has little impact on message recipients when their level of processing is low enough to prevent recipients from identifying this affect through attentional processes. Thus, level of processing has a nonlinear influence on the impact of affect: The affective impact is greater when processing level is moderate (when people are able or motivated to identify it but they are unable to evaluate its relevance) than when it is either high or low. Regardless of the attitude source, when a message is actionable, these attitudes are likely to influence future intentions and behaviors.

As shown in the bottom half of Figure 7.1, cognitive and motivational processes differ when people have a prior attitude. First, the sequence of processes of attitude change (vs. formation) is longer, which according to a stochastic model should result in less impact on final attitudes and persuasion. Second, people may retrieve their prior attitude and use it as a basis for exposure decisions, which often results in people seeking congenial messages and processing these messages through the lens of their attitudes. Third, people may be incidentally or forcefully exposed to a persuasive message that in turn leads to retrieving a prior attitude. In this case, the prior attitude may influence information identification, information selection, attitude, and behavior. Chapter 8 covers my research related to selective exposure and the effects of prior attitudes and behaviors on the processing of persuasive communications and behavioral interventions.

> **Principle 17. Influence of prior attitudes and behavioral patterns on the impact of messages and interventions.** The outcomes of persuasive communications and behavioral interventions depend first and foremost on whether prior attitudes and related information are accessible at the time of receiving the message or behavioral intervention.

A related assumption is that **goals of action (to do something) control the formation and change of attitudes and behaviors.** On the one hand, the goal to respond to an object may stimulate attitude formation when one lacks a prior attitude. On the other hand, the goal to respond to an object may stimulate recall of a prior attitude when a prior attitude exists. Thus, unless there is an additional need to change one's attitude to adapt to the environment, the goal to act tends to yield attitude maintenance.

Streams of Information in Persuasion

Persuasive communications and behavioral interventions come in many forms but typically include a set of arguments, affective feelings, a communicator, and behavioral recommendations (e.g., actionability, number of recommendations). The arguments, affective feelings, and the communicator are described in the coming sections and illustrate the sources of information that are typical in persuasive communication. Behavioral recommendations are covered in Chapter 9, along with my conceptualization of the processes that lead to recipients ultimately performing a behavior.

The Arguments

The arguments contained in a message or intervention are clearly an important message factor. Argument quality has a specific role in models of persuasion, such as the elaboration-likelihood model, which conceptualizes it as message contents that influence message recipients who have the ability and motivation to think about the message (i.e., the central route to persuasion according to Petty & Cacioppo, 1986). Other message factors, such as argument length, supposedly affect persuasion even when message recipients lack the ability and motivation to think about the communication in a careful manner (Langer, Blank, & Chanowitz, 1978).

Arguments that recipients characterize as "strong" often include statistical data as opposed to anecdotal evidence (Petty & Cacioppo, 1986). Unfortunately, however, the inclusion of statistical data does not imply that the arguments contain truthful data or are logically valid. *New York Times* writer William Davies characterized the 2016 presidential campaign in the United States "The Age of Post-Truth Politics." In a similar vein, *Politico* wrote about "Donald Trump's Fictional America," and a number of intellectual streams have analyzed widespread misinformation in the general population. Most of the knowledge about the world comes from indirect sources, and "fake" news and videos abound. Therefore, verification of the premises is not always possible and message recipients must inspect sources and congruence with other information to decide what to believe. In the absence of such verification, many subjectively strong arguments lack empirical validity.

Aristotle (384–322 BC; 1938) delineated two types of valid arguments: (a) deductively valid and (b) inductively valid. An argument is deductively valid when the validity of the premises forces the conclusion to be true. An argument is inductively valid when the premises make the conclusion likely. Naive audiences rarely apply the rules of logic to the persuasive arguments they encounter. Rather, they use practical reasoning, much like the reasoning used in scientific and legal contexts. Walton, Reed, and Macagno (2008) identified 44 rules at stake in both producing and judging arguments including expert opinion, argument from example, argument from cause to effect, the sunk costs argument, argument from analogy, *ad hominem* argument, and the slippery slope argument. For example, the expert opinion argument has the following structure:

Source E is an expert in subject domain S containing proposition A.
E asserts that proposition A is true (false).

A is true (false).

Other arguments that follow practical reasoning can be analyzed in the same way and confer strength to most of the messages we encounter in daily life.

Finally, a message type that has been gaining popularity is the narrative. Narrative persuasion involves real or fictional stories that discuss target issues, or portray characters who enact what the messages recommend. Experience taking (identifying with and simulating a characters' inner experience; Kaufman & Libby, 2012) and transportation into the story (see van Laer, de Ruyter, Visconti, & Wetzels, 2014) are important mechanisms of narrative persuasion. People who are transported into the story and identify with characters internalize the message position (Beentjes et al., 2012; De Graaf et al., 2009; Green, 2006; Mazzocco et al., 2010; Niederdeppe, Heley, & Barry, 2015), in part because the narrative facilitates attention to the message and elaboration of its contents (Igartua & Barrios, 2012; Slater & Rouner, 2002).

Despite our logical and practical reasoning abilities, message recipients are unfortunately gullible. For example, online exposure to user-generated content on YouTube shapes young people's perceptions of tobacco (Bromberg, Augustson, & Backinger, 2012; Carroll, Shensa, & Primack, 2013; Elkin, Thomson, & Wilson, 2010; Forsyth & Malone, 2010; Freeman, 2012; Hong & Cody, 2002; Luo et al., 2013; Paek et al., 2014; Peters & Kashima, 2015; Richardson & Vallone, 2014; Seidenberg et al., 2012). There are at least three reasons why YouTube influences attitudes. First, there are large quantities of tobacco-related messages on YouTube (Bromberg, Augustson, & Backinger, 2012; Carroll, Shensa, & Primack, 2013; Elkin, Thomson, & Wilson, 2010; Forsyth & Malone, 2010; Freeman & Chapman, 2007; K. Kim, Paek, & Lynn, 2010; Luo et al., 2013; Paek et al., 2014; Richardson & Vallone, 2014; Seidenberg et al., 2012), with more messages presenting favorable than unfavorable views on tobacco (Bromberg, Augustson, & Backinger, 2012; Carroll, Shensa, & Primack, 2013; Elkin, Thomson, & Wilson, 2010; Forsyth & Malone, 2010; Freeman & Chapman, 2007; K. Kim, Paek, & Lynn, 2010; Luo et al., 2013; Paek et al., 2014; Richardson & Vallone, 2014; Seidenberg et al., 2012). Second, YouTube has more than 1 billion users who collectively watch hundreds of millions of hours of video per day (YouTube, n.d.), and is the favorite website for more than half of today's teenagers (Wasserman, 2013).

We experimentally examined whether YouTube videos create favorable attitudes toward featured tobacco products by comparing attitudes with a control group that viewed a video unrelated to tobacco. We also measured attitudes toward cigarette smoking. We focused on four different tobacco products: (a) chewing tobacco, (b) e-cigarettes, (c) hookahs, and (d) pipe smoking. Four highly viewed messages that independent coders judged to be low in credibility were presented online to a sample of 18- to 24-year-olds (final $N = 350$) with varied prior use of tobacco products. This selection of low-credibility messages allowed for the most stringent test of the consequences of seemingly harmless amateur videos posted on YouTube. Results indicated that the videos about e-cigarettes and hookahs yielded more positive attitudes toward the respective products than did the control video or the video about pipe smoking. Also, the video about pipe smoking led to more positive attitudes toward cigarette smoking than all other videos, supporting the idea that audiences are rather uncritical of obviously dubious contents presented by noncredible communicators.

Extraneous Affect and Specific Emotions Like Fear

Affective or emotional feelings are a primary basis for attitudes. For instance, people might believe that the chance of winning the lottery is low but still feel like purchasing a ticket each time they enter a gas station. In these situations, their feelings toward the object can override their beliefs about it and thus play a dominant role in shaping behavior. In addition to the feelings elicited by the attitude object itself, affect elicited by other relevant sources, such as experiencing a happy or sad mood, can also influence attitudes (Schwarz & Clore, 2007). Experimentally induced irrelevant affect influences judgments about products (Pham, 1998), personal risks (Gasper & Clore, 2000), and politics (Forgas & Bower, 1987). These effects, however, occur only when people are unaware of the true source of their feelings (Gasper & Clore, 2000).

One of the more investigated emotional factors in the area of persuasion and behavioral interventions is fear (for other specific emotions, see Graton, Ric, & Gonzalez, 2016; Skurka, Niederdeppe, & Romero-Canyas, 2018). Fear appeals are attempts to arouse fear by highlighting a threat or danger to promote a behavior (Dillard, Plotnick, Godbold, Freimuth, & Edgar, 1996; Maddux & Rogers, 1983). My colleagues and I (Tannenbaum et al., 2015) meta-analyzed the effects of fear appeals and found an overall moderate and significant effect on a combination of attitudes, intentions, and behaviors. Clearly, interventions benefit from eliciting emotional responses that are relevant to the recommended behavior.

Our meta-analyses of fear appeals found that the effects of fear vary as a function of behaviors and samples. For example, fear worked better for messages targeting behaviors circumscribed in time, like MMR (Measles, Mumps, and Rubella) vaccination, more than it did for messages targeting lifetime behaviors like exercise (d = 0.43 vs. 0.21). Fear was also more effective in collectivistic cultures than in individualistic ones (d = 0.47 vs. 0.26).

The effects of fear also varied as a function of topic. As shown in Table 7.1, fear appeals had smaller effects in the domains of dental hygiene,

Table 7.1 *Effect of fear appeals as a function of message topic*

Topic	d	95% CI	k
Dental hygiene	0.06	−0.16, 0.28	14
Driving safety	0.11	−0.10, 0.33	27
HIV/STDs	0.37	0.20, 0.54	33
Drinking/drugs	0.49	0.25, 0.74	20
Smoking	0.26	0.13, 0.40	40
Cancer prevention	0.16	−0.01, 0.34	26
Disease prevention	0.40	0.19, 0.61	51
General safety	0.22	0.03, 0.40	13
Environment/society	0.24	0.02, 0.45	13
Other	0.39	0.11, 0.68	11

driving safety, smoking, as well as general and environmental safety, as opposed to drinking and drug use, HIV/STIs, and disease prevention. Also, fear appeals that discuss the susceptibility of the audience had higher impact than those that discuss the severity of the problem (e.g., how grave symptoms are and number of deaths) (d = 0.43 vs. 0.23). As described by protection motivation theory, stating that the recommended behavior is efficacious produced more change than not doing so (d = 0.43 vs. 0.21). However, contrary to the claim that moderate fear is better than high fear (Hovland, Janis, & Kelley, 1953), there was no evidence of any curvilinear effect. Both moderate and high levels of fear led to stronger effects than low fear but did not differ from each other.

We (Albarracín et al., 2005) also examined the influence of fear in a meta-analysis of the effects of fear arguments in the context of interventions to increase condom use. This meta-analysis compared the effects of introducing or not introducing fear along with a variety of other strategies. In contrast to our meta-analysis of the experimental fear literature (Tannenbaum et al., 2015), including fear arguments in these more complex interventions was less efficacious than not including them (d = 0.35 vs. 0.14; for comparison, control group d = 0.08, 95% CI = 0.06 to 0.10). The two exceptions were fear arguments in samples with an average age under 21 and interventions without behavioral skills training. In those two instances, including fear arguments made no difference.

The differences between fear in the simple verbal messages tested in laboratory experiments and synthesized in Tannenbaum et al. (2015) and fear in the more complex behavioral interventions in Albarracín et al. (2005) is intriguing. First, the audience of a health intervention typically knows it is at risk for a disease. Therefore, introducing fear takes them away from the mindset of implementing the recommended behavior. Second, the audience of a health intervention is typically not able to carry out fairly complex behaviors like reducing alcohol and drug use in sexual contexts or negotiating condom use. Therefore, the introduction of fear when recipients are trying to acquire these skills can lead them to interpret the fear they experience as lack of confidence in their ability to perform the recommended behaviors. Both of these possibilities received support because fear was counterproductive when audiences had higher risk (e.g., in clinical settings) and when the interventions included behavioral skills training. In contrast, the effect of fear was null when these conditions were not met.

The Communicator or Source

As practical argumentation shows, the source or communicator is often used to judge how sound an argument is. However, source effects have received much attention in the literature and are often manipulated independently of the arguments. Some of the characteristics of communicators include expertise and similarity to the recipient, which affect trust in the competence and benevolence of the source. Generally, experts have been deemed more effective in experimental work on persuasion, whereas naive peers have been deemed more effective in behavioral intervention work. My collaborators and I thus contrasted experts with peers and sources who are similar to the message recipients with sources who are not (Durantini et al., 2006).

Many interventions have relied on the use of community members to spread new behavioral practices in a community. A fascinating study using peers was conducted by Kelly et al. (2002). The researchers applied the principle that innovations would spread through the network. They demonstrated that tightly knit groups like gay men in the South benefit from changing the attitudes of popular opinion leaders and using these individuals to transmit their attitudes to others (diffusion of innovation; Kelly et al., 1991, 1992). This creative approach was adopted by Fisher, Fisher, Bryan, and Misovich (2002), also in the HIV-prevention domain. In this latter work, participants were over 1,500 inner-city high school students from Connecticut. The study compared a teacher-delivered intervention, a peer-delivered intervention, a teacher-plus-peer-delivered intervention, and a control group. The teacher intervention attempted to increase knowledge, attitudes, norms, HIV threat, and skills to implement condom use. The format was relatively standard and the intervention was delivered in class. The peer intervention followed Kelly's (1992) natural opinion leader model. Kids from the target schools were recruited and provided with distinctive shirts. Schools were also decorated in ways that matched the shirts. Posters displayed the SWAAT acronym, designating the peers as "Students Working Against AIDS Together." Each of the kids recruited into the project was asked to discuss safe sex and teach behavioral skills to five other kids over the course of 3 weeks. Findings are shown in Figure 7.2 and revealed that the peer-led intervention was more effective at increasing condom use at a 3-month follow-up. However, the classroom intervention was more effective than the peer intervention at a 1-year follow-up. The superiority of the teacher-led intervention suggests that, at least in some conditions, the effect of experts is superior to the effect of lay peers. The reason is that, over a period of a year, the sources themselves probably contradicted their own recommendations and were seen as hypocritical instead of as credible.

In a meta-analysis (Durantini et al., 2006), my colleagues and I investigated the associations between source characteristics, including

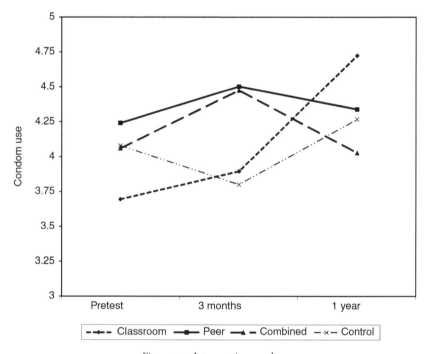

Figure 7.2 Intervention results.

similarity between the source and the recipient, and the recipients' actual behavioral change after the interventions. This work compared two hypotheses. On the one hand, some researchers have argued that persuasive communications (and therefore behavioral interventions) should use experts as sources (Hovland, Janis, & Kelley, 1953). On the other hand, other researchers have favored the use of laypersons selected from the target community (Freire & da Veiga Coutinho, 1972; Putnam, 1993).

By dividing interventions into ones presented by experts (e.g., public health educators, physicians, nurses, research staff) and ones presented by lay community members (i.e., community leaders, artists, religious ministers), our meta-analysis (Durantini et al., 2006) could establish what type of source was more effective and for whom. Findings indicated that expert sources were more effective than lay community members for most populations (see Figure 7.3). There were, however, two exceptions. For teens, lay community members were more effective. For European Americans, both types of sources were equally effective. In addition, the results from this review revealed that experts were more effective, particularly for populations that typically have restricted power in society. That is, the beneficial impact of having an expert source was much stronger for ethnic minorities and women than for ethnic majorities and men.

It is also important for experts to share some of the characteristics of the audience. Not only are women and ethnic minorities more sensitive to the expertise of the communicator than are men and ethnic majorities, they are more responsive to sources who share whatever characteristic makes an audience different from the mainstream. That is, women change more in response to other women, and ethnic minorities changed more in response to other ethnic minorities. Moreover, most populations at risk for HIV (injection drug users, multiple-partner heterosexuals, low condom users) benefited from having both an expert and somebody at risk as intervention facilitators.

Information Identification and Selection Processes

Message recipients must identify or direct attention to potential information that is available at the time and assess the extent to which this information is relevant to the judgment they are about to make. These identification and selection processes appear in Figure 7.4 and determine which source of information ultimately shapes behavior. Neither the arguments contained in a message nor extraneous affect can bias inferences unless people first identify or direct attention to them. After the

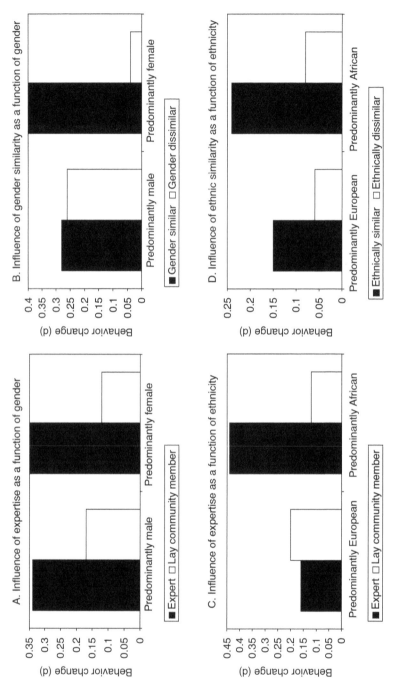

Figure 7.3 Effects of source expertise for different populations.

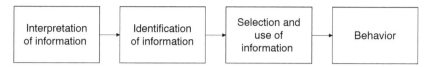

Figure 7.4 Identification and selection model.

information is selected, people may use it as a basis for various judgments. These judgments include beliefs, attitudes, and intentions regarding a particular behavior.

As mentioned before, decreases in ability and motivation disrupt the identification and selection of the information, as well as the judgments based on this information. That is, people attend to the information more effectively when they have the ability and motivation to think about it than when they do not. Moreover, decreases in ability and motivation should first affect the processing of information that is more difficult to identify. For example, greater decreases in ability and motivation may be necessary to disrupt identification of the message arguments than to disrupt identification of affect and emotions, which are more immediate (Albarracín, 2002).

The identification and selection processes imply directing attention to pieces of information and selecting them as bases for judgment. Imagine that the recipients of an ad must make a behavior decision. The probability of recipients identifying the arguments mentioned in the ad increases with the salience of the message information (Higgins, 1996; Wyer & Srull, 1989). The probability of recipients identifying their affective reactions increases with the intensity of affective feelings at any given time. These processes typically unfold without awareness, although they can also operate under conscious monitoring (see Smith, 1994).

In general, the effects of ability and motivation on the likelihood of *identifying* each type of information should be similar across different types of information. That is, decreases in ability and motivation may decrease attention to the content of a persuasive message as well as to extraneous affect (for related claims, see Gilbert & Hixon, 1991). However, different types of information may be selected at different rates. Some information may be *selected* more often than other because it is perceived as more relevant. Relevance is the perceived appropriateness of the information to reach a given conclusion.

In combination, the mechanisms of information identification and selection imply that decreases in ability and motivation are likely to reduce the influence of the arguments contained in the message in a monotonic fashion. Generally, a decrease in the likelihood of identifying and establishing the relevance of persuasive arguments should decrease their impact. However, the influence of ability and motivation on the use of other information, such as extraneous affective reactions, can be curvilinear. That is, moderate decreases in ability and motivation may increase the influence of less relevant cues by preventing assessment of the information relevance, which happens to be low. However, further decreases in ability and motivation may prevent information identification. Such further decreases may thus reduce the influence of subjectively irrelevant information, such as extraneous affect.

In my research described presently, message recipients could base their judgment on the arguments contained in the message and on the extraneous affect they experienced at the time. Naturally, the arguments of the persuasive message were likely to appear more relevant than the extraneous affect. We (Albarracín, 2002; Albarracín & Kumkale, 2003a; Handley et al., 2009) induced participants to experience a positive or negative mood and to read a strong or weak persuasive message about the institution of comprehensive exams. To examine the consequences of ability and motivation, we independently varied both the personal relevance of the message and the distraction participants experienced at the time they read it. The motivation conditions involved either low or high distraction induced via environmental noise. The motivation conditions involved a policy that would either affect participants or would not. We were able to observe if these manipulations had linear or nonmonotonic effects on the influence of extraneous affect and argument strength.

Our conceptualization appears in Figure 7.5. We hypothesized that extraneous affect is unlikely to bias judgments unless people identify or direct attention to it when making a judgment. There are three conditions that may allow people to identify their feelings as a potential source of information. First, people who have both ability and motivation to think about their affective reactions should identify these reactions with ease. Second, recipients who are distracted by environmental information may need considerable motivation to assess their affective states but may nevertheless do so successfully. Third, recipients who have the ability may identify their affective reactions even in the absence of motivation, as attentional resources may be sufficient to do so (see, e.g., Schwarz & Clore, 2007). In other words, having either or both ability and motivation may facilitate identification.

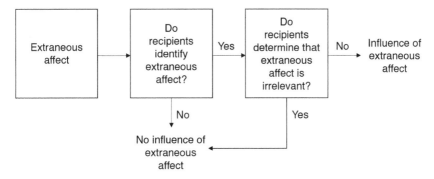

Figure 7.5 Selection and identification of affect in persuasion.

According to our model, however, identification is not sufficient for information to have an influence. Using the information is likely to depend on judging it as relevant. For example, people's attempts to determine the relevance of their experienced affect are likely to be more successful when they have ability and motivation to think about the information than when they do not. Consequently, when recipients have ability and motivation, they are likely to discount extraneous affect as a legitimate basis for their attitudes. However, when able recipients have low motivation, they may perform this analysis less carefully and misperceive the advocacy as the extraneous source of their feelings. Similarly, motivated participants with low ability may fail to discount extraneous affect because of a disruption of the selection process.

The data from the first two experiments we (Albarracín, 2002; Albarracín & Kumkale, 2003) conducted are summarized in Figure 7.6. After reading a message advocating comprehensive exams, participants reported their attitudes, their perception that the policy would lead to the outcomes described in the message (i.e., outcome beliefs), and their evaluations of these outcomes. They also reported their beliefs and evaluations of outcomes that recipients of the messages were likely to generate spontaneously on the basis of prior knowledge. Intentions and actual straw votes in support of the policy were also measured in some of the experiments. As shown by mean attitude differences in Figure 7.2, the influence of affect was greatest when either ability or motivation was low but not when both were low or both were high.

The data from this experiment also revealed that the influence of argument strength decreased linearly along with motivation and ability. That is, argument strength had an influence when either or both ability or motivation were high. However, argument strength had no influence when ability and motivation were both low. This finding suggests that message recipients in low ability and motivation conditions failed to form attitudes on the basis of information available at the time. Supplementary analyses suggested that this inability was present even when participants had encoded the arguments in the message. Specifically, participants had used arguments as a basis for outcome beliefs and evaluations but these cognitions had not been integrated into attitudes.

In sum, people's ability and motivation at the time they receive a persuasive message have a curvilinear impact on the influence of irrelevant affect and a linear impact on the influence of argument strength. An analysis of other findings (Albarracín, 2002; Albarracín & Kumkale, 2003) leads to the same conclusion. In an earlier experiment (Experiment 1 of Albarracín, 1997) report, all participants had 5 min to read the message (short time) and received the communication in conditions of either low or high ability (i.e., high or low distraction at the time of the message presentation). However, in this experiment, motivation was confounded with ability. That is, participants in high-ability conditions were told that they would have to take the exams if instituted (high motivation), whereas participants in conditions of low ability were told that they would not have to take the exams if instituted (low motivation). In other work (Albarracín & Wyer, 2001), we induced moderate motivation by telling participants that they would have to vote in a referendum to decide on the institution of comprehensive exams, although they would not have to take the exams if the policy were instituted. Moreover, in this series, the time participants had to read the message was 5 min in Experiment 1 (short time) and 10 min in Experiment 3 (long time). Because of the different time allocations and the different levels of motivation across the three experiments, the combination of these data also offers three levels of amount of thought.

The arrangement of conditions from the three experiments along the continuum of amount of thought appears in Table 7.2. The high level of thought comprises (a) the high-ability condition of Albarracín's (1997) Experiment 1 (high motivation, short time), (b) the high-ability condition in Albarracín and Wyer's (2001) Experiment 1 (moderate motivation, short time), and (c) the high-ability condition of Albarracín and Wyer's (2001) Experiment 3 (moderate motivation, long time). The moderate level of thought includes (a) the low-ability condition of Albarracín and Wyer's (2001) Experiment 1 (moderate motivation, short time) and (b) the low-ability condition of Albarracín and Wyer's (2001) Experiment 3 (moderate motivation, long time). The low-ability condition of Albarracín's (1997) Experiment 1 represents the low level of thought (low motivation, short time). A summary of the effects of affect and argument strength across these three levels appears in the second and third sections of Table 7.2. The mean differences show that the influence of amount of thought on the impact of argument strength was linear, whereas the influence of affect was quadratic. However, such a pattern may not become apparent when researchers manipulate ability and motivation over only two levels (Avnet & Higgins, 2006; Petty & Cacioppo, 1986a).

We (Albarracín, 2002; Albarracín & Kumkale, 2003) validated our interpretation of our findings by means of directly manipulating the processes that are theoretically involved. We induced a mood in an independent group of participants and then presented the persuasive messages used in Experiment 1 of the same series. Motivation was kept constant at a low level and ability was varied over two levels (high vs. low). According to the model in Figure 7.5, participants in the low-motivation–high-ability conditions should identify but not discount their affective reactions, which should result in evidence of affective bias in those conditions. In contrast, participants in conditions of low ability and motivation should be unable to identify the affect they experience when they read the communication. In turn, this inability should result in a lack of impact of affect.

The critical change in Albarracín and Kumkale's (2003) Experiment 3, however, was the introduction of instructions to manipulate the amount of affect-relevant thought by participants at the time of receiving the message. We told some participants to read the message while trying to become sensitive to the affect and emotions they experienced at the time and to attempt to separate their mood from their reactions to the persuasive communication. This manipulation was expected to accelerate the processes spontaneously performed by participants. Therefore, when ability is high and motivation is low, participants who are forced to think about their affect may be able to discount their affective reactions because they are already able to identify these reactions. In contrast, when both ability and motivation are low, being forced to focus on affective reactions may enable participants to identify their mood but may not be sufficient to induce discounting (for other conditions leading to affect identification, see Lu & Sinha, 2017).

The data from Experiment 3 are summarized in Tables 7.2 and 7.3 and provide strong support for the model in Figure 7.5. Participants with high ability and low motivation who were instructed to attend to their affect were

Table 7.2 *Effects of affect and argument strength on attitudes (Adapted from Albarracín, 2002)*

Conditions	Level or amount of thought		
	High	Moderate	Low
Arrangement of conditions along thought continuum			
Albarracín's (1997; short time) Experiment 1			
High ability (high motivation)	x	–	–
Low ability (low motivation)	–	–	x
Albarracín and Wyer's (2001) Experiment 1 (short time; moderate motivation)			
High ability	x	–	–
Low ability	–	x	–
Albarracín and Wyer's (2001) Experiment 3 (long time; moderate motivation)			
High ability	x	–	–
Low ability	–	x	–
Effect of affect			
Albarracín's (1997; short time) Experiment 1			
High ability (high motivation)	–0.40	–	–
Low ability (low motivation)	–	–	0.20
Albarracín and Wyer's (2001) Experiment 1 (short time; moderate motivation)			
High ability	–0.73	–	–
Low ability	–	1.79*	–
Albarracín and Wyer's (2001) Experiment 3 (long time; moderate motivation)			
High ability	–0.28	–	–
Low ability	–	1.16*	–
Effect of argument strength			
Albarracín's (1997; short time) Experiment 1			
High ability (high motivation)	1.50*	–	–
Low ability (low motivation)	–	–	0.3
Albarracín and Wyer's (2001) Experiment 1 (short time; moderate motivation)			
High ability	2.61*	–	–
Low ability	–	0.62	–
Albarracín and Wyer's (2001) Experiment 3 (long time; moderate motivation)			
High ability	1.05*	–	–
Low ability	–	1.10*	–

Note: Table entries are mean differences representing the influence of affect and argument strength. The effect of affect is represented with the difference between attitudes when affect was positive and attitudes when affect was negative. The effect of argument strength is inferred from the difference between attitudes when the presented arguments were strong and attitudes when the presented arguments were weak. An "x" indicates the amount of thought a given condition represents.
$^{*}p < 0.05.$

no longer influenced by affect. In contrast, participants with low ability and motivation who received the instructions became influenced by affect.

As suggested by the unimodel and by my research on information identification and selection, most information has equal chances of being identified as long ability and motivation are sufficient. Kruglanski and his colleagues (Kruglanski & Thompson, 1999a, 1999b) argued that a single process governs the formation of subjective knowledge, including attitudes. Forming an attitude is a process of hypothesis testing and inference. It is influenced by (a) the structure of the evidence presented, (b) the cognitive ability affecting inferential activity, and (c) the motivational factors impacting the extent and direction of information processing. According to these researchers, elements of the message itself (e.g., quality, complexity, and humor), the information source (e.g., credibility, attractiveness, and speech), and context variables or environmental cues (e.g., ambient noise, lighting, and message modality) can all be relevant to the conclusion that a person makes about an issue.

As explained before, one factor that equalizes the relevance of source information and message arguments is the length of the passages describing these factors. In a study by Pierro, Mannetti, Erb, Spiegel, and Kruglanski (2005), college students were presented with arguments about comprehensive exams. Some of the participants were told that the exams would be implemented during or after their time at the university. Thus, this manipulation created either a high or a low level of personal relevance. In addition, the source of the message (i.e., "Mr. Davide Biancato") was

Table 7.3 *Effects of ability and instructional set on the influence of affect on attitudes: Experiment 3 (low motivation)*

Condition	Positive affect	Negative affect	Difference
High ability			
Control	0.6	−0.7	1.3*
Affect focus	−0.7	0.3	−1.0
Low ability			
Control	−0.1	0.1	−0.2
Affect focus	0.3	−1.2	1.5*

Note: Differences represent the influence of affect on attitudes. They were derived by subtracting mean attitudes when affect was negative from mean attitudes when affect was positive.
*$p < 0.05$.
Source: Adapted from Albarracín and Kumkale (2003).

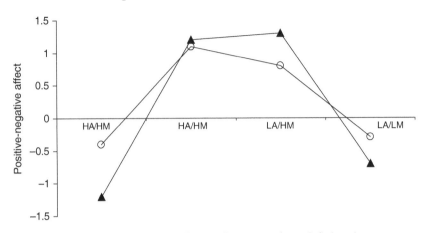

Figure 7.6 Influence of affect in Albarracín and Kumkale (2003).

introduced as an expert in testing and assessment (high-credibility condition) or as an expert in fitness and physical coordination (low-credibility condition). Finally, the expertise information was also either long (a page) or short (50 words).

The influence of the source depended on both its length and the participants' motivation. Brief descriptions had more influence when participants had low motivation to process the message and thus relied exclusively on those descriptions. When motivation was high, however, long descriptions had the same impact as the communication arguments.

One important question is why brief descriptions of the source have an influence even when ability is low. Pierro, Mannetti, Kruglanski, and Sleeth-Keppler (2004) conducted work to answer this very question. They argued that message recipients who have low motivation to think about the communication are likely to settle for whatever relevant cue appears first in the communication (see Chaiken, 1980). Thus, they are likely to ignore the message arguments when the arguments follow the source description. In contrast, recipients who have high motivation are likely to first process the implications of the cue (in this case the source information) but continue processing the information afterward. Thus, if the cue is followed by the arguments and the arguments are more relevant than the cue, then the arguments should override the earlier influence of the cue. As a result, participants with high ability may show an influence of the arguments but not of the cue. The authors' research manipulating the relevance of two ordered sets of information supported this possibility.

Importantly, assessment of the information relevance should be only one of the stages involved in processing a persuasive communication. Given the identification and selection model, the influence of relevant information should be monotonically disrupted by decreases in processing ability and motivation. For example, it may take some ability to comprehend the implications of a source description and even greater ability to decide if this information is relevant. Identifying and assessing the relevance of this information should each increase its impact on persuasion. In contrast, processing ability and motivation have been shown to have a nonmonotonic impact on the influence of subjectively irrelevant information. As a result, increases in ability and motivation may increase the use of that information as long as these factors are not high enough to facilitate discounting on the basis of irrelevance. This notion is summarized in the following principle:

> **Principle 18. Impact of ability and motivation on identification, selection, and impact.** The impact of a specific type of information depends on criteria of information relevance as well as the ability and motivation to judge this relevance. Increases in ability and motivation produce a linear influence of information deemed relevant but an inverted-U influence of information deemed irrelevant.

In sum, people use the information received at the time a message or intervention is presented as a basis for their attitudes and beliefs and evaluations. However, the way in which they select it depends on their ability to pay attention to it and the subjective relevance of this information. Highly relevant information is most impactful when people have the ability and motivation to identify it and assess its relevance. In contrast, less relevant information such as extraneous affect is most impactful when people have sufficient ability and motivation to identify but not sufficient ability and motivation to identify to discount it.

Differences in the Impact of Persuasion in Attitude Formation and Change Contexts

Also key to this book, accessing one's prior attitude is a key deterrent of persuasion in attitude change contexts. Because past attitudes are a highly diagnostic criteria for current evaluations, people who can retrieve them can make judgments without further cognitive work. After all, existing attitudes provide a "ready aid" for evaluating the attitude object the next time one faces the object (Driscoll, Blascovich, & Fazio, 1992; Fazio, Maio,

& Olson, 2000; Shavitt, 1989). Thus, although I propose that identification and selection processes are relevant when recipients *change* their prior attitudes, they are insufficient to explain the impact of persuasive communications in attitude change contexts. Message recipients can use their prior attitudes and related information as a standard of comparison and engage in either perceptual or inferential validation processes. Prior attitudes and associated beliefs also guide processing of a message or intervention in ways that make the impact of messages about prior attitudes dramatically smaller than the impact of messages concerning new issues.

Differences in the impact of the message arguments. The dramatic effect of having a prior attitude is clear in the domain of misinformation correction. Misinformation on consequential subjects includes claims that affect health behaviors and voting decisions. For instance, the rumor that genetically modified mosquitoes caused the Zika virus outbreak in Brazil is misinformation, a claim unsupported by scientific evidence (Chan et al., 2017). Despite retraction of the scholarly article claiming a causal link between autism and the measles, mumps, and rubella (MMR) vaccine, some people are still convinced of this unfounded claim (Chan et al., 2017). Others continue to believe that there were weapons of mass destruction in Iraq prior to the US invasion in 2003, a belief that should be undercut by the fact that none was found there after the invasion (Chan et al., 2017).

My colleagues and I (Chan et al., 2017) meta-analyzed the experimental literature of misinformation correction in news types of settings. The overall effects are presented in Table 7.4. Our synthesis revealed large effects for presenting misinformation (ds = 2.41–3.08), for correction (ds = 1.14–1.33), and for persistence of misinformation following the correction (ds = 0.75–1.06). Also, there was less correction and more persistence when audiences generated reasons in support of the initial misinformation at the time they received it.

The greater impact of communications for new than known topics is also apparent in the effects of informal messages on social media. For example, a meta-analysis of 1,532 effect sizes across 96 studies covered 40 platforms and 26 product categories (Rosario et al., 2016). On average, electronic word of mouth was positively correlated with sales (r = 0.09), but its effectiveness differed across platform, product, and metric factors. The association of electronic word of mouth and sales was stronger for the sales of new products than that of mature products (r = 0.13 and 0.07, respectively).

Table 7.4 *Results of effect size estimates*

	Random-effects model			
	k	$d.$	95% CI	τ^2
Misinformation	16	3.08	2.02–4.15	4.48 (1.66)
Debunking	30	1.14	0.68–1.61	1.65 (0.44)
Misinformation-persistence	42	0.97	0.60–1.35	1.46 (0.33)
Misinformation	14	2.46	1.73–3.19	1.87 (0.77)
Misinformation-persistence	40	0.75	0.50–1.00	0.60 (0.14)

Note: k = number of samples; $d.$ = mean Hedges's d; 95% CI = 95 percent confidence interval; Q = Cochran's Q test; τ^2 = estimated amount of total heterogeneity (and standard error); I^2 = level of between-sample heterogeneity. Random-effects model with weights used standardized N residuals as weights.
Source: Adapted from Chan et al. (2017).

Differences in the impact of source information. When prior attitudes are not available, individuals may construct new ones on the basis of their prior knowledge or information presented in a message. For instance, students may derive an attitude toward a specific type of exam (e.g., comprehensive exams) from their knowledge about and attitudes toward other exams. They may also conclude that a new type of exam is in their best interest when a credible source says so or when a message presents sound arguments. This latter effect, however, is more likely to take place when recipients have no prior attitude about comprehensive exams.

A meta-analysis we (Kumkale, Albarracín, & Seignourel, 2010) conducted actually tested the hypothesis that the effects of source credibility are more pronounced when people lack prior attitudes, prior knowledge about the topic, or both. We selected 46 data sets in which participants received a persuasive communication from credible and noncredible sources, and examined the influence of source credibility on participants' attitudes and beliefs after the communication.

Table 7.5 presents the results relevant to these analyses, organized by whether or not participants had a prior attitude toward the topic (left and right panels) and by the levels of prior knowledge in a particular sample. As can be seen, the effect of source credibility was greater when recipients had neither initial attitudes nor prior knowledge on the issue discussed in the message (d = 0.75) than when either or both prior knowledge was low or prior attitudes were present (ds between 0.24 and 0.46).

Table 7.5 *Meta-analysis of the effects of prior knowledge and prior attitudes on the impact of source expertise to compare the magnitude of persuasion in attitude formation and attitude change conditions*

	Prior knowledge	Prior attitudes
Prior knowledge	Absent	Present
Low	0.75	0.33
High	0.46	0.24

Note: Entries are *d*s = mean attitudes or beliefs immediately after the communication when the source was credible minus when the source was not.
Source: Adapted from Kumkale et al. (2010).

The Impact of Action Goals on the Formation and Change of Attitudes and the Initiation and Change of Behavioral Procedures

Attitude formation and change. Action and inaction goals have intriguing, divergent implications for attitude formation and change. Because action goals require an attitude, they facilitate attitude formation in some cases but attitudes retrieval in others. We (Albarracín & Handley, 2007) tested these predictions in a series of experiments using goal priming. Over two experiments, we first primed goals with a word completion task containing either action- or inaction-connoting words. Participants then received negative or positive information about a topic that was familiar or unfamiliar to them. Participants in attitude change conditions had received positive information about a fictitious grain and thus had formed a prior, positive attitude; for them, the second, negative message countered those prior attitudes. Participants in attitude formation conditions had not received any prior information and saw the countermessage *tabula rasa*. As predicted, the impact of the second message in the attitude formation condition was greater in action (vs. inaction) goal conditions. In contrast, the impact of the second message in the attitude change condition was greater in inaction (vs. action) goal conditions.

When it comes to prior attitudes, priming general action and inaction goals has been shown to moderate the ease with which attitudes are reported. In a relevant study (Albarracín & Handley, 2011, Experiment 11), participants received action and inaction primes and then were asked questions about their attitudes toward abortion. Results indicated that attitudes were reported significantly faster when participants received action primes than when they received inaction primes (*M*s = 2.54 vs. 3.71 s). Importantly, this effect was independent of the extremity of the prior attitudes and general response speed. Moreover, the effect occurred because participants were forewarned about the topic of the upcoming message. Thus, in Experiment 2 of the same series, we manipulated forewarning such that some participants expected the message and others did not. Participants who were forewarned about gun control reported their attitudes toward gun control more rapidly when action was primed than when inaction was primed (*M*s = 1.96 vs. 3.99 s). However, participants who were forewarned about the control topic of euthanasia showed similar speed when they reported attitudes toward gun control (*M*s = 2.77 vs. 2.46 s), which presumably had not been retrieved due to lack of forewarning.

We (Albarracín & Handley, 2011) followed up these experiments by examining if retrieving prior attitudes in response to the action prime decreased the probability of being influenced by a persuasive message countering those attitudes. For example, in Experiment 3 of the same series, we measured attitudes after participants received the primes and then again after they were presented with a counterattitudinal message about vegetarianism. Analyses of change scores as a function of prime revealed less attitude change in the direction of the message following action (vs. inaction) primes (*M*s = 0.31 vs. 1.34), respectively. Another experiment (Experiment 5) provided further evidence that participants in inaction conditions had processed the message more than participants in action conditions. Specifically, the attitude difference between strong and weak arguments was significant in the inaction prime conditions but not in action prime conditions.

Importantly, performing a goal-directed activity should release the energy initially mobilized by the goal (Shah, Friedman, & Kruglanski, 2002; Shah & Kruglanski, 2000). In the case of general action and inaction goals, any activity perceived as action or inaction has the potential to satisfy these goals. For instance, if people who set an action goal construe a specific movement as an action, this movement may satisfy the action goal. By the same token, if people who set an inaction goal construe a behavior as rest, resting may satisfy the inaction goal. Consequently, general action or inaction primes may combine with physical movement or rest to produce conditions of satisfied and unsatisfied action and inaction goals.[1]

---

[1] These effects of physical movement and rest, however, should not be apparent unless researchers can induce *general* action and inaction goals. Without the setting of general goals, any incidental movement or rest is unlikely to produce these effects. People may set specific action and inaction goals that are satisfied *only* by a correspondingly specific activity. For example, if they decide to go

To test these predictions, we conducted an experiment (Experiment 7) in which participants with negative attitudes toward vegetarianism received a countermessage after the priming task. In addition to priming either action or inaction goals, we introduced a task that could satisfy either action or inaction goals. Some participants were asked to perform a physical action (doodling or making a paper plane) for a short amount of time, whereas others were asked to simply rest on their seats for the same amount of time. By crossing the goal and the actual action, we determined that the satisfaction of the goal reduced the effects observed for unsatisfied goals. Specifically, satisfied action goals as well as unsatisfied inaction goals produced greater attitude change than did unsatisfied action goals and satisfied inaction goals.

In sum, these experiments provided support for the possibility that general action goals increase attitude maintenance whereas inaction goals increase attitude change. Furthermore, performing an unrelated task that could satisfy the action or inaction goal reversed the earlier findings. This result suggested that the effects of general goals were motivational and ceased when the goals were satisfied. In addition, the effects of the general goals were apparent only when prior attitudes were highly accessible due to practice using these attitudes.

Yet another experiment from that series (Experiment 6) validated the assumption that *accessible* attitudes are most reluctant to change when action goals are in place. All participants had favorable attitudes toward vegetarianism at the beginning of the study. Half of them were then presented with a variety of food coupons with instructions to select some to take with them. The other half of the participants performed a filler task. The food-coupon-practice condition should facilitate attitude mainten-ance by eliciting attitude retrieval in response to action goals. As predicted, action goals led to attitude maintenance when people had accessible prior attitudes. All in all, these results support the following principle:

Principle 19. Effects of action and inaction goals on attitudinal forma-tion and change, as well as behavioral initiation and change. All else being equal, action goals increase attitudinal formation and behavioral initiation but reduce attitudinal and behavioral change.

There are situations, however, in which generalized action goals could trigger change instead of maintenance. For example, a person who mildly

---

running, running is necessary to satisfy the goal. In these situations, other movements are unlikely to satisfy the goal of running. Hence, mere movement should have no effect.

favors a political candidate may intend to vote in favor of the candidate, without planning to donate money for the candidate's campaign. In this context, developing a more polarized positive attitude facilitates various actions (donation in addition to voting). If this is so, action goals may increase the impact of new positive information about the candidate and yield attitude polarization. Similarly, if attitude polarization improves execution of a behavior, action tendencies could also yield polarization. For instance, changing from ambivalent to decisive attitudes may decrease hesitation. Consequently, people with action goals may change ambivalent attitudes.

Harmon-Jones, Harmon-Jones, and Levy (2015) actually developed similar ideas as part of an action-orientation model to understand cognitive dissonance. They attempted to explain why experiencing conflict when making a decision leads to various strategies to reduce the conflict. For instance, if one chooses between two equally attractive alternatives, the chosen alternative is rated as more attractive after the decision. According to Harmon-Jones, Harmon-Jones, and Levy (2015), the motivation to reduce dissonance evolved to allow people to carry out actions despite uncertainty. That is, when we commit to a course of action, the proximal motivation to reduce cognitive discrepancy is to reduce the negative affect associated with dissonance. More importantly, however, the distal motivation is preserving action effectiveness (for related ideas, see Heider, 1946).

Harmon-Jones and Harmon-Jones (2002) tested their predictions by asking participants to choose between similarly desirable alternatives (Brehm, 1956). In action-orientation conditions, participants wrote about implementing a decision they later did or did not face. Findings suggested that priming action orientation (previously writing about this decision) increased the typical spreading of alternatives relative to control conditions. This finding is important because, without considering action orientation, dissonance can be predicted to be high in both conditions.

Formation and change of behavioral procedures. Suppose one learns to classify circles by clicking a computer mouse and to classify squares by not clicking the mouse. Now suppose that one encounters a similar classification task later on. Activating an action goal or an inaction goal immediately prior to the classification should have different effects depending on whether or not the task has changed. Imagine that a group of people is asked to again click the mouse in response to circles, whereas another group is asked to now click the mouse in response to squares. An action goal should have facilitating effects for those still clicking in response to circles (the same behavior as before) but disruptive effects for those now clicking in response to squares (a different behavior).

An experiment we (Brown, Rick, & Albarracín, 2003) conducted tested exactly this prediction. Participants were first trained in a "go"/"no-go" task, in which they had to classify either circles or squares by either clicking the mouse or not clicking the mouse. Following a brief time interval, participants were presented with action and inaction word primes and were then instructed to either move or rest using the same procedures. Both satisfied action goals as well as unsatisfied inaction goals facilitated switching from one behavior to the other. Participants saved time when the target was known and the goal end state was action. That is, satisfied inaction goals as well as satisfied inaction goals produced savings in the time required to repeat the task. However, these conditions decreased savings in the time required to switch tasks.

In a different study, we (Brown, Rick, & Albarracín, 2004) examined the effects of action and inaction goals on the application of previously trained evaluation procedures. Participants were trained in performing evaluations using a series of 200 trials in which moderately positive or negative pictures of landscapes, people, and objects were presented. The participants were asked to evaluate how pleasant or unpleasant each picture was. They then took a break, after which they were primed with either action or inaction, received a new set of pictures, and were asked to write comments about each picture they saw.

The comments participants spontaneously wrote in response to the picture were coded as evaluative or nonevaluative. That is, comments such as "I like this picture" were coded as evaluative, and a proportion of evaluative thoughts over total number of thoughts was calculated for each participant. The mean proportion of evaluations reflected the influence of the priming manipulation on the reapplication of prior evaluative procedures. They showed that participants were more likely to generate evaluative comments of the pictures when they were in action end states than when they were in inaction end states.

In summary, action goals facilitate procedures that have been practiced recently more than do inaction goals. Notably, satisfying action goals produces outcomes similar to those of not satisfying inaction goals. Correspondingly, not satisfying action goals produces outcomes similar to those of satisfying inaction goals. Therefore, both unsatisfied inaction and satisfied action goals (inaction end states) facilitated procedural change, whereas satisfied inaction and unsatisfied action goals (action end states) facilitated procedural repetition.

Summary

Previous models of persuasion have typically not articulated the mechanisms underlying the use of different pieces of information as a basis for judgment. The proposed model assumes that all information available at the time (e.g., arguments, extraneous affect, past behavior) has the chance of being identified and used in judgment. After message recipients identify different pieces of information, they select information relevant to the judgment they are about to make (Albarracín, 2002). Because of these two stages of information identification and selection, decreases in ability and motivation are likely to have a negative, linear effect on the influence of argument strength. However, the influence of ability and motivation on the use of other, less relevant information is likely to be curvilinear.

McGuire (1968a) and Wyer (1974a, 1974b) conceptualized how recipients of a message engage in a sequence of cognitive activities. This sequence includes being presented with the content of the message, paying attention and comprehending its arguments, and then yielding to its recommendations. According to them, the success of a persuasive message depends on its ability to elicit each of these cognitive activities. In many ways, the model proposed in this chapter extends McGuire and Wyer's conceptualization. For example, it assumes that the information one receives is critical for the outcome of a persuasive message and, therefore, that the message content is critical.

In other ways, however, the model in this chapter departs from McGuire's (1968a) and Wyer's (1974a, 1974b) formulations. For example, it incorporates other sources of information that more contemporary models of persuasion have identified as critical (see Chaiken, 1980; Petty & Cacioppo, 1986a), and identifies conditions in which different types of information can have an influence. Our conceptualization also describes the contingencies of various judgments (e.g., outcome beliefs and evaluations) and how recipients can integrate these cognitions into their attitudes.

Of course, my model bears some resemblance to the elaboration-likelihood model and the heuristic systematic model. Like these dual-process models, it deals with information coming from the message arguments. It also deals with competing and often less relevant information, such as the affect one experiences for reasons unrelated to the message. However, the resemblance is in many ways apparent, as several of the predictions of our model contradict the predictions of dual-processing models. Most notably, the elaboration-likelihood model and the heuristic systematic model both assume that decreases in motivation and ability should be accompanied by increased influence of irrelevant information. In contrast, my model assumes that these restrictions will ultimately impair identification and use of any information whatsoever. Furthermore, dual-process models do not propose stages of processing, nor do they describe the order in which different stages develop.

Past research on persuasion has been driven by stage models of persuasion as well as the cognitive response model, the elaboration-likelihood model, the heuristic systematic model, and the unimodel. However, it is necessary to differentiate processes of attitude formation and change, with special attention to the influence of prior attitudes on the decision to seek out a persuasive message and the ultimate impact of a message or behavioral intervention, particularly in combination with goals of action and inaction. The key elements of persuasive communications and interventions to change behavior include behavioral recommendations, persuasive arguments, the communicator, and affective feelings. Message actionability and the elements and the processes leading to behavior are discussed in the coming chapters.

CHAPTER 8

Persuasive Communications and Behavioral Interventions in the Context of Prior Attitudes and Behaviors

Understanding persuasion requires understanding of how prior attitudes and behaviors influence attention and exposure to relevant information. Research on attention to attitude-relevant information has uncovered weak or nonexistent biases favoring attention to pro-attitudinal information (Eagly et al., 2001). Nonetheless, research on selective exposure has uncovered a strong selective approach bias in the decision to seek attitude- and behavior-consistent materials (Hart et al., 2009; Howell & Shepperd, 2012; Melnyk & Shepperd, 2012; Sweeny, Melnyk, Miller, & Shepperd, 2010).

Selective exposure to pro-attitudinal or pro-behavioral information stems from both cognitive and motivational factors. Among them, people who are confident in their ability to resist change seek contradictory information more than people who are not. The effects of this bias are both desirable and undesirable. On the one hand, selective exposure can maintain internal stability as we cope with constantly changing environments. On the other, selective exposure can prevent necessary changes from happening. For example, a person who engages in risky behavior would benefit from exposure to materials that question that behavior.

Sometimes, exposure can be gained by reassuring people that they will be able to resist the pressure to change. This strategy is designed to reduce the selective approach to attitude-consistent information when such strategy has undesirable consequences. After discussing these strategies, I describe identification and selection of information in contexts of attitude change and finish the chapter with a review of attitude change processes.

Selective Exposure

Many factors play a role in the decision to seek information, including of course persuasive messages and interventions. For example, people are likely to seek communications that appear targeted to one's gender, such as women seeking out messages that are obviously designed for women (Durantini & Albarracín, 2012; McCulloch, Albarracín, & Durantini, 2008), as well as interventions that appear likely to meet one's needs (Durantini & Albarracín, 2009; Earl et al., 2009). People are more likely to make conscious decisions to participate in interventions when they have time (Albarracín, Wilson, Durantini, & Livingood, 2013) and seek more involved programs after participating in easy ones (Albarracín, Leeper, Earl, & Durantini, 2008). People seek programs that match cultural beliefs (Wilson, Durantini, Albarracín, Crause, & Albarracín, 2013), but can get turned off when they believe that programs are targeted toward their racial group (Earl, Crause, Vaid, & Albarracín, 2016; Earl, Nisson, & Albarracín, 2015).

Important to this book, exposure to persuasive communications and behavioral interventions does not happen in an attitudinal vacuum. Attitudes, beliefs, and past behaviors shape the decision to read a message or to click a hyperlink embedded in a tweet. My colleagues and I (Hart et al., 2009) meta-analyzed the experimental literature on selective exposure to determine associations with attitudes, beliefs, and behaviors in a variety of contexts. Included were studies with an initial attitude, belief, or behavior measure and then a measure of voluntary exposure to materials that either agreed or disagreed with their initial position. Participants could, for example, report their attitudes toward gun control and then decide if they wanted to read an article that favored or opposed gun control.

The average effect was moderate and the bias was present across all domains. As shown in Figure 8.1, political and religious attitudes were more likely to produce a selective approach to pro-attitudinal information, but consumer and health attitudes were not that far behind. Effects on health information seeking are particularly troubling. For example, my colleagues (Bae, Maloney, Albarracín, & Cappella, 2018) conducted a selective exposure experiment with a national sample of youths (ages 15–21 years; $n = 614$). During a 10-min browsing session, participants saw a set of 16 videos (eight smoking and eight nonsmoking) and could view the video or videos of their choice. Behavioral data showed that youth with higher interest in smoking selected and spent more time watching pro-smoking videos than did youth with lower interest in smoking.

According to our meta-analysis (Hart et al., 2009), Easier to retrieve prior attitudes influenced exposure decisions, as attitudes that are tied to issues people consider personally relevant. Specifically, presenting

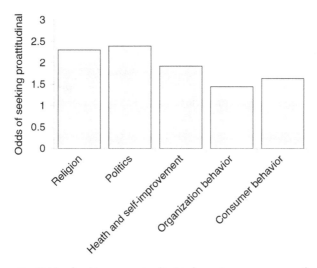

Figure 8.1 Odds of seeking pro-attitudinal information as a message of topic.

information in ways that facilitate retrieval of prior attitudes increase exposure to attitude-consistent information. For example, presenting more pieces of information to choose from, using longer descriptions of the available options, and having people perform several behaviors relevant to an issue, each increase exposure to pro-attitudinal information. Apparently, offering multiple retrieval cues for attitudes strengthens the effect of attitudes on exposure decisions.

There are, however, many determinants of selective exposure. For example, one's commitment to a position increases the tendency to seek information that confirms this position. In two studies by Brock and Balloun (1967), participants listened to an audio tape that supported or opposed their attitudes toward church or smoking. The tape contained static and participants learned to reduce the static by pressing a designated button. As hypothesized, committed churchgoers and smokers made more attempts at reducing the static when they listened to a supportive communication than when they listened to an unsupportive communication. In contrast, the effect was smaller for noncommitted churchgoers or smokers.

The quality of the information can also influence selective exposure. Festinger (1964) argued that the selective approach to attitude-consistent information diminishes if the counterattitudinal information can be refuted. Lowin (1967) created four sets of information that crossed the similarity between the message position and the participants' attitudes (supportive vs. challenging) with the strength of the arguments contained in the message (weak vs. strong). Participants received one of these messages in the mail and were instructed to send in a postcard if they wanted to receive additional brochures. As expected, more participants requested additional brochures when they received strong supporting information and weak challenging information relative to the other conditions. Hence, people are more likely to select challenging information when they believe that they can counterargue it. This possibility is considered presently.

Selective Exposure to Digital and Legacy Media

The searching and customization potential of digital media, along with electronic targeting of messages, create the perfect climate for both de facto exposure to a selective slice of materials (Barnidge & Peacock, 2019) and selective exposure. Thus, one might expect biases in exposure to be present.

A study on the relation between liberal attitudes toward sexuality ("To what extent do you consider acceptable that a minor has sex?" "To what extent do you consider acceptable that a minor has multiple sexual partners?") and exposure to pornography on the internet. A crossed-lagged longitudinal design (Martyniuk & Štulhofer, 2018) revealed that adolescents who had liberal attitudes toward sexuality were more likely to have higher frequency of consumption of pornography on the internet than adolescents who had conservative attitudes toward sexuality. The effects varied across cities and by gender between $d = 0.06$ and $d = 0.47$, with an average $d = 0.25$.

A critical dimension of selective exposure in digital media is the selection of discussion networks. In research conducted by Lyons (2019), participants nominated discussion network members on various topics, including political issues, self-driving cars, and vaccines. For political issues, participants were more likely to select ideologically homogeneous networks for the discussion of congenial than uncongenial information ($d = 0.16$). Moreover, this selection was motivated by the goal of choosing people who shared the nominators' own beliefs.

In terms of strength, estimates of congenial selective exposure in digital media suggest that the role of intentional selection of information is weaker for social media than the materials in the experiments that yielded a $d = 0.36$ in Hart et al.'s (2009) meta-analysis. Therefore, one can conclude that, first, both legacy and social media provide the conditions for people to de facto affiliate on the basis of similarity (i.e., homophily) without any need of further biased selection. Second, the media have an information-complex environment that may dilute congenial biases. For example, the media might offer 10 different articles at the same time, but many of which are on unrelated topics. As a result, it may be more difficult for a reader to select a pro- or anti-gun control article.

Beliefs in Self-Defense

Historical examples abound of people who strongly advocate and defend a given attitude and then change this position, becoming "converted" to points of view that contradict their initial position. One reason for such changes is likely the perception that one can defend one's attitudes from attack. Ironically, however, this confidence can make a person vulnerable to attitude change.

My research has shown that people who are confident that their attitudes resist future challenges are more willing to examine evidence that both supports and contradicts their attitudes. In contrast, people who doubt their defensive ability prefer information that supports their attitudes over information that contradicts their attitudes (Byrne, 1961; Olson & Zanna, 1982). Although, in many ways, denial is a primitive defense mechanism, avoiding counterattitudinal information ensures attitude maintenance. In contrast, seeking counterattitudinal information can make attitudes weaker. Obviously, people exposed to counterattitudinal information are often able to counterargue the information. However, strong messages still exert an influence regardless of the level of defensive confidence of an audience.

Several lines of research on selective exposure are relevant to understanding beliefs in self-defense. First, the seminal inoculation research by McGuire and Papageorgis (1961) suggests that counterattitudinal information strengthens resistance more than simply bolstering attitudes. Furthermore, my research (Albarracín & Mitchell, 2004) studied whether defensive confidence produces more exposure to conflicting information. For example, Wilson, Gilbert, and Wheathey (1998) hypothesized that people are more willing to view supraliminal messages than subliminal messages. Presumably, they believe that supraliminal messages are easier to resist. We argued that such theories are also present in more general beliefs in one's defensive ability.

Evidence of the influence of confidence on selective exposure also comes from research on more specific forms of confidence. In Cannon's (1964) work, participants who thought that they failed on a previous intellectual problem (low confidence) were more likely to approach decision-consistent information than people who believed that they performed well (high confidence; but see lack of replication by Freedman, 1965).

In my work, defensive confidence entails stable and temporary individual differences that relate specifically to people's attitudes and their responses to persuasion. People who are high in defensive confidence are more open to receiving counterattitudinal information. Therefore, they change their attitudes more than people who doubt their defensive abilities. In terms of mediators, people who are high in defensive confidence may expect to trust their initial attitudes. Similarly, people who are high (vs. low) in defensive confidence may expect to effectively counterargue counterattitudinal information and to feel better about themselves. They may also expect the counterattitudinal information to be less novel and weaker. The mediating influence of these perceptions appears in Figure 8.2.

We (Albarracín & Mitchell, 2004; Albarracín, Wang, & Albarracín, 2012) developed a scale to measure defensive confidence on the basis of in-depth interviews. For that purpose, we first constructed a large pool of items to measure defensive confidence. Items were developed on the basis of a series of qualitative interviews with political and religious activists as well as lay participants and students. During these qualitative interviews, participants described their feelings and thoughts when their personal

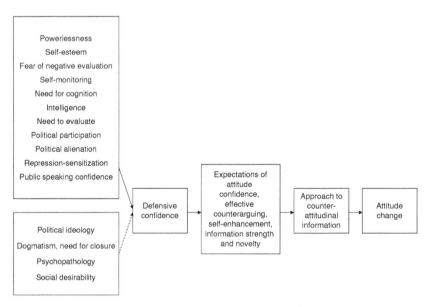

Figure 8.2 Processes involving defensive confidence.

attitudes were under attack and discussed their experiences defending their attitudes. The resulting items were pretested and selected on the basis of factor analysis. These procedures resulted in 12 items such as "During discussions of issues I care about, I can successfully defend my ideas" and "No matter what I read or hear, I am always capable of defending my feelings and opinions." Participants responded to the defensive confidence questions by providing their judgment on a scale from 1 (*not at all characteristic of me*) to 5 (*extremely characteristic of me*). The sum of responses to these items was used as an overall index of defensive confidence after reverse-scoring items as appropriate.

We administered the scale to several groups of participants. The scale had adequate test–retest reliability. Consistent with expectations, defensive confidence correlated positively with need for cognition, verbal intelligence, need to evaluate, and political participation. Overall, however, these six associations predicted a total 31 percent of the variance in defensive confidence. Thus, they suggested that the construct was unique.

We also designed a study to determine whether defensive confidence influences selective exposure to attitude-relevant information. During the first part of the study, participants completed the defensive confidence scale. Then, as part of an ostensibly unrelated study, we indicated that we were conducting research for a fictitious organization, which was presented as the "Bureau of Sociology Education Research." The Bureau was described as a longstanding, prestigious organization responsible for collecting data to design introductory sociology textbooks. We further stated that one of the objectives of the Bureau was to ensure clarity and comprehension of theories and key terms in sociology.

The experimenter told participants that the study involved reading and discussing passages on either abortion or euthanasia. Moreover, participants were informed that, before going into the group discussion, they would have time to prepare by reading a selection of two passages, each of which would be on a different issue. After these instructions, participants received a text request form to select one of the two issues in the study. Thus, on a scale from 0 to 100, they indicated how interested they would be to read about (a) abortion from the point of view of pro-choice groups, (b) abortion from the point of view of pro-life groups, (c) euthanasia from the point of view of groups that are in favor of it, and (d) euthanasia from the point of view of groups that are against it. They also considered two pairs of choices, one pair representing the favoring and opposing sides of each topic, and ranked the options of each pair. After participants made text ratings and selections, the experimenter explained that it was important to determine the composition of the group of students participating in the study to make sure that the sample had diverse points of view. Participants then indicated their attitudes toward each of the topics.

We hypothesized that people who are confident that they can defend their attitudes would show less bias in favor of pro-attitudinal information than people who are not. To examine this prediction, we created measures of selective exposure concerning each issue in the study. First, we computed differences in interest ratings by subtracting interest in reading materials against each issue from interest in reading materials supporting each issue. These measures reflect relative approach to materials in favor of abortion and euthanasia. Next, we created indicator variables from the rankings to represent selection of materials favoring abortion and euthanasia. Finally, we computed an overall measure of exposure that incorporated differences in preference and rankings for the alternative positions.

For descriptive purposes, the correlations between attitudes and the exposure measures appear in the top section of Table 8.1, organized by

Table 8.1 *Correlations between attitudes toward abortion and preference for abortion-relevant information as a function of defensive confidence: Study 3*

	Preference for	
Analysis	Pro-abortion information	Pro-euthanasia information
Simple correlations		
High	0.35	0.28
Low	0.80***	0.85***
Multiple regression		
Attitudes	2.05**	2.49**
Defensive confidence	0.94*	1.36*
Interaction	−1.96*	−2.24*

Note: Coefficients in the top panel are Pearson correlations across high and low defensive confidence. The bottom panel presents standardized regression coefficients, βs. Negative interaction terms imply that the positive association between pro-abortion attitudes and preference for pro-abortion materials was higher when confidence was low rather than high. Mean attitudes toward abortion were 4.07 (SD = 1.67) and 4.09 (SD = 1.41) for the high- and low-confidence groups, respectively; F (1, 38) = 0.002, *ns*; Levene's test for equality of variances = 0.39, *ns*. Mean attitudes toward abortion were 3.92 (SD = 1.46) and 4.39 (SD = 1.07) for the high- and low-confidence groups, respectively; F (1, 38) = 1.30, *ns*; Levene's test for equality of variances F(1, 38) = 0.97, *ns*.
***p < 0.001. **p < 0.01. *p < 0.05.
Source: Adapted from Albarracín and Mitchell (2004).

topic and by each of the two levels of defensive confidence determined by a median split. Significant positive correlations imply that participants approached pro-attitudinal information to a greater extent than counter-attitudinal information. Nonsignificant correlations suggest absence of attitudinal selectivity. These data show that the attitudes of participants who scored high on the defensive confidence scale did not significantly correlate with exposure to pro-attitudinal materials. That is, these participants adopted an open-minded approach to the material. In contrast, people who were low in defensive confidence had strong positive correlations between their attitudes and seeking pro-attitudinal information. That is, these participants demonstrated increased preference for material that confirmed their prior attitudes.

The correlations for each level of the median split only have descriptive value. However, to formally test whether defensive confidence decreases bias in favor of pro-attitudinal information, we regressed the summary measures representing selective exposure on attitudes toward each issue, defensive confidence, and the interaction between attitudes and defensive confidence. A summary of these findings appears in the bottom section of Table 8.1. As predicted, the interactions were significant for both abortion and euthanasia, suggesting that more confident people approached pro-attitudinal information to a lesser extent than less confident ones.

Another study (Albarracín & Mitchell, 2004, Study 4) was designed to provide a replication of the findings in Table 8.1. Unlike those findings, however, this study included an experimental manipulation of defensive confidence. Participants were asked to write about an episode in which they either did or did not defend their attitudes well. Following this manipulation, participants were given an opportunity to select information that either favored or opposed abortion. Thus, we were able to observe if exposure preferences varied as a function of manipulated defensive confidence.

The procedures to measure selective exposure were the same used in the prior study, although we restricted consideration to attitudes toward abortion. Thus, participants indicated their interest in reading the texts in favor of and against abortion, ranked each text, and reported their attitudes toward abortion. Again, we created a summary measure of preference for the pro-abortion text and analyzed this preference as a function of participants' attitudes, the manipulation of defensive confidence, and the interaction between these two variables.

The findings from this study appear in Table 8.2 and replicated the ones from the earlier study. As the top section of the table shows, participants in low defensive confidence conditions preferred pro-attitudinal information

Table 8.2 *Correlations as a function of defensive confidence and multiple-regression analyses: Study 5*

Variable	Exposure measures		Expectations about information					Postexposure attitudes
	Preferences	Actual exposure	Differential counterarguing success a	Differential attitude confidence	Differential self-enhancement	Differential novelty	Differential strength	
Simple correlations								
High	0.30**	0.30**	0.38***	0.21*	0.41***	0.24**	0.43***	0.37***
Low	0.54***	0.50***	0.68***	0.48***	0.47***	0.50***	0.53***	0.70***
Multiple regressions								
Attitudes[a]	1.28**	1.11**	1.12**	1.18**	0.68*	1.08**	0.90**	1.01**
Defensive confidence	0.01	0.04	0.02	-0.15	0.01	0.07	0.04	0.08
Interaction	-0.87*	-0.72*	-0.65*	-0.90*	-0.28	-0.74*	-0.43	-0.96**

Note: Coefficients in the top panel are Pearson correlations across high and low defensive confidence. The bottom panel presents standardized regression coefficients, βs. Negative interaction terms imply that the positive associations between pro-abortion attitudes and preference, expectations, or postexposure attitudes were higher when confidence was low rather than high. Mean attitudes were -1.73 (SD = 2.22) and -1.30 (SD = 2.50) for the high- and low-confidence groups, respectively; $F(1, 191) = 1.56$, *ns*. Levene's test for equality of variances $F(1, 191) = 3.37$; $p < 0.07$.
[a] In this analysis, this variable was reverse-scored so that positive numbers indicate expectations of greater counterargument in response to the counterattitudinal position.

***$p < 0.001$. **$p < 0.01$. *$p < 0.05$.

Source: Adapted from Albarracín and Mitchell (2004).

to a greater extent than participants in high defensive confidence conditions. The difference between the correlations across the two groups was statistically significant, as indicated by a significant interaction between attitudes and the defensive confidence manipulation. Thus, these findings provided support for the earlier findings using our personality measure.

Effects of Defensive Confidence on Exposure-Mediated Attitude Change

The studies we just presented preliminary evidence that individuals with high defensive confidence are less likely to prefer pro-attitudinal information relative to individuals with low defensive confidence. In another study, in addition to recording reading preferences and decisions, participants actually read the text they selected. After exposure to the selected text, participants reported their attitudes toward abortion one more time. Thus, it was possible to examine whether greater exposure to pro-attitudinal materials among participants who were low in defensive confidence led to greater stability in their initial attitudes relative to those who were low in this trait. In addition, we included assessments of attitude confidence and the potential mediators presented in Figure 8.2. Hence, we could gauge the processes that drive the influence of defensive confidence on selective approach to pro-attitudinal information.

We analyzed differential exposure to attitude-relevant materials by regressing the measure of preference for pro-attitudinal materials and whether or not they read the pro-attitudinal materials on their prior attitudes, their level of defensive confidence, and the interaction between the two. A summary of this regression analysis as well as the correlations between attitudes and the two exposure measures under high (above *Md*) and low (below *Md*) levels of defensive confidence appear in the first two columns of Table 8.2. As the top rows of those columns show, the new analyses provided a replication of our earlier findings.

In this study, we also investigated the perceptions that mediated the influence of defensive confidence on decisions to approach attitude-relevant information. A first step in showing mediation was to determine whether differential expectations about pro- and counterattitudinal information indeed varied as a function of attitudes and defensive confidence. Thus, we first regressed the measures of differential expectations of counterarguing success, attitude confidence, self-enhancement, novelty, and strength on initial attitudes, defensive confidence, and the interaction between attitudes and defensive confidence. These analyses appear in the middle columns of Table 8.2. As shown, the interaction was significant for counterarguing success, attitude confidence, and differential novelty. That is, participants generally thought that they would counterargue the message less, trust their attitudes more, and find more novel information when the message was pro-attitudinal than when the message was counterattitudinal. However, the differences in perceptions of pro- and counterattitudinal messages were less pronounced when defensive confidence was high (vs. low).

We then determined whether participants who are high and low in defensive confidence differed in their selection of information because of their expectations about counterarguing success, attitude confidence, and/ or novelty. We reran the multiple-regression equations to predict actual exposure to the pro-attitudinal text (see the second column of Table 8.2) including expectations about counterarguing success, attitude confidence, and novelty. Adding differential counterarguing success, attitude confidence, and novelty reduced the interaction between attitude and defensive confidence to nonsignificance. Of the three predictors, however, only expected counterarguing success and attitude confidence remained as significant predictors of exposure and were significant mediators of the interaction between prior attitudes and defensive confidence. All in all, these analyses suggested that differential counterarguing success and attitude confidence mediated the influence of defensive confidence on exposure to pro-attitudinal information.

Finally, we tested whether people with high defensive confidence are vulnerable to attitude change (Table 8.3). We regressed postmessage attitudes on initial attitudes, defensive confidence, and the interaction between initial attitudes and defensive confidence. These analyses appear in the last column of Table 8.1 and show more change (i.e., smaller r between prior and poststudy attitudes) among participants with high (vs. low) defensive confidence. Moreover, when exposure decisions were added into the equation, the significant interaction between initial attitudes and defensive confidence became nonsignificant. This finding as well as a final mediation test suggested that defensive confidence affected exposure to counterattitudinal information and ultimately attitude change.[1]

---

[1] At least two conditions could potentially produce different effects of defensive confidence on selective exposure and attitude change. First, communications are more persuasive when they contain strong arguments than when they contain weak arguments. Communications containing weak arguments, however, produce either no effect or a boomerang effect, making recipients even more inclined to oppose the advocacy after receiving the communication (Johnson, Maio, & Smith-McLallen, 2005). Therefore, greater defensive confidence will not universally produce greater attitude change. Second, people do not let their defensive perceptions guide their actions without attempting to control these effects. As a result, making people aware of the bias of defensive confidence could well change our findings.

Table 8.3 *Correlations between attitudes toward abortion and preference for pro-abortion*

Analysis	Preference
Simple correlations	
High	0.36*
Low	0.69***
Multiple regression	
Attitudes	1.27***
Defensive confidence	0.61*
Interaction	−0.97**

Note: Coefficients in the top panel are Pearson correlations across high and low defensive confidence. The bottom panel presents standardized regression coefficients, βs. Negative interaction terms imply that the positive association between pro-abortion attitudes and preference for pro-abortion materials was higher when confidence was low rather than high. Mean attitudes were 3.97 (SD = 1.61) and 3.86 (SD = 1.63) for the high- and low-confidence groups, respectively; F $(1, 73)$ = 0.76, *ns*. Levene's test for equality of variances, F $(1, 73)$ = 0.29, *ns*.
***p < 0.001. **p < 0.01. *p < 0.05.

Like prior individual difference measures, the defensive confidence scale provides a tool for identifying clusters of people who might adopt confirmatory strategies and, thus, are vulnerable to the errors associated with such strategies. For example, people with low defensive confidence are less receptive to information that counters their attitudes. As a result, these individuals may seek therapy less often if they fear that the therapist will question their perceptions of the world. They may even seek medical assistance less frequently with the objective of maintaining unrealistic health beliefs. The implications of defensive confidence for behavioral interventions are discussed presently.

Selective Exposure to Behavioral Interventions

Large amounts of resources have been dedicated to the design of programs to persuade people to engage in behaviors that are beneficial for them or the societies in which they live. However, much less work has been done to identify the characteristics of messages and interventions that increase exposure to or participation in these programs. In fact, programs are typically tested under conditions that reduce attrition and self-selection and provide strong incentives for participation (e.g., money or other goods, the symbolic rewards of contributing to the scientific enterprise). However, when behavioral interventions are implemented in the real world, potential target recipients have a choice concerning participation. People may not read the brochures, watch the videos played at the health department in their area, or participate in the individual or group counseling that is available in nearby health or community settings.

Consider some examples of refusal to participate in a condom use intervention. John knows that unprotected sex is dangerous but does not use condoms because condoms decrease his sexual pleasure and perform-ance. A blunt offer to participate in multisession counseling to get him to use condoms is likely to elicit reactance (Brehm, 1972; J. Liu et al., 2014). Put simply, he wants to continue doing what he is doing and feels that others have no right to interfere. The intervention is an "interference" he needs to avoid. Consequently, he refuses to participate.

Like John, Mary is not using condoms with her regular partner. She would use condoms if she could convince her partner but feels unable to achieve this objective. She does not think that any intervention could change that, because "her partner is more stubborn than usual." Therefore, she is as unlikely to participate.

The two examples above illustrate how people's intentions and behav-iors may influence decisions to participate in an HIV-prevention program. In particular, people who are not yet using condoms may deem an intervention a threat to their personal decisions or a challenge to which they cannot rise.

Despite the importance of understanding exposure to interventions to change behavior, progress in this domain has been slow. One reason is that past research often had suboptimal correspondence. For example, Feather (1963) asked smokers and nonsmokers to rank 13 articles according to how desirable they were to read. Of the 13 articles, one stated that there was no link between lung cancer and cigarette smoking and another stated that there was a link. Contrary to the author's expectation, smokers' and nonsmokers' ratings of the two articles did not differ. One notable aspect of this research, however, is that there is no correspondence between the target of the message (a belief) and the subject variable (a prior behavior) (Earl et al., 2009). Thus, corresponding operationalizations might be essential.

The possibility that the association between exposure patterns and past behavior may be more clear when the measures of exposure and past behavior correspond was supported in a study by Earl et al. (2009; see also Wilson & Albarracín, 2015). We argued that, to understand exposure to interventions to increase condom use, one must look at attitudes toward condom use and actual condom use. In contrast, a lot of research on selective exposure has concerned social, religious, or political attitudes. However, when the target of an intervention is a behavior or an increase in knowledge, prior behaviors and knowledge must be taken into account.

We (Noguchi, Albarracín, & Durantini, 2007) actually meta-analyzed enrollment in behavioral interventions to increase condom use as a function of past condom use. We found a linear relation, such that higher condom use predicted higher enrollment than lower condom use. This finding points to the fact that our programs often preach to the choir and that we need creative ways of engaging vulnerable, unwilling audiences.

How to Increase Participation among People Not Currently Engaging in the Behavior

An important question is how to increase participation in a strategic way. Back to our examples, John does not want to participate because he experiences reactance. He thinks that the intervention is intrusive. How can we better "sell" the intervention for him? One may be able to make him feel that he is able to defend his position and to walk out of the intervention doing just what he was doing before the intervention (i.e., not using condoms). Such a message should decrease intervention avoidance by increasing the perception that he will be able to resist the intervention successfully (defensive confidence).

The reason why Mary does not participate, however, is not reactance. She happens to doubt the ability of the intervention to help her use condoms. Nonetheless, one should be able to convince her to participate by persuading her that the program has been helpful for other women with equally stubborn partners. If the program has helped others like her, it may be helpful to her as well.

Findings with dieting behavior. Preliminary support for these hypotheses comes from a study of dieting behavior by Glasman and Albarracín

(2003a). In this research, women were presented with options of different types of diets. A brief explanation about the different diets was followed by an opportunity to choose one for further reading. Thus, the main dependent measure was whether a particular diet was selected. The diets were introduced in ways that mapped onto intentions to diet and intentions to not diet. One program was described as highly effective to lose weight. The other was described as a program that would inform audiences but not necessarily impose any perspective (control message). Participants were asked to indicate their interest in reading more about the program.

The results from the dieting study are presented in Figure 8.3, as a function of whether the women were dieting at the time and whether they intended to lose weight. As can be seen, which message was presented mattered most when participants intended to lose weight but were currently not dieting. When participants intended to lose weight and were already successful at dieting, the type of program also made a difference on interest, but not as much as when participants were not yet successful at dieting. Finally, there was no difference in interest in the program when participants had no intention to lose weight.

In sum, there is evidence that describing a program as effective is important to attract participants who want to change, particularly those

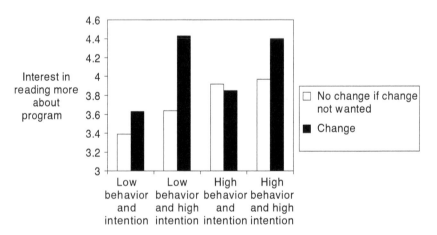

Figure 8.3 Interest in dietary program.

who are not yet successful. The preliminary data, however, do not support the possibility of greater success for telling nonintenders that the program is not imposing. In this context, the nature of the program was irrelevant for these participants.

Findings with HIV Interventions. The conclusions from a randomized control trial conducted at a state health department in Florida supported that the framing of the intervention offer matters a great deal to nonintenders as well. Participants were community members recruited through flyers or direct referrals in Gainesville, FL. Referrals and flyers described the study as a "health survey" and participants who called were asked various questions about health, including sexual activity. Only participants who were sexually active in the last 6 months, not currently pregnant, and using condoms rarely or sometimes (but not always) were eligible and scheduled to come in for an interview. At the time of this interview, the participant responded to a questionnaire administered by a member of the research team. Halfway through the interview, the interviewer paused the administration, announcing a 30-min break.

The critical manipulations and observations of the study occurred during the ostensible break. At that point, a confederate entered the room pretending to do work unrelated to the interview. The true purpose, however, was to record the participant's exposure behavior. After the confederate entered the room, the interviewer exited after explaining that s/he had to enter the data. While the confederate was in the room, the participant had 10 min to peruse six brochures sitting on the table. After 10 min elapsed, the interviewer knocked on the door, apologized for a delay in the data entry, and offered the participant a 10-min video about HIV. The client could either accept or decline to play the video. Next, the interviewer returned and offered the participant the option of participating in a HIV-risk-reduction counseling session. If the participant previously accepted the video, the interviewer waited 10 min before returning to offer the counseling. If the participant declined to watch the video, the interviewer waited 5 min before returning to the room and offering the counseling to the participant. After the interviewer offered the counseling, if the participant accepted, the confederate was asked to counsel the participant. If the participant declined, however, the interviewer exited the room and returned 5 min later to administer a posttest questionnaire.

The critical manipulations were the way in which the program was introduced. For example, at the moment the counseling session was offered to the participant, the interviewer could give one of the introductions:

A. While you are waiting, you have the choice to speak with a certified HIV-prevention counselor. The counseling session provides information about HIV and condom use. It will also help you figure out your risk for HIV infection. The point of the counseling session is to provide you with the most current information, not to influence your opinion or make you use condoms if you don't want to. [Would you be interested?]

B. While you are waiting, you have the choice to speak with a certified HIV-prevention counselor. The counseling session provides information about HIV and condom use. It will also help you figure out your risk for HIV infection. A counselor can show you ways to help you make your behavior safer. Most of the people who participate in counseling said that it improved their lives and they wished they had participated sooner. [Would you be interested?]

C. While you are waiting, you have the choice to speak with a certified HIV-prevention counselor. The counseling session provides information about HIV and condom use. It will also help you figure out your risk for HIV infection. [Would you be interested?]

D. Would you be interested in participating in an HIV counseling sessions?

Thus, some participants were induced to experience high defensive confidence or empowerment with respect to the intervention (A), others were induced to experience high change confidence (B), and two groups served as controls (C and D). Group C had a descriptive introduction and Group D had no introduction. As shown in Figure 8.4, results supported the expectation that increasing defensive confidence would increase exposure to the program. That is, acceptance of the program was higher when participants were introduced to the program in a way that would increase their perceived ability to resist the intervention. In contrast, the other two conditions did not differ from each other.

Retention in HIV-prevention interventions can also be understood as a form of selective exposure to information (Albarracín & Mitchell, 2004; Earl et al., 2015; Noguchi, Albarracín, & Durantini, 2007). We thus examined the possibility that people would expose themselves to persuasive communications if they believe that they can resist their influence

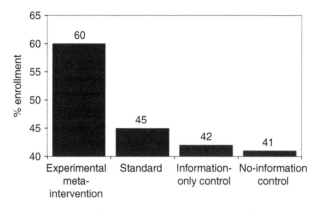

Figure 8.4 Effects of meta-intervention on enrollment.

(Albarracín & Mitchell, 2004; Brehm, 1966). If the dynamic of enrollment is similar to retention (Noguchi, Albarracín, Durantini, & Glasman, 2007), similar messages may also increase retention in an HIV-prevention counseling program by meeting the motivations of potential clients (Earl et al., 2009; McCulloch, Albarracín, & Durantini, 2008; Noguchi, Albarracín, Durantini et al., 2007). For HIV risk-reduction interventions, objective outcomes include HIV-risk reduction (Floyd, Prentice-Dunn, & Rogers, 2000), as well as emotional and instrumental support (Durantini & Albarracín, 2009).

   We conducted a randomized control trial to test the impact of video meta-interventions designed to either promote defensive confidence or remind clients of the various objective goals fulfilled by the HIV counseling program, and to compare these videos with control videos. The defensive confidence or empowering meta-intervention entailed describing the *recipient* as the motor of the behavior change (Albarracín, Durantini, Earl, Gunnoe, & Leeper, 2008). This strategy suggested that the program could not change behavior unless the individual wanted it to. The instrumental video involved descriptions of the information and referrals the counselor could provide, in addition to giving information and guidance about HIV prevention. We also included a condition that combined the empowering and instrumental messages, as well as two control conditions. One control entailed stories about people living with HIV that were used in all experimental videos. The other control simply presented educational information on reducing STIs.

The outcome of the randomized controlled trial was completion of the counseling program, which had additional sessions. The design involved another manipulation related to introducing a questionnaire at the end of the first session, before attendance to the second session could be measured. When no questionnaire was introduced, the instrumental message alone was better than any of the other messages. Also, the instrumental message was more effective than the empowering message in the absence of measures of mediating expectations. The overall gains in completion as a result of the instrumental message were 16 percent.

One aspect of our findings is noteworthy. First, the defensive confidence or empowering meta-intervention, which had impressive results with acceptance of HIV-prevention counseling (Albarracín et al., 2008), did not yield more completion than the control conditions. This result highlights that the determinants of enrollment and retention are different, with defensiveness playing a key role in initiation, but lack of outcome relevance seemingly underlying drop out.

Identification, Selection, and Attitude Change

Responses to persuasive communications also depend on the identification and selection of information after exposure. The mechanisms of attitude change have been of interest to attitude researchers for several decades. In particular, the information-integration theory (Anderson, 1981) and social judgment theory (Sherif & Hovland, 1961) explicitly addressed change. These theories consider the role of prior attitudes vis-à-vis new information. In addition, models of attitude strength propose that stronger attitudes last longer than weaker ones. Thus, according to these models, change is largely a function of intrinsic properties of the attitude being considered. For example, the elaboration-likelihood model (Petty & Cacioppo, 1986) posits that attitude formation and change involve the same processes. In the case of formation, the attitude is weak; in the case of change, the attitude is strong.

Although invaluable, each of these models has limitations. First, the information-integration theory describes how different pieces of information can be combined. However, it does not explicate how people arrive at specific weights. Second, social judgment theory emphasizes a perceptual comparative process through which attitudes and new information are compared. However, it does not address other forms of comparison or indicate how ability and motivation may influence these stages. Third, the elaboration-likelihood model proposes important roles for ability and motivation. However, this model addresses what is specific to attitude formation rather than change. In the following section, I analyze the implications of identification and selection of information about a communicator by considering the sleeper effect.

Sleeper Effect

Processes surrounding attitude change include the *sleeper effect*. This effect involves an increase in persuasion following a delay after a message is presented by a noncredible source. For example, recipients of political communications may discount a message from a political opponent because they do not perceive the source of the message as credible (for reviews, see Cook & Flay, 1978; Kumkale & Albarracín, 2004). As time goes by, however, the recipients may recall the arguments in the message but not its source. Failing to recall a source that is not credible results in being more persuaded by the message arguments at the point of the delayed follow-up (Kumkale & Albarracín, 2004). Simply put, during reception, the source of the message acts as a *discounting cue* and temporarily decreases the impact of the message, leaving recipients unpersuaded immediately after they receive the communication. Over time, however, people do not spontaneously recall the discounting cue and reconstruct their attitudes on the basis of the information they recall, which is the arguments.

The sleeper effect was first identified during research on interventions to improve the morale of the enlisted US soldiers during World War II. An army propaganda film was presented to soldiers and their opinions were measured either 5 days or 9 weeks after the message presentation (Hovland & Lumsdaine, 1949; for a review, see Kumkale & Albarracín, 2004b). Findings indicated that the positive effect of the message relative to a control was greater 9 weeks after presenting the film than 5 days after presenting the film. In addition, the opinions of message recipients had increased significantly, which led Hovland et al. (1949) to designate the phenomenon as the *sleeper effect*. The sleeper effect is counterintuitive because the impact of persuasive communications typically decays over time (Cook & Flay, 1978; Kumkale & Albarracín, 2004). For this reason, this persuasion pattern has stimulated a large amount of research to understand its conditions and mechanisms.

Explanations of the sleeper effect. Initial explanations of the sleeper effect assumed that message recipients forget the noncredible communicator as time goes by (e.g., Hovland & Weiss, 1951; Kumkale & Albarracín, 2004).

To test this hypothesis, Hovland and his colleagues (Hovland & Weiss, 1951; Kelman & Hovland, 1953) conducted experiments in which participants received messages attributed to either trustworthy or untrustworthy sources and then completed measures of opinions as well as of recall of the message content and the source. As in their seminal study, messages with credible sources produced greater initial persuasion than messages delivered by noncredible sources. However, as time went by, the impact of the messages presented by credible sources decayed, whereas the impact of the messages presented by noncredible sources either remained the same or increased slightly.

Although the second experimental phase on the sleeper effect (Hovland & Weiss, 1951; Kelman & Hovland, 1953) reproduced the initial findings, the recall data called their hypothesis into question. Surprisingly, recipients of messages with discounting cues could still remember the noncredible sources of the messages at the time of the delayed follow-up. Therefore, Hovland and Weiss (1951) replaced the forgetting hypothesis with the dissociation hypothesis. That is, message recipients may not entirely forget the cue, yet the association between the representations of the discounting cue and the message content may fade over time (Hovland & Weiss, 1951).

The forgetting hypothesis implies that the traces of the cue disappear or become unavailable in memory over time, whereas the dissociation hypothesis implies that the cue remains available in memory but is simply less accessible in relation to the topic of the communication. A third hypothesis, proposed by Greenwald, Pratkanis, and colleagues decades after the effect was first proposed, is similar to the forgetting hypothesis (Greenwald, Pratkanis, Leippe, & Baumgardner, 1986; Pratkanis, Greenwald, Leippe, & Baumgardner, 1988). However, rather than stating that message recipients recall the arguments but forget the source at the time of the delay follow-up, this hypothesis describes differential decay. That is, recipients forget both the arguments and the source but they forget the source more than the arguments.

But why would the discounting cue decay at a faster rate than the arguments? To address this question, Greenwald, Pratkanis, and their colleagues (Greenwald, Pratkanis, Leippe, & Baumgardner, 1986; Pratkanis, Greenwald, Leippe, & Baumgardner, 1988) implemented a result-centered approach to identify the preconditions for the sleeper effect. In an impressive series of 17 experiments, participants received the discounting cue either before or after the message. The sleeper effect was more likely when the cue followed the message than when the cue preceded the message (Pratkanis et al., 1988). Clearly then, the position of the discounting cue is essential to produce the effect because information presented first lasts longer, whereas more recent information dissipates more rapidly (Miller & Campbell, 1959).

Empirical definitions of the sleeper effect. Figure 8.5 presents several distinct patterns of change in attitudes over time including the (a) nonpersisting boomerang effect (A), (b) absolute sleeper effect (B), and (C) relative sleeper effect (C; Kumkale et al., 2004). All of these patterns show that a message presented by a credible source, which constitutes an acceptance cue, decays over time. Each of these patterns, however, differs in what takes place when the people receive a discounting cue.

Figure 8.5A shows a nonpersisting boomerang effect, in which a message initially produces attitude change opposite to the direction of the advocacy but this opposition fades over time. Because recipients initially disagree with the advocacy more than do baseline participants (dotted line in Figure 8.5), the observed increase in persuasion stems from the dissolution of a boomerang effect rather than a sleeper effect.

Panels B1 and B2 of Figure 8.5 present sleeper effects. Both depict a key requisite for the effect, which is for initial agreement to not fall below the level of agreement in baseline conditions (Kumkale & Albarracín, 2004). For a sleeper effect to be present, recipients of discounting cues should be at least as persuaded as baseline participants (see Figure 8.5, panels B1 and B2). Of course, recipients of discounting cues could be more persuaded of the advocacy than baseline participants. However, a strong discounting cue typically suppresses the impact of the message arguments, generating attitudes at the same level of baseline attitudes.

Absolute sleeper effects involve an increase in persuasion among recipients of discounting cues, in addition to verifying that the increase is not due to an initial boomerang effect. Figure 8.5, panel B1 shows an absolute sleeper effect, which is a statistically significant increase in persuasion among recipients of discounting cues with no corresponding baseline increase. Figure 8.5, panel B2 shows another absolute sleeper effect, in which the persuasion increase among recipients of discounting cues is greater than the increase baseline conditions.

Relative sleeper effects involve discounting-cue conditions showing either less decay, stability, or a decay that is also visible in the baseline. Figure 8.5, panel C1 shows that persuasion among recipients of discounting cues decays less than among those in acceptance-cue conditions. Figure 8.5, panel C2 shows that persuasion among recipients of discounting cues persists over time, whereas persuasion in acceptance-cue conditions decays.

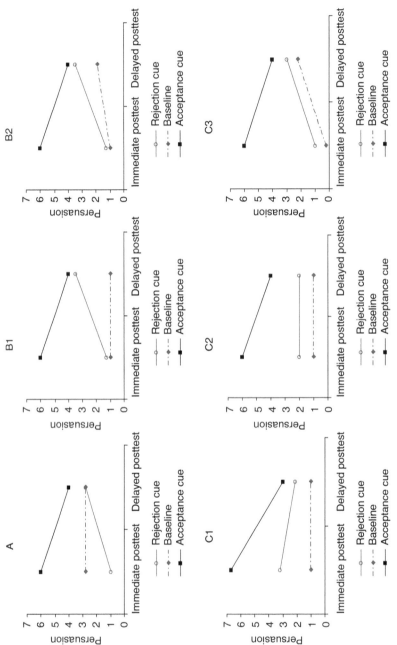

Figure 8.5 Patterns of immediate and delayed persuasion following exposure to a persuasive message: (A) boomerang effect; (B) absolute sleeper effects; (C) relative sleeper effects.

Figure 8.5, panel C3 shows increases over time in the discounting-cue condition but the same increase appears in the baseline condition.

Meta-analysis of the sleeper effect. Kumkale and I conducted a meta-analysis of the sleeper effect to determine which empirical pattern predominated and what were the necessary conditions for the effect (Kumkale & Albarracín, 2004).

We hypothesized that stronger sleeper effects, such as the absolute one (Figure 8.5B), would be more likely when the initial message and the cue are sufficiently strong to exert an influence. For example, an absolute sleeper effect should be more likely when the cue initially suppresses the impact of a message that otherwise is persuasive (e.g., initial change or difference in discounting-cue conditions vs. baseline conditions is close to 0; see Figure 8.5B). This initial suppression of the effect of the arguments ensures that there is room for persuasion if the discounting goes away. We also tested the hypothesis that the sleeper effect occurs only when the cue appears at the end of the communication.

Our hypotheses imply that adequate impacts of the message arguments and the discounting cue are necessary to generate the sleeper effect. In addition, however, we hypothesized that high ability or motivation to think about a communication would be necessary for the initial arguments to be processed in a way that would ensure strong and long-lasting impact.

Our selection criteria generated a database of 72 data sets (k). We calculated effect sizes for (a) persuasion and (b) recall/recognition of the message content. Specifically, we calculated differences among experimental and control groups at each time of measurement. For example, we obtained the difference in agreement with the message between discounting-cue and baseline conditions at the immediate posttest, which allowed us to examine the possibility of a nonpersisting boomerang effect. We also obtained differences over the different time points within each condition.

The overall results from our meta-analysis suggested the presence of a relative sleeper effect. We then tested if the sleeper effect was a negative function of the amount of initial change, as hypothesized. The sleeper effect was indeed greater when the initial change was closer to zero. In contrast, there was no sleeper effect but rather decay when recipients were initially persuaded by the arguments, presumably because of the ineffectiveness of the discounting cue. The negative relation between amount of initial change and the sleeper effect appears in Figure 8.6.

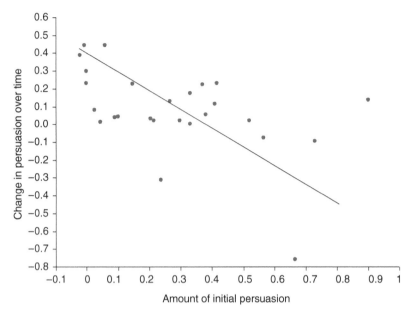

Figure 8.6 Negative association between amount of initial change and sleeper effect.

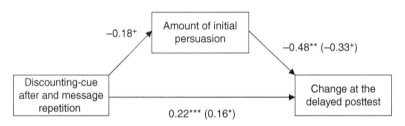

Figure 8.7 Influence of cue position on sleeper effect.

Next, we tested the hypothesis that the sleeper effect would occur only when the discounting cues followed the message arguments and when message elaboration was high. Message elaboration was assumed to be high when there was message repetition, issue relevance was high, and prior knowledge about the message topic was high. Figure 8.7 shows the effect of the position of the cue on amount of initial change and delayed change, that is, on the sleeper effect. As shown, presenting the cue after the arguments correlated positively with the size of the sleeper effect, and this effect was mediated by the amount of initial change (see Figure 8.6). In addition, elaboration mattered. As presented in Figure 8.8, absolute

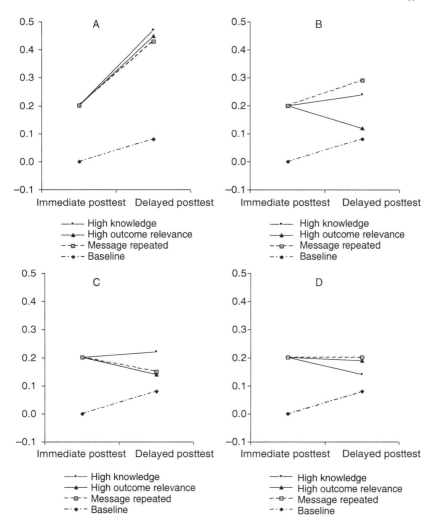

Figure 8.8 Results from the sleeper effect meta-analysis. (Reproduced from Kumkale & Albarracín, 2004)

sleeper effects were most apparent when repetition, issue relevance, and knowledge were high than when they were low.

Identification and selection of information model and new sleeper effect. The model in Figure 7.4 has shed further light on the processes that produce the sleeper effect. Our primary underlying assumption was that different aspects of the communication are available when the communication is first received relative to later, when delayed attitudes are reported. Delayed effects should therefore depend on whether people identify or attend to the source versus the arguments, but there is no reason why message recipients should always attend to the message arguments more than the source. In other words, sleeper effects studied for over 60 years could be fundamentally different if one were to generate situations in which the source of the message were the focus (Albarracín, Kumkale et al., 2017).

Although a source-based sleeper effect had not been identified in the past, we questioned the premise that the influence of the message source necessarily decays more than the influence of the message arguments (Hovland et al., 1949; Hovland & Weiss, 1951). Instead, we (Albarracín, Kumkale et al., 2017) saw no a priori reason to take this assumption for granted. To take one example, the personal characteristics of political candidates are often more important and memorable than the issues discussed in political campaigns (for reviews, see Albarracín, Kumkale et al., 2017). Most middle-aged Americans might remember that Michael Dukakis was a longtime governor of Massachusetts, but very few would remember his arguments concerning prison reform. In such situations, the attributes of the source may remain more memorable than the arguments (Kruglanski, Fishbach, Erb, Pierro, & Mannetti, 2004).

One reason sleeper effects for the source had not been observed is that all research on the sleeper effect had used strong arguments (Albarracín, Kumkale et al., 2017). Weak arguments, however, are common in everyday communication contexts. When a credible source introduces weak arguments, the initial influence of a credible communicator may decrease with the realization that the arguments are weak (i.e., reason for discounting). This discounting may produce no impact at the point of the immediate follow-up (see Table 8.4). Nonetheless, as the reason for discounting (i.e., weak arguments) becomes less accessible, a source-based sleeper effect may occur.

How a focus on the communicator would change the results of messages over time is not at all far-fetched. Decades of social cognition research supported the idea that representations can be organized around the attributes of the communicator or source of a persuasive message (Devine & Ostrom, 1985; Lingle & Ostrom, 1981; Wyer et al., 1994; Wyer, Budesheim, & Lambert, 1990). Presidential elections, for example, are contexts that motivate recipients to primarily form impressions of the candidates (Ottati & Wyer, 1993; Ottati, Edwards, & Krumdick, 2005).

Consequently, attitude-relevant information may be organized around the identity of the candidates rather than the candidates' arguments. When the focus of attention is on the source, the representation of the arguments may become less accessible over time and produce a sleeper effect for the source. These representations are depicted in Figure 8.9.

The focus of attention while a message is presented may be incidentally produced by presenting the message arguments before the source of the communication, which is the only condition under which absolute sleeper effects have been generated (Kumkale & Albarracín, 2004). But researchers like Pratkanis thought that the message arguments decayed less because of a primacy effect without explicating the mechanism. If focus of attention is the key factor, we should be able to produce it by giving participants the goal of evaluating the suitability of a candidate for public office (a source focus) or the desirability of the candidate's policy (an argument focus) (Albarracín, Kumkale et al., 2017). We should also be able to produce it by asking participants questions about selected aspects of the communication content (Albarracín, Kumkale et al., 2017; Feldman & Lynch, 1988; Fitzsimons & Williams, 2000), by repeating either information about the source versus the arguments, or by varying the visual vividness of each piece of information.

To examine the intriguing possibility of a sleeper effect for the source, we systematically manipulated recipients' focus of attention on the communication source versus the arguments, both at the time of exposure and at the point of the delayed follow-up. These manipulations along with

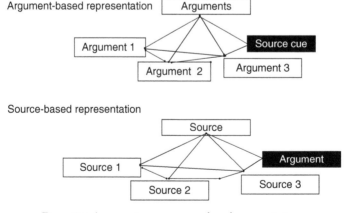

Figure 8.9 Argument- versus source-based representations.

manipulations of both the credibility of the source and the strength of the message arguments provided the grounds for testing for both the traditional argument-based sleeper effect as well as the source-based sleeper effect. Findings from three experiments showed a sleeper effect for the source when the focus of attention was the communicator and when credible sources presented weak arguments. In contrast, we found the traditional sleeper effect for the arguments when the focus of attention was the arguments and strong arguments were presented by a noncredible communicator.

In Experiments 1 and 2, participants evaluated the ostensible campaign of a fictitious political party running for the student government on campus. Each participant received two ads. One ad described the arguments of the party and contained either strong or weak arguments, and the other ad introduced the attributes of the candidates running for the office, who were portrayed as either credible or noncredible. These ads allowed us to generate two conditions, one with strong arguments presented by a noncredible source and the other with weak arguments presented by a credible source. The messages were also crossed with manipulations of attentional focus on either the arguments or the source. In Experiment 1, the focus manipulation was introduced in between the immediate and delayed follow ups using questions about either the source or the arguments (Feldman & Lynch, 1988; Fitzsimons & Williams, 2000; Killeya & Johnson, 1998). In Experiment 2, the participants were asked to examine either the argument ad or the source ad twice during message exposure, once for content and another for style.

The results from our first two experiments appear in Table 8.4. The change scores in this table imply sleeper effects when they are positive and decay when they are negative. As predicted, a focus on arguments produced the traditional sleeper effect (e.g., $d = 0.40$ in Experiment 1), but a focus on the source produced a sleeper effect for the source ($d = 0.55$ in Experiment 1). Experiment 2 also showed that the source focus had produced a better memory for the source, whereas the argument focus had produced a better memory for the argument. Even more, relative recall of arguments versus source attributes mediated each type of sleeper effect.

In sum, the communicator can be the focus of attention producing sleeper effects for the source. This finding is consistent with the idea source and other cues to persuasion can have multiple roles (Wegener et al., 2010).

Table 8.4 *Attitudes and attitude change as a function of information set and focus of attention*

| Dependent measure | Weak arguments–credible source | | Strong arguments–noncredible source | |
	Focus on arguments (n = 62)	Focus on source (n = 48)	Focus on arguments (n = 48)	Focus on source (n = 57)
Experiment 1 (Attitudes)				
Immediate attitudes	−0.17	−0.37	0.17	0.35
	(2.43)	(2.64)	(2.35)	(2.16)
Delayed attitudes	−0.43	0.03	0.73	−0.18
	(2.62)	(2.63)	(2.52)	(2.43)
Attitude change	−0.26[+]	0.40[*]	0.55[*]	−0.53[*]
	(−0.58/0.06)	(0.04/0.76)	(0.20/0.91)	(−0.86/−0.21)
Experiment 2 (Attitudes)				
Immediate attitudes	0.40	0.93	0.34	−0.10
	(2.75)	(2.01)	(2.47)	(1.89)
Delayed attitudes	−0.05	1.43	1.06	−0.06
	(3.22)	(1.95)	(2.49)	(3.21)
Attitude change	−0.46[+]	0.50[*]	0.72[*]	0.04[ns]
	(−0.93/0.06)	(0.02/0.98)	(0.23/1.21)	(−0.42/0.49)
Recall for message arguments and source attributes				
Message arguments	2.74	1.61	2.71	2.00
	(2.31/3.17)	(1.17/2.05)	(2.25/3.16)	(1.58/2.42)
Source attributes	0.90	2.00	0.82	2.00
	(0.31/1.48)	(1.43/2.58)	(0.20/1.44)	(1.43/2.58)

Note: Immediate and delayed attitudes were measured using scales that ranged from −5 to 5. Values in parentheses are standard deviations for immediate and delayed attitudes; for attitude change scores, they are 95 percent confidence intervals around the means. Recall scores could range from 0 to 4 for both arguments and source attributes. Values in parentheses are 95 percent confidence intervals around the means.
[+] $p < 0.06$. [*] $p < 0.05$.
Source: Adapted from Albarracín, Kumkale, and Vento (2017).

One demonstration of this possibility came from research on the attitude–behavior relation. Attitudes formed on the basis of extensive information about a source, which supposedly elicits high levels of processing, were more persistent and predicted behavior more than did attitudes formed on the basis of brief information about the source (Pierro et al., 2012). As persistence and impact on behavior are frequent consequences of high levels of elaboration (Barden & Tormala, 2014; Howe & Krosnick, 2015), our work shows that communicators can be the target of much attention and thinking and may influence behaviors as well. For other research on the effects of concentrating on the communication source, see Clark, Wegener, Sawicki, Petty, and Brinol (2013), and Clark and Evans (2014).

Identification and Comparison in Attitude Change

Without a doubt, responses to persuasive communications are in part driven by how accessible prior attitudes are. As described previously, Fazio (1989) showed that highly accessible attitudes are activated by the mere presence of the attitude object. The more times people evaluate an object, the faster they can evaluate it, and the more automatic the evaluation becomes. For that reason, highly accessible prior attitudes can guide final attitudes and thus reduce consideration of other information (Fazio, Ledbetter, & Towles-Schwen, 2000). The influence of attitude accessibility on change has been studied in the context of persuasive communication as well.

There is evidence that the reception of comparable information across different time points is also an important predictor of attitude change (Muthukrishnan, Pham, & Mungalé, 2001; Muthukrishnan, Pham, & Mungalé, 1999; Pham & Muthukrishnan, 2002). According to this research, attitudes change when the prior and the new information are "alignable." Thus, a challenge to a prior attitude is successful when the new information maps onto the old information. This research is highly relevant to this chapter and will be reviewed in the following sections.

My colleagues and I summarized the role of attitude accessibility and comparison in the model of Figure 8.10 (Albarracín, Wallace, & Glasman, 2004). As shown in Figure 8.10, three key processes are presumably involved in attitude change. People can activate their prior attitude and also pay attention to additional information relevant to those attitudes. For example, people planning to vote in an upcoming election may recall their prior favorable attitude toward the candidate. They may access attitude-consistent or -inconsistent memories about the object, or they might consider the attitude-consistent or -inconsistent implications of external stimuli. For example, during election time, people who activate prior attitudes toward political candidates may also recall prior knowledge about the candidates (internal attitude-related information) and analyze political propaganda available in their environment (external attitude-related information). People may also consider feelings of familiarity

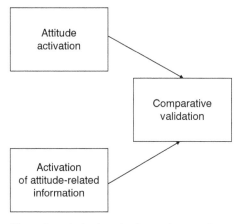

Figure 8.10 Attitude activation and comparison.

(Krosnick et al., 2007), the mood they experience at the time (DeSteno et al., 2000; Forgas & Bower, 1987; Schwarz & Clore, 1983, 2007), the credibility or attractiveness of the communication source (Chaiken, 1979; Hovland & Weiss, 1951), their past behavioral decisions (Albarracín & Wyer, 2000a; Janis & King, 1954), or the threat posed by attitude-inconsistent information (Festinger, 1957; for a proposal of modes of resolution of belief conflict, see Abelson, 1959).

The prior attitude may be seen as a summary of the additional information associated with the attitude, such as the object attributes that led to a positive attitude toward the object (Albarracín et al., 2004). In some cases, the additional information is redundant, and people simply rely on their attitude. However, if the additional information is new, people are likely to attempt to integrate the prior attitude with the additional information. Integrating this information may entail assigning equal weights by default and averaging the prior attitudes with the evaluative implications of the additional information.

As shown in Figure 8.10, however, people sometimes compare their prior attitude with the evaluative implications of the additional information (Albarracín et al., 2004). Comparison can proceed in a bottom-up or top-down fashion. By definition, two objects must be activated for any comparison to occur. Moreover, alignable objects (two types of fruits) are more likely to elicit comparison than unalignable objects (a fruit and a desk). In our case, activation of a prior attitude and additional information can trigger spontaneous comparative processing. This processing may lead to assimilation or contrast effects as described by social judgment theory and can lead to the two pieces of information receiving different weights.

Other times, the comparison develops in a top-down fashion (Albarracín et al., 2004). For example, people may receive direct instructions to reconsider their prior position on an issue in light of newly available information (e.g., during a judicial trial). When this happens, they must activate the new specific information as well as their prior attitude to perform the comparison.

The order of activation and comparison has important consequences for attitude change (Albarracín et al., 2004). In particular, the goal to compare may produce biases in what information is selected. One is likely to use the features of the new information to select additional information. Furthermore, the goal to compare may trigger activation of either the prior information or the new information.

The activation-comparison model specifies situations in which comparative motivation can facilitate the activation and maintenance of prior attitudes without triggering comparison. Figure 8.11 presents a case in which comparison precedes attitude activation (Albarracín et al., 2004). Any disruption that leaves comparison incomplete may enhance the effect of the prior information or the new information depending on which one was activated first.

In contrast, Figure 8.12 presents situations in which the attitude is retrieved before comparison is a goal. If the attitude was retrieved first, attitude maintenance is more likely than attitude change. Attitude and information accessibility may have similar effects. When prior attitudes are not easy to recall, having the goal of comparing new information with the prior attitude should first elicit the recall of the prior attitude. In the process, however, people may decide to simply use that prior attitude and give up on comparing it with other information. Thus, when prior attitudes are low in accessibility, attempts at comparison could produce attitude maintenance.

Comparison may nonetheless occur (Albarracín et al., 2004). There are lower-level, perceptual types of comparative processes, as well as inferential forms of comparative validation. Either form of comparison can involve a number of elements processed sequentially but we restrict consideration to only two. One may simply wish to compare one's prior attitude with new information to determine if one's attitude must change. Or one may compare the direction or validity of the prior information with the direction or validity of the current information. Importantly, these comparisons may be performed quickly with increasing process automation.

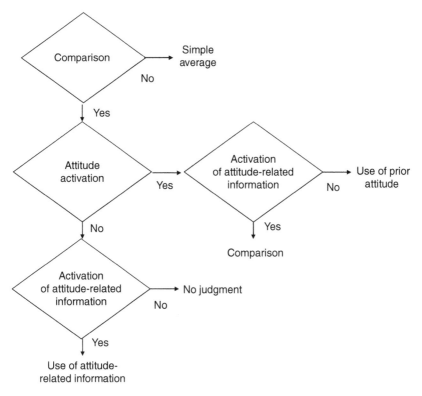

Figure 8.11 Comparison following attitude activation.

Attitude Change as a Combined Function of Activation and Comparison

The model in Figure 8.11 also implies that attempts at comparison will trigger a retrieval of the prior attitude to make the comparison possible. Therefore, the motivation to compare a prior attitude with other information is likely to activate the prior attitude. Interestingly, however, the process may stop at the point of the attitude retrieval. If such an interruption occurred, comparison would decrease attitude change (Albarracín et al., 2004). People who receive new information will not always retrieve a prior attitude. Suppose that people are induced to compare a new persuasive message with their prior attitude and associated information. Suppose also that these individuals have not yet retrieved their attitude and associated information. In this situation, the comparison induction may promote the activation of the prior attitude, which is a precondition for

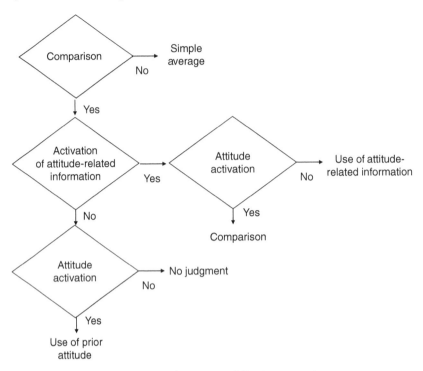

Figure 8.12 Attitude activation following comparison.

attitude comparison. However, the comparison motivation may only be sufficient to elicit attitude activation but not comparison. Consequently, people may simply report the attitude they retrieved in their attempt at the comparison (Albarracín et al., 2004).

The evidence presented in Figure 8.11 (Albarracín et al., 2004) supported the notion that comparison inductions sometimes yield activation and maintenance of a prior attitude. Less accessible attitudes changed when participants received neither an attitude reminder nor a comparison inducement. This finding suggested that these participants formed attitudes online on the basis of the second (negative) message alone. However, less accessible attitudes did not change when participants received the comparison inducement, suggesting that the comparison inducement produced attitude activation. However, the sequence of processing presumably stopped before the comparison stage needed for the new information to be integrated with prior attitudes.

If a given comparison inducement is sufficient to activate the prior attitude but falls short of inducing actual comparison, an even stronger comparison inducement might achieve both. Relevant to this hypothesis are data on attitude change among participants who previously received information that a product was either positive or negative (Muthukrishnan, 2003). After reporting their attitude at the point of the pretest, participants received an ad that challenged the consumer information they received previously. The ad had either a comparative or a noncomparative format, and contained information that concerned either the same or different dimensions as the first information set. The four combinations of format and dimension alignability provide three levels of comparison induction, namely, (a) high (both comparative format and same dimensions), (b) moderate (either comparative format or same dimensions), and (c) low (neither comparative format nor same dimensions). Now, if prior attitudes are difficult to access, the moderate-comparison induction might be sufficient to instill attitude activation but not comparison, leading to maintenance of the recalled attitude. In contrast, the highest-comparison induction should promote attitude comparison as well as activation, leading to change.

Muthukrishnan (2003) found that negative initial attitudes were more difficult to access than positive initial attitudes. Given this accessibility difference, the moderate level of comparison induction may only increase activation of and, therefore, maintenance in the less accessible (negative) attitudes. In contrast, the moderate-comparison induction might elicit comparison and thus change of more accessible (positive) attitudes. Furthermore, the high-comparison induction may successfully produce comparison and therefore change regardless of the accessibility of prior attitudes (Albarracín et al., 2004). As can be seen from Figure 8.13, these predictions were supported. First, when prior attitudes were more accessible (Figure 8.13A), moderate- or high-comparison conditions had more change. Second, when attitudes were less accessible (Figure 8.13B), low- and high-comparison conditions had the most change. Participants in the low-comparison condition probably formed an attitude on the basis of the online information, which contradicted their prior attitudes. Participants in the moderate-comparison condition probably retrieved their prior attitude but the induction was not strong enough to promote comparison. Participants in the high-comparison condition performed the comparison regardless of the accessibility of their prior attitude.

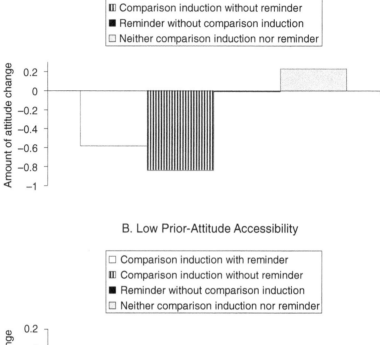

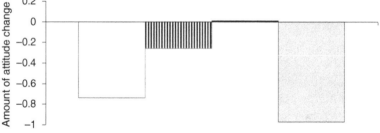

Figure 8.13 Effects of low, moderate, and high comparison as a function of prior attitude accessibility.

Process of Comparison

A lot of the research on comparative processes has concerned *direction of comparison* effects. This research has revealed that the way in which one performs the comparison influences what information is activated. When two elements (*A* and *B*) are presented in a sequence, the second element (*B*) is more frequently compared with the first (*A*) than the first is compared with the second. One starts the comparison when one is considering *B*. Therefore, one is more likely to compare *B* with *A*, thus driving attention to the features of *B* – the *subject*. Then, comparing entails determining what features the subject shares with the alternative and what features are unique to the subject. In this process, the unique features of *A* are overlooked.

Consider the options of rental places used by de Bruin and Keren (2003). As shown in Table 8.5, if one went through a "for rent" list provided by a student housing service, when reading the characteristics of room *A,* one would have to consider *A* by itself. By the time one gets to read about room *B*, however, one may be compelled to compare the two rooms. While reading about *B*, the characteristics of *B* are more salient than those of *A*.

Table 8.5 *Room rent scenarios to illustrate direction of comparison effects*

Valence of unique features	Room A	Room B	Room C
Negative	Own phone line	Nice roommates	Cute layout
	Old carpet	*Difficult to park bike*	*High security deposit*
	Near supermarket	Sink in room	Near (night) bus stop
	Difficult to park bike	*Old carpet*	*Old carpet*
	Student recommended	Near park	Includes washer
	High security deposit	*Dirty kitchen*	*Dirty kitchen*
	Safe neighborhood	Lots of windows/ light	Pretty view
	Dirty kitchen	*High security deposit*	*Difficult to park bike*
	Shared balcony	Lots of closet space	Friendly landlord
Positive	*Own phone line*	*Student recommended*	*Own phone line*
	Old carpet	Thin walled	Messy corridor
	Near supermarket	*Near supermarket*	*Safe neighborhood*
	Difficult to park bike	Overdue maintenance	Discolored wall paper
	Student recommended	*Own phone line*	*Shared balcony*
	High security deposit	Two months' notice	Poor bathroom heating
	Safe neighborhood	*Shared balcony*	*Near supermarket*
	Dirty kitchen	Unfriendly landlord	Nosy neighbors
	Shared balcony	*Safe neighborhood*	*Student recommended*

Source: Adapted from de Bruin and Keren (2003).

Thus, in comparing the two, one is likely to use the features of *B* as a sort of checklist. As one encounters each feature of *B*, one may quickly check if the feature is also present in *A*. Common features will be ignored, and any unique features of *B* will define the outcome of the comparison. As a result, the outcome of the comparison will ultimately depend on whether the unique features of *B* are positive or negative. One should select *B* if its unique features are positive, but *A* if the unique features of *B* are negative.

The direction of comparison effect has received considerable attention in various domains. In this regard, de Bruin and Keren (2003) explored it as a function of sequential versus simultaneous types of presentations. Across five experiments, the authors presented the three scenarios (A–C) in Table 8.5 in one of three ways: (a) sequential (one description was presented at a time and consideration of the next was allowed only after the first one had been considered), (b) semi-simultaneous presentation (one description was presented first, followed by the simultaneous presentation of that same description on one side of the visual field and the next one on the other side), and (c) simultaneous (descriptions were presented simultaneously, each on one side of the visual field). In addition, across the five studies, judgments were measured either (a) sequentially (one after the sequential presentation of the target image), or (b) simultaneously (the items measuring both judgments were presented on the same page, below the simultaneously presented descriptions).[2] In all cases, participants reported their judgment of each option on a scale from 1 (*very unattractive*) to 9 (*very attractive*).

A summary of their results for the room choice scenarios appears in Table 8.6. This summary includes the *p*-value of the linear trends of order. If there is a direction of comparison effect, the second item should appear more extreme than the first. Likewise, the third item should appear more extreme than the second. If the unique features are positive, judgments should become more positive if they come later than earlier in the sequence. Conversely, if the unique features are negative, judgments should become more negative if they come later than earlier in the sequence. Consistent with these expectations, the judgments in Table 8.6 show an effect of the positive and negative features of the most recently judged room. This effect, however, was more pronounced when conditions facilitated the sequential judgment of the attractiveness of each room. As a visual inspection of the table suggests, the direction of comparison

---

[2] For simplicity, we only discuss the findings for the presentation of two elements. In this research, however, the researchers repeated their procedures with a third list and with a different set of stimuli. The findings we report generalized to these other conditions.

Table 8.6 *Judgments of preference in response to room rent scenarios*

	Unique positive	Unique negative
A. Sequential judgments of sequentially presented options (Experiment 1)		
First	4.92	5.04
Second	5.13	4.24
Third	5.51	4.33
p-value of linear trend	0.001	0.006
B. End of sequence judgments of sequentially presented options (Experiment 2)		
First	5.84	5.72
Second	5.97	4.87
Third	6.20	4.99
Linear trend	0.13	0.02
C. Sequential judgments in semi-simultaneously presented options (Experiment 3)		
First	5.19	4.84
Second	5.69	4.26
Third	6.10	4.43
Linear trend	0.0001	0.11
D. Sequential judgments of simultaneously presented options (Experiment 4, judged left to right)		
First	5.81	5.80
Second	6.40	5.55
Third	6.25	5.32
Linear trend	0.06	0.11
E. Sequential judgments of simultaneously presented options (Experiment 4, judged right to left)		
First	5.79	5.59
Second	6.38	5.71
Third	6.97	4.94
Linear trend	0.0001	0.04
F. Simultaneously requested judgments of simultaneously presented options (Experiment 5, judged left to right)		
First	5.94	4.18
Second	6.63	4.73
Third	6.31	4.27
Linear trend	0.21	0.79
G. Simultaneously requested judgments of simultaneously presented options (Experiment 5, judged right to left)		
First	5.39	4.93
Second	6.33	5.07
Third	6.42	5.00
Linear trend	0.03	0.84

Source: Adapted from de Bruin and Keren (2003).

effects were more frequently significant when the materials were presented sequentially and the judgments were made sequentially than when either or both activities were simultaneous.

Alignability Effects

Interestingly, the direction of comparison effect depends on the nature of the differences. There are truly unique attributes of the focal alternative (*B* in the earlier example) that cannot be compared with the attributes of the other element. However, there are also unique attributes that are *alignable* with other attributes and thus should not produce direction of comparison effects (see, e.g., Sanbonmatsu, Kardes, & Gibson, 1991). For example, one brand of microwave popcorn may pop in a bag and another brand may come with a special microwave bowl. These two attributes are clearly different, but they are also alignable because both are containers. When differences are alignable, they can be easily compared and are thus difficult to miss.

One important prediction with respect to alignability is that a better alternative would be preferred only if the differences with the worse alternative are alignable. If it is difficult to perform the comparison, the superior attributes of the better alternative may remain unnoticed. Table 8.7 presents the stimuli used by Zhang and Markman (2001) in a study of the effects of alignability on consumer attitudes. Importantly, the two brands in Table 8.7 were equally attractive when evaluated individually. However, as shown in Figure 8.14A, when both brands were judged one next to the other, the one that was more attractive based on alignable differences was judged more desirable than the one than was more attractive based on nonalignable differences.

Even when nonalignable differences are likely to be ignored in many situations, Zhang and Markman (2001) have shown that high involvement reduces this difference. Figures 8.14B,C present the number of participants choosing each brand as a function of the alignability of attributes and involvement level. The high-involvement participants were told that they were part of a very small group of people whose opinions would contribute to making final adjustments to a product to be soon marketed in their area. The low-involvement participants were told that their data would be pooled with those of many participants and that the products were being considered for development. As shown in Figure 8.14, when involvement was low, the better alignable brand was selected more frequently. In contrast, when involvement was high, both brands were similarly attractive. Apparently then, a high motivation to process information allows

Table 8.7 *Commonalities, alignable differences, and nonalignable differences of stimulus brands*

Better brand given alignable differences	Better brand given nonalignable differences
Commonalities	
Low cost per serving	Low cost per serving
Low level of sodium	Low level of sodium
Not salty	Not salty
Easy to prepare	Easy to prepare
Alignable differences	
Large-size kernels	Medium-size kernels
Pops in its own bag	Requires a microwave bowl
Calories equal to a slice of bread	Calories equal to a tablespoon of sugar
Crunchiness lasts long	Crunchiness lasts for 3 hours
Nonalignable differences	
Slightly low in corn and grain flavor	Easy to swallow
Tastes a bit sweet	Not likely to burn
Has some citric acid	Not tough
With waterproof wrapping	Kind of crispy

Source: Adapted from Zhang and Markman (2001, Experiments 1 and 2).

individuals to accurately estimate the value of a product even when the differences are difficult to assess.

Assimilation and Contrast Effects

The goal to compare two elements can produce interesting effects. For example, comparisons with extreme standards generally lead to contrast effects, whereas comparisons with moderate standards generally lead to assimilation effects. For example, Mussweiler, Rüter, and Epstude (2004) recruited water polo players and asked them to estimate their athletic abilities. Participants were told that people often need to have a reference standard in mind. Half of the participants received a description of an athlete who typically makes a good impression during competition and receives occasional praise from the coach (moderately high standard). The other half received a description of an athlete who is clearly the best member of the team and is exclusively responsible for the team's victory (extremely high standard). After receiving either of these descriptions, all participants evaluated their swimming speed and their average contribution to the team's performance.

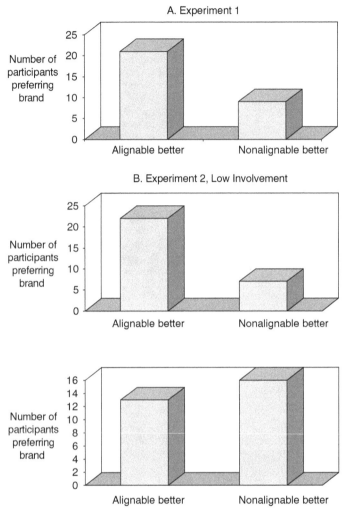

Figure 8.14 Zhang and Markman's (2001) experiments.

As expected, the water polo players evaluated their own athletic abilities as higher when they previously received the moderately high standard than when they received the extremely high standard. In this regard, other studies have conclusively demonstrated that assimilation and contrast effects are contingent on focusing on similarities versus differences. For example, in a related study by Mussweiler, Rüter, and Epstude (2004), participants who assimilated their self-assessed intelligence to a high standard spontaneously mentioned their similarities with the target. Conversely, participants who contrasted their self-assessed intelligence with a high standard spontaneously mentioned their differences from the target.

Inferential Comparative Processes

Considering *inferential processes*, comparative validation is the joint analysis of a prior attitude with its associated information (the attitude basis) vis-à-vis new information along with its summary evaluation. This is graphically presented in Figure 8.15. In this case, the correspondence between the two elements on the right is compared with the correspondence between the two elements on the left. For example, if the fit between the elements on the right is tighter than the fit between the elements on the left, the prior attitude is likely to appear more valid than the new information. Comparative validation relies on validation principles and ability and motivation to perform the validation.

Our model (Albarracín et al., 2004; Albarracín, Wallace, Hart, & Brown, 2012) specified a *corroboration principle* by which agreement between the prior attitude and subjectively valid attitude-related information should increase confidence in the validity of both elements (Treadwell & Nelson, 1996) and may increase the extremity of the prior attitude. Several studies support this notion. For instance, female participants who evaluated pictures of male models had more confident and extreme evaluations when their ratings were corroborated by other raters (Baron et al., 1996). Moreover, corroborating

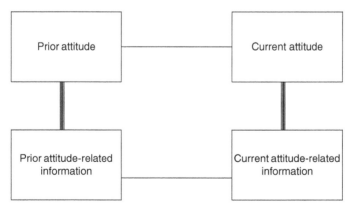

Figure 8.15 Comparison followed by activation of attitude-related information.

evidence appears to derive not only from external sources but also from internal ones. Tesser (1978) proposed that merely thinking about an issue results in attitude polarization because people normally produce ideas that are consistent with their prior attitudes. Moreover, people who are knowledgeable about an issue have more thoughts in line with their attitudes than people who have little knowledge about the issue. Consistent with this possibility, when men and women reflected about football plays and women's fashion, men's attitudes toward football and women's about fashion were more polarized than the corresponding attitudes in women and men (Tesser & Leone, 1977). Presumably, retrieving knowledge consistent with prior attitudes increases the subjective validity of the attitude.

Our own research (Albarracín et al., 2012) has shown that comparison of two messages leading to the same conclusion increases the perceived strength of the second message. Both messages advocated instituting comprehensive exams at the university. Participants who received the second message in a format that could be easily compared with the first (see also Kalro, Sivakumaran, & Marathe, 2013) developed more positive judgments than participants who did not receive the information in this format. These effects were mediated by differences in strength. This analysis appears in Figure 8.16. This effect was replicated in several experiments.

Discussions with other people can also polarize attitudes (Isenberg, 1986). Interactions with others who agree can yield more extreme attitudes (Moscovici & Zavalloni, 1969). Why attitudes polarize during discussion with similar others is intriguing (for a review, see Prislin & Wood, 2005). Polarization may be the result of exchanging evaluatively consistent arguments that are new to one of the individuals (Burnstein & Vinokur, 1977). The new, corroborating arguments may cause shift toward a more extreme position. In addition, simply repeating one's own arguments can polarize judgments as well (Brauer, Judd, & Gliner, 1995).

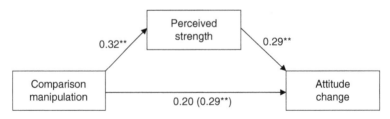

Figure 8.16 Mediation of the effects of comparison.

A *defensive confidence principle* applies to situations in which people compare a prior attitude and evaluatively inconsistent attitude-related information. In this case, people may develop more confident and extreme attitudes after outweighing valid information of conflicting implications than before they consider conflicting information (McGuire, 1961; Papageorgis & McGuire, 1961). The defensive confidence principle entails determining the validity of two conflicting pieces of information on the basis of their relative perceived success. People may more strongly endorse evaluations they have successfully defended from challenge than evaluations that were not challenged. However, the associated polarization in either the prior attitude or the implications of the attitude-related information should not occur when the prior attitudes and the attitude-related information are both subjectively valid. Such situations should stimulate a compromise between the prior attitude and the attitude-related information.

One example of defensive confidence comes from McGuire and Papageorgis's (1961) research on beliefs that are deeply held but weakly supported (i.e., "truism"; e.g., brushing one's teeth frequently is beneficial). In this research, participants received a communication attacking a truism after having defended the truism from a mild attack (a message) or after having received no such attack. The study showed that participants who received an attack after being immunized by the earlier mild attack were better able to maintain their belief in the truism than people who were not previously inoculated. It is possible that realizing that one's prior attitude has survived attack strengthens one's confidence in that attitude.[3]

Research by Tormala and Petty (2002) also speaks to the defensive confidence principle. In one of their studies, experimental participants were asked to resist messages that were described as strong or weak, whereas control participants received no information about the strength of the messages they received. Results indicated that participants had equally extreme attitudes regardless of the supposed strength of the message they resisted. However, participants were more certain about their attitudes after resisting an ostensibly strong message than after resisting both an

---

[3] My model assumes that people may polarize their prior attitudes either by receiving valid supporting information or by refuting inconsistent information. However, McGuire and Papageorgis (1961) demonstrated that refutational defenses increase resistance to future persuasion to a greater extent than supportive information, although receiving supportive arguments is better than receiving no arguments at all. In the context of our model, people may engage in more comparison when the information they receive disagrees with their attitudes. If this is true, polarization may in fact be more frequent when the attitude-related information is inconsistent with the prior attitude.

ostensibly weak or undetermined strength message. Tormala and Petty concluded that people interpret their personal success in defending their attitudes from a strong attack as a sign that their attitude is correct. Therefore, they increase their attitude certainty.

Consider the case of incoming college students who are prejudiced against African Americans but learn that their aspirational group rejects racism. The students may judge both pieces of information vis-à-vis their current goal to be accepted by the aspirational group. They may thus judge the ingroup's opinion to be valid and their prior racist attitude to be invalid. In comparing their prior attitude with the attitude of their aspirational group, however, students may conclude that the ingroup opinion ought to be particularly sound to convince them despite their prior prejudice. As a result, they may endorse an egalitarian position that is more confident and extreme because of the comparison with their prior conflicting attitudes.

Other evidence is also illustrative of this principle. Rucker and Petty (2004) presented participants with a strong ad promoting a pharmaceutical product and instructed them either to list negative thoughts or to simply list their thoughts about the message. Presumably, participants who listed only negative thoughts attempted to resist the communication more than those who were free to list any (positive, negative, and/or neutral) thoughts. Findings indicated that participants were persuaded regardless of what thoughts they listed, supposedly because the ad was difficult to refute. However, participants who attempted to resist the message (and failed) were more confident in their attitude than those who did not make such an attempt. Although Rucker and Petty examined attitude formation rather than change, failure to invalidate attitude-inconsistent information appears to reassure individuals of the validity of that information.

Unanticipated Changes in Beliefs and Behaviors

Fishbein and Ajzen (1981) also conceptualized persuasion with particular attention to both beliefs in the message and beliefs generated by recipients. According to them, understanding persuasion requires taking three aspects into account. First, people may believe in the arguments presented in the message (i.e., "acceptance"). Second, "yielding" may occur when these primary beliefs are more novel or stronger than prior beliefs. Third, a persuasive message may have indirect "impact" effects on other, unmentioned beliefs. Thus, both yielding and impact can predict behavior change. Yielding represents beliefs in the message, whereas impact represents beliefs based on prior knowledge.

To examine the importance of acceptance, yielding and impact, Fishbein, Ajzen, and McArdle (1980) developed messages to persuade alcoholics to participate in a rehabilitation program. The two messages of concern for my analyses advocated signing up for the program and described the consequences of this behavior. The arguments contained in the two messages were the same. One of them, however, was framed positively and concerned reductions in negative outcomes and increases in positive outcomes as consequences of enrollment. The other message was framed negatively. It argued that not signing up for the program would lead to an increase in negative consequences and a decrease in positive ones.

The two messages used in the study allowed for an examination of acceptance, yielding, and impact. Acceptance was assessed by measuring beliefs in the arguments of the persuasive message after message exposure. Yielding was represented by the difference between beliefs in the outcomes the message described across experimental and control conditions. Impact was represented as the difference between beliefs in outcomes not described in the message across experimental and control conditions. For example, the message stated that not signing up for the program would lead to a poorer relationship with one's family and employer. Hence, acceptance and yielding were assessed with beliefs that "not signing up for the program would lead to a poorer relationship with family and employer." The impact counterpart stated that signing up for the program would facilitate a "better relationship with family and employer." The key study outcome, signing up for a program, showed acceptance, that is, people accepted what the message proposed. If the message indicated that "not signing up for the program would lead to a poorer relationship with family and employer," participants were likely to endorse that belief. To determine if there is actual change (i.e., yielding, or movement toward the advocacy), this absolute acceptance score, however, needs to be examined in relation to a baseline (i.e., in this case, the control condition). To determine if knowledge-based beliefs changed, one needs to examine if these beliefs were stronger in the experimental conditions than in the control conditions. Results indicated that the message had been successful on all three counts. Recipients accepted the message, that is, the absolute level of enrollment in the program was high. In addition, recipients showed yielding, that is, there was greater acceptance in the experimental than in the control group. Finally, recipients showed impact, that is, trickle-down effects from mentioned beliefs to other conclusions participants made based on their prior knowledge of the issue.

In the context of this chapter, the distinction between acceptance and impact is important. For example, persuasive messages may lead to beliefs unanticipated by persuaders. However, the acceptance-yielding-impact model did not specify the relation between message- and knowledge-based beliefs and attitudes.

We explored whether change in behavioral measures was greater when outcomes were targeted in comparison to when outcomes were not targeted by a behavioral recommendation. Specifically, we examined whether single-behavior interventions assessed change in behavioral outcomes untargeted by the recommendation, as this allowed for the comparison of change in targeted versus untargeted measures. Taking interventions making a single-behavior recommendation that included multiple behavioral measures ($k = 5$), we computed a weighted mean effect size for change in targeted and untargeted measures. Whether a measure was targeted by the recommendation significantly predicted overall change. The weighted mean effects sizes from the fixed-effects analyses showed that, compared to untargeted behaviors ($d = 0.04$; 95% CI = 0.01, 0.06), change was significantly greater in targeted behaviors ($d = 0.33$; 95% CI = 0.31, 0.36).

Change in Action and Inaction Patterns

The homogeneity in action and inaction recommendations can influence behavior change, such that only changing actions or only changing inactions is easier than changing a mix of actions and inactions. My colleagues and I investigated implications of the notion of general action and inaction concepts for message actionability (Albarracín et al., 2017). We proposed that a health recommendation of action would facilitate other health recommendations of action but hinder recommendations of inaction. Likewise, a health recommendation of inaction would facilitate other inaction recommendations but hinder action recommendations. In sum, a homogeneous set of health recommendations should be more efficacious than a heterogeneous set. For example, recommending increases in physical activity may be more efficacious when combined with the recommendation to increase fruit and vegetable intake than when combined with the recommendation to decrease in fat intake. Correspondingly, recommending a decrease in fat intake may be more efficacious when combined with reducing sugar intake or quitting smoking than when combined with increasing exercise.

We used the data from our multiple-behavior meta-analysis to test the hypothesis that homogeneous behavioral recommendations were more efficacious than heterogeneous ones (Albarracín, Sunderrajan, Dai, et al., 2019). We coded (a) the domain of the recommendation (e.g., diet, exercise) and (b) whether the recommendation was for action (e.g., increase physical activity; increase fruit intake) or inaction (e.g., reduce fat intake; quit smoking; rest and relax). We created a variable that classified interventions as recommending predominately action behaviors, an equal number of action and inaction behaviors, or predominately inaction behaviors. We also created a variable that averaged all behavioral and clinical measures of change available in a study. Table 8.8 shows the average effect of that variable on overall change, as well as Q_B statistics, which indicate a significant effect of the recommendation combination on overall change. As hypothesized, homogeneous recommendations for either action or action were more effective than mixed action/inaction recommendations. In addition, interventions with equal numbers of action and inaction recommendations did not differ significantly from single-behavior programs or control conditions (see subscripts e and d in Table 8.8), and a predominance of inaction recommendations produced

Table 8.8 *Change as a function of the homogeneity of action and inaction recommendations*

	Predominately inaction	Equal	Predominately action	Q_{B_2}	k
k	30	106	80		
Fixed-effects d.	0.35_a	0.11_{bde}	0.19_c	395.84^{***}	216
Random-effects d.	0.48_a	0.16_b	0.23_c	35.73^{***}	216

Note: d. = weighted means. No-intervention control groups (k = 39, d. = 0.06, confidence interval = −0.01, 0.12) and single-behavior intervention groups (k = 15, d. = 0.07, confidence interval = 0.02, 0.13) were excluded. Following the means, we present the Q_B for the action/inaction index. Q_B = homogeneity coefficient for the difference across levels of a factor, distributed as a chi-square with degrees of freedom equal to the number of factor levels − 1. ds with similar subscripts a–c are not significantly different from one another. Subscript d indicates that change is not different from change in the no-intervention control group. Subscript e indicates that change is not different from change in the single-behavior control group. k = number of conditions.
$^*p$ < 0.05, $^{**}p$ < 0.01, $^{***}p$ < 0.001.
Source: Adapted from Albarracín et al. (2017).

more change than a predominance of action recommendations. Whatever the case, interventions with homogeneous recommendations were more actionable than interventions with heterogeneous recommendations.

Summary

Prior attitudes shape the processing of persuasive messages and behavioral interventions in fundamental ways. First, people select messages and interventions in ways that minimize their likely impact. They seek pro-violence messages when they already espouse pro-violence beliefs and healthy eating messages when they already follow healthy diets. These decisions of course decrease the probability of changing attitudes and behaviors that have negative social and health effects, which has led to my research on finding methods to decrease selective exposure biases. For example, because selective exposure is often tied to a low sense of one's ability to self-defend if one's attitudes or behaviors come under attack, reassuring an audience that they will only change if they want to is often sufficient to increase exposure to messages and enrollment in behavioral interventions. In addition, understanding attitude and behavior change requires understanding activation of prior attitudes and other information contained in the message. For example, easy to access prior attitudes generally decrease change in response to new information but may also increase change when they facilitate comparison with new information. Furthermore, when people who are called to report an attitude retrieve the initial basis for their attitude, the structure of that information in memory drives the degree of attitude change in that situation.

CHAPTER 9

Actionability, Sources of Actionability, and Behavioral Impact of Persuasive Communications and Behavioral Interventions

Some messages target attitudes and beliefs, such as messages to increase the popularity of a president or instill the belief in God. Other messages are designed with the intent of having an impact on behavior. So are behavioral interventions, which introduce counseling, role-playing, tasks, and various forms of training to ensure an impact on behavior. When messages are designed to affect behavior, success equals "actionability." I define *actionability* as the probability that the message or intervention communicates or enables performance of behavioral recommendations (Albarracín, Sunderrajan, & Dai, 2018; Cohen & Andrade, 2018). As such, it entails a message that can induce the cognitive, motivational, or behavioral processes that will lead to the recommended behavior within the individual. It also concerns the fit of the behavioral recommendations within the world in which recipients will attempt to perform a behavior. In this chapter, I first distinguish actionality from other concepts, namely, argument strength and desirability. I then turn to actionability factors that pertain to instilling the desired behavior in the person and promoting a behavior that will fit the environment in which the behavior is executed.

Distinguishing Actionability from Argument Strength

Actionability is conceptually different from the believability or strength of the message arguments because a message may be highly credible without having any implications for behavior. We tested perceptions of actionability and argument strength by assigning participants to read either a positive review or a negative review of a juice that could ostensibly be customized by buyers (Albarracín, Sunderrajan et al., 2019). The high-actionability form of the message indicated that the juice offered a variety of flavors and could satisfy different needs for a wide range of customers; the low-actionability form of the message indicated that the juice had an

Table 9.1 *Ratings of argument strength and actionability as a function of message type*

	Argument strength M (SD)	Actionability M (SD)
High-actionability message	1.39 (0.88)	2.05 (0.71)
Low-actionability message	1.59 (0.99)	1.13 (1.11)

Source: Albarracín et al. (2018).

inefficient and wasteful manufacturing process. Participants read the message and then rated their reactions. The actionability scales had items such as "this piece of information influences my behavioral decision" and "this piece of information is relevant to my behavioral goal." The argument strength scale had items such as "this information is persuasive" and "this information is compelling." Table 9.1 shows participants' ratings of each message. As shown in this table, the two messages were identical in argument strength but their actionability differed markedly. The message that discussed customization and allowed participants to imagine what they would do with the product was perceived as more actionable than the message that discussed the product manufacturing.

Although actionability is not the same as argument strength, when a message is explicitly behavioral, stronger evidence or reasoning makes the message more actionable. This notion is apparent when a message recommending voting in favor of an upcoming policy is analyzed not only in terms of perceived argument strength but also in terms of its behavioral effects. For example, in research I have conducted with behavioral versions of earlier messages developed by Petty and Cacioppo (1986b), participants' perceptions of argument strength were highly correlated with their intentions to vote for the policy in an upcoming referendum and with the ballots they actually cast in a straw vote.

Distinguishing Actionability from Desirability

Actionability is also theoretically different from the desirability of the object or behavior promoted in an intervention. For instance, a message may communicate that a future product will be more or less environmentally friendly. Nevertheless, if the primary barrier to purchasing the product is its high cost, arguing that it is environmentally friendly is not likely to have much effect on behavior. In this case, the message describes attributes that are desirable but not actionable.

Although actionability is different from desirability, including action contents in a message can elicit positive feelings. As mentioned previously, for example, words like *action* are rated as more active than words like *freeze* or *relax* (McCulloch et al., 2012). Correspondingly, words rated as active are generally perceived more positively than words rated as inactive. In advertising contexts, Nike's "Just do it!" says little about the trademark's sport products but likely capitalizes on the associations between doing and positive feelings. "Just do it" is also actionable in a broad sense because it applies to any of the activities for which athletic gear is designed.

Person Factors and Context Factors of Actionability

I propose a Lewin's (1951) understanding of message or intervention actionability as a function of (a) effects on the action–person factors and (b) the action–context factors. First, messages or interventions may induce high *action potential* within the person by eliciting cognitive, affective, skills, and motivational factors conducive to the behavior. Second, messages or interventions have high *context action potential* when they recommend a behavior that fits with the context. Note that an intervention's context potential extends Fishbein and Ajzen's (1975) correspondence principle, which is the idea that attitudes and intentions predict behavior as long as they correspond in target, action, time, and context. However, I propose context potential as the degree to which recipients can perform the recommended behavior when they go into the world, which requires considering the fit between message recommendation and the surrounding environment and upcoming opportunities.

Factors That Elicit Action within the Person

Communications and interventions are actionable when they instill the cognitive responses, motivational responses, as well as skills and motor responses that recipients need to implement a behavioral recommendation. These psychological responses include (a) activation of concepts, (b) formation of beliefs and attitudes, (c) emotional feelings, (d) behavioral skills, and (e) perceptions of control. Intentions may also be involved, except that some behaviors are relatively automatic. The person's action potential is thus the degree to which a message or intervention promotes cognitions, feelings, and skills that in turn predict behavior by the

Table 9.2 *Message contents related to actionability via processes related to the person*

Content category	Examples
Activation of specific contents	Words like "polite"
Activation of broad contents	Words like "action" and "go"
Behavioral control arguments	Describing that the person is in charge and fully controls her behavior
Behavioral skills arguments and training	Arguments: Explaining what to do when partners do not want to use a condom, when recipients or their partners are sexually excited, and when alcohol or drugs are involved; Training: Role-playing of interpersonal conflict over condom use and initiation of discussions about protection
Behavioral defaults	Prechecked option to order a low-calorie meal
Informational and attitudinal arguments	Informational: Presenting data on the reduced probability of contracting a disease; Attitudinal: Discussing positive implications of using condoms for the health of sexual partners
Number of behavioral recommendations	2 Recommendations: to increase exercise and quit smoking
Homogeneity of behavioral recommendations	Homogeneous: Increasing exercise and increasing fruit and vegetable intake; Heterogeneous: Increasing exercise and decreasing fat intake; or Increasing fruit and vegetable intake and quitting smoking

individual (see Table 9.2). The person's action potential is also related to the number and homogeneity of the behavioral recommendations contained in a message or behavioral intervention.

Activation of specific action concepts. Past research has shown that external signals such as words and pictures can influence performance of subsequent behavioral tasks by activating behavioral concepts. Subtle influence of simple signals that precede a judgment or behavior is known as a priming effect (for a review, see Weingarten et al., 2016a). In classic findings, college students who unscrambled words denoting rudeness during a sentence unscramble task were more likely to interrupt a conversation than were those who unscrambled words about either politeness or neutral topics (Bargh et al., 1996). In the same research, participants who accessed words relevant to the elderly stereotype walked down the hallway more slowly than did control participants. Despite the fact that some of these priming effects have been difficult to reproduce (Doyen, Klein, Pichon, & Cleeremans, 2012; Harris, Coburn, Rohrer, & Pashler, 2013), in a large meta-analysis of behavioral priming, we found a small but robust effect (d = 0.332) (Weingarten et al., 2016a). We also found that behavioral concepts that were valued more (vs. less) had stronger priming effects.

Based on the ability of simple concepts to stimulate behavior, interventions that can activate behavioral concepts have higher action potential. For example, a message that primes the concept "efficiency" by containing words like "fast," "speed," or "quickness" may have greater potential to speed up recipients' behaviors than a similar message without these words. Actionable interventions are often able to activate at least one and often multiple behavioral concepts relevant to the recommended behaviors. However, even though activating concepts is important, priming concepts alone is unlikely to exert predictable effects because the direction of the effects often depends on preexisting motivations in the recipients (Hart & Albarracín, 2009; Strahan, Spencer, & Zanna, 2002). Therefore, more elaborate propositions are generally necessary for messages to be actionable.

Activation of broad action concepts. Messages that promote broad action concepts in the media may have effects of recipient behaviors. We (Ireland et al., 2016) investigated associations between action tweets and HIV prevalence across US counties, testing the alternate hypotheses that action goals could predict either higher or lower HIV rates depending on whether they promote either protective or risky behavior. We analyzed 150 million tweets that could be geolocated in relation to US counties. We analyzed them by creating an action dictionary by compiling LIWC's motion and verb categories and supplementing those with synonyms of core action words (work, go, plan, and think). The resulting action dictionary contained 854 words and stems that are related to general motor (e.g., fly, gaming, gym) and cognitive activity (e.g., plan, deduce, realize). We regressed HIV prevalence on presence of action words while controlling for socioeconomic disease determinants, including wealth disparity (Gini index), percentage of the population that identifies as Black, percentage of the population that is foreign born, total population, and population density. We found that action language correlated negatively with HIV prevalence (see also Ireland, Schwartz, Chen, Ungar, & Albarracín, 2015).

We have also found that trying to promote one action can inadvertently lead to promoting another action. For example, my colleagues and I found that presenting exercise ads can promote eating (Albarracín et al., 2009).

We adapted existing exercise ads to have a set of image and text ads for exercise and a parallel set of control ads that might induce positive affect. Figure 9.1 shows these advertisements. The affect-matched controls were selected to ensure that any effects of the exercise ads would be related to "Go skating" rather than to the positive affect generated by the icon. We found that participants ate more raisins after viewing the exercise ads than after viewing the control ads.

Our study (Albarracín et al., 2009) generated a lot of interest and several conceptual replications. For example, van Kleef, Shimizu, and Wansink (2011) ran a similar experiment in which participants evaluated ads promoting exercise paraphernalia. They found that the exercise ad led to less food consumption during the buffet meal that followed the ad. However, after the meal, recipients of the exercise ad were hungrier and left less relaxed and more active than recipients of control ads. One difference with our study was that, whereas our study was done in a laboratory and described to participants as a judgment study, van Kleef et al.'s experiment was done during lunch and described to participants as a study of eating behavior. This difference might have created a motivation to self-present as healthier among participants in van Kleef et al.'s study. In fact, in their study, recipients of exercise ads reported being healthier and in better shape than did control participants.

In another conceptual replication of our study, Fishbach, Steinmetz, and Tu (2016) used specific exercise words like running and found no effects of food intake during a meal. From the point of view of general action and inaction goals, this result is predictable. General action goals should influence a variety of behaviors, but specific action goals should influence specific behaviors. Therefore, whereas "go" might influence both eating and exercise (Hepler, Wang, & Albarracín, 2012), words like "running" may only influence exercise.

Finally, as indicated by Principle 13, general action goals can promote both approach and avoidance, creating active approach, active avoidance, and doing nothing. In an experiment conducted by Nisson and Earl (2016), participants viewed one of four ads recommending "At the grocery store . . ." (a) "seek out healthy snacks" (approach/action), (b) "keep an eye out for healthy snacks" (approach/inaction), (c) "steer away from unhealthy snacks" (avoidance/action), and (d) "pass by unhealthy snacks" (avoidance/inaction). As predicted, action promoted both active approach and active avoidance, producing more snack consumption in the action/approach condition than the action/avoidance condition. Interestingly, this effect was present for both healthy snacks (i.e., grapes) and unhealthy snacks (potato chips), indicating generalized effects instead of effects on

(a)

(b)

Figure 9.1 Exercise and control ads.

only healthy snacks. The approach and avoidance conditions did not differ when paired with inaction concepts.

Behavioral control arguments. According to Bandura and Wood (1989), a high sense of self-efficacy is key to human agency and attempts at changing one's circumstances and behaviors. In general, perceptions of control refer to people's appraisals of their ability to direct their own behavior. Numerous prior studies have shown that measuring perceived behavioral control improves the prediction of behavior (Ajzen et al., 2019). Meta-analyses have also found that perceptions of control predict behavior, although the amount of explained variance over and above behavioral intentions is generally low (Armitage & Conner, 2001; Cheung & Chan, 2000). However, the contribution of perceived behavioral control depends largely on the degree to which the behavior is under volitional control. When volitional control is high, perceived behavioral control carries little weight because intentions are good predictors of behavior. In contrast, when volitional control is low, perceptions of control carry more weight (Madden, Ellen, & Ajzen, 1992). For example, persuasive communications and interventions to promote condom use are more successful when they include arguments designed to persuade recipients that they have control over their behavior and these recipients have low behavioral control to begin (Albarracín et al., 2003). Hence, actionable interventions must induce the perception that recipients will have control over the recommended behavior.

Behavioral skills arguments and training. Decades ago, Atkinson (1964) introduced a formula to calculate the tendency to act using three determinants: (a) the motivation to act, (b) the incentive for success, and (c) the probability of success. The probability of success is often based on behavioral skills. Based on Atkinson's model, even when a person has both motivation and incentives to act, behavioral skills are key for the person to perform the behavior.

There is considerable support for the importance of behavioral skills in the impact of behavioral interventions. For example, interventions to promote condom use are more successful when they include behavioral skills training than when they do not (Albarracín et al., 2005). A lack of behavioral skills also predicts failures to quit smoking (Tait et al., 2007), whereas behavioral skills training increases quitting success (Conner & Higgins, 2010). Similar results have been found in the area of alcohol use, where skills training reduces alcohol use (Koning, Eijnden, Verdurmen,

Engels, & Vollebergh, 2013). Therefore, actionable interventions promote the skills necessary to execute the recommended behavior.

Behavioral defaults. Explicit behavioral recommendations include "exercise every day," "reduce alcohol drinking," "vote in 2020," and "try our new product." But there are also implicit recommendations. For example, 82 percent of potential organ donors chose to become donors in countries with organ donation as the default choice, compared with only 42 percent in countries without this default (Johnson & Goldstein, 2003). Similarly, 86 percent of new employees sign up for a specific retirement plan when the plan is set as the default, compared with only 50 percent when there is no default (Madrian & Shea, 2001).

One of the reasons default options can be effective is that they offer clues concerning normative or evaluative information in a particular case (McKenzie, Liersch, & Finkelstein, 2006). If people believe that policy makers set the default because most people favor it (Everett et al., 2015), then norms should mediate the advantage of the action default. Also, the default may prime endorsement of an option in a relatively incidental and efficient way, via a heuristic. For example, people who make decisions quickly should be more likely to use the default as a heuristic without much awareness of doing so. Thus, my collaborators and I (White, Jiang, & Albarracín, 2019) expected to find action-default advantages when participants are in a hurry and thus it is convenient for them to follow the default.

We conducted four studies to examine the effects of decision times on donation to a charitable organization using an action-default format or a no-action-default format. Some of the studies had a naturalistic measure of decision time when people made donation choices. Results were consistent with our predictions. Defaults had strong effects for participants who made quicker decisions but no effects for those who made slower decisions. When decision time was manipulated, participants in shorter-time conditions were more likely to donate in response to action-default options than were participants in longer-time conditions. In addition, we found that the effect of the action-default advantage was not mediated by either norms or attitudes, implying a fairly simple, heuristic mechanism of the type "if this behavior is offered, I will follow it."

Informational and attitudinal arguments. A persuasive message designed to modify a target behavior usually describes the positive consequences of performing a behavior. It may also describe how the behavior will avoid negative consequences. For example, a communication designed to stimulate consumption of wholewheat bread may state that the behavior will facilitate weight loss and prevent colon cancer. Therefore, recipients of the message may assess the likelihood that these outcomes will actually occur as a result of the behavior (outcome beliefs). They may also estimate the desirability of these outcomes (outcome evaluations). In addition, recipients could spontaneously think of previously unmentioned consequences of the behavior (e.g., a less pleasing taste of wholewheat bread relative to white bread). Thus, they may construe the likelihood and desirability of these knowledge-based consequences as well.

The implications of both message-related and knowledge-based beliefs and evaluations may then be combined to form an attitude. This combination may be done in the manner postulated by Fishbein and Ajzen (Ajzen & Fishbein, 1980; Fishbein & Ajzen, 1975). This attitude, along with other possible factors (e.g., social norms or perceptions of control; see Ajzen, 1985, 1991; Ajzen & Driver, 1991; Ajzen & Madden, 1986; Doll, Ajzen, & Madden, 1991; Fishbein & Ajzen, 2010; Hassan, Shiu, & Parry, 2016; Schifter & Ajzen, 1985), may influence the recipients' intention to perform the behavior. Later, this intention may provide the basis for their future actions (Ajzen & Fishbein, 1980; Fishbein & Ajzen, 1975).

Messages and interventions may allow recipients to form new beliefs or alter preexisting beliefs that are linked to the recommended behavior. Forming new beliefs can help to form new attitudes and therefore develop new behaviors, whereas altering prior beliefs can change preexisting attitudes toward certain objects, and therefore, change habits. Many messages designed to curb smoking, for example, emphasize that smoking is bad for health. However, such messages are often ineffective because the primary preexisting beliefs leading to smoking related to the attractive social image of smoking (e.g., looking "cool") and the seemingly uplifting effects of smoking on smokers' moods. Thus, actionable messages to change smoking require changing these beliefs.

Figure 9.2 suggests that beliefs and evaluations can be a basis for attitudes and ultimately behavioral decisions. One question, however, is whether outcome beliefs are formed before or after the outcomes are evaluated. Message recipients may first assess how likely an outcome is and then gauge its desirability if they believe that the outcome is likely to occur. In this scenario, the perceived likelihood of the outcome could bias estimates of its desirability. Alternatively, message recipients could first evaluate the desirability of an outcome and then gauge how likely it is to occur (Bargh et al., 1992). In this case, evaluations could affect beliefs, as well as attitudes and ultimately behavior independently of beliefs.

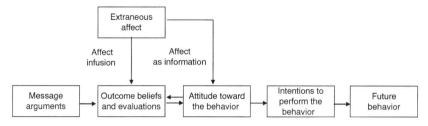

Figure 9.2 Processing of behavior-relevant communications.

When people have high processing ability and motivation, receiving a strong actionable persuasive message is likely to result in strong beliefs in and favorable evaluations of the outcomes described in the message. We (Albarracín & Wyer, 2001) conducted three experiments to investigate the cognitive sequence activated when they receive a persuasive message. We found that, when participants were not distracted by external noise, they first formed beliefs and evaluations of behavioral outcomes and then integrated the implications of these cognitions into their attitudes. In one of the path models we tested, argument strength influenced message-based cognitions. Once formed, these cognitions stimulated the message recipient to generate other cognitions based on prior knowledge (e.g., counterarguments). Both message-based and knowledge-based cognitions were the basis for attitudes and intentions. This model appears in the top panel of Figure 9.3 and fits well for the lower-distraction data. In contrast, the fit of this model was significantly less satisfactory for higher-distraction conditions (not shown).

In the same research, we also used response-time techniques to observe how one type of outcome cognition (e.g., beliefs) facilitated the report of the others (e.g., evaluations). Participants completed a computerized questionnaire that included questions about outcome beliefs and evaluations. The outcomes were selected from the persuasive messages presented in the other experiments of the series. However, participants were not exposed to any message and were thus unlikely to have estimated the likelihood and desirability of these outcomes before being asked to do so.

The time taken to report outcome beliefs and evaluations was analyzed as a function of presentation order and type of cognition (beliefs vs. evaluations). Averaged over the two order conditions, outcome beliefs and outcome evaluations were reported equally quickly. Therefore, neither type of cognition was inherently easier to compute than the other. However, evaluations were made more quickly when beliefs had been

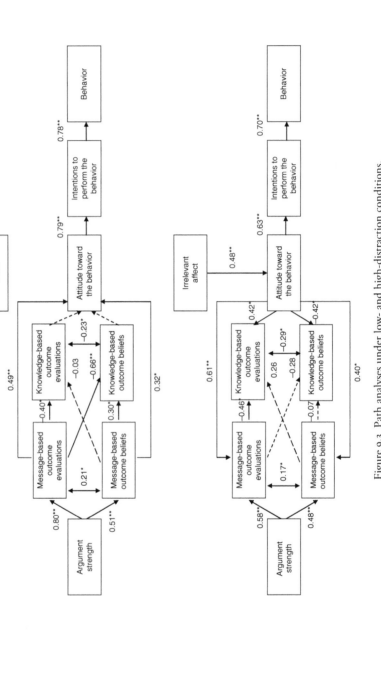

Figure 9.3 Path analyses under low- and high-distraction conditions.

reported beforehand than when they had not. This difference was significantly greater than the difference in time required to report beliefs when evaluations had and had not been reported earlier. In conclusion, these findings provided support for the hypothesis that outcome beliefs are formed prior to outcome evaluations.

As shown in Figure 9.2, people may also base their attitudes on information other than the message and independently of outcome beliefs and evaluations. In these situations, however, their attitudes could have reciprocal effects on their beliefs (Rosenberg, 1960b). McGuire and McGuire (1991), for example, identified tendencies to engage in both wishful thinking (i.e., judging that a desirable event will occur or that an undesirable event will not on the basis of its desirability) and rationalization (i.e., judging that a likely event is desirable or that an unlikely event is undesirable on the basis of its probability). Participants in one of their studies received information that experts judged an event (e.g., development of a vaccine) to be either positive or negative. They then judged the event to be more likely when they had received information that the event was desirable (vs. undesirable). These findings suggest that, although outcome beliefs and evaluations may be determinants of attitudes under some conditions, outcome cognitions could also be the result of attitudes formed ahead of time. However, these conditions were not discussed by McGuire and McGuire (1991).

Consider now what happens when people have a deficit in motivation or ability to think about the message they receive. Albarracín and Wyer (2001) reported that participants who were distracted at the time of receiving the message based their attitudes on the mood they experienced for reasons unrelated to the message. When distraction was higher (actually moderate; see Albarracín & Kumkale, 2003), affect had a positive influence on not only attitudes but also behavioral intentions, actual behavior, and outcome beliefs and evaluations (Albarracín & Wyer, 2001). In contrast, when distraction was low, affect had little influence, and, if anything, the influence was negative in direction (Albarracín & Wyer, 2001).

The data from path analyses provided further evidence concerning the influence of affect. These data appear in the bottom panel of Figure 9.3. Under higher-distraction conditions, participants who experienced positive affect were more likely to develop positive attitudes than participants who experienced negative affect. Thus, the data from higher-distraction conditions suggest that certain factors, such as one's mood, can have direct influences on attitudes. Furthermore, when affect influenced attitudes, these attitudes can affect outcome beliefs and evaluations. This conclusion was suggested by an improvement in the goodness of fit of the model in which attitudes influenced outcome beliefs and evaluations rather than reverse.[1]

Number of behavioral recommendations. The presence and number of behavioral recommendations are primary considerations in thinking about the actionability of a message or behavioral intervention. What is the optimal number of behavior recommendations to maximize an intervention's impact? In response to this question, my colleagues and I conducted a meta-analysis of multiple-domain health-promotion interventions. We included multiple-behavior interventions in the area of lifestyle (diet, exercise, and smoking). Eligible reports included a pretest assessment of clinical and/or behavioral outcomes, which were averaged, and the final database included 216 multiple-behavior change intervention groups ($N =$ 74,000 participants). We coded the recommendations by identifying the goals, or behavioral categories, targeted by the interventions. These goals involved specific prescriptions about dietary, exercise, and/or smoking behaviors (e.g., reducing sedentary time). We counted the total number of primary goals (e.g., three when the recommendations were to reduce calories, to increase fruit and vegetable intake, and to increase physical activity).

We calculated Becker's (1988) g to indicate a change between the pre- and the posttest measures. The measures of behavioral outcomes in the area of *diet* were energy intake (e.g., kcal/week), carbohydrate, protein, fiber, fat, fruit, and vegetable intake (in grams or servings), number of meals per day, whether participants achieved dietary recommendations, whether participants achieved recommendations for fruit and vegetable intake, whether participants checked their blood pressure in the past 12 months, presence of unhealthy eating, and presence of overeating. The behavioral measures in the *exercise* domain entailed whether participants engaged in daily exercise, weekly hours of physical activity, whether participants engaged in occupational physical activity, whether participants had regular physical activity, whether participants achieved certain exercise recommendations, whether participants were sedentary, whether participants reported high- impact physical activity, self-monitoring of pulse and blood pressure, self-monitoring with pedometer (daily pace), time spent in physical activity, energy expenditure in physical activity (k/cal.), and number of TV hours

---

[1] Correspondingly, reversing the paths linking outcome beliefs and evaluations with attitudes led to decreases in goodness of fit when distraction was low.

per day. The behavioral measures in the *smoking* domain included current smoking status, number of cigarettes smoked per day (often via diaries), number of years of smoking, whether participants were ex-smokers, and longest quit duration. We also calculated clinical measures. For example, the clinical measures in the *exercise* area included body weight in kilograms, body mass index, hip size, waist size, hip/waist ratio, body fat, whether participants were overweight, whether participants were obese, systolic/diastolic blood pressure, triglycerides level, HDL/LDL cholesterol, fasting blood glucose, presence of diabetes, presence of metabolic syndrome, pulse, results from spirometer tests, results from VO_2 Max tests, results from chest X-ray, presence of nicotine in blood, lab tests to confirm right dose of medication in blood, lab tests for diabetes, results from PAP tests, results from mammogram reports, results from dental records, and results from colonoscopy reports.

The findings from this meta-analysis appear in Table 9.3. They show that moderate numbers (2–3) of recommended behaviors produce better clinical and behavioral outcomes than both fewer (0–1) and greater (4+) numbers (Wilson et al., 2015). Thus, in this context, piling up behavioral recommendations seems ineffective beyond a point (see also Mata, Todd, & Lippke, 2010). However, the linear trend was strong and significant as well, implying that more recommendations produce greater effects.

Some of our experimental research has also supported the hypothesis that the effects of the number of recommendations levels out beyond a point. In two laboratory experiments (McDonald, McDonald, Hughes, & Albarracín, 2017), we investigated the effects of the number of health recommendations (e.g., quit smoking; relax for a day) contained in a health-promotion message on participants' recommendation recall and intentions to enact the recommendations in the future. We hypothesized that, if recommendations are stored in memory as individual bits of information, a higher number of presented recommendations should increase the number of recalled recommendations. Beyond a point, however, recipients may summarize a group of recommendations as part of a single, more general recommendation (i.e., a theme or header). This summarization process should then result in a decrease in the proportion of recalled recommendations. The results from Experiment 1 appear in Figure 9.4. As shown, as the number of recommendations went up, the total number of recalled recommendations increased but the proportion of recalled recommendations decreased. Experiment 2 obtained the same pattern with the number and the proportion of intended behaviors. Therefore, an important implication of this research is that interventionists should go for higher or lower numbers depending on their objectives.

Table 9.3 *Change as a function of number of recommendations controlling for duration, domain targeted, and self-selected sample*

| | d (95% CI) | | | | |
| | No. of recommendations | | | | |
Outcome	0	1	2–3	4 or more	Random-effects Q_B
Behavioral	0.05_a (−0.07, 0.17)	0.11_b (−0.11, 0.33)	0.29_c (0.17, 0.41)	0.14_b (0.03, 0.25)	34.87^{***}
Clinical	0.17_a (0.04, 0.30)	0.12_a (−0.13, 0.36)	0.27_b (0.13, 0.40)	0.22_c (0.12, 0.33)	12.07^{**}
Overall	0.10_a (0.01, 0.20)	0.17_b (−0.02, 0.36)	0.33_c (0.23, 0.43)	0.19_b (0.10, 0.27)	33.74^{***}

Note: Change for intervention and control groups as a function of number of recommendations. CI = confidence interval. d = fixed-effects weighted means. Q_B = homogeneity coefficient for the difference across levels of a factor, distributed as a chi-square with degrees of freedom equal to the number of factor levels − 1. Within each row, ds with similar subscripts are not significantly different from one another.
$^*p < 0.05.$ $^{**}p < 0.01.$ $^{***}p < 0.001.$
Source: Adapted from Wilson et al. (2015).

When behaviors are interchangeable, such as when the same benefit can be derived from any of 10 forms of exercise, recommending all 10 will maximize the benefit by increasing the sheer number of executed behaviors. In contrast, when behaviors form a set and must be recalled jointly to be of benefit, then a lower number of behaviors should be better to maximize a high *proportion* of executed behaviors. For example, medications are often prescribed as a combination. It is desirable for people to take a drug that depletes a vitamin along with the vitamin. Hence, in these situations, a lower number of intervention recommendations should produce more complete adherence.

Homogeneity of behavioral recommendations. As explained previously, The way in which recommendations of action and inaction are packaged within a message or intervention contributes to actionability because the combination can trigger either synergistic or antagonistic processes of action initiation and inhibitory control over behavior. Action recommendations

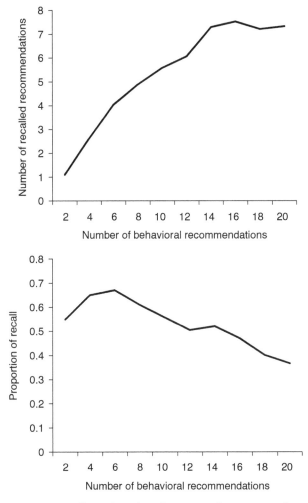

Figure 9.4 Effects of number of recommendations on recall.

should elicit action preparation, that is, an executive process that orchestrates a response (Jennings & Molen, 2005), whereas inaction recommendations (to quit smoking) should elicit inhibition of active behaviors. Although the responses vary, the executive mechanisms of action preparation and inhibitory processes appear to generalize across tasks and behaviors. A meta-analysis of 18 experiments conducted by Tuk, Zhang, and Sweldens (2015) demonstrated that engaging self-control in one domain (i.e., controlling thoughts, attention, food consumption, or emotions) facilitates self-control in other domains. Furthermore, Berkman, Burklund, and Lieberman (2009) reported that inhibitory signals originate in the same areas of the brain across a variety of responses, suggesting a general inhibitory process. These findings are also consistent with my work on general action and inaction goals controlling a great variety of behaviors. In any event, as shown in Table 9.3, recommending that people begin exercise and eat more healthy food is more effective than recommending that they begin exercise and reduce fat intake. Behavioral change was greater when either all actions or all inactions were recommended than when the program included a mixture of actions and inactions.

In closing, the notion of person's action potential is summarized in the following principle:

> **Principle 20. Person's action potential.** Action potential is a function of activation of action concepts, the number and homogeneity of behavioral interventions, and contents (e.g., words or images) that are likely to influence beliefs about behavioral antecedents and evaluations of behavioral antecedents and outcomes, behavioral skills, as well as perceptions of control.

Context's Action Potential

Action–context fit is another important consideration because behavioral recommendations may not apply to a context, either because of level of abstraction discrepancies or structural discrepancies.

Level of abstraction and structural discrepancies. Discrepancies in the level of abstraction imply that the behavior recommended in a message or intervention is either too general or too specific to be implemented in reality. The recommendation to pursue "a healthy diet" for weight loss can evoke many high-calorie diets that include "healthy foods" but are too high in calories to promote weight loss. Therefore, this recommendation is too general to promote appropriate behaviors in real contexts. Furthermore, highly specific recommendations may lack context potential for a different reason. A message that recommends a pharmaceutical drug identified with its commercial name may be too specific to promote the flexibility of choosing generic substitutes when people cannot afford the specific brand, or when a pharmacy does not carry the specific brand.

Recipients construct a mental model of what behaviors should be executed when and where. Discrepancies with reality may also come in the form of structural discrepancies (Avishai, Conner, & Sheeran, 2019). Structural discrepancies might imply that the behavior recommended in a message or intervention does not exist in reality. A message that recommends preventing the flu by taking a pill will produce a discrepancy between the structure of the behavior as recommended in the message and the structure of flu prevention behavior as it exists in reality. For example, recipients of a message to prevent the flu with a pill may go to a health clinic to get the flu pill but find out that only an injection is available.

Space and time are additional considerations. A message that recommends getting a flu shot at a health clinic has less action potential than a message that recommends getting the flu shot at a health clinic or a pharmacy. With respect to time, deadlines are likely to produce discrepancies between the effort of meeting a deadline and the effort message recipients are ready to invest. Jiang and I assumed that, when a behavior has a close deadline, people with a general action goal may be more likely to perform the behavior than those with a general inaction goal. In contrast, when a behavior has a distant deadline, people may not see their current goals as relevant. In our research, we manipulated action and inaction goals by measuring or manipulating movement, such as whether people were walking versus standing. We expected that, for close deadlines, compared to participants in inaction conditions (e.g., standing), those in action conditions (e.g., walking) would be more willing to get a flu shot recommended in a message presented to them. In Study 1, we distributed coupons with different deadlines to participants who were walking or sitting inside the student union. In Studies 2 and 3, we measured intentions to get the flu shots with different deadlines after imagining walking or sitting. Finally, Study 4 tested whether a greater sense of fit (Avnet, Laufer, & Higgins, 2013; Fennis & Stel, 2011; Fransen et al., 2011; Gerlach et al., 2003; Lee & Aaker, 2004; Meier et al., 2012; Montoya et al., 2017) was involved in the interplay between time deadlines and goals.

Generally, behavioral goals follow the principle of effort conservation (Silvestrini & Gendolla, 2013), implying that decisions are made when necessary and timely. For example, in Silvestrini and Gendolla's (2013) research, priming action and inaction words led to more or less effort mobilization only when the task was feasible, a situation that is more likely when a deadline is close. Likewise, our research showed that the message was effective when it was temporally relevant, that is in the close deadline. Study 1 showed that walking participants were more likely to redeem coupons with a close (vs. distant) deadline than were those who were seated. Table 9.4

presents the results from the remaining studies. As shown, when the deadline for a behavior was close, people with action goals had stronger behavioral intentions than those with inaction goals. In contrast, when the deadline was distant and thus less relevant, the general goals were not influential.

To summarize, context's action potential is described in the following principle:

> **Principle 21. Context's action potential.** The context's action potential is the degree to which recipients can perform the recommended behavior in the available contexts. It depends on the fit between the recommended behavior and the context (opportunities, realism of the prescribed behavior, and correspondence between the prescribed behavior and the person's time and space).

Cultural and historical considerations. A final consideration concerning the contextual fit between behavioral recommendations and the surrounding world is the degree to which cultural and historical contexts might promote certain types of behavioral recommendations by favoring general action and inaction. For example, in the United States, the number of diagnoses of manic episodes in children was reported to increase between the years 1995 and 2000 (Harpaz-Rotem et al., 2005) (see Figure 9.5). This finding may reflect a myriad of factors. One of these factors, however, may be an increase in the general action goals set for children and their families. The increase in the number of working hours, combined with the pressure to exercise, consume, excel in sports, and organize leisure activities could produce such bottom-up effects.

Rates of manic episodes also vary across different ethnic groups in the United States. As shown in Figure 9.6, White Americans have the highest lifetime prevalence, followed by Black Americans, Hispanic Americans, and Asian Americans, in that order. Even among Hispanic Americans, who fall in the middle, being born in the United States is a risk factor for manic episodes, as Figure 9.6 also reflects. Again, these data may stem from underlying causes that cannot be fully unconfounded here. Nonetheless, they support the intuition that different communities differ in the degree to which they pursue general action and inaction goals.

Cross-country differences in manic symptoms also suggest that general action and inaction goals reflect cultural differences. I reanalyzed the incidence of impulsivity-related disorders across 14 countries using data collected house-to-house using an international psychiatric DSM-IV standardized interview (Kessler et al., 2004). Using cluster analysis (see Figure 9.7), different solutions identified different sets of countries.

Table 9.4 *Effects of deadlines in combination with movement-induced goals*

	Deadline	
Behavioral intentions	Close, *M* (*SD, n*)	Distant, *M* (*SD, n*)
Study 2: Flu shot and real movement		
Action	3.65[a] (2.95, 34)	3.11[a] (2.59, 42)
Control	3.82[a] (3.31, 36)	2.27[a] (2.77, 35)
Inaction	1.93[b] (1.93, 37)	3.68[a] (2.63, 34)
d (action–inaction)	0.70	−0.22
d (action–control)	−0.05	0.31
d (inaction–control)	−0.72	0.52
Study 3: Flu shot and imagined movement		
	Close *M* (*SD, n*)	Distant *M* (*SD, n*)
Action	4.60[a] (3.83, 54)	3.96[a] (3.75, 51)
Inaction	0.97[b] (1.58, 46)	3.16[a] (3.40, 52)
d (action–inaction)	1.34	0.22
Study 4: Flu shot and imagined movement		
	Close *M* (*SD, n*)	Distant *M* (*SD, n*)
Action	4.00[a] (3.03, 49)	2.79[a] (2.69, 48)
Control	4.09[a] (2.70, 48)	3.51[a] (2.95, 48)
Inaction	2.50[b] (2.73, 49)	3.55[a] (2.79, 47)
d (action–inaction)	0.52	−0.28
d (action–control)	−0.03	−0.26
d (inaction–control)	−0.59	0.01
Control	3.99[a] (2.48, 48)	3.14[a] (2.11, 48)
d (action–inaction)	0.49	−0.23
d (action–control)	−0.07	−0.17
d (inaction–control)	−0.54	0.08

Note: Cells with different superscripts in a column differ at $p < 0.05$.
Different subscripts represent significantly different means, d = Cohen's d.
Source: Adapted from Jiang and Albarracín's (2019) studies.

Notably, however, analyses placed the United States in a cluster with the highest prevalence of impulse control, mood disorders, and substance abuse. The second cluster included China, Japan, and Nigeria and had the lowest prevalence of impulse control, mood disorders, and substance abuse. The third cluster included the Netherlands and fell between the

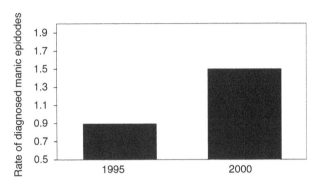

Figure 9.5 Rate of manic episode diagnoses.

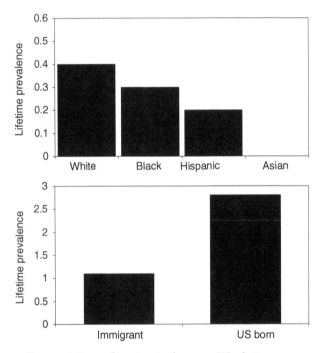

Figure 9.6 Rates of manic episodes across US ethnic groups.

other two clusters in terms of the same disorders. Again, even though many factors could account for these national differences, cultural variability in the setting of action and inaction goals may play a role.

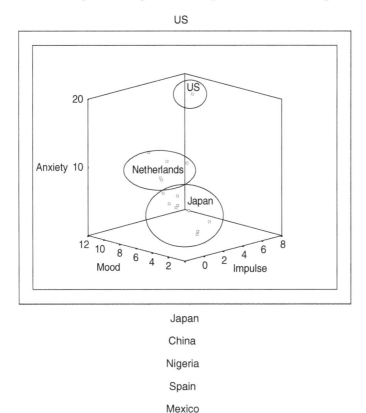

US

Japan

China

Nigeria

Spain

Mexico

Figure 9.7 Cluster analysis of prevalence of impulse control disorders.

Cultural research conducted by my group has revealed that the desir-ability of the concepts of action (e.g., "action is good") and inaction (e.g., "inaction is good") varies across countries (Ireland, Hepler, Li, & Albarracín, 2015; Zell et al., 2013). We administered questionnaires about attitudes toward action and inaction in 19 countries (see Zell et al., 2013). College students and samples of general adults rated action and inaction as positive or negative via two almost identical scales assessing the extent to which (a) action was important for happiness and contributed to society (i.e., action is important in people's lives, action is essential for life, actions contribute to society, being active makes people happy, and action is good) and (b) inaction was important for happiness and contributed to society (i.e., inaction is important in people's lives, being inactive is unpleasant, inaction is good, inaction is necessary in one's life, and inaction offers many benefits). Scales went from 1 (*strongly disagree*) to 7 (*strongly agree*). A summary of these data appears in Table 9.5. As shown, people generally liked action more than inaction, although both means were generally positive. The exceptions were Japan and China, where both attitudes were similarly positive.

As one might expect, attitudes toward action and inaction correlated negatively in 10 out of 19 countries (Table 9.5). We predicted that cultural differences in dialecticism, the tendency to hold contradictory beliefs (Spencer-Rodgers, Williams, & Peng, 2010), would be related to the strength of this negative correlation. East Asians, who are dialectical, more often report contradictory evaluations of themselves and their groups, recognizing that both positive and negative characteristics coexist (Ma-Kellams, Spencer-Rodgers, & Peng, 2011; Spencer-Rodgers, Boucher, Mori, Wang, & Peng, 2009). Our study included the Dialectical Self-Scale (Spencer-Rodgers et al., 2010), which contains statements such as *I sometimes believe two things that contradict each other* and *If there are two opposing sides to an argument, they cannot both be right* (reverse-scored) on 1 (*strongly disagree*) to 7 (*strongly agree*) scales. As shown in Table 9.5, dialecticism varied across countries. Importantly, dialecticism correlated with the correlation between attitudes toward action and inaction. Specifically, participants in more dialectical countries (e.g., Japan, r = 0.50) had a more positive correlation between action and inaction attitudes than participants in less dialectical countries.

We also examined the influence of the distribution of responsibility for action within societies. *Horizontality* entails equal distribution of control and responsibility among members of a group, and can be distinguished from *verticality*, which entails the concentration of control and responsibility in those with authority and high status (Singelis, Triandis, Bhawuk, & Gelfand, 1995; Shavitt, Lalwani, Zhang, & Torelli, 2006; Triandis & Gelfand, 1998). Horizontal cultures are illustrated by Denmark, Australia, or the Israeli Kibbutz, where responsibility for action is widely distributed and this distribution is valued. Vertical cultures are illustrated by Japan and the United States, which discourage independent action for most members of a group or society. We (Albarracín, Jones, Hepler, & Li, 2017) hypothesized that, if verticality places greater social constraints on action, attitudes toward general action would be less positive in vertical countries than in horizontal ones. Thus, our cross-cultural study included the vertical/horizontal individualism-collectivism scale (Singelis et al., 1995) to assess vertical individualism (e.g., *It is important that I do my job better than others*), vertical collectivism (e.g., *It is my duty to take care of my family, even when*

Table 9.5 *Means for attitudes toward action and inaction and dialecticism in 19 countries*

Country	Mean dialecticism	Mean attitude toward action	Mean attitude toward inaction	Correlation (*r*)
Argentina	3.63	5.39	3.96	−0.28
Bolivia	3.60	5.70	3.25	−0.25
China	4.11	5.41	5.58	0.61
Colombia	3.52	5.74	3.61	−0.23
England	3.92	5.83	5.54	0.14
Guatemala	3.31	5.89	3.96	−0.19
Hong Kong	4.20	5.49	5.36	0.56
Israel	3.59	5.76	3.81	−0.05
Italy	3.48	5.64	3.44	−0.28
Japan	4.19	5.48	5.48	0.50
Mexico	3.56	5.42	3.72	−0.10
Norway	3.84	5.72	4.95	0.33
Philippines	3.80	5.85	3.98	−0.10
Portugal	3.52	5.83	3.43	−0.18
Singapore	3.93	5.44	4.30	0.13
Spain	3.61	5.39	4.00	0.03
Switzerland	3.73	5.59	4.57	0.22
Turkey	3.43	5.71	3.19	−0.31
United States	*3.54*	*5.65*	*4.6*	*0.16*

Source: Adapted from Zell et al. (2013).

I have to sacrifice what I want), horizontal individualism (e.g., *I rely on myself most of the time; I rarely rely on others*), and horizontal collectivism (e.g., *I feel good when I cooperate with others*). Individualism and collectivism were not associated with attitudes toward action, which led to the decision to simply create a horizontal scale and a vertical scale. However, findings indicated that attitudes toward action correlated more positively with the horizontal than the vertical dimensions of the scale. Attitudes toward inaction, however, were unrelated to either dimension.

In other analyses of the same cross-cultural study, we (Ireland et al., 2015) investigated whether neuroticism was linked to attitudes toward action and whether this link was mediated by depression and anxiety. Attitudes toward action correlated negatively with neuroticism, an association explained by the greater anxiety associated with neuroticism. Also, attitudes toward inaction correlated positively with neuroticism. Thus, our research suggests that neuroticism is linked to anxiety, which is known to paralyze people. However, our research also implies that these personality traits have important attitudinal correlates, namely, that people who score high in neuroticism dislike action and like inaction.

Regardless of the origins of general attitudes toward action and inaction, a context that favors action may be a context that should increase the impact of messages designed to increase action. For example, recommendations to increase consumerism and fast food may be easier to follow when audiences are on the go and looking for ways to act without paying attention to whether the actions are beneficial for themselves or others. Future research should investigate such contextual effects along with the way in which specific and global goals come into play.

Summary

Messages designed with the intent of influencing behavior and behavioral interventions are successful when they influence factors in the person and the situation that ultimately make those programs actionable. Actionability is the probability that the message or intervention communicates or enables performance of behavioral recommendations (Albarracín et al., 2018). First, a message or behavioral intervention can stimulate the cognitive, motivational, or behavioral processes that ultimately make the individual perform the recommended behavior. Second, it can promote behavioral recommendations that fit within the world in which potential actors live.

PART V

Conclusion

CHAPTER 10

Conclusions and Future Directions

This book has presented a framework that integrates three streams of research: (a) my work on action and inaction; (b) my basic research on attitudes, persuasion, and goals; and (c) my applications to health, primarily HIV and drug use prevention. Following an introduction in Chapter 1, Chapter 2 discussed formation of beliefs and types of beliefs, including expectations, beliefs in antecedents and outcomes, beliefs about action and inaction, and the biases introduced by beliefs. The chapter also detailed the effects of beliefs about objects and experiences, and later the effects of beliefs about the antecedents and consequences of behavior.

Chapter 3 concerned attitudes as well as attitude dimensions and structure, including ambivalence. Attitudes have both a memory component and a judgment component. This aspect is important because recognizing attitude change is not possible without recognizing that these two components are part of attitudes. The chapter also covered the relation between attitude-relevant memories and evaluative judgments, my research on specific and *general* attitudes toward objects and behaviors, including actions and inactions, and the degree to which attitudes predict behavior, including a meta-analysis of the attitude–behavior relation.

Chapter 4 covered behavior, intentions, and goals. It described my view of intentionality, including subtle intention formation and the psychological representation of intention. Goals vary in terms of content, level of conscious involvement, and type of object. Goals are either general (get tenure) or specific (publish a paper), focus on actions or inactions (effortful behavior vs. rest), and have either psychological end states (i.e., behavioral, affective, and cognitive) or objective end states (e.g., a financial or health outcome).

Chapters 5 and 6 covered the influence of past behavior, practice, and experience, as well as the past or present situational influences of other people and normative factors. Chapter 5 described the influences of concrete experience, and three processes underlying the influence of past behavior: biased scanning, self-perception, and cognitive dissonance. Chapter 6 presented a mode of different forms of social influence: This influence stems from other people's verbal expressions and behaviors, which can influence behavior, beliefs, attitudes, and procedures. For example, people exert normative and informational influences on others, train and provide practice opportunities to others, and exert influences on automatic processes such as mimicry.

Chapter 7 concerned the influence of persuasive communications and behavioral interventions. It addressed classic stage models of persuasion, followed by the cognitive response model, the elaboration-likelihood model, the heuristic systematic model, and the unimodel. It then drew important distinctions between processes of attitude formation and change, with special attention to the influence of prior attitudes on the decision to seek out a persuasive message. In addition, it addressed the opposing influences of action and inaction goals for attitude formation and change, as well as behavior initiation and change.

Chapter 8 covered the stages of processing of persuasive communications and behavioral interventions in the presence of prior attitudes. It included selective exposure and interventions to increase exposure to messages and enrollment in behavioral interventions, in addition to detailing identification and selection of information in attitude change contexts. Chapter 9 concluded this book by exploring the processes that lead from a persuasive message or behavioral intervention to actual behavioral performance. I described the notion of actionability and explore actionability factors related to the person who must enact the behavior and the context in which the behavior is enacted. I closed with a reflection of the cultural and historical trends that provide greater actionability for action than inaction.

Book Principles

The book moved through a systematic analysis of the cognitive and motivational processes underlying attitudes and behavior change. This analysis is summarized in the following principles.

Principle 1. Type of goal objects. The objects of goals are either states or processes, and both can be behavioral, cognitive, social, or affective. Process goals can be means in and of themselves, means to meet state goals, and means to meet other process goals.

Principles of Cognitive Functioning

Principle 2. **Effects of action goals on other psychological variables.** Goals of action stimulate the formation and use of behavioral beliefs, behavioral procedures, and intentions, which are themselves informed by personal experience and practice with a behavior, behavioral procedures, other people, as well as persuasive communications (i.e., verbal and visual messages delivered in a standard format to all members of an audience) and behavioral interventions (i.e., more complex programs that involve role-playing, client-centered counseling, or other strategies in which the audience is active).

Principle 3. **Salience, accessibility, and nature of information used as a basis for attitudes, beliefs, and behaviors.** People form and change attitudes and beliefs, as well as initiate and change behavior, on the basis of whatever is salient and accessible at a particular time.

Principle 4. **Selection of salient and accessible information depends on processing ability and motivation, as well as relevance criteria.** People consciously select salient and accessible information on the basis of their ability and motivation to think about the information.

Principle 5. **Intentionality and awareness of cognitive and behavioral processes.** People are generally unintentional about and unaware of the cognitive processes that underlie judgments and behavior.

Principle 6. **Formation of representations and judgments.** People form better-defined, richer, and more consequential representations when they pay attention to a stimulus, concept, or behavior. Representations include beliefs, attitudes, and intentions, as well as memories.

Principle 7. **Reciprocity in the relations among beliefs, attitudes, intentions, goals, behavioral procedures, and behavior.** Most relations among psychological variables involved in the understanding and change of attitudes and behavior (beliefs, attitudes, intentions, goals, behavioral procedures, and behavior) are reciprocal in nature, so that, if a first variable influences a second variable, the second variable influences the first given the right inferential and retrieval mechanisms.

Principles Related to Beliefs

Principle 8. **Impact of beliefs on attitudes.** Changing beliefs about the outcomes and antecedents of a behavior generally changes attitudes.

Principle 9. **Relative numerosity of beliefs about action and inaction.** There are more beliefs about general action than about general inaction.

Principle 10. **Influence of beliefs about action and inaction on specific beliefs.** Beliefs about action and inaction can influence beliefs about any specific behavior that can be construed as action or inaction.

Principles Related to Attitudes

Principle 11. **Function of general attitudes.** General attitudes are a means to integrating all objects and behaviors, all actions, and all inactions.

Principle 12. **Representation of attitudes toward action and attitudes toward inaction.** Attitudes toward action are better represented than attitudes toward inaction. As a result, attitudes toward action may have more influence on other judgments and on behavior.

Principles Related to Behavior, Intentions, and Goals

Principle 13. **Hierarchical position of general goals of action and inaction.** General goals of action and inaction either begin a motivational process, or become active in the service of other high-level goals such as seeking pleasure. For example, general goals of action or inaction can be met through prevention and promotion, yielding active approach, active avoidance, and doing nothing. Likewise, general goals of action and inaction can be met through locomotion and assessment goals, yielding locomotion, assessment, and doing nothing. In addition, general goals of action and inaction can be met through specific goals construed as action or inaction, respectively.

Principle 14. **General action and inaction goals and active/inactive means.** General action and inaction goals are satisfied through active (e.g., running, or suddenly interrupting a run), or passive processes (e.g., continuing to lie down in bed, or remaining still on a conveyor belt).

Principle 15. **Conditions for behavior without goal or intention mediation.** Goals (relatively abstract aims) and intentions are unnecessary only when behaviors are conditioned responses to stimuli.

Principle 16. **Nature of intentional behavior.** Intentional behavior is rarely executed algorithmically. Hence, intentions are represented as full-fledged mental propositions ("I will climb the wall"), but also as feelings (conative feelings), or as a haphazard string of fragmentary stimuli or words that imply an intention ("will climbing").

Principles Related to Persuasive Communications and Behavioral Interventions

Principle 17. **Influence of prior attitudes and behavioral patterns on the impact of messages and interventions.** The outcomes of persuasive communications and behavioral interventions depend first and foremost on whether prior attitudes and related information are accessible at the time of receiving the message or behavioral intervention.

Principle 18. **Impact of ability and motivation on identification, selection, and impact.** The impact of a specific type of information depends on criteria of information relevance as well as the ability and motivation to judge this relevance. Increases in ability and motivation produce a linear influence of information deemed relevant but an inverted-U influence of information deemed irrelevant.

Principle 19. **Effects of action and inaction goals on attitudinal formation and change, as well as behavioral initiation and change.** All else being equal, action goals increase attitudinal formation and behavioral initiation but reduce attitudinal and behavioral change.

Principle 20. **Person's action potential.** Action potential is a function of activation of action concepts, the number and homogeneity of behavioral interventions, and contents (e.g., words or images) that are likely to influence beliefs about behavioral antecedents and evaluations of behavioral antecedents and outcomes, behavioral skills, as well as perceptions of control.

Principle 21. **Context's action potential.** The context's action potential is the degree to which recipients can perform the recommended behavior in the available contexts. It depends on the fit between the recommended behavior and the context (opportunities, realism of the prescribed behavior, and correspondence between the prescribed behavior and the person's time and space).

Future Directions

Each of the chapters in this book has covered a broad landscape that begins with the very reasons why we form beliefs and attitudes and the complex interactions involving beliefs, attitudes, behaviors, and socio-contextual factors. This book has brought together concepts from different areas and research traditions, and emphasized that action goals are key to the success of persuasive communications and behavioral interventions at changing attitudes and behaviors. This notion, however, suggests new avenues of research. To begin, how can we decouple prior attitudes and behavioral patterns through real world interventions? How can we make prior dysfunctional attitudes and behaviors unnecessary or even dysfunctional? How can we introduce rest as a way of disconnecting people's present from past attitudes and behaviors they would like to change? What are the necessary persuasive and interventional devices that we can use to facilitate optimal sequences of processing and train people to disrupt processing of counterproductive messages? Finally, when and how will we study the processes described here in people's natural social networks and in connection to the cultures that give meaning to their lives?

References

Aarts, H., Dijksterhuis, A., & Midden, C. (1999). To plan or not to plan? Goal achievement or interrupting the performance of mundane behaviors. *European Journal of Social Psychology, 29*(8), 971–979. https://doi.org/10.1002/(SICI)1099-0992(199912)29:8<971::AID-EJSP963>3.0.CO;2-A

Abelson, R. P. (1959). Modes of resolution of belief dilemmas. *Journal of Conflict Resolution, 3*(4), 343–352.

Abrams, D., & Hogg, M. A. (2008). Collective identity: Group membership and self-conception. In *Blackwell handbook of social psychology: Group processes* (pp. 147–181). Malden, MA: Blackwell. https://doi.org/10.1002/9780470998458.ch18

Abrams, D., Thomas, J., & Hogg, M. A. (1990). Numerical distinctiveness, social identity and gender salience. *British Journal of Social Psychology, 29*(1), 87–92. https://doi.org/10.1111/j.2044-8309.1990.tb00889.x

Abrams, D., Wetherell, M., Cochrane, S., Hogg, M. A., & Turner, J. C. (1990). Knowing what to think by knowing who you are: Self-categorization and the nature of norm formation, conformity and group polarization. *British Journal of Social Psychology, 29*(2), 97–119. https://doi.org/10.1111/j.2044-8309.1990.tb00892.x

Ackerman, J. M., Nocera, C. C., & Bargh, J. A. (2010). Incidental haptic sensations influence social judgments and decisions. *Science, 328*(5986), 1712–1715. https://doi.org/10.1126/science.1189993

Adaval, R., & Wyer, R. S., Jr. (1998). The role of narratives in consumer information processing. *Journal of Consumer Psychology, 7*(3), 207–245.

Ahluwalia, R. (2002). How prevalent is the negativity effect in consumer environments? *Journal of Consumer Research, 29*(2), 270–279.

Ajzen, I. (1985). From intentions to actions: A theory of planned behavior. In J. Kuhl & J. Beckmann (Eds.), *Action control* (pp. 11–39). Berlin, Germany: Springer. https://doi.org/10.1007/978-3-642-69746-3_2

Ajzen, I. (1991). The theory of planned behavior. *Organizational Behavior and Human Decision Processes, 50*(2), 179–211. https://doi.org/10.1016/0749-5978(91)90020-T

Ajzen, I. (2001). Nature and operation of attitudes. *Annual Review of Psychology, 52*, 27–58. https://doi.org/10.1146/annurev.psych.52.1.27

Ajzen, I. (2002). Residual effects of past on later behavior: Habituation and reasoned action perspectives. *Personality and Social Psychology Review, 6*(2), 107–122. https://doi.org/10.1207/S15327957PSPR0602_02

Ajzen, I. (2019). *TPB measurement.* Retrieved from https://people.umass.edu/aiz en/pdf/tpb.measurement.pdf

Ajzen, I., Czasch, C., & Flood, M. G. (2009). From intentions to behavior: Implementation intention, commitment, and conscientiousness. *Journal of Applied Social Psychology, 39*(6), 1356–1372. https://doi.org/10.1111/j.1559-1816 .2009.00485.x

Ajzen, I., & Driver, B. L. (1990). Application of the theory of planned behavior to leisure choice. *Journal of Leisure Research, 24*(3), 157–162.

Ajzen, I., & Driver, B. L. (1991). Prediction of leisure participation from behavioral, normative, and control beliefs: An application of the theory of planned behavior. *Leisure Sciences, 13*(3), 185–204. https://doi.org/10.1080/0149040 9109513137

Ajzen, I., & Fishbein, M. (1972). Attitudes and normative beliefs as factors influencing behavioral intentions. *Journal of Personality and Social Psychology, 21*(1), 1–9. https://doi.org/10.1037/h0031930

Ajzen, I., & Fishbein, M. (1980). *Understanding attitudes and predicting social behavior.* Upper Saddle River, NJ: Prentice Hall.

Ajzen, I., & Fishbein, M. (2005). Theory-based behavior change interventions: Comments on Hobbis and Sutton. *Journal of Health Psychology, 10*(1), 27. https://doi.org/10.1177/1359105305048552

Ajzen, I., Fishbein, M., Lohmann, S., & Albarracín, D. (2019). The influence of attitudes on behavior. In B. T. Albarracín & D. Johnson (Eds.), *Handbook of attitudes: Vol. 1. Basic principles* (2nd ed., pp. 197–255). Hoboken, NJ: John Wiley.

Ajzen, I., & Madden, T. J. (1986). Prediction of goal directed behavior: Attitudes, intentions, and perceived behavioral control. *Journal of Experimental Social Psychology, 22*, 453–474. https://doi.org/10.1016/0022-1031(86)90045-4

Albarracín, D. (1997). *Processing of behavior-related communications as a function of cognitive elaboration: A multiple-stage model* (PhD dissertation). Retrieved from ProQuest Dissertations and Theses database.

Albarracín, D. (2002). Cognition in persuasion: An analysis of information processing in response to persuasive communications. *Advances in Experimental Social Psychology, 34*, 61–130. Retrieved from www.sciencedirect.com/science/article/pii/ S0065260102800041

Albarracín, D. (2012). Craving activity and losing objectivity: Effects of general action concepts on approach to decision-consistent information. *Social Psychological and Personality Science, 3*(1), 55–62. https://doi.org/10.1177 /1948550611408620

Albarracín, D. (2017). *Action and inaction content in message.* Unpublished raw data, University of Illinois Urbana Champaign.

Albarracín, D., Cohen, J., & Kumkale, G. T. (2003). When communications collide with recipients' actions: Effects of post-message behavior on intentions to follow the message recommendation. *Personality and Social Psychology Bulletin, 29*(7), 834–845. https://doi.org/10.1177/0146167203029007003

Albarracín, D., Durantini, M. R., Earl, A., Gunnoe, J. B., & Leeper, J. (2008). Beyond the most willing audiences: A meta-intervention to increase exposure to HIV-prevention programs by vulnerable populations. *Health Psychology*, *27*(5), 638–644. https://doi.org/10.1037/0278-6133.27.5.038

Albarracín, D., Gillette, J. C., Earl, A. N., Glasman, L. R., Durantini, M. R., & Ho, M.-H. (2005). A test of major assumptions about behavior change: A comprehensive look at the effects of passive and active HIV-prevention interventions since the beginning of the epidemic. *Psychological Bulletin*, *131* (6), 856–897. https://doi.org/10.1037/0033-2909.131.6.856

Albarracín, D., & Handley, I. M. (2007). The time for doing is not the time for change: Effects of general action and inaction goals on attitude retrieval and attitude change. *Journal of Personality and Social Psychology*, *100*, 983–998. https://doi.org/10.1037/a0023245

Albarracín, D., Handley, I. M., Albarracín, D., & Handley, I. M. (2011). The time for doing is not the time for change: Effects of general action and inaction goals on attitude retrieval and attitude change. *Journal of Personality and Social Psychology*, *100*(6), 983–998. https://doi.org/10.1037/a0023245

Albarracín, D., Handley, I. M., Noguchi, K., McCulloch, K. C., Li, H., Leeper, J., . . . Hart, W. (2008). Increasing and decreasing motor and cognitive output: A model of general action and inaction goals. *Journal of Personality and Social Psychology*, *95*(3), 510–523. https://doi.org/10.1037/a0012833

Albarracín, D., & Hart, W. (2011). Positive mood plus action = negative mood plus inaction: Effects of general action and inaction concepts on decisions and performance as a function of affect. *Emotion*, *11*(4), 951–957. https://doi.org/10.1037/a0024130

Albarracín, D., Hart, W., & McCulloch, K. C. (2006). Associating versus proposing or associating what we propose: Comment on Gawronski and Bodenhausen (2006). *Psychological Bulletin*, *132*, 732–735. https://doi.org/10.1037/0033-2909.132.5.732

Albarracín, D., Hepler, J., & Tannenbaum, M. (2011). General action and inaction goals: Their behavioral, cognitive, and affective origins and influences. *Current Directions in Psychological Science*, *20*(2), 119–123. https://doi.org/10.1177/0963721411402666

Albarracín, D., Ho, R. M., McNatt, P. S., Williams, W. R., Rhodes, F., Malotte, C. K., . . . Grp, P. R. S. (2000). Structure of outcome beliefs in condom use. *Health Psychology*, *19*(5), 458–468. https://doi.org/10.1037//0278-6133.19.5.458

Albarracín, D., Hornik, R., & Ajzen, I. (2007). *Prediction and change of health behavior: Applying the reasoned action approach*. Mahwah, NJ: Erlbaum.

Albarracín, D., Johnson, B. T., Fishbein, M., & Muellerleile, P. A. (2001). Theories of reasoned action and planned behavior as models of condom use: A meta-analysis. *Psychological Bulletin*, *127*(1), 142–161. https://doi.org/10.1037/0033-2909.127.1.142

Albarracín, D., Johnson, B. T., & Zanna, M. P. (Eds.) (2005). *The handbook of attitudes*. New York, NY: Psychology Press.

Albarracín, D., Jones, C., Hepler, J., & Li, I. H. (2017). Liking for action and the vertical/horizontal dimension of culture in nineteen nations: Valuing equality over hierarchy promotes positivity towards action. *Interamerican Journal of Psychology, 51*(3), 335–343. https://doi.org/10.30849/rip/ijp.v51i3.359

Albarracín, D., & Kumkale, G. T. (2003). Affect as information in persuasion: A model of affect identification and discounting. *Journal of Personality and Social Psychology, 84*(3), 453–469. https://doi.org/10.1037/0022-3514.84.3.453

Albarracín, D., Kumkale, G. T., & Poyner-Del Vento, P. (2017). How people can become persuaded by weak messages presented by credible communicators: Not all sleeper effects are created equal. *Journal of Experimental Social Psychology, 68*, 171–180.

Albarracín, D., Leeper, J., Earl, A., & Durantini, M. R. (2008). From brochures to videos to counseling: Exposure to HIV-prevention programs. *AIDS and Behavior, 12*, 354–262. https://doi.org/10.1007/s10461-007-9320-x

Albarracín, D., McNatt, P. S. P., Klein, C. T. F., Ho, R., Mitchell, A. L., & Kumkale, G. T. (2003). Persuasive communications to change actions: An analysis of behavioral and cognitive impact in HIV prevention. *Health Psychology, 22*(2), 166–177. https://doi.org/10.1037/0278-6133.22.2.166

Albarracín, D., & Mitchell, A. L. (2004). The role of defensive confidence in preference for proattitudinal information: How believing that one is strong can sometimes be a defensive weakness. *Personality and Social Psychology Bulletin, 30* (12), 1565–1584. https://doi.org/10.1177/0146167204271180

Albarracín, D., Noguchi, K., & Earl, A. N. (2006). Joyce's "Ulysses" and Woolf's "Jacob's Room" as the phenomenology of reasoning: Intentions and control as emergent of language and social interaction. *Psychological Inquiry, 17*(3), 236–245.

Albarracín, D., Noguchi, K., & Fischler, I. (2011). The syntax of defection and cooperation: The effects of the implicit sentences nice act versus act nice on behavior change. *Social Psychological and Personality Science, 2*(3), 298–305.

Albarracín, D., & Shavitt, S. (2018). Attitudes and attitude change. *Annual Review of Psychology, 69*, 299–327. https://doi.org/10.1146/annurev-psych-122216-011911

Albarracín, D., Sunderrajan, A., & Dai, W. (2018). Action, inaction, and action-ability: Definitions and implications for communications and interventions to change behaviors. In R. A. Bevins & D. Hope (Eds.), *The 65th annual Nebraska Symposium on Motivation: Change and maintaining change* (pp. 75–99). New York, NY: Springer.

Albarracín, D., Sunderrajan, A., Dai, W., & White, B. X. (2019). The social creation of action and inaction: From concepts to goals to behaviors. *Advances in Experimental Social Psychology, 60*, 223–271. https://doi.org/10.1016/bs .aesp.2019.04.001

Albarracín, D., Sunderrajan, A., Lohmann, S., Chan, M. S., Jiang, D., Chan, M. P. S., & Jiang, D. (2019). The psychology of attitudes, motivation, and persuasion. In B. T. Albarracín & D. Johnson (Eds.), *Handbook of attitudes: Vol. 1. Basic principles* (2nd ed., pp. 3–44). Hoboken, NJ: John Wiley.

Albarracín, D., & Vargas, P. (2010). Attitudes and persuasion: From biology to social responses to persuasive intent. In B. T. Albarracín & D. Johnson (Eds.), *Handbook of attitudes: Vol. 1. Basic principles* (2nd ed., pp. 394–427). Hoboken, NJ: John Wiley. https://doi.org/10.1146/annurev.psych.57.102904.190034

Albarracín, D., Wallace, H. M., & Glasman, L. R. (2004). Survival and change in judgments: A model of activation and comparison. *Advances in Experimental Social Psychology, 36*, 251–315. https://doi.org/10.1016/S0065-2601(04)36005-3

Albarracín, D., Wallace, H. M., Hart, W., & Brown, R. D. (2012). How judgments change following comparison of current and prior information. *Basic and Applied Social Psychology, 34*(1). https://doi.org/10.1080/01973533.2011.637480

Albarracín, J., Wang, W., & Albarracín, D. (2012). Are confident partisans disloyal? The role of defensive confidence in party defection. *Journal of Applied Social Psychology, 42*(7), 1576–1598. https://doi.org/10.1111/j.1559-1816.2012.00896

Albarracín, D., Wang, W., & Leeper, J. (2009). Immediate increase in food intake following exercise messages. *Obesity, 17*(7), 1451–1452. https://doi.org/10.1038/oby.2009.16

Albarracín, D., Wang, W., Li, H., & Noguchi, K. (2011). Structure of attitudes: Judgments, memory, and implications for change. In W. D. Crano & R. Prislin (Eds.), *Attitudes and attitude change* (pp. 19–39). New York, NY: Psychology Press. https://doi.org/10.4324/9780203838068

Albarracín, D., Wang, W., & McCulloch, K. C. (2018). Action dominance: The performance effects of multiple action demands and the benefits of an inaction focus. *Personality and Social Psychology Bulletin, 44*, 966–1007.

Albarracín, D., Wilson, K., Chan, M., Pui, S., Durantini, M., & Sanchez, F. (2017). Action and inaction in multi-behaviour recommendations: A meta-analysis of lifestyle interventions. *Health Psychology Review*, 1–24. https://doi.org/10.1080/17437199.2017.1369140

Albarracín, D., Wilson, K., Durantini, M. R., & Livingood, W. (2013). When is retention in health promotion interventions intentional? Predicting return to health promotion interventions as a function of busyness. *Acta de Investigacion Psicologica, 3*(3), 1311–1321.

Albarracín, D., & Wyer, R. S., Jr. (2000). The cognitive impact of past behavior: Influences on beliefs, attitudes, and future behavioral decisions. *Journal of Personality and Social Psychology, 79*(1), 5.

Albarracín, D., & Wyer, R. S., Jr. (2001). Elaborative and nonelaborative processing of a behavior-related communication. *Personality and Social Psychology Bulletin, 27*(6), 691–705. https://doi.org/10.1177/0146167201276005

Albarracín, D., Zanna, M. P., Johnson, B. T., & Kumkale, T. (2005). Attitudes: Introduction and scope. In D. Albarracín, B. T. Johnson, & M. P. Zanna (Eds.), *The handbook of attitudes* (pp. 3–19). New York, NY: Psychology Press.

Allison, S. T., & Messick, D. M. (1988). The feature-positive effect, attitude strength, and degree of perceived consensus. *Personality and Social Psychology Bulletin, 14*(2), 231–241. https://doi.org/10.1177/0146167288142002

Alwin, D. F., Cohen, R. L., & Newcomb, T. M. (1991). *Political attitudes over the life span: The Bennington women after fifty years.* Madison, WI: University of Wisconsin Press.

American Psychiatric Association (2000). *Diagnostic and statistical manual of mental disorders* (Vol. 4th ed.). Washington, DC: Author. https://doi.org/10.1097/00001888-195209000-00035

Anderson, C. (1983). The causal structure of situations: The generation of plausible causal attributions as a function of type of event situation. *Journal of Experimental Social Psychology, 19*(2), 185–203. https://doi.org/http://dx.doi.org/10.1016/0022-1031%2883%2990037-9

Anderson, J. R. (2013). *The architecture of cognition.* New York, NY: Psychology Press.

Anderson, N. H. (1968). Application of a linear-serial model to a personality-impression task using serial presentation. *Journal of Personality and Social Psychology, 10*(4), 354.

Anderson, N. H. (1974). Information integration theory: A brief survey. *Contemporary Developments in Mathematical Psychology, 2,* 236–305.

Anderson, N. H. (1981). *Foundations of information integration theory* (Vol. 578). New York, NY: Academic Press.

Aristotle (1938). *The Organon, The Categories* (H. Tredennick, Trans.). Cambridge, MA: Harvard University Press.

Armitage, C. J. (1995). Can the theory of planned behavior predict the maintenance of physical activity? *Health Psychology, 24*(2), 235–245. https://doi.org/10.1037/0278-6133.24.3.235

Armitage, C. J., & Conner, M. (2001). Efficacy of the theory of planned behaviour: A meta-analytic review. *British Journal of Social Psychology, 40*(4), 471–499. https://doi.org/10.1348/014466601164939

Aronson, E. (1968). Dissonance theory: Progress and problems. In *Theories of cognitive consistency: A sourcebook* (pp. 5–27). Chicago: Rand-McNally.

Aronson, E., & Carlsmith, J. M. (1963). Effect of severity of threat on devaluation of forbidden behavior. *Journal of Abnormal Psychology, 66*(6), 584. https://doi.org/10.1037/h0039901

Aronson, E., & Mills, J. (1959). The effect of severity of initiation on liking for a group. *The Journal of Abnormal and Social Psychology, 59*(2), 177.

Asch, S. E. (1940). Studies in the principles of judgments and attitudes: II. Determination of judgments by group and by ego standards. *Journal of Social Psychology, 12*(2), 433–465.

Asch, S. E. (1952). *Social psychology.* Englewood, NJ: Prentice Hall.

Asch, S. E. (1957). An experimental investigation of group influence. In *Symposium on preventive and social psychiatry* (pp. 15–17). Washington, DC: National Academies Press.

Atkinson, J. W. (1964). *An introduction to motivation: Vol. 9. Engineering.* Oxford, England: Van Nostrand.

Avishai, A., Conner, M., & Sheeran, P. (2019). Setting realistic health goals: Antecedents and consequences. *Annals of Behavioral Medicine, 53*, 1020–1031. https://doi.org/10.1093/abm/kaz012

Avnet, T., & Higgins, E. T. (2003). Locomotion, assessment, and regulatory fit: Value transfer from "how" to "what." *Journal of Experimental Social Psychology, 39*(5), 525–530. https://doi.org/10.1016/S0022-1031(03)00027-1

Avnet, T., & Higgins, E. T. (2006). How regulatory fit affects value in consumer choices and opinions. *Journal of Marketing Research, 43*(1), 1–10.

Avnet, T., Laufer, D., & Higgins, E. T. (2013). Are all experiences of fit created equal? Two paths to persuasion. *Journal of Consumer Psychology, 23*(3), 301–316. https://doi.org/10.1016/j.jcps.2012.10.011

Bae, R. E., Maloney, E. K., Albarracín, D., & Cappella, J. N. (2018). Does interest in smoking affect youth selection of pro-smoking videos? A selective exposure experiment. *Nicotine and Tobacco Research, 21*, 539–546.

Baer, R. A. (2003). Mindfulness training as a clinical intervention: A conceptual and empirical review. *Clinical Psychology: Science and Practice, 10*(2), 125–143. https://doi.org/10.1093/clipsy/bpg015

Bagozzi, R. P., & Warshaw, P. R. (1990). Trying to consume. *Journal of Consumer Research, 17*(2), 127–140. https://doi.org/10.1086/208543

Bailenson, J. N., & Blascovich, J. (2004). Avatars. In *Encyclopedia of human–computer interaction* (pp. 64–68). Great Barrington, MA: Berkshire.

Bailenson, J. N., & Yee, N. (2005). Digital chameleons – Automatic assimilation of nonverbal gestures in immersive virtual environments. *Psychological Science, 16*(10), 814–819. https://doi.org/10.1111/j.1467-9280.2005.01619.x

Bamberg, S., Ajzen, I., & Schmidt, P. (2003). Choice of travel mode in the theory of planned behavior: The roles of past behavior, habit, and reasoned action. *Basic and Applied Social Psychology, 25*(3), 175–187. https://doi.org/10.1207/S15324834BASP2503_01

Banaji, M. R., Lemm, K. M., & Carpenter, S. J. (2001). The social unconscious. In A. Tesser & N. Schwarz (Eds.), *Blackwell handbook of social psychology: Intraindividual processes* (pp. 134–158). Oxford, England: Blackwell.

Bandura, A. (1986). *Social foundations of thought and action: A social cognitive theory* (Series in Social Learning Theory Vol. 1). Upper Saddle River, NJ: Prentice Hall.

Bandura, A. (1997). *Self-efficacy: The exercise of control.* New York, NY: Macmillan.

Bandura, A. (2001). Social cognitive theory: An agentic perspective. *Annual Review of Psychology, 6*, 1–60. https://doi.org/10.1146/annurev.psych.52.1.1

Bandura, A., & Wood, R. (1989). Effect of perceived controllability and performance standards on self-regulation of complex decision making. *Journal of Personality and Social Psychology, 56*(5), 805–814. https://doi.org/10.1037/0022-3514.56.5.805

Barden, J., & Tormala, Z. L. (2014). Elaboration and attitude strength: The new meta-cognitive perspective. *Social and Personality Psychology Compass, 8*(1), 17–29. https://doi.org/10.1111/spc3.12078

Bargh, J. A. (1994). The four horsemen of automaticity: Intention, awareness, efficiency, and control as separate issues. In R. S. Wyer (Ed.), *Handbook of social cognition* (pp. 1–40). Mahwah, NJ: Erlbaum.

Bargh, J. A. (2014, January). Unconscious impulses and desires impel what we think and do in ways Freud never dreamed of. *Scientific American*. https://doi .org/10.1038/scientificamerican0114-30

Bargh, J. A. (2016). Awareness of the prime versus awareness of its influence: implications for the real-world scope of unconscious higher mental processes. *Current Opinion in Psychology*, *12*, 49–52. https://doi.org/10.1016/j.copsyc.2016 .05.006

Bargh, J. A., Chaiken, S. R., Govender, R., & Pratto, F. (1992). The generality of the automatic activation effect. *Journal of Personality and Social Psychology*, *62* (6), 893–912. https://doi.org/10.1037/0022-3514.62.6.893

Bargh, J. A., Chaiken, S. R., Raymond, P., & Hymes, C. (1996). The automatic evaluation effect: Unconditional automatic attitude activation with a pronunciation task. *Journal of Experimental Social Psychology*, *32*(1), 104–128. https://doi.org/10.1006/jesp.1996.0005

Bargh, J. A., Chen, M., & Burrows, L. (1996). Automaticity of social behavior: Direct effects of trait construct and stereotype activation on action. *Journal of Personality and Social Psychology*, *71*(2), 230–244. https://doi.org/10.1037/0022-3514.71.2.230

Bargh, J. A., Gollwitzer, P. M., Lee-Chai, A., Barndollar, K., & Trötschel, R. (2001). The automated will: Nonconscious activation and pursuit of behavioral goals. *Journal of Personality and Social Psychology*, *81*(6), 1014.

Barnidge, M., & Peacock, C. (2019). A third wave of selective exposure research? The challenges posed by hyperpartisan news on social media. *Media and Communication*, *7*(3), 4–7. https://doi.org/10.17645/mac.v7i3.2257

Baron, R. S., Hoppe, S. I., Kao, C. F., Brunsman, B., Linneweh, B., & Rogers, D. (1996). Social corroboration and opinion extremity. *Journal of Experimental Social Psychology*, *32*(6), 537–560. https://doi.org/10.1006/jesp.1996.0024

Bar-Tal, D., Raviv, A., & Goldberg, M. (1982). Helping behavior among preschool children: An observational study. *Child Development*, *53*(2), 396–402. https://doi.org/10.2307/1128982

Bassili, J. N., & Brown, R. D. (2005). Implicit and explicit attitudes: Research, challenges, and theory. In D. Albarracín, B. T. Johnson, & M. P. Zanna (Eds.), *The handbook of attitudes* (pp. 543–574). New York, NY: Psychology Press.

Becker, B. J. (1988). Synthesizing standardized mean change measures. *British Journal of Mathematical and Statistical Psychology*, *41*, 257–278. https://doi.org /10.1111/j.2044-8317.1988.tb00901.x

Beentjes, J. W. J., de Graaf, A., Hoeken, H., Sanders, J., & Beentjes, J. W. J. (2012). Identification as a mechanism of narrative persuasion. *Communication Research*, *39*(6), 802–823. https://doi.org/10.1177/0093650211408594

Bem, D. J. (1965). An experimental analysis of self-persuasion. *Journal of Experimental Social Psychology*, *1*, 199–218.

Bem, D. J. (1967). Self-perception: An alternative interpretation of cognitive dissonance phenomena. *Psychological Review, 74*(3), 183–200. https://doi.org/10.1037/h0024835

Bem, D. J. (1968). The epistemological status of interpersonal simulations: A reply to Jones, Linder, Kiesler, Zanna, and Brehm. *Journal of Experimental Social Psychology, 4*(3), 270–274. https://doi.org/10.1016/0022-1031(68)90055-3

Bem, D. J. (1972). Self-perception theory. *Advances in Experimental Social Psychology, 6*, 1–62. https://doi.org/10.1016/S0065-2601(08)60024-6

Bem, D. J., & McConnell, H. K. (1970). Testing the self-perception explanation of dissonance phenomena: On the salience of premanipulation attitudes. *Journal of Personality and Social Psychology, 14*(1), 23–31. https://doi.org/10.1037/h0020916

Bensley, L. S., & Wu, R. (1991). The role of psychological reactance in drinking following alcohol prevention messages. *Journal of Applied Social Psychology, 21*(13), 1111–1124. https://doi.org/10.1111/j.1559-1816.1991.tb00461.x

Berger, I. E., & Mitchell, A. A. (1989). The effect of advertising on attitude accessibility, attitude confidence, and the attitude-behavior relationship. *Journal of Consumer Research, 16*(3), 269–279.

Berkman, E. T., Burklund, L., & Lieberman, M. D. (2009). Inhibitory spillover: Intentional motor inhibition produces incidental limbic inhibition via right inferior frontal cortex. *NeuroImage, 47*(2), 705–712. https://doi.org/10.1016/j.neuroimage.2009.04.084

Betsch, T., Fiedler, K., & Brinkmann, J. (1998). Behavioral routines in decision making: The effects of novelty in task presentation and time pressure on routine maintenance and deviation. *European Journal of Social Psychology, 28*(6), 861–878.

Bettes, B. A., Dusenbury, L., Kerner, J., James-Ortiz, S., & Botvin, G. J. (1990). Ethnicity and psychosocial factors in alcohol and tobacco use in adolescence. *Child Development, 61*(2), 557–565. https://doi.org/10.1111/j.1467-8624.1990.tb02800.x

Birnbaum, M. H., & Stegner, S. E. (1979). Source credibility in social judgment: Bias, expertise, and the judge's point of view. *Journal of Personality and Social Psychology, 37*(1), 48–74. https://doi.org/10.1037/0022-3514.37.1.48

Bizer, G. Y., Tormala, Z. L., Rucker, D. D., & Petty, R. E. (2006). Memory-based versus on-line processing: Implications for attitude strength. *Journal of Experimental Social Psychology, 42*(5), 646–653. https://doi.org/10.1016/j.jesp.2005.09.002

Blankenship, K. L., Allen, J. J., Kane, K. A., & Anderson, C. A. (2019). The role of attitudes in violence and aggression. In B. T. Albarracín & D. Johnson (Eds.), *Handbook of attitudes: Vol. 2. Applications* (2nd ed., pp. 299–336). Hoboken, NJ: John Wiley.

Blascovich, J., Loomis, J., Beall, A. C., Swinth, K. R., Hoyt, C. L., & Bailenson, J. N. (2002). Immersive virtual environment technology as a methodological tool for social psychology. *Psychological Inquiry, 13*(2), 103–124. https://doi.org/10.1207/S15327965PLI1302_01

Blei, D., Ng, A., & Jordan, M. (2003). Latent dirichlet allocation. *Journal of Machine Learning Research, 3*, 993–1022.

Block, L. G., & Keller, P. A. (1995). When to accentuate the negative: The effects of perceived efficacy and message framing on intentions to perform a health-related behavior. *Journal of Marketing Research, 32*(2), 192–203.

Bluemke, M., & Friese, M. (2008). Reliability and validity of the Single-Target IAT (ST-IAT): Assessing automatic affect towards multiple attitude objects. *European Journal of Social Psychology, 38*(6), 977–997.

Bond, R., & Smith, P. B. (1996). Culture and conformity: A meta-analysis of studies using Asch's (1952b, 1956) line judgment task. *Psychological Bulletin, 119* (1), 111–137. https://doi.org/10.1037/0033-2909.119.1.111

Bornstein, R. F. (1989). Exposure and affect: Overview and meta-analysis of research, 1968–1987. *Psychological Bulletin, 106*(2), 265.

Boulding, W., Kalra, A., Staelin, R., & Zeithaml, V. A. (1993). A dynamic process model of service quality: From expectations to behavioral intentions. *Journal of Marketing Research, 30*(1), 7–27.

Bradley, M. M., Codispoti, M., Cuthbert, B. N., & Lang, P. J. (2001). Emotion and motivation I: Defensive and appetitive reactions in picture processing. *Emotion, 1*(3), 276.

Bradley, M. M., Hamby, S., Löw, A., & Lang, P. J. (2007). Brain potentials in perception: Picture complexity and emotional arousal. *Psychophysiology, 44*(3), 364–373.

Brandstatter, V., Lengfelder, A., & Gollwitzer, P. M. (2001). Implementation intentions and efficient action initiation. *Journal of Personality and Social Psychology, 81*(5), 946–960. https://doi.org/10.1037//0022-3514.81.5.946

Brauer, M., Judd, C. M., & Gliner, M. D. (1995). The effects of repeated expressions on attitude polarization during group discussions. *Journal of Personality and Social Psychology, 68*(6), 1014. https://doi.org/10.4324 /9780203647585

Brehm, J. W. (1956). Postdecision changes in the desirability of alternatives. *The Journal of Abnormal and Social Psychology, 52*(3), 384.

Brehm, J. W. (1966). *A theory of psychological reactance.* Oxford, England: Academic Press. https://doi.org/10.1002/hrdq.20027

Brehm, J. (1972). *Responses to loss of freedom: A theory of psychological reactance.* Morristown, NJ: General Learning Press.

Brewer, W. F., & Lichtenstein, E. H. (1981). Event schemas, story schemas, and story grammars. In J. Long & A. Baddeley (Eds.), *Attention and performance IX* (pp. 363–379). Hillsdale, NJ: Erlbaum.

Brindal, E., Freyne, J., Saunders, I., Berkovsky, S., Smith, G., & Noakes, M. (2012). Features predicting weight loss in overweight or obese participants in a web-based intervention: Randomized trial. *Journal of Medical Internet Research, 14*(6), 114–129. https://doi.org/10.2196/jmir.2156

Brinol, P., & Petty, R. E. (2003). Overt head movements and persuasion: A self-validation analysis. *Journal of Personality and Social Psychology, 84*(6), 1123–1139. https://doi.org/10.1037/0022-3514.84.6.1123

Brock, T. C., & Balloun, J. L. (1967). Behavioral receptivity to dissonant information. *Journal of Personality and Social Psychology, 6*(4), 413. https://doi .org/10.1037/h0021225

Bromberg, J. E., Augustson, E. M., & Backinger, C. L. (2012). Portrayal of smokeless tobacco in YouTube videos. *Nicotine and Tobacco Research, 14*(4), 455–462. https://doi.org/10.1093/ntr/ntr235

Brown, P. (1995). The role of the evaluator in comprehensive community initiatives. In J. P. Connel, A. C. Kubisch, L. B. Schorr, & C. H. Weiss (Eds.), *New approaches to evaluating community initiatives* (pp. 201–237). Washington, DC: Aspen.

Brown, R., & Albarracín, D. (2003). Unpublished data.

Brown, R., & Albarracín, D. (2004). Unpublished data on evaluative procedures.

Brown, S. A., Christiansen, B. A., & Goldman, M. S. (2015). The Alcohol Expectancy Questionnaire: An instrument for the assessment of adolescent and adult alcohol expectancies. *Journal of Studies on Alcohol, 48*(5), 483–491. https://doi.org/10.15288/jsa.1987.48.483

Brunel, F. F., Collins, C. M., Greenwald, A. G., & Tietje, B. C. (1999). Making the private public, accessing the inaccessible: Marketing applications of the Implicit Association Test. Paper presented at the annual meeting of the Association for Consumer Research, Columbus, OH.

Bruner, J. S. (1957). On perceptual readiness. *Psychological Review, 64*(2), 123.

Bryan, W. L., & Harter, N. (1899). The acquisition of a hierarchy of habits. *Psychological Review, 6*, 345–375.

Bryant, J., & Oliver, M. B. (2009). *Media effects: Advances in theory and research.* https://doi.org/10.1017/CBO9781107415324.004

Burchell, K., Rettie, R., & Patel, K. (2013). Marketing social norms: Social marketing and the "social norm approach." *Journal of Consumer Behaviour, 9*, 1–9. https://doi.org/10.1002/cb.1395

Burger, J. M. (1999). The foot-in-the-door compliance procedure: A multiple-process analysis and review. *Personality and Social Psychology Review, 3*(4), 303–325. https://doi.org/10.1207/s15327957pspr0304_2

Burger, J. M., & Caldwell, D. F. (2003). The effects of monetary incentives and labeling on the foot-in-the-door effect: Evidence for a self-perception process. *Basic and Applied Social Psychology, 25*(3), 235–241. https://doi.org/10.1207 /S15324834BASP2503_06

Burnstein, E., & Vinokur, A. (1977). Persuasive argumentation and social comparison as determinants of attitude polarization. *Journal of Experimental Social Psychology, 13*(4), 319–332. https://doi.org/10.1016/0022-1031(77)90002-6

Byrne, D. (1961). Response to attitude similarity-dissimilarity as a function of affiliation need. *American Psychologist, 16*(7), 358.

Byrne, R. M. J., & Johnson-Laird, P. N. (1989). Spatial reasoning. *Journal of Memory and Language, 28*(5), 564–575. https://doi.org/10.1016/0749-596X(89) 90013-2

Cacioppo, J. T., Berntson, G. G., & Crites, S. L. (1996). Social neuroscience: Principles of psychophysiological arousal and response. In *Social psychology: Handbook of basic principles* (pp. 72–101). New York, NY: Guilford Press.

Cacioppo, J. T., Gardner, W. L., & Berntson, G. G. (1997). Beyond bipolar conceptualizations and measures: The case of attitudes and evaluative space. *Personality and Social Psychology Review*, *1*(1), 3–25.

Cameron, C. D., Brown-Iannuzzi, J. L., & Payne, B. K. (2012). Sequential priming measures of implicit social cognition: A meta-analysis of associations with behavior and explicit attitudes. *Personality and Social Psychology Review*, *16*(4), 330–350.

Camus, T., Hommel, B., Brunel, L., & Brouillet, T. (2018). From anticipation to integration: the role of integrated action-effects in building sensorimotor contingencies. *Psychonomic Bulletin and Review*, *25*, 1059–1065. https://doi.org/10.3758/s13423-017-1308-6

Cannon, L. K. (1964). Self-confidence and selective exposure to information. In L. Festinger (Ed.), *Conflict, decision and dissonance* (pp. 83–95). Stanford, CA: Stanford University Press.

Cappella, J. N. (1981). Mutual influence in expressive behavior. Adult-adult and infant-adult dyadic interaction. *Psychological Bulletin*, *89*(1), 101–132. https://doi.org/10.1037/0033-2909.89.1.101

Cappella, J. N., & Planalp, S. (1981). Talk and silence sequences in information conversations: Interspeaker influence. *Human Communication Research*, *7*(2), 117–132. https://doi.org/10.1111/j.1468-2958.1981.tb00564.x

Carpenter, C. J., & Boster, F. J. (2013). The relationship between message recall and persuasion: More complex than it seems. *Journal of Communication*, *63*(4), 661–681. https://doi.org/10.1111/jcom.12042

Carrera, P., Muñoz, D., Caballero, A., Fernández, I., Aguilar, P., & Albarracín, D. (2014). Cómo el tiempo verbal afecta a la interpretación de las acciones: El pasado simple conduce a las personas a un nivel de representación abstracto. *Psicologica*, *35*, 209–223.

Carrera, P., Muñoz, D., Caballero, A., Fernández, I., & Albarracín, D. (2012). The present projects past behavior into the future while the past projects attitudes into the future: How verb tense moderates predictors of drinking intentions. *Journal of Experimental Social Psychology*, *48*(5), 1196–1200. https://doi.org/10.1016/j.jesp.2012.04.001

Carroll, M. V., Shensa, A., & Primack, B. A. (2013). A comparison of cigarette- and hookah-related videos on YouTube. *Tobacco Control*, *22*, 319–323. https://doi.org/10.1136/tobaccocontrol-2011-050253

Carver, C. S., Ganellen, R. J., Froming, W. J., & Chambers, W. (1983). Modeling: An analysis in terms of category accessibility. *Journal of Experimental Social Psychology*, *19*, 403–421. https://doi.org/10.1016/0022-1031(83)90019-7

Carver, C. S., & White, T. L. (1994). Behavioral inhibition, behavioral activation, and affective responses to impending reward and punishment: The BIS/BAS Scales. *Journal of Personality and Social Psychology*, *67*, 319–333. https://doi.org/10.1037/0022-3514.67.2.319

Casadio, M., Pressman, A., Acosta, S., Danzinger, Z., Fishbach, A., Mussa-Ivakli, F. A., . . . Chen, D. (2011). *Body machine interface: Remapping motor skills after spinal cord injury.* Paper presented at the IEEE International Conference on Rehabilitation Robotics (ICORR).

Cavallo, D. N., Tate, D. F., Ries, A. V., Brown, J. D., DeVellis, R. F., & Ammerman, A. S. (2012). A social media-based physical activity intervention: A randomized controlled trial. *American Journal of Preventive Medicine, 43*(5), 527–532. https://doi.org/10.1016/j.amepre.2012.07.019

Centola, D. (2010). The spread of behavior in an online social network experiment. *Science, 329,* 1194–1197. https://doi.org/10.1126/science.1185231

Centola, D. (2011). An experimental study of homophily in the adoption of health behavior. *Science, 334,* 1269–1272. https://doi.org/10.1126/science .1207055

Chaiken, S. R. (1979). Communicator physical attractiveness and persuasion. *Journal of Personality and Social Psychology, 37*(8), 1387–1397. https://doi.org/10 .1037/0022-3514.37.8.1387

Chaiken, S. R. (1980). Heuristic versus systematic information processing and the use of source versus message cues in persuasion. *Journal of Personality and Social Psychology, 39,* 752–766. https://doi.org/10.1037/0022-3514.39.5.752

Chaiken, S. R., & Bargh, J. A. (1993). Occurrence versus moderation of the automatic evaluation effect: Reply. *Journal of Personality and Social Psychology, 64*(5), 759–765. https://doi.org/10.1037/0022-3514.64.5.759

Chaiken, S. R., & Eagly, A. H. (1976). Communication modality as a determinant of message persuasiveness and message comprehensibility. *Journal of Personality and Social Psychology, 34*(4), 605–614. https://doi.org/10.1037//0022-3514 .34.4.605

Chan, M. P. S., Jones, C., & Albarracín, D. (2017). Countering false beliefs: An analysis of the evidence and recommendations of best practices for the retraction and correction of scientific misinformation. In K. H. Jamieson, D. M. Kahan, & D. A. Scheufele (Eds.), *The Oxford handbook of the science of science communication.* Oxford, England: Oxford University Press. https://doi .org/10.1093/oxfordhb/9780190497620.013.37

Chan, M. P. S., Jones, C. R., Hall Jamieson, K., & Albarracín, D. (2017). Debunking: A meta-analysis of the psychological efficacy of messages countering misinformation. *Psychological Science, 28*(11), 1531–1546. https://doi.org/10 .1177/0956797617714579

Chan, M. P. S., Lohmann, S., Morales, A., Zhai, C., Ungar, L. H., Holtgrave, D. R., & Albarracín, D. (2018). An online risk index predicting HIV and other STIs across US counties and across years. *AIDS and Behavior, 22,* 2322–2333.

Chan, M. P. S., Morales, A., Farhadloo, M., Palmer, R. P., & Albarracín, D. (2019). Harvesting and harnessing social media data for psychological research. In H. Blanton & G. D. Webster (Eds.), *Social psychological research methods: Social psychological measurement* (pp. 228–264). New York, NY: Routledge/ Taylor and Francis.

Chandler, J., & Schwarz, N. (2009). How extending your middle finger affects your perception of others: Learned movements influence concept accessibility. *Journal of Experimental Social Psychology, 45,* 123–128. https://doi.org/10.1016/j.jesp.2008.06.012

Chang, C. (2004). The interplay of product class knowledge and trial experience in attitude formation. *Journal of Advertising, 33*(1), 83–92. https://doi.org/10.1080/00913367.2004.10639156

Chartrand, T. L., & Bargh, J. A. (1999). The Chameleon effect: The perception–behavior link and social interaction. *Journal of Personality and Social Psychology, 76*(6), 893–910. https://doi.org/10.1037/0022-3514.76.6.893

Chatzisarantis, N. L. D., & Hagger, M. S. (2007). Mindfulness and the intention–behavior relationship within the theory of planned behavior. *Personality and Social Psychology Bulletin, 33*(5), 663–676. https://doi.org/10.1177/0146167206297401

Chen, S., & Chaiken, S. (1999). The heuristic–systematic model in its broader context. In *Dual process theories in social psychology* (pp. 73–96). New York, NY: Guilford Press.

Cheng, C. M., & Chartrand, T. L. (2003). Self-monitoring without awareness: using mimicry as a nonconscious affiliation strategy. *Journal of Personality and Social Psychology, 85*(6), 1170.

Cheung, S.-F., & Chan, D. K.-S. (2000). *The role of perceived behavioral control in predicting human behavior: A meta-analytic review of studies on the theory of planned behavior.* Unpublished manuscript, Chinese University of Hong Kong.

Cialdini, R. B., & Goldstein, N. J. (2004). Social influence: Compliance and conformity. *Annual Review of Psychology, 55,* 591–621. https://doi.org/10.1146/annurev.psych.55.090902.142015

Cialdini, R. B., Herman, C. P., Levy, A., Kozlowski, L. T., & Petty, R. E. (1976). Elastic shifts of opinion: Determinants of direction and durability. *Journal of Personality and Social Psychology, 34*(4), 663–672. https://doi.org/10.1037//0022-3514.34.4.663

Cialdini, R. B., Levy, A., Herman, C. P., & Evenbeck, S. (1973). Attitudinal politics: The strategy of moderation. *Journal of Personality and Social Psychology, 25,* 100–108. https://doi.org/10.1037/h0034265

Cialdini, R. B., & Trost, M. (1998). Social influence: Social norms, conformity, and compliance. In *The handbook of social psychology* (pp. 151–192). New York, NY: McGraw-Hill.

Cialdini, R. B., Wosinska, W., Barrett, D. W., Butner, J., & Gornik Durose, M. (2001). The differential impact of two social influence principles on individualists and collectivists in Poland and the United States. In W. Wosinska, R. B. Cialdini et al. (Eds.), *The practice of social influence in multiple cultures: Applied social research* (pp. 33–50). Mahwah, NJ: Erlbaum.

Cioffi, D., & Garner, R. (1996). On doing the decision: Effects of active versus passive choice on commitment and self-perception. *Personality and Social Psychology Bulletin, 22,* 133–147.

Clark, J. K., & Evans, A. T. (2014). Source credibility and persuasion: The role of message position in self-validation. *Personality and Social Psychology Bulletin, 40* (8), 1024–1036. https://doi.org/10.1177/0146167214534733

Clark, J. K., & Wegener, D. T. (2008). Attitudinal ambivalence and message-based persuasion: Motivated Processing of Proattitudinal Information and Avoidance of Counterattitudinal Information, *Personality and Social Psychology Bulletin, 34*(4), 565–577. https://doi.org/10.1177/0146167207312527

Clark, J. K., Wegener, D. T., Sawicki, V., Petty, R. E., & Briñol, P. (2013). Evaluating the message or the messenger? Implications for self-validation in persuasion. *Personality and Social Psychology Bulletin, 39*(12), 1571–1584. https://doi.org/10.1177/0146167213499238

Clore, G. L., & Schnall, S. (2005). The influence of affect on attitude. In D. Albarracín, B. T. Johnson, & M. P. Zanna (Eds.), *The handbook of attitudes* (pp. 437–489). New York, NY: Psychology Press.

Cohen, J. B., & Andrade, E. B. (2018). The ADF framework: A parsimonious model for developing successful behavior change interventions. *Journal of Marketing Behavior, 3*(2), 81–119. https://doi.org/10.1561/107.00000046

Conner, M., & Higgins, A. R. (2010). Long-term effects of implementation intentions on prevention of smoking uptake among adolescents: A cluster randomized controlled trial. *Health Psychology, 29*(5), 529–538. https://doi.org/10.1037/a0020317

Converse, P. E., & Apter, D. (1964). *Ideology and discontent.* New York, NY: Free Press of Glencoe.

Cook, T. D., & Flay, B. R. (1978). The persistence of experimentally induced attitude change. *Advances in Experimental Social Psychology, 11*, 1–57. https://doi.org/10.1016/S0065-2601(08)60004-0

Cooper, J., Zanna, M. P., & Taves, P. A. (1978). Arousal as a necessary condition for attitude change following induced compliance. *Journal of Personality and Social Psychology, 36*(10), 1101–1106. https://doi.org/10.1037/0022-3514.36.10.1101

Cooper, R. P., & Shallice, T. (2006). Hierarchical schemas and goals in the control of sequential behavior. *Psychological Review, 113*, 887–916. https://doi.org/10.1037/0033-295X.113.4.887

Crano, W. D., & Hannula-Bral, K. A. (1994). Context/categorization model of social influence: Minority and majority influence in the formation of a novel response norm. *Journal of Experimental Social Psychology, 30*, 247–276. https://doi.org/10.1006/jesp.1994.1012

Cuthbert, B. N., Schupp, H. T., Bradley, M. M., Birbaumer, N., & Lang, P. J. (2000). Brain potentials in affective picture processing: covariation with autonomic arousal and affective report. *Biological Psychology, 52*(2), 95–111.

Czyzewska, M., & Ginsburg, H. J. (2007). Explicit and implicit effects of anti-marijuana and anti-tobacco TV advertisements. *Addictive Behaviors, 32* (1), 114–127. https://doi.org/10.1016/j.addbeh.2006.03.025

Dalton, A. N., Chartrand, T. L., & Finkel, E. J. (2010). The schema-driven chameleon: How mimicry affects executive and self-regulatory resources,

Journal of Personality and Social Psychology, 98(4), 605–617. https://doi.org/10.1037/a0017629

Darkes, J., & Goldman, M. S. (1998). Expectancy challenge and drinking reduction: Process and structure in the alcohol expectancy network. *Experimental and Clinical Psychopharmacology, 6,* 64–76. https://doi.org/10.1037/1064-1297.6.1.64

Dasgupta, N. (2013). Implicit attitudes and beliefs adapt to situations: A decade of research on the malleability of implicit prejudice, stereotypes, and the self-concept. *Advances in Experimental Social Psychology, 47,* 233–279. https://doi.org/10.1016/B978-0-12-407236-7.00005-X

Davies, M. (2008). *The corpus of contemporary American English (COCA): 400+ million words, 1990–present.* Harvard Dataverse.

Davis, J. P., Smith, D. C., & Briley, D. A. (2017). Substance use prevention and treatment outcomes for emerging adults in non-college settings: A meta-analysis. *Psychology of Addictive Behaviors, 31,* 242–254. https://doi.org/10.1037/adb0000267

Davis, L. E., Ajzen, I., Saunders, J., & Williams, T. (2002). The decision of African American students to complete high school: An application of the theory of planned behavior. *Journal of Educational Psychology, 94*(4), 810–819. https://doi.org/10.1037//0022-0663.94.4.810

de Bruin, W. B., & Keren, G. (2003). Order effects in sequentially judged options due to the direction of comparison. *Organizational Behavior and Human Decision Processes, 92*(1–2), 91–101. https://doi.org/10.1016/S0749-5978(03)00080-3

De Graaf, A., Hoeken, H., Sanders, J., & Beentjes, H. (2009). The role of dimensions of narrative engagement in narrative persuasion. *Communications, 34*(4). https://doi.org/10.1515/COMM.2009.024

de la Corte, L., Kruglanski, A. W., de Miguel, J., Manuel Sabucedo, J., & Diaz, D. (2007). Seven psychosocial principles to explain terrorism. *Psicothema, 19*(3), 366–374.

De Leeuw, A., Valois, P., Ajzen, I., & Schmidt, P. (2015). Using the theory of planned behavior to identify key beliefs underlying pro-environmental behavior in high-school students: Implications for educational interventions. *Journal of Environmental Psychology, 42,* 128–138. https://doi.org/10.1016/j.jenvp.2015.03.005

DeSteno, D., Petty, R. E., Wegener, D. T., & Rucker, D. D. (2000). Beyond valence in the perception of likelihood: The role of emotion specificity. *Journal of Personality and Social Psychology, 78*(4), 707. https://doi.org/10.1037/0022-3514.78.3.397

Deutsch, M., & Gerard, H. B. (1955). A study of normative and informational social influences upon individual judgment. *The Journal of Abnormal and Social Psychology, 51*(3), 629.

Devine, P. G., & Ostrom, T. M. (1985). Cognitive mediation of inconsistency discounting. *Journal of Personality and Social Psychology, 49*(1), 5.

DiGirolamo, A., Thompson, N., Martorell, R., Fein, S., & Grummer-Strawn, L. (2005). Intention or experience? Predictors of continued breastfeeding. *Health Education and Behavior*, *32*(2), 208–226.

Dillard, J. P., Plotnick, C. A., Godbold, L. C., Freimuth, V. S., & Edgar, T. (1996). The multiple affective outcomes of AIDS PSAs: Fear appeals do more than scare people. *Communication Research*, *23*(1), 44–72. https://doi.org/10.1177/009365096023001002

Dittrich, W. H., & Lea, S. E. (1993). Motion as a natural category for pigeons: Generalization and a feature-positive effect. *Journal of the Experimental Analysis of Behavior*, *59*, 115–129. https://doi.org/10.1901/jeab.1993.59-115

Dolcos, S., & Albarracín, D. (2014). The inner speech of behavioral regulation: Intentions and task performance strengthen when you talk to yourself as a You. *European Journal of Social Psychology*, *44*(6), 636–642. https://doi.org/10.1002/ejsp.2048

Doll, J., Ajzen, I., & Madden, T. J. (1991). Optimal-scaling and judgment in different domains: A reanalysis. *Zeitschrift für Sozialpsychologie*, *22*(2), 102–111.

Dovidio, J. F., Schellhaas, F. M. H., & Pearson, A. R. (2019). The role of attitudes in intergroup relations. In B. T. Albarracín & D. Johnson (Eds.), *Handbook of attitudes: Vol. 2. Applications* (2nd ed., pp. 419–454). Hoboken, NJ: John Wiley.

Doyen, S., Klein, O., Pichon, C. L., & Cleeremans, A. (2012). Behavioral priming: It's all in the mind, but whose mind? *PLoS ONE*, *7*(1). https://doi.org/10.1371/journal.pone.0029081

Driscoll, D. M., Blascovich, J., & Fazio, R. H. (1992). On the functional value of attitudes: The influence of accessible attitudes on the ease and quality of decision making. *Personality and Social Psychology Bulletin*, *18*, 388–401. https://doi.org/10.1177/0146167292184002

Dulany, D. E. (2006). Review of consciousness and behavior. *Contemporary Psychology: A Journal of Reviews*, *30*, 243. https://doi.org/10.1037/023670

Dunning, D., Anderson, J. E., Schlösser, T., & Ehlebracht, D. (2014). Trust at zero acquaintance: More a matter of respect than expectation of reward. *Journal of Social and Personality Psychology*, *107*(1), 122–141.

Durantini, M. R., & Albarracín, D. (2009). Material and social incentives to participation in behavioral interventions: A meta-analysis of gender disparities in enrollment and retention in experimental human immunodeficiency virus prevention interventions. *Health Psychology*, *28*(5), 631–640. https://doi.org/10.1037/a0015200

Durantini, M. R., & Albarracín, D. (2012). Men and women have specific needs that facilitate enrollment in HIV-prevention counseling. *AIDS Care*, *24*(10). https://doi.org/10.1080/09540121.2012.661834

Durantini, M. R., Albarracín, D., Mitchell, A. L., Earl, A. N., & Gillette, J. C. (2006). Conceptualizing the influence of social agents of behavior change: A meta-analysis of the effectiveness of HIV-prevention interventionists for different groups. *Psychological Bulletin*, *132*(2), 212.

Eagly, A. H. (1974). Comprehensibility of persuasive arguments as a determinant of opinion change. *Journal of Personality and Social Psychology*, *29*(6), 758–773. https://doi.org/10.1037/h0036202

Eagly, A. H., & Chaiken, S. (1993). Psychology of attitudes. In *Psychology of attitudes*. San Diego, CA: Harcourt Brace Jovanovich.

Eagly, A. H., & Chaiken, S. R. (2005). Attitude research in the 21st century: The current state of knowledge. In D. Albarracín, B. T. Johnson, & M. P. Zanna (Eds.), *The handbook of attitudes* (pp. 743–767). New York, NY: Psychology Press.

Eagly, A. H., & Chaiken, S. (2007). The advantages of an inclusive definition of attitude. *Social Cognition*, *25*(5), 582–602. https://doi.org/10.1521/soco.2007.25.5.582

Eagly, A. H., Kulesa, P., Chen, S., & Chaiken, S. R. (2001). Do attitudes affect memory? Tests of the congeniality hypothesis. *Current Directions in Psychological Science*, *10*(1), 5–9. https://doi.org/10.1111/1467-8721.00102

Earl, A., Albarracín, D., Durantini, M. R., Gunnoe, J. B., Leeper, J., & Levitt, J. H. (2009). Participation in counseling programs: High-risk participants are reluctant to accept HIV-prevention counseling. *Journal of Consulting and Clinical Psychology*, *77*(4), 668.

Earl, A., Crause, C., Vaid, A., Albarracín, D., & Albarracín, D. (2016). Disparities in attention to HIV-prevention information. *AIDS Care*, *28*(1), 79–86. https://doi.org/10.1080/09540121.2015.1066747

Earl, A., Hart, W., Handley, I., & Albarracín, D. (2004). *Effects of action goals on prevention and promotion*. Unpublished manuscript.

Earl, A., Nisson, C. A., & Albarracín, D. (2015). Stigma cues increase self-conscious emotions and decrease likelihood of attention to information about preventing stigmatized health issues. *Acta de Investigación Psicológica*, *5*(1), 1860–1871. https://doi.org/10.1016/S2007-4719(15)30006-5

Eckes, T., & Six, B. (1994). Fakten und Fiktionen in der Einstellungs-Verhaltens-Forschung: Eine Meta-Analyse. *Zeitschrift Für Sozialpsychologie*, *25*, 253–271.

Economist. (2018). American attitudes towards gun control. Retrieved from www.economist.com/graphic-detail/2018/02/23/american-attitudes-towards-gun-control

Eisenstadt, D., & Leippe, M. R. (2005). Dissonance and importance: Attitude change effects of personal relevance and race of the beneficiary of a counterattitudinal advocacy. *Journal of Social Psychology*, *145*(4), 447–467. https://doi.org/10.3200/SOCP.145.4.447-468

Eiser, J. R. (1973). Judgement of attitude statements as a function of judges' attitudes and the judgemental dimension. *British Journal of Social and Clinical Psychology*, *12*(3), 231–240.

Eiser, J. R., & White, C. J. M. (1973). Affirmation and denial in evaluative descriptions. *British Journal of Psychology*, *64*(3), 399–403.

Ekman, P. (1973). Universal facial expressions in emotion. *Studia Psychologica*, *15*, 140–147.

Ekman, P. (1994). Strong evidence for universals in facial expressions: A reply to Russell's mistaken critique. *Psychological Bulletin, 115*, 268–287. https://doi.org /10.1037/0033-2909.115.2.268

Elkin, L., Thomson, G., & Wilson, N. (2010). Connecting world youth with tobacco brands: YouTube and the internet policy vacuum on Web 2.0. *Tobacco Control, 19*, 361–366. https://doi.org/10.1136/tc.2010.035949

Elkin, R. A., & Leippe, M. R. (1986). Physiological arousal, dissonance, and attitude change: Evidence for a dissonance arousal link and a don't remind effect. *Journal of Experimental Social Psychology, 51*(1), 55–65. https://doi.org/10 .1037/0022-3514.51.1.55

Elliot, A. J., & Church, M. A. (1997). A hierarchical model of approach and avoidance achievement motivation. *Journal of Personality and Social Psychology, 72*(1), 218.

Elsner, B., & Hommel, B. (2001). Effect anticipation and action control. *Journal of Experimental Psychology: Human Perception and Performance, 27*, 229–240. https://doi.org/10.1037/0096-1523.27.1.229

Elsner, B., & Hommel, B. (2004). Contiguity and contingency in action-effect learning. *Psychological Research, 68*, 138–154. https://doi.org/10.1007/s00426-0 03-0151-8

Epstude, K., Scholl, A., & Roese, N. J. (2016). Prefactual thoughts: Mental simulations about what might happen. *Review of General Psychology, 20*(1), 48–56. https://doi.org/10.1037/gpr0000064

Erb, H. P., & Bohner, G. (2007). Social influence and persuasion: Recent theoretical developments and integrative attempts. In K. Fiedler (Ed.), *Social communication* (pp. 191–221). New York, NY: Psychology Press.

Erb, H. P., & Bohner, G. (2010). Consensus as the key: Towards parsimony in explaining majority and minority influence. In M. Martin & R. Hewstone (Eds.), *Minority influence and innovation: Antecedents, processes, and consequences* (pp. 79–103). Hove, England: Psychology Press.

Esses, V. M., Hamilton, L. K., & Gaucher, D. (2019). The role of attitudes in migration. In B. T. Albarracín & D. Johnson (Eds.), *Handbook of attitudes: Vol. 2. Applications* (2nd ed., pp. 455–487). Hoboken, NJ: John Wiley.

Etter, J., Humair, J., Bergman, M., & Perneger, T. (2000). Development and validation of the Attitudes Towards Smoking Scale (ATS-18). *Addiction, 95*(4), 613–625.

Everett, J. A. C., Caviola, L., Kahane, G., Savulescu, J., & Faber, N. S. (2015). Doing good by doing nothing? The role of social norms in explaining default effects in altruistic contexts. *European Journal of Social Psychology, 45*(2), 230–241. https://doi.org/10.1002/ejsp.2080

Eysenck, H. J. (1967). *The dynamics of anxiety and hysteria: An experimental application of modern learning theory to psychiatry.* New York, NY: Routledge and Kegan Paul.

Eysenck, H. J., & Eysenck, M. W. (1985). *Personality and individual differences: A natural science approach.* New York, NY: Plenum.

Fabrigar, L. R., MacDonald, T. K., & Wegener, D. T. (2005). The structure of attitudes. In D. Albarracín, B. T. Johnson, & M. P. Zanna (Eds.), *The handbook of attitudes* (pp. 79–124). New York, NY: Psychology Press.

Farhadloo, M., Winneg, K., Chan, M.-P. S., Jamieson, K. H., & Albarracín, D. (2018). Associations of topics of discussion on twitter with survey measures of attitudes, knowledge, and behaviors related to Zika: Probabilistic study in the United States. *Journal of Medical Internet Research*, *20*(2). https://doi.org/10 .2196/publichealth.8186

Fazio, R. H. (1989). On the power and functionality of attitudes: The role of attitude accessibility. In A. R. Pratkanis, S. J. Breckler, & A. G. Greenwald (Eds.), *Attitude structure and function* (pp. 153–179). Hillsdale, NJ, Lawrence Erlbaum.

Fazio, R. H. (1990). Multiple processes by which attitudes guide behavior: The mode model as an integrative framework. *Advances in Experimental Social Psychology*, *23*, 75–109. https://doi.org/10.1016/S0065-2601(08)60318-4

Fazio, R. H. (2007). Attitudes as object – evaluation associations of varying strength. *Social Cognition*, *25*(5), 603–637.

Fazio, R. H., Chen, J.-M., McDonel, E. C., & Sherman, S. J. (1982). Attitude accessibility, attitude-behavior consistency, and the strength of the object-evaluation association. *Journal of Experimental Social Psychology*, *18*(4), 339–357.

Fazio, R. H., Jackson, J. R., Dunton, B. C., & Williams, C. J. (1995). Variability in automatic activation as an unobtrusive measure of racial attitudes: A bona fide pipeline? *Journal of Personality and Social Psychology*, *69*, 1013–1027. https://doi .org/10.1037/0022-3514.69.6.1013

Fazio, R. H., Ledbetter, J. E., & Towles-Schwen, T. (2000). On the costs of accessible attitudes: Detecting that the attitude object has changed. *Journal of Personality and Social Psychology*, *78*, 197–210. https://doi.org/10.1037/0022-3514 .78.2.197

Fazio, R. H., Maio, G. R., & Olson, J. M. (2000). Accessible attitudes as tools for object appraisal: Their costs and benefits. In *Why we evaluate: Functions of attitudes* (pp. 1–36). Mahwah, NJ: Erlbaum.

Fazio, R. H., Powell, M. C., & Herr, P. M. (1983). Toward a process model of the attitude behavior relation: Accessing one's attitude upon mere observation of the attitude object. *Journal of Personality and Social Psychology*, *44*(4), 723–735. https://doi.org/10.1037/0022-3514.44.4.723

Fazio, R. H., Powell, M. C., & Williams, C. J. (1989). The role of attitude accessibility in the attitude-to-behavior process. *Journal of Consumer Research*, *16*(3), 280–288.

Fazio, R. H., Sanbonmatsu, D. M., Powell, M. C., & Kardes, F. R. (1986). On the automatic activation of attitudes. *Journal of Personality and Social Psychology*, *50* (2), 229.

Fazio, R. H., Sherman, S. J., & Herr, P. M. (1982). The feature-positive effect in the self-perception process: Does not doing matter as much as doing? *Journal of Personality and Social Psychology*, *42*, 404–411. https://doi.org/10.1037/0022-3514 .42.3.404

Fazio, R. H., & Williams, C. J. (1986). Attitude accessibility as a moderator of the attitude-perception and attitude-behavior relations: An investigation of the 1984 presidential election. *Journal of Personality and Social Psychology, 51*, 505–514. https://doi.org/10.1037/0022-3514.51.3.505

Fazio, R. H., Zanna, M. P., & Cooper, J. (1978). Direct experience and attitude-behavior consistency: Information processing analysis. *Personality and Social Psychology Bulletin, 4*(1), 48–51. https://doi.org/10.1177/014616727800400109

Feather, N. T. (1963). Cognitive-dissonance, sensitivity, and evaluation. *Journal of Abnormal Psychology, 66*(2), 157. https://doi.org/10.1037/h0049383

Feldman, G., & Albarracín, D. (2017). Norm theory and the action-effect: The role of social norms in regret following action and inaction. *Journal of Experimental Social Psychology, 69*, 111–120. https://doi.org/10.1016/j.jesp.2016.07.009

Feldman, J. M., & Lynch, J. G. (1988). Self-generated validity and other effects of measurement on belief, attitude, intention, and behavior. *Journal of Applied Psychology, 73*(3), 421.

Fennis, B. M., & Stel, M. (2011). The pantomime of persuasion: Fit between nonverbal communication and influence strategies. *Journal of Experimental Social Psychology, 47*(4), 806–810. https://doi.org/10.1016/j.jesp.2011.02.015

Ferguson, M. J., & Bargh, J. A. (2004). Liking is for doing: The effects of goal pursuit on automatic evaluation. *Journal of Personality and Social Psychology, 87* (5), 557–572. https://doi.org/10.1037/0022-3514.87.5.557

Festinger, L. (1950). Informal social communication. *Psychological Review, 57* (5), 271.

Festinger, L. (1954). A theory of social comparison processes. *Human Relations, 7*, 117–140. https://doi.org/10.1177/001872675400700202

Festinger, L. (1957). *A theory of cognitive dissonance.* Stanford, CA: Stanford University Press.

Festinger, L. (1964). *Conflict, decision, and dissonance.* Palo Alto, CA: Stanford University Press.

Festinger, L., & Carlsmith, J. M. (1959). Cognitive consequences of forced compliance. *Journal of Abnormal and Social Psychology, 58*(2), 203–210. https://doi.org/10.1037/h0041593

Fishbach, A., Steinmetz, J., & Tu, Y. (2016). Motivation in a social context: Coordinating personal and shared goal pursuits with others. In A. Elliot (Ed.), *Advances in motivation science* (Vol. 3, pp. 35–79). San Diego, CA: Elsevier. https://doi.org/10.1016/bs.adms.2015.12.005

Fishbein, M. (1963). An investigation of the relationships between beliefs about an object and the attitude toward that object. *Human Relations, 16*(3), 233–239. https://doi.org/10.1177/001872676301600302

Fishbein, M. (2008). A reasoned action approach to health promotion. *Medical Decision Making: An International Journal of the Society for Medical Decision Making, 28*(6), 834–844. https://doi.org/10.1177/0272989X08326092

Fishbein, M., & Ajzen, I. (1974). Attitudes towards objects as predictors of single and multiple behavioral criteria. *Psychological Review, 81*(1), 59–74. https://doi .org/10.1037/h0035872

Fishbein, M., & Ajzen, I. (1975). *Belief, attitude, intention, and behavior: An introduction to theory and research*. Reading, MA: Addison-Wesley. https://doi .org/10.1017/CBO9781107415324.004

Fishbein, M., & Ajzen, I. (1981). Acceptance, yielding and impact: Cognitive processes in persuasion. In R. E. Petty, T. M. Ostrom, & T. C. Brock (Eds.), *Cognitive responses in persuasion* (pp. 339–359). Hillsdale, NJ: Erlbaum.

Fishbein, M., & Ajzen, I. (2010). *Predicting and changing behaviour: The reasoned action approach*. New York, NY: Psychology Press. https://doi.org/10.4324 /9780203937082

Fishbein, M., & Ajzen, I. (2011a). Attitudes, norms, and control as predictors of intentions and behavior. In *Predicting and changing behavior: The reasoned action approach* (pp. 179–219). New York, NY: Psychology Press.

Fishbein, M., & Azjen, I. (2011b). *Predicting and changing behavior: The reasoned action approach*. New York, NY: Taylor and Francis. https://doi.org/10.1080/0 0224545.2011.563209

Fishbein, M., Ajzen, I., & Hanson, M. J. S. (1999). *Fishbein–Ajzen–Hanson Questionnaire*. Retrieved from https://cancercontrol.cancer.gov/brp/tcrb/nci guide_measure/Fishbein-Ajzen-Hanson_Questionnaire.pdf

Fishbein, M., Ajzen, I., & McArdle, J. (1980). Changing the behavior of alcoholics: Effects of persuasive communication. In *Understanding attitudes and predicting social behavior* (pp. 217–242). Englewood Cliffs, NJ: Prentice Hall.

Fisher, J. D., Fisher, W. A., Bryan, A. D., & Misovich, S. J. (2002). Information-motivation-behavioral skills model-based HIV risk behavior change intervention for inner-city high school youth. *Health Psychology, 21*(2), 177–186. https:// doi.org/10.1037/0278-6133.21.2.177

Fisher, W. A., Fisher, J. D., & Rye, B. J. (1995). Understanding and promoting AIDS-preventive behavior: Insights from the theory of reasoned action. *Health Psychology, 14*, 255–264. https://doi.org/10.1037/0278-6133.14.3.255

Fiske, S. T., & Taylor, S. E. (1991). *Social cognition* (2nd ed.). New York, NY: McGraw-Hill.

Fitzsimons, G. J., & Williams, P. (2000). Asking questions can change choice behavior: Does it do so automatically or effortfully? *Journal of Experimental Psychology: Applied, 6*(3), 195.

Floyd, D. L., Prentice-Dunn, S., & Rogers, R. W. (2000). A meta-analysis of research on protection motivation theory. *Journal of Applied Social Psychology, 30*, 407–429. https://doi.org/10.1111/j.1559-1816.2000.tb02323.x

Fong, C. P. S., & Wyer, R. S. (2003). Cultural, social, and emotional determinants of decisions under uncertainty. *Organizational Behavior and Human Performance, 90*(2), 304–322. https://doi.org/10.1016/S0749-5978(02)00528-9407

Forgas, J. P. (1995). Mood and judgment: The affect infusion model (AIM). *Psychological Bulletin*, *117*(1), 39.

Forgas, J. P., & Bower, G. H. (1987). Mood effects on person-perception judgments. *Journal of Personality and Social Psychology*, *53*(1), 53–60. https://doi .org/10.1037/0022-3514.53.1.53

Förster, J., & Strack, F. (1996). Influence of overt head movements on memory for valenced words: A case of conceptual-motor compatibility. *Journal of Personality and Social Psychology*, *71*(3), 421.

Forsyth, S. R., & Malone, R. E. (2010). "I'll be your cigarette – light me up and get on with it": Examining smoking imagery on YouTube. *Nicotine and Tobacco Research*, *12*, 810–816. https://doi.org/10.1093/ntr/ntq101

Fransen, M. L., Fennis, B. M., Pruyn, A. T. H., & Vohs, K. D. (2011). When fit fosters favoring: The role of private self-focus. *Journal of Experimental Social Psychology*, *47*(1), 202–207. https://doi.org/10.1016/j.jesp.2010.09.004

Fraser, R. T., Johnson, K., Hebert, J., Ajzen, I., Copeland, J., Brown, P., & Chan, F. (2010). Understanding employers' hiring intentions in relation to qualified workers with disabilities: Preliminary findings. *Journal of Occupational Rehabilitation*, *20*(4), 420–426. https://doi.org/10.1007/s10926-009-9220-1

Freedman, J. L. (1965). Confidence, utility, and selective exposure: A partial replication. *Journal of Personality and Social Psychology*, *2*(5), 778.

Freedman, J. L., & Fraser, S. C. (1966). Compliance without pressure: The foot-in-the-door technique. *Journal of Personality and Social Psychology*, *4*, 195–202. https://doi.org/10.1037/h0023552

Freedman, J. L., & Sears, D. O. (1966). Selective exposure. *Advances in Experimental Social Psychology*, *2*, 57–97. https://doi.org/10.1016/S0065-2601 (08)60103-3

Freeman, B. F. (2012). New media and tobacco control. *Tobacco Control*, *21*, 139–144.

Freeman, B., & Chapman, S. (2007). Is "YouTube" telling or selling you something? Tobacco content on the YouTube video-sharing website. *Tobacco Control*, *16*, 207–210. https://doi.org/10.1136/tc.2007.020024

Freire, P., & da Veiga Coutinho, J. (1972). *Cultural action for freedom* (Vol. 48). London, England: Penguin Harmondsworth.

Freitas, A. L., & Higgins, E. T. (2002). Enjoying goal-directed action: The role of regulatory fit. *Psychological Science*, *13*(1), 1–6. https://doi.org/10.1111/1467-9280 .00401

Freud, S. (1912). La dynamique du transfert. *La Technique Psychanalytique*, *16*, 50–60.

Freund, P. A., Kuhn, J. T., & Holling, H. (2011). Measuring current achievement motivation with the QCM: Short form development and investigation of measurement invariance. *Personality and Individual Differences*, *51*, 629–634. https://doi.org/10.1016/j.paid.2011.05.033

Galante, J., Galante, I., Bekkers, M.-J., & Gallacher, J. (2014). Effect of kindness-based meditation on health and well-being: A systematic review and meta-analysis. *Journal of Consulting and Clinical Psychology*, *82*(6), 1101–1114. https://doi.org/10.1037/a0037249

Gangestad, S. W., & Snyder, M. (2000). Self-monitoring: Appraisal and reappraisal. *Psychological Bulletin*, *126*, 530–555. https://doi.org/10.1037/0033-2909.126.4.530

Garcia-Retamero, R., & Galesic, M. (2009). Communicating treatment risk reduction to people with low numeracy skills: A cross-cultural comparison. *American Journal of Public Health*, *99*(12), 2196–2202. https://doi.org/10.2105/AJPH.2009.160234

Garling, T., Bamberg, S., & Friman, M. (2019). The role of attitude in choice of travel, satisfaction with travel, and change to sustainable travel. In B. T. Albarracín & D. Johnson (Ed.), *Handbook of attitudes: Vol. 2. Applications* (2nd ed., pp. 562–586). Hoboken, NJ: John Wiley.

Gartner, L. M., Morton, J., Lawrence, R. A., Naylor, A. J., O'Hare, D., Schanler, R. J., & Eidelman, A. I. (2005). Breastfeeding and the use of human milk. *Pediatrics*, *115*(2), 496–506.

Gasper, K., & Clore, G. L. (2000). Do you have to pay attention to your feelings to be influenced by them? *Personality and Social Psychology Bulletin*, *26*(6), 698–711. https://doi.org/10.1177/0146167200268005

Gawronski, B., & Bodenhausen, G. V. (2006). Associative and propositional processes in evaluation: Conceptual, empirical, and metatheoretical issues: Reply to Albarracín, Hart, and McCulloch (2006), Kruglanski and Dechesne (2006), and Petty and Brinol (2006). *Psychological Bulletin*, *132*, 745–750. https://doi.org/10.1037/0033-2909.132.5.745

Gawronski, B., & Bodenhausen, G. V. (2007). Unraveling the processes underlying evaluation: Attitudes from the perspective of the APE model. *Social Cognition*, *25*(5), 687–717.

Gawronski, B., & Brannon, S. M. (2019). Attitudes and the implicit-explicit dualism. In B. T. Albarracín & D. Johnson (Eds.), *Handbook of attitudes: Vol. 1. Basic principles* (2nd ed., pp. 158–196). Hoboken, NJ: John Wiley

Gawronski, B., & Strack, F. (2004). On the propositional nature of cognitive consistency: Dissonance changes explicit, but not implicit attitudes. *Journal of Experimental Social Psychology*, *40*(4), 535–542. https://doi.org/10.1016/j.jesp.2003.10.005

Gawronski, B., Strack, F., & Bodenhausen, G. V. (2012). Attitudes and cognitive consistency: The role of associative and propositional processes. In *Attitudes: Insights from the new implicit measures* (pp. 85–117). New York, NY: Psychology Press. https://doi.org/10.4324/9780203809884

Gebauer, J. E., Maio, G. R., & Pakizeh, A. (2013). Feeling torn when everything seems right: Semantic incongruence causes felt ambivalence. *Personality and Social Psychology Bulletin*, *39*(6), 777–791. https://doi.org/10.1177/0146167213481679

Geers, A. L., Brinol, P., & Petty, R. E. (2019). An analysis of the basic processes of formation and change of placebo expectations. *Review of General Psychology*, *23*(2), 211–229. https://doi.org/10.1037/gpr0000171

Geers, A. L., Helfer, S. G., Kosbab, K., Weiland, P. E., & Landry, S. J. (2005). Reconsidering the role of personality in placebo effects: dispositional optimism, situational expectations, and the placebo response. *Journal of Psychosomatic Research, 58*(2), 121–127.

Geers, A. L., & Lassiter, G. D. (1999). Affective expectations and information gain: Evidence for assimilation and contrast effects in affective experience. *Journal of Experimental Social Psychology, 35*(4), 394–413.

Gendolla, G. H. E., & Silvestrini, N. (2010). The implicit "go": Masked action cues directly mobilize mental effort. *Psychological Science, 21*, 1389–1393. https://doi.org/10.1177/0956797610384149

Gentner, D., & Gentner, D. R. (1983). Flowing waters and teeming crowds: Mental models of electricity. In *Mental models* (pp. 99–129). Hillsdale, NJ: Erlbaum.

Gerbner, G., Gross, L., Morgan, M., & Signorielli, N. (1980). The mainstreaming of America: Violence profile no 11. *Journal of Communication, 30*(3), 10–29. https://doi.org/10.1111/j.1460-2466.1980.tb01987.x

Gerbner, G., Gross, L., Morgan, M., & Signorielli, N. (1982). Charting the mainstream: Television's contributions to political orientations. *Journal of Communication, 32*(2), 100–127. https://doi.org/10.1111/j.1460-2466.1982.tb00500.x

Gerbner, G., Gross, L., Signorielli, N., & Morgan, M. (1980). Television violence, victimization, and power. *American Behavioral Scientist, 23*(5), 705–716. https://doi.org/10.1177/000276428002300506

Gerlach, J. T., Diepolder, H. M., Zachoval, R., Gruener, N. H., Jung, M. C., Ulsenheimer, A., . . . Pape, G. R. (2003). Acute hepatitis C: High rate of both spontaneous and treatment-induced viral clearance. *Gastroenterology, 125*(1), 80–88. https://doi.org/10.1016/S0016-5085(03)00668-1

Gilbert, D. T., & Hixon, J. G. (1991). The trouble of thinking: Activation and application of stereotypic beliefs. *Journal of Personality and Social Psychology, 60*(4), 509–517. https://doi.org/10.1037/0022-3514.60.4.509

Gilovich, T., Medvec, V. H., & Kahneman, D. (1998). Varieties of regret: A debate and partial resolution. *Psychological Review, 105*, 602–605. https://doi.org/10.1037/0033-295X.105.3.602

Gist, M., Rosen, B., & Schwoerer, C. (1988). The influence of training method and trainee age on the acquisition of computer skills. *Personnel Psychology, 41*, 255–265. https://doi.org/10.1111/j.1744-6570.1988.tb02384.x

Glasman, L. R., & Albarracín, D. (2003a). Models of health-related behavior. *AIDS and Behavior, 7*(2), 183–193.

Glasman, L. R., & Albarracín, D. (2003b). Unpublished data.

Glasman, L. R., & Albarracín, D. (2006). Forming attitudes that predict future behavior: a meta-analysis of the attitude–behavior relation. *Psychological Bulletin, 132*(5), 778–822. https://doi.org/10.1037/0033-2909.132.5.778

Glasman, L. R., & Scott-Sheldon, L. A. J. (2019). The role of attitudes in HIV prevention, testing, and treatment. In B. T. Albarracín & D. Johnson (Eds.),

Handbook of attitudes: Vol. 2. Applications (2nd ed., pp. 121–151). Hoboken, NJ: John Wiley.

Godin, G., Bélanger-Gravel, A., Vézina-Im, L.-A., Amireault, S., & Bilodeau, A. (2012). Question-behaviour effect: A randomised controlled trial of asking intention in the interrogative or declarative form. *Psychology and Health*, *27* (9), 1086–1099. https://doi.org/10.1080/08870446.2012.671617

Godin, G., & Kok, G. (1996). The theory of planned behavior: A review of its applications to health-related behaviors. *American Journal of Health Promotion*, *11*(2), 87–98.

Gollwitzer, P M. (1996). How goals and plans affect social behavior. *International Journal of Psychology*, *31*(3–4), 2642.

Gollwitzer, P. M. (1999). Implementation intentions: Strong effects of simple plans. *American Psychologist*, *54*(7), 493–503. https://doi.org/10.1037/0003-066X .54.7.493

Gollwitzer, P. M. (2004). The psychology of goals. *International Journal of Psychology*, *39*(5–6), 502.

Gollwitzer, P. M., & Bayer, U. (1999). Deliberative versus implemental mindsets in the control of action. In *Dual-process theories in social psychology* (pp. 403–422). New York, NY: Guilford Press.

Gollwitzer, P. M., Heckhausen, H., & Steller, B. (1990). Deliberative and implemental mindsets: Cognitive tuning toward congruous thoughts and information. *Journal of Personality and Social Psychology*, *59*(6), 1119–1127. https://doi.org/10.1037/0022-3514.59.6.1119

Gowans, C. W. (2004). Philosophy of the Buddha. *International Philosophical Quarterly*, *44*, 1–240. https://doi.org/10.4324/9780203480793

Graham, A., Cobb, N., Papandonatos, G., Moreno, J. L., Kang, H., Tinkelman, D. G., … Abrams, D. B. (2011). A randomized trial of internet and telephone treatment for smoking cessation. *Archives of Internal Medicine*, *171*, 46–53.

Graton, A., Ric, F., & Gonzalez, E. (2016). Reparation or reactance? The influence of guilt on reaction to persuasive communication. *Journal of Experimental Social Psychology*, *62*, 40–49. https://doi.org/10.1016/j.jesp.2015.09.016

Gray, J. A. (1991). The neuropsychology of temperament. In *Explorations in temperament* (pp. 105–128). New York, NY: Springer.

Gray, J. A., & McNaughton, N. (2000). Fundamentals of the septo-hippocampal system. In *The neuropsychology of anxiety: An enquiry into the functions of septo-hippocampal system* (2nd ed., pp. 204–232). Oxford, England: Oxford University Press.

Green, M. C. (2006). Narratives and cancer communication. *Journal of Communication*, *56*(Suppl. 1), S163–S183. https://doi.org/10.1111/j.1460-2466 .2006.00288.x

Greenwald, A. G. (1968). Cognitive learning, cognitive response to persuasion, and attitude change. *Psychological Foundations of Attitudes*, pp. 147–170.

Greenwald, A. G., & Albert, R. D. (1968). Acceptance and recall of improvised arguments. *Journal of Personality and Social Psychology, 8*(1, Pt. 1), 31–34. https://doi.org/10.1037/h0021237

Greenwald, A. G., & Banaji, M. R. (1995). Implicit social cognition: Attitudes, self-esteem, and stereotypes. *Psychological Review, 102*(1), 4–27.

Greenwald, A. G., Banaji, M. R., Rudman, L. A., Farnham, S. D., Nosek, B. A., & Mellott, D. S. (2002). A unified theory of implicit attitudes, stereotypes, self-esteem, and self-concept. *Psychological Review, 109*(1), 3.

Greenwald, A. G., Draine, S. C., & Abrams, R. L. (1996). Three cognitive markers of unconscious semantic activation. *Science, 273*(5282), 1699–1702.

Greenwald, A. G., & Farnham, S. D. (2000). Using the implicit association test to measure self-esteem and self-concept. *Journal of Personality and Social Psychology, 79*(6), 1022.

Greenwald, A. G., McGhee, D. E., & Schwartz, J. L. (1998). Measuring individual differences in implicit cognition: The implicit association test. *Journal of Personality and Social Psychology, 74*, 1464–1480. https://doi.org/10.1037/0022-3514.74.6.1464

Greenwald, A. G., Poehlman, T. A., Uhlmann, E. L., & Banaji, M. R. (2009). Understanding and using the Implicit Association Test: III. Meta-analysis of predictive validity. *Journal of Personality and Social Psychology, 97*(1), 17–41. https://doi.org/10.1037/a0015575

Greenwald, A. G., Pratkanis, A. R., Leippe, M. R., & Baumgardner, M. H. (1986). Under what conditions does theory obstruct research progress? *Psychological Review, 93*(2), 216.

Grier, S., & Bryant, C. A. (2004). Social marketing in public health. *Annual Review of Public Health, 26*(1), 319–339. https://doi.org/10.1146/annurev.publhealth.26.021304.144610

Griffith, D. A., & Chen, Q. (2004). The influence of virtual direct experience (VDE) on online ad effectiveness. *Journal of Advertising, 33*(1), 55–68. https://doi.org/10.1080/00913367.2004.10639153

Guimond, S. (1999). Attitude change during college: Normative or informational social influence? *Social Psychology of Education, 2*, 237–261.

Gunther, A. C., Bolt, D., Borzekowski, D. L. G., Liebhart, J. L., & Dillard, J. P. (2006). Presumed influence on peer norms: How mass media indirectly affect adolescent smoking. *Journal of Communication, 56*(1), 52–68. https://doi.org/10.1111/j.1460-2466.2006.00002.x

Haggard, P., & Clark, S. (2003). Intentional action: Conscious experience and neural prediction. *Consciousness and Cognition, 12*(4), 695–707. https://doi.org/10.1016/S1053-8100(03)00052-7

Hagger, M. S. (2019). The role of attitudes in physical activity. In B. T. Albarracín & D. Johnson (Eds.), *Handbook of attitudes: Vol. 2. Applications* (2nd ed., pp. 92–120). Hoboken, NJ: John Wiley.

Hagger, M. S., & Chatzisarantis, N. L. D. (2014). An integrated behavior change model for physical activity. *Exercise and Sport Sciences Reviews, 42*, 62–69. https://doi.org/10.1249/JES.0000000000000008

Hagger, M. S., Luszczynska, A., de Wit, J., Benyamini, Y., Burkert, S., Chamberland, P.-E., . . . Gollwitzer, P. M. (2016). Implementation intention and planning interventions in Health Psychology: Recommendations from the Synergy Expert Group for research and practice. *Psychology and Health, 31*(7), 814–839. https://doi.org/10.1080/08870446.2016.1146719

Handley, I. M., Albarracín, D., & Brown, R. (2007). Inferential and perceptual influences of affective expectations on judgments of experienced affect. *ACR North American Advances.*

Handley, I. M., Albarracín, D., Brown, R. D., Li, H., Kumkale, E. C., & Kumkale, G. T. (2009). When the expectations from a message will not be realized: Naive theories can eliminate expectation-congruent judgments via correction. *Journal of Experimental Social Psychology, 45*(4), 933–939. https://doi.org/10.1016/j.jesp.2009.05.010

Hansen, K. T., & Singh, V. (2015). *Choice concentration.* Working paper.

Hanson, M. J. S., & Laffrey, S. C. (1999). Cross-cultural study of beliefs about smoking among teenaged females. *Western Journal of Nursing Research, 21*(5), 635–651.

Harmon-Jones, E., & Harmon-Jones, C. (2002). Testing the action-based model of cognitive dissonance: The effect of action orientation on postdecisional attitudes. *Personality and Social Psychology Bulletin, 28*(6), 711–723. https://doi.org/10.1177/0146167202289001

Harmon-Jones, E., Harmon-Jones, C., & Levy, N. (2015). An action-based model of cognitive-dissonance processes. *Current Directions in Psychological Science, 24,* 184–189. https://doi.org/10.1177/0963721414566449

Harpaz-Rotem, I., Leslie, D. L., Martin, A., & Rosenheck, R. A. (2005). Changes in child and adolescent inpatient psychiatric admission diagnoses between 1995 and 2000. *Social Psychiatry and Psychiatric Epidemiology, 40*(8), 642–647.

Harris, C. R., Coburn, N., Rohrer, D., & Pashler, H. (2013). Two failures to replicate high-performance-goal priming effects. *PLoS ONE, 8*(8), 0072467. https://doi.org/10.1371/journal.pone.0072467

Hart, W., & Albarracín, D. (2009). The effects of chronic achievement motivation and achievement primes on the activation of achievement and fun goals. *Journal of Personality and Social Psychology, 97,* 1129–1141.

Hart, W., & Albarracín, D. (2009). What I was doing versus what I did: Verb aspect influences memory and future actions. *Psychological Science, 20*(2), 238–244. https://doi.org/10.1111/j.1467-9280.2009.02277.x

Hart, W., Albarracín, D., Eagly, A. H. A. H., Brechan, I., Lindberg, M. J., & Merrill, L. (2009). Feeling validated versus being correct: A meta-analysis of selective exposure to information. *Psychological Bulletin, 135*(4), 555–588. https://doi.org/10.1037/a0015701

Hart, W., & Gable, P. A. (2013). Motivating goal pursuit: The role of affect motivational intensity and activated goals. *Journal of Experimental Social Psychology, 49,* 922–926.

Hasking, P., Lyvers, M., & Carlopio, C. (2011). The relationship between coping strategies, alcohol expectancies, drinking motives and drinking behaviour. *Addictive Behaviors, 36*, 479–487. https://doi.org/10.1016/j.addbeh.2011.01.014

Hassan, L. M., Shiu, E., & Parry, S. (2016). Addressing the cross-country applicability of the theory of planned behaviour (TPB): A structured review of multi-country TPB studies. *Journal of Consumer Behaviour, 15*(1), 72–86. https://doi.org/10.1002/cb.1536

Hatfield, E., Cacioppo, J. T., & Rapson, R. L. (1994). *Emotional contagion.* Cambridge, England: Cambridge University Press.

Hatzivassiloglou, V., Klavans, J., Holcombe, M., Barzilay, R., Kan, M.-Y., & McKeown, K. (2001). *SIMFINDER: A flexible clustering tool for summarization.* Paper presented at the Workshop on Summarization in NAACL-01.

Hatzivassiloglou, V., & McKeown, K. R. (1997). Predicting the semantic orientation of adjectives. In *Proceedings of the 35th Annual Meeting of the ACL and the 8th Conference of the European Chapter of the ACL* (pp. 174–181). Madrid, Spain: Association for Computational Linguistics.

Hatzivassiloglou, V., & Wiebe, J. (2000). *Effects of adjective orientation and gradability on sentence subjectivity.* Paper presented at the Conference on Computational Linguistics (COLING-2000).

Hausenblas, H. A., Carron, A. V., & Mack, D. E. (1997). Application of the theories of reasoned action and planned behavior to exercise behavior: A meta-analysis. *Journal of Sport and Exercise Psychology, 19*(1), 36–51.

Hayes, S. C., et al. (Eds.) (2004). *Mindfulness and acceptance: Expanding the cognitive-behavioral tradition.* New York, NY: Guilford Press.

Heider, F. (1946). Attitudes and cognitive organization. *The Journal of Psychology, 21*, 107–112.

Heim, E., Ajzen, I., Schmidt, P., & Seddig, D. (2018). Women's decisions to stay in or leave an abusive relationship: Results from a longitudinal study in Bolivia. *Violence Against Women, 24*(14), 1639–1657. https://doi.org/10.1177/1077801217741993

Hepler, J., & Albarracín, D. (2009). Change blindness. Unpublished manuscript.

Hepler, J., & Albarracín, D. (2013). Attitudes without objects: Evidence for a dispositional attitude, its measurement, and its consequences. *Journal of Personality and Social Psychology, 104*(6), 1060–1076. https://doi.org/10.1037/a0032282

Hepler, J., & Albarracín, D. (2014). Liking more means doing more: Dispositional attitudes predict patterns of general action. *Social Psychology, 45*(5), 391–398. https://doi.org/10.1027/1864-9335/a000198

Hepler, J., Albarracín, D., McCulloch, K. C., & Noguchi, K. (2012). Being active and impulsive: The role of goals for action and inaction in self-control. *Motivation and Emotion, 36*(4), 416–424. https://doi.org/10.1007/s11031-011-9263-4

Hepler, J., Wang, W., & Albarracín, D. (2012). Motivating exercise: The interactive effect of general action goals and past behavior on physical activity.

Motivation and Emotion, 36(3), 365–370. https://doi.org/10.1007/s11031-011-92 67-0

Higgins, E. T. (1996). Knowledge activation: Accessibility, applicability and salience. In E. T. Higgins & A. W. Kruglanski (Eds.), *Handbook of basic principles* (pp. 133–168). New York, NY: Guilford Press.

Higgins, E. T. (1997). Beyond pleasure and pain. *American Psychologist, 52*, 1280–1300.

Higgins, E. T. (2012). Regulatory focus theory. In *Handbook of theories of social psychology* (Vol. 1, pp. 483–504). Thousand Oaks, CA: Sage. https://doi.org/10 .4135/9781446249215.n24

Hoch, S. J., & Deighton, J. (1989). Managing what consumers learn from experience. *Journal of Marketing, 53*(2), 1–20.

Hoegg, J., & Alba, J. W. (2006). Taste perception: More than meets the tongue. *Journal of Consumer Research, 33*(4), 490–498.

Hofmann, T. (1999). Probabilistic latent semantic analysis. In *Proceedings of Uncertainty in Artificial Intelligence, UAI'99* (pp. 289–296).

Hofmann, W., Gawronski, B., Gschwendner, T., Le, H., & Schmitt, M. (2005). A meta-analysis on the correlation between the Implicit Association Test and explicit self-report measures. *Personality and Social Psychology Bulletin, 31*(10), 1369–1385.

Holtgrave, D. (2007). Applied aspects of health promotion interventions based on theory of reasoned action and theory of planned behavior. In *Prediction and change of health behavior: Applying the reasoned action approach* (pp. 273–280). Mahwah, NJ: Erlbaum.

Homer, P. M., & Batra, R. (1994). Attitudinal effects of character-based versus competence-based negative political communications. *Journal of Consumer Psychology, 3*(2), 163–185.

Hommel, B. (1997). Toward an action-concept model of stimulus response compatibility. In B. Hommel & W. Prinz (Eds.), *Theoretical issues in stimulus-response compatibility* (pp. 281–320). Amsterdam: Elsevier.

Hong, T., & Cody, M. J. (2002). Presence of pro-tobacco messages on the web. *Journal of Health Communication, 7*, 273–307. https://doi.org/10.1080 /10810730290088148

Hong, T., Rice, J., & Johnson, C. (2012). Ethnic group and temporal influences of social norms: Smoking behavior among a panel of adolescents. *Journal of Communication, 62*(1), 158–174. https://doi.org/10.1111/j.1460-2466.2011.01623.x

Hornik, R., Ajzen, I., & Albarracín, D. (2007). An extension of the theory of reasoned action and its successors to multiple behavior interventions. In *Prediction and change of health behavior: Applying the reasoned action approach* (pp. 53–67). Mahwah, NJ: Erlbaum.

Hovland, C. I. (1959). Reconciling conflicting results derived from experimental and survey studies of attitude change. *American Psychologist, 14*(1), 8.

Hovland, C. I., Janis, I. L., & Kelley, H. H. (1953). Communication and persuasion.

Howe, L. C., & Krosnick, J. A. (2015). Attitude strength. *Annual Review of Psychology*, *67*, 327–351. https://doi.org/10.1146/annurev-psych-122414-033600

Hovland, C. I., Lumsdaine, A. A., & Sheffield, F. D. (1949). *Experiments on mass communications*. Princeton, NJ: Princeton University Press.

Hovland, C. I., & Weiss, W. (1951). The influence of source credibility on communication effectiveness. *Public Opinion Quarterly*, *15*(4), 635–650.

Howell, J. L., & Shepperd, J. A. (2012). Reducing information avoidance through affirmation. *Psychological Science*, *23*, 141–145. https://doi.org/10.1177/0956797611424164

Hsee, C. K., Yang, A. X., & Wang, L. (2010). Idleness aversion and the need for justifiable busyness. *Psychological Science*, *21*(7), 926–930. https://doi.org/10.1177/0956797610374738

Huang, M., Hollis, J., Polen, M., Lapidus, J., & Austin, D. (2005). Stages of smoking acquisition versus susceptibility as predictors of smoking initiation in adolescents in primary care. *Addictive Behaviors*, *30*, 1183–1194. https://doi.org/10.1016/j.addbeh.2004.12.009

Hui, Y., See, M., & Petty, R. E. (2008). Affective and cognitive meta-bases of attitudes: Unique effects on information interest and persuasion. *Journal of Personality and Social Psychology*, *94*(6), 938–955. https://doi.org/10.1037/0022-3514.94.6.938

Humphreys, G. W., & Forde, E. M. E. (2001). Hierarchies, similarity, and interactivity in object recognition: "Category-specific" neuropsychological deficits. *Behavioral and Brain Sciences*, *24*(3), 453–476.

Hurlbert, J. S. (1989). The Southern region: A test of the hypothesis of cultural distinctiveness. *Sociological Quarterly*, *30*(2), 245–266. https://doi.org/10.1111/j.1533-8525.1989.tb01521.x

Igartua, J., & Barrios, I. (2012). Changing real-world beliefs with controversial movies: Processes and mechanisms of narrative persuasion. *Journal of Communication*, *62*(3), 514–531. https://doi.org/10.1111/j.1460-2466.2012.01640.x

Ireland, M. E., Chen, Q., Schwartz, H. A. A., Ungar, L. H. L. H., & Albarracín, D. (2016). Action tweets linked to reduced county-level HIV prevalence in the United States: Online messages and structural determinants. *AIDS and Behavior*, *20*(6), 1256–1264. https://doi.org/10.1007/s10461-015-1252-2

Ireland, M. E., Hepler, J., Li, H., & Albarracín, D. (2015). Neuroticism and attitudes toward action in 19 countries. *Journal of Personality*, *83*, 243–250. https://doi.org/10.1111/jopy.12099

Ireland, M. E., Schwartz, H. A., Chen, Q., Ungar, L. H., & Albarracín, D. (2015). Future-oriented tweets predict lower county-level HIV prevalence in the United States. *Health Psychology*, *34*(Suppl), 1252–1260. https://doi.org/10.1037/hea0000279

Isenberg, D. J. (1986). Group polarization: A critical review and meta-analysis. *Journal of Personality and Social Psychology*, *50*(6), 1141.

Izard, C. E. (2005). Innate and universal facial expressions: Evidence from developmental and cross-cultural research. *Psychological Bulletin, 115,* 288–299. https://doi.org/10.1037/0033-2909.115.2.288

Jaccard, J. J., & King, G. W. (1977). The relation between behavioral intentions and beliefs: A probabilistic model. *Human Communication Research, 3,* 326–334.

Jacobson, R. P., Mortensen, C. R., & Cialdini, R. B. (2011). Bodies obliged and unbound: Differentiated response tendencies for injunctive and descriptive social norms. *Journal of Personality and Social Psychology, 100*(3), 433–448. https://doi.org/10.1037/a0021470

Janis, I. L., & King, B. T. (1977). The influence of role playing on opinion change. *Journal of Abnormal and Social Psychology, 49*(2), 211–218. https://doi.org/10.1037/h0056957

Janis, I. L., & Milholland, H. C., Jr. (1954). The influence of threat appeals on selective learning of the content of a persuasive communication. *Journal of Psychology, 37*(1), 75–80. https://doi.org/10.1080/00223980.1954.9916132

Jennings, J. R., & Van Der Molen, M. W. (2005). Preparation for speeded action as a psychophysiological concept. *Psychological Bulletin, 131*(3), 434–459. https://doi.org/10.1037/0033-2909.131.3.434

Jeong, S. S., & Hwang, Y. (2012). Does multitasking increase or decrease persuasion? Effects of multitasking on comprehension and counterarguing. *Journal of Communication, 62*(4), 571–587. https://doi.org/10.1111/j.1460-2466.2012.01659.x

Jiang, D., & Albarracín, D. (2019). Acting by a deadline: The interplay between deadline distance and movement induced goals. *Journal of Experimental Social Psychology, 85.*

Jiang, D., Albarracín, D., & Jiang, D. (2014). The embodied psychology of time limits: How unrelated motion states shape intentions to act by a deadline. *ACR North American Advances, 42,* 531–532. https://doi.org/10.2139/ssrn.429963

Johnson, B. T., Lin, H.-Y., Symons, C. S., Campbell, L. A., & Ekstein, G. (1995). Initial beliefs and attitudinal latitudes as factors in persuasion. *Personality and Social Psychology Bulletin, 21*(5), 502–511.

Johnson, B. T., Maio, G. R., & Smith-McLallen, A. (2005). Communication and attitude change: Causes, processes, and effects. In D. Albarracín, B. T. Johnson, & M. P. Zanna (Eds.), *The handbook of attitudes* (pp. 617–670). New York, NY: Psychology Press.

Johnson, B. T., Smith-McLallen, A., Killeya, L. A., & Levin, K. D. (2004). Truth or consequences: Overcoming resistance to persuasion with positive thinking. In *Resistance and persuasion* (pp. 215–233). Mahwah, NJ: Erlbaum.

Johnson, B. T., Wolf, L. J., Maio, G. R., & Smith-McLallen, A. (2019). Communication induced persuasion or resistance: Processes and effects of who says what to whom. In B. T. Albarracín & D. Johnson (Eds.), *Handbook of attitudes: Vol. 1. Basic principles* (2nd ed., pp. 557–601). Hoboken, NJ: John Wiley.

Johnson, E. J., & Goldstein, D. (2003). *Do defaults save lives?* American Association for the Advancement of Science. https://doi.org/10.1126/science .1091721

Jonas, K., Diehl, M., & Brömer, P. (1997). Effects of attitudinal ambivalence on information processing and attitude-intention consistency. *Journal of Experimental Social Psychology, 33*(2), 190–210.

Jones, R. A., Linder, D. E., Kiesler, C. A., Zanna, M., & Brehm, J. W. (1968). Internal states or external stimuli: Observers' attitude judgments and the dissonance-theory-self-persuasion controversy. *Journal of Experimental Social Psychology, 4*, 247–269. https://doi.org/10.1016/0022-1031(68)90054-1

Jones, S. S. (2007). Imitation in infancy: The development of mimicry. *Psychological Science, 18*, 593–599. https://doi.org/10.1111/j.1467-9280 .2007.01945.x

Jost, J. T., Kruglanski, A. W., & Nelson, T. O. (1998). Social metacognition: An expansionist review. *Personality and Social Psychology Review, 2*(2), 137–154.

Judd, C. M., & Kulik, J. A. (1980). Schematic effects of social attitudes on information processing and recall. *Journal of Personality and Social Psychology, 38*(4), 569.

Kabat-Zinn, J. (1990). *Full catastrophe living: Using the wisdom of your body and mind to face stress, pain, and illness.* New York, NY: Delta.

Kahneman, D., & Miller, D. T. (1986). Norm theory: Comparing reality to its alternatives. *Psychological Review*, pp. 348–366. https://doi.org/10.1037/0033-29 5X.93.2.136

Kahneman, D., & Tversky, A. (1982). The psychology of preferences. *Scientific American, 246*(1), 160–173. https://doi.org/10.1038/scientificamerican0182-160

Kalro, A. D., Sivakumaran, B., & Marathe, R. R. (2013). Direct or indirect comparative ads: The moderating role of information processing modes. *Journal of Consumer Behavior, 147*, 133–147. https://doi.org/10.1002/cb

Kamb, M. L., Fishbein, M., Douglas, J. M., Jr., Rhodes, F., Rogers, J., Bolan, G., ... Peterman, T. A. (1998). Efficacy of risk-reduction counseling to prevent human immunodeficiency virus and sexually transmitted diseases: A randomized controlled trial. *JAMA, 280*, 1161–1167.

Kaufman, G. F., & Libby, L. K. (2012). Changing beliefs and behavior through experience-taking. *Journal of Personality and Social Psychology, 103*(1), 1–19. https://doi.org/10.1037/a0027525

Keillor, J. M., Barrett, A. M., Crucian, G. P., Kortenkamp, S., & Heilman, K. M. (2002). Emotional experience and perception in the absence of facial feedback. *Journal of the International Neuropsychological Society, 8*, 130–135. https://doi.org /10.1017/s1355617701020136

Kelley, H. H. (1973). The process of causal attribution. *American Psychologist, 28*, 107–128.

Kelly, J. A., St Lawrence, J. S., Diaz, Y. E., Stevenson, L. Y., Hauth, A. C., Brasfield, T. L., ... Andrew, M. E. (1991). HIV risk behavior reduction following intervention with key opinion leaders of population: an experimental analysis. *American Journal of Public Health, 81*(2), 168–171.

Kelly, J. A., St Lawrence, J. S., Stevenson, L. Y., Hauth, A. C., Kalichman, S. C., Diaz, Y. E., . . . Morgan, M. G. (1992). Community AIDS/HIV risk reduction: The effects of endorsements by popular people in three cities. *American Journal of Public Health, 82*(11), 1483–1489.

Kelman, H. C., & Hovland, C. I. (1953). "Reinstatement" of the communicator in delayed measurement of opinion change. *Journal of Abnormal and Social Psychology, 48*(3), 327.

Kendon, A. (1970). Movement coordination in social interaction: Some examples described. *Acta Psychologica, 32,* 101–125. https://doi.org/10.1016/0001-6918(70) 90094-6

Kerr, M., Stattin, H., Biesecker, G., & Ferrer-Wreder, L. (2002). *Handbook of psychology: Developmental psychology.* Hoboken, NJ: John Wiley.

Kessler, R. C., Demyttenaere, K., Bruffaerts, R., Posada-Villa, J., Gasquet, I., Kovess, V., . . . Chatterji, S. (2004). WHO World Mental Health Survey Consortium 2004. Prevalence, severity and unmet need for treatment of mental disorders in the World Health Organization World Mental Health Surveys. *JAMA, 291,* 2581–2590.

Kiesler, C. A. (1971). *The psychology of commitment.* New York, NY: Academic Press.

Killeya, L. A., & Johnson, B. T. (1998). Experimental induction of biased systematic processing: The directed-thought technique. *Personality and Social Psychology Bulletin, 24*(1), 17–33.

Kim, K., Paek, H. J., & Lynn, J. (2010). A content analysis of smoking fetish videos on YouTube: Regulatory implications for tobacco control. *Health Communication, 25,* 97–106. https://doi.org/10.1080/10410230903544415

Kim, M. S., & Hunter, J. E. (1993). Relationships among attitudes, behavioral intentions, and behavior: A meta-analysis of past research, part 2. *Communication Research, 20*(3), 331–364.

Kleinke, C. L., Peterson, T. R., & Rutledge, T. R. (1998). Effects of self-generated facial expressions on mood. *Journal of Personality and Social Psychology, 74,* 272–279. https://doi.org/10.1037/0022-3514.74.1.272

Kline, R. B., Canter, W. A., & Robin, A. (1987). Parameters of teenage alcohol use: A path analytic conceptual model. *Journal of Consulting and Clinical Psychology, 55,* 521–528. https://doi.org/10.1037/0022-006X.55.4.521

Koning, I. M., van den Eijnden, R. J. J. M., Verdurmen, J. E. E., Engels, R. C. M. E., & Vollebergh, W. A. M. (2013). A cluster randomized trial on the effects of a parent and student intervention on alcohol use in adolescents four years after baseline; no evidence of catching-up behavior. *Addictive Behaviors, 38*(4), 2032–2039. https://doi.org/10.1016/j .addbeh.2012.12.013

Kopalle, P. K., & Lehmann, D. R. (1995). The effects of advertised and observed quality on expectations about new product quality. *Journal of Marketing Research, 32*(3), 280–290.

Kopalle, P. K., & Lehmann, D. R. (2001). Strategic management of expectations: The role of disconfirmation sensitivity and perfectionism. *Journal of Marketing Research, 38*(3), 386–394.

Koriat, A. (2000). The feeling of knowing: Some metatheoretical implications for consciousness and control. *Consciousness and Cognition, 9*(2), 149–171.

Kosinski, M., Stillwell, D., & Graepel, T. (2013). Private traits and attributes are predictable from digital records of human behavior. *Proceedings of the National Academy of Sciences, 110*(15), 5802–5805. https://doi.org/10.1073/pnas.1218772110

Kraus, S. J. (1995). Attitudes and the prediction of behavior: A meta-analysis of the empirical literature. *Personality and Social Psychology Bulletin, 21*(1), 58–75.

Krosnick, J. A., & Abelson, R. P. (1992). The case for measuring attitude strength in surveys. In *Questions about questions: Inquiries into the cognitive bases of surveys* (pp. 177–203). New York, NY: Russell Sage Foundation.

Krosnick, J. A., Betz, A. L., Jussim, L. J., & Lynn, A. R. (2007). Subliminal conditioning of attitudes. *Personality and Social Psychology Bulletin, 18*, 152–162. https://doi.org/10.1177/0146167292182006

Krosnick, J. A., Charles, M. J., & Wittenbrink, B. (2005). The measurement of attitudes. In D. Albarracín, B. T. Johnson, & M. P. Zanna (Eds.), *The handbook of attitudes* (pp. 21–76). New York, NY: Psychology Press. https://doi.org/10.4324/9781410612823.ch2

Krueger, J., & Clement, R. W. (1997). Estimates of social consensus by majorities and minorities: The case for social projection. *Personality and Social Psychology Review, 1*, 299–313. https://doi.org/10.1207/s15327957pspr0104_2

Kruglanski, A. (1996). Goals as knowledge structures. In *The psychology of action: Linking cognition and motivation to behavior* (pp. 599–618). New York, NY: Guilford Press. https://doi.org/10.3748/wjg.v23.i28.5086

Kruglanski, A. W., Fishbach, A., Erb, H.-P., Pierro, A., & Mannetti, L. (2004). The parametric unimodel as a theory of persuasion. In G. Haddock & G. Maio (Eds.), *Contemporary perspectives on the psychology of attitudes* (pp. 399–422). New York, NY: Psychology Press.

Kruglanski, A. W., & Higgins, E. T. (2007). The goal construct in social psychology. In *Social psychology: Handbook of basic principles* (pp. 334–352). New York, NY: Guildford Press.

Kruglanski, A. W., & Thompson, E. P. (1999a). Persuasion by a single route: A view from the unimodel. *Psychological Inquiry, 10*(2), 83–109. https://doi.org/10.1207/S15327965PLI1002_01

Kruglanski, A. W., & Thompson, E. P. (1999b). The illusory second mode or, the cue is the message. *Psychological Inquiry, 10*(2), 182–193. https://doi.org/10.1207/S15327965PLI1002_17

Kuhl, J. (1984). Volitional aspects of achievement motivation and learned helplessness: Toward a comprehensive theory of action control. *Progress in Experimental Personality Research, 13*, 99–171. https://doi.org/10.1016/B978-0-12-541413-5.50007-3

Kumkale, G. T., & Albarracín, D. (2004). The sleeper effect in persuasion: a meta-analytic review. *Psychological Bulletin, 130*(1), 143–172. https://doi.org/10.1037/0033-2909.130.1.143

Kumkale, G. T., Albarracín, D., & Seignourel, P. J. (2010). The effects of source credibility in the presence or absence of prior attitudes: Implications for the design of persuasive communication campaigns. *Journal of Applied Social Psychology, 40*(6), 1325–1356. https://doi.org/10.1111/j.1559-1816 .2010.00620.x

Kunda, Z. (1987). Motivated inference: Self-serving generation and evaluation of causal theories. *Journal of Personality and Social Psychology, 53,* 636–647. https:// doi.org/10.1037/0022-3514.53.4.636

LaFrance, M., & Broadbent, M. (1976). Group rapport: Posture sharing as a nonverbal indicator. *Group and Organization Management, 1,* 328–333. https://doi.org/10.1177/105960117600100307

Landman, J. (1987). Regret and elation following action and inaction: Affective responses to positive versus negative outcomes. *Personality and Social Psychology Bulletin, 13,* 524–536. https://doi.org/10.1177/0146167287134009

Lang, P. J., Ohman, A., & Vaitl, D. (1988). *The international affective picture system* [Photographic slides]. Gainesville, FL: Center for Research in Psychophysiology, University of Florida.

Langer, E. J., Blank, A., & Chanowitz, B. (1978). The mindlessness of ostensibly thoughtful action: The role of "placebic" information in interpersonal inter-action. *Journal of Personality and Social Psychology, 36,* 635–642. https://doi.org /10.1037/0022-3514.36.6.635

Laranjo, L., Arguel, A., Neves, A. L., Gallagher, A. M., Kaplan, R., Mortimer, N., . . . Lau, A. Y. S. (2014). The influence of social networking sites on health behavior change: A systematic review and meta-analysis. *Journal of the American Medical Informatics Association, 22*(1), 243–256. https://doi.org /10.1136/amiajnl-2014-002841

Lassiter, G. D., Geers, A. L., & Apple, K. J. (2002). Communication set and the perception of ongoing behavior. *Personality and Social Psychology Bulletin, 28,* 158–171. https://doi.org/10.1177/0146167202282003

Lau-Barraco, C., Braitman, A. L., Leonard, K. E., & Padilla, M. (2012). Drinking buddies and their prospective influence on alcohol outcomes: Alcohol expect-ancies as a mediator. *Psychology of Addictive Behaviors, 26,* 747–758. https://doi .org/10.1037/a0028909

Law, S., Schimmack, U., & Braun, K. A. (2003). Cameo appearances of branded products in TV shows: How effective are they. Manuscript in preparation.

Ledgerwood, A., Callahan, S. P., Ledgerwood, A., & Callahan, S. P. (2019). The social side of abstraction: Psychological distance enhances conformity to group norms. *Psychological Science, 23*(8), 907–913. https://doi.org/10.1177 /0956797611435920

Lee, A. Y., & Aaker, J. L. (2004). Bringing the frame into focus: the influence of regulatory fit on processing fluency and persuasion. *Journal of Personality and Social Psychology, 86*(2), 205.

Lemmer, G., & Wagner, U. (2015). Can we really reduce ethnic prejudice outside the lab? A meta-analysis of direct and indirect contact interventions. *European Journal of Social Psychology, 45*, 152–168. https://doi.org/10.1002/ejsp.2079

Leonardelli, G. J., Pickett, C. L., & Brewer, M. B. (2010). Optimal distinctiveness theory: A framework for social identity, social cognition, and intergroup relations. *Advances in Experimental Social Psychology, 43*, 63–113. https://doi.org/10.1016/S0065-2601(10)43002-6

Lepper, M. R., Greene, D., & Nisbett, R. E. (1973). Undermining children's intrinsic interest with extrinsic reward: A test of the "overjustification" hypothesis. *Journal of Personality and Social Psychology, 28*, 129–137. https://doi.org/10.1037/h0035519

Levelt, W. J. M., & Kelter, S. (1982). Surface form and memory in question answering. *Cognitive Psychology, 14*, 78–106. https://doi.org/10.1016/0010-0285(82)90005-6

Levine, J. M., & Moreland, R. L. (2002). Group reactions to loyalty and disloyalty. *Advances in Group Processes*, pp. 203–228. https://doi.org/10.1016/S0882-6145(02)19008-4

Levitan, L. C., & Visser, P. S. (2008). The impact of the social context on resistance to persuasion: Effortful versus effortless responses to counter-attitudinal information. *Journal of Experimental Social Psychology, 44* (3), 640–649. https://doi.org/10.1016/j.jesp.2007.03.004

Lewin, K. (1951). *Field theory in social science: Selected theoretical papers*. New York, NY: Harper.

Lieberman, M. D., Ochsner, K. N., Gilbert, D. T., & Schacter, D. L. (2001). Do amnesiacs exhibit cognitive dissonance reduction? The role of explicit memory and attention in attitude change. *Psychological Science, 12*, 135–140. https://doi.org/10.1111/1467-9280.00323

Lichtenstein, S., & Slovic, P. (1971). Reversals of preference between bids and choices in gambling decisions. *Journal of Experimental Psychology, 89*(1), 46–55.

Lingle, J. H., & Ostrom, T. M. (1981). Principles of memory and cognition in attitude formation. In R. Petty, T. M. Ostrom, & T. C. Brock (Eds.), *Cognitive responses in persuasion* (pp. 399–420). New York, NY: Psychology Press.

Liu, J., Jones, C., Wilson, K., Durantini, M. R., Livingood, W., Albarracín, D., & Albarracín, D. (2014). Motivational barriers to retention of at-risk young adults in HIV-prevention interventions: Perceived pressure and efficacy. *AIDS Care, 26*(10), 1242–1248. https://doi.org/10.1080/09540121.2014.896450

Liu, J., Zhao, S., Chen, X., Falk, E., & Albarracín, D. (2017). The influence of peer behavior as a function of social and cultural closeness: A meta-analysis of normative influence on adolescent smoking initiation and continuation. *Psychological Bulletin, 143*(10), 1082–1115. https://doi.org/10.1037/bul0000113

Liu, S., Huang, J. L., & Wang, M. (2014). Effectiveness of job search interventions: A meta-analytic review. *Psychological Bulletin, 140*(4), 1009–1041. https://doi.org/10.1037/a0035923

Locke, E. A., Latham, G. P., & Erez, M. (1988). The determinants of goal commitment. *The Academy of Management Review, 13*(1), 23. https://doi.org/10.2307/258352

Lockwood, P., Jordan, C. H., & Kunda, Z. (2002). Motivation by positive or negative role models: Regulatory focus determines who will best inspire us. *Journal of Personality and Social Psychology, 83*, 854–864. https://doi.org/10.1037/0022-3514.83.4.854

Logan, G. D. (1988). Toward an instance theory of automatization. *Psychological Review, 95*(4), 492.

Lohmann, S., & Albarracín, D. (2019). *The feeling of intention.* Unpublished manuscript.

Lohmann, S., Jones, C., & Albarracín, D. (2019). The modulating role of self-posed questions in repeated choice: Integral and incidental questions can increase or decrease behavioral rigidity. *Journal of Experimental Social Psychology, 85*.

Loomis, J. M., Blascovich, J. J., & Beall, A. C. (1999). Immersive virtual environment technology as a basic research tool in psychology. *Behavior Research Methods, Instruments, and Computers, 31*, 557–564. https://doi.org/10.3758/BF03200735

Lopez, M. L., & Stack, C. (2001). Social capital and the culture of power: Lessons from the field. In *Social capital and poor communities* (pp. 31–59). New York, NY: Russell Sage Foundation.

Losch, M. E., & Cacioppo, J. T. (1990). Cognitive dissonance may enhance sympathetic tonus, but attitudes are changed to reduce negative affect rather than arousal. *Journal of Experimental Social Psychology, 26*, 289–304. https://doi.org/10.1016/0022-1031(90)90040-S

Lowin, A. (1967). On choice between supportive and nonsupportive information. *American Psychologist, 22*(7), 530.

Lu, F. C., & Sinha, J. (2017). Speaking to the heart: Social exclusion and reliance on feelings versus reasons in persuasion. *Journal of Consumer Psychology, 27*(4), 409–421. https://doi.org/10.1016/j.jcps.2017.03.004

Ludvigh, E. J., & Happ, D. (1974). Extraversion and preferred level of sensory stimulation. *British Journal of Psychology, 65*(3), 359–365.

Lund, M. (2016). Exploring smokers' opposition to proposed tobacco control strategies. *NAD Nordic Studies on Alcohol and Drugs, 33*(4), 321–334. https://doi.org/10.1515/nsad-2016-0027

Lundgren, S. R., & Prislin, R. (1998). Motivated cognitive processing and attitude change. *Personality and Social Psychology Bulletin, 24*(7), 715–726. https://doi.org/10.1177/0146167298247004

Luo, C., Zheng, X., Zeng, D. D., Leischow, S., Cui, K., Zhang, Z., & He, S. (2013). Portrayal of electronic cigarettes on YouTube. In D. Zeng et al. (Eds.), *Smart health: ICSH 2013* (Lecture Notes in Computer Science Vol. 8040, pp. 1–6). Berlin, Germany: Springer. https://doi.org/10.1007/978-3-642-39844-5_1

Lyons, B. A. (2019). Discussion network activation: An expanded approach to selective exposure. *Media and Communication, 7*(3), 32–41. https://doi.org/10 .17645/mac.v7i3.2112

MacDonald, T. K., & Zanna, M. P. (1998). Cross-dimension ambivalence toward social groups: Can ambivalence affect intentions to hire feminists? *Personality and Social Psychology Bulletin, 24*(4), 427–441.

Madden, T. J., Ellen, P. S., & Ajzen, I. (1992). A comparison of the theory of planned behavior and the theory of reasoned action. *Personality and Social Psychology Bulletin, 18*(1), 3–9. https://doi.org/10.1177/0146167292181001

Maddux, J. E., & Rogers, R. W. (1983). Protection motivation and self-efficacy: A revised theory of fear appeals and attitude change. *Journal of Experimental Social Psychology, 19*(5), 469–479. https://doi.org/10.1016/0022-1031(83)90023-9

Madrian, B. C., & Shea, D. F. (2001). The power of suggestion: Inertia in 401(k) participation and savings behavior. *Quarterly Journal of Economics, 116*(4), 1149–1187. https://doi.org/10.1162/003355301753265543

Maglione, M. A., Maher, A. R., Ewing, B., Colaiaco, B., Newberry, S., Kandrack, R., . . . Hempel, S. (2017). Efficacy of mindfulness meditation for smoking cessation: A systematic review and meta-analysis. *Addictive Behaviors, 69*, 27–34. https://doi.org/10.1016/j.addbeh.2017.01.022

Maio, G. R., Bell, D. W., & Esses, V. M. (1996). Ambivalence and persuasion: The processing of messages about immigrant groups. *Journal of Experimental Social Psychology, 32*(6), 513–536.

Maio, G. R., & Olson, J. M. (1995). Relations between values, attitudes, and behavioral intentions: The moderating role of attitude function. *Journal of Experimental Social Psychology, 31*(3), 266–285.

Ma-Kellams, C., Spencer-Rodgers, J., & Peng, K. (2011). I am against us? Unpacking cultural differences in ingroup favoritism via dialecticism. *Personality and Social Psychology Bulletin, 37*(1), 15–27. https://doi.org/10.1177 /0146167210388193

Mandler, J. M., & DeForest, M. (1979). Is there more than one way to recall a story? *Child Development, 50*, 886–889.

Mannetti, L., Levine, J. M., Pierro, A., & Kruglanski, A. W. (2010). Group reaction to defection: The impact of shared reality. *Social Cognition, 28*(3,SI), 447–464. https://doi.org/10.1521/soco.2010.28.3.447

Markman, A. B., & Gentner, D. (2001). Thinking. *Annual Review of Psychology, 52* (1), 223–247.

Marks, L. J., & Kamins, M. A. (1988). The use of product sampling and advertising: Effects of sequence of exposure and degree of advertising claim exaggeration on consumers' belief strength, belief confidence, and attitudes. *Journal of Marketing Research, 25*(3), 266–281. https://doi.org/10.2307/3172529

Markus, H. R., & Kitayama, S. (1991). Culture and the self: Implications for cognition, emotion, and motivation. *Psychological Review, 98*, 224–253. https:// doi.org/10.1037/0033-295X.98.2.224

Marques, J. M., Abrams, D., & Serôdio, R. G. (2001). Being better by being right: Subjective group dynamics and derogation of in-group deviants when generic norms are undermined. *Journal of Personality and Social Psychology, 81*, 436–447. https://doi.org/10.1037/0022-3514.81.3.436

Martyniuk, U., & Štulhofer, A. (2018). A longitudinal exploration of the relationship between pornography use and sexual permissiveness in female and male adolescents. *Journal of Adolescence, 69*, 80–87. https://doi.org/10.1016/j.adolescence.2018.09.006

Mata, J., Dallacker, M., Vogel, T., & Hertwig, R. (2019). The role of attitudes in diet, eating, and body weight. In B. T. Albarracín & D. Johnson (Eds.), *Handbook of attitudes: Vol. 2. Applications* (2nd ed., pp. 67–91). Hoboken, NJ: John Wiley.

Mata, J., Todd, P. M., & Lippke, S. (2010). When weight management lasts. Lower perceived rule complexity increases adherence. *Appetite, 54*, 37–43. https://doi.org/10.1016/j.appet.2009.09.004

Matheson, H., White, N., & McMullen, P. (2015). Accessing embodied object representations from vision: A review. *Psychological Bulletin, 141*(3), 511–524. https://doi.org/10.1037/bul0000001

Mathew, R. J., Weinman, M. L., & Barr, D. L. (1984). Personality and regional cerebral blood flow. *British Journal of Psychiatry, 144*, 529–532. https://doi.org/10.1192/bjp.144.5.529

Matsumoto, D. (1987). The role of facial response in the experience of emotion: More methodological problems and a meta-analysis. *Journal of Personality and Social Psychology, 52*(4), 769.

Matthews, D., & Dietz-Uhler, B. (1998). The black-sheep effect: How positive and negative advertisements affect voters' perceptions of the sponsor of the advertisement 1. *Journal of Applied Social Psychology, 28*(20), 1903–1915.

Mayer, F. S., Duval, S., & Duval, V. H. (1980). An attributional analysis of commitment. *Journal of Personality and Social Psychology, 39*, 1072–1080. https://doi.org/10.1037/h0077726

Mazzocco, P. J., Green, M. C., Sasota, J. A., & Jones, N. W. (2010). This story is not for everyone: Transportability and narrative persuasion. *Social Psychological and Personality Science, 1*(4), 361–368. https://doi.org/10.1177/1948550610376600

McCulloch, K. C., Albarracín, D., & Durantini, M. R. (2008). A door to HIV-prevention interventions: How female-targeted materials can enhance female participation. *Journal of Applied Social Psychology, 38*(5), 1211–1229. https://doi.org/10.1111/j.1559-1816.2008.00345.x

McCulloch, K. C., Fitzsimons, G. M. G. M., Chua, S. N. S. N., & Albarracín, D. (2011). Vicarious goal satiation. *Journal of Experimental Social Psychology, 47*(3), 685–688. https://doi.org/10.1016/j.jesp.2010.12.019

McCulloch, K. C., Li, H., Hong, S., & Albarracín, D. (2012). Naïve definitions of action and inaction: The continuum, spread, and valence of behaviors. *European Journal of Social Psychology, 42*(2), 227–234. https://doi.org/10.1002/ejsp.860

McDonald, J., McDonald, P., Hughes, C., & Albarracín, D. (2017). Recalling and intending to enact health recommendations: Optimal number of prescribed behaviors in multibehavior messages. *Clinical Psychological Science, 5*(5), 858–865. https://doi.org/10.1177/2167702617704453

McEachan, R. R. C., Conner, M., Taylor, N. J., & Lawton, R. J. (2011). Prospective prediction of health-related behaviours with the theory of planned behaviour: A meta-analysis. *Health Psychology Review, 5*(2), 97–144.

McGregor, I., Newby-Clark, I. R., & Zanna, M. P. (1999). "Remembering" dissonance: Simultaneous accessibility of inconsistent cognitive elements moderates epistemic discomfort. In E. Harmon-Jones & J. Mills (Eds.), *Cognitive dissonance: Progress on a pivotal theory in social psychology* (pp. 325–353). Washington, DC: American Psychological Association.

McGuire, W. J. (1960). Cognitive consistency and attitude change. *Journal of Abnormal and Social Psychology, 60*, 345–353. https://doi.org/10.1037/h0048563

McGuire, W. J. (1961). Resistance to persuasion conferred by active and passive prior refutation of the same and alternative counterarguments. *Journal of Abnormal and Social Psychology, 63*, 326–332. https://doi.org/10.1037/h0048344

McGuire, W. J. (1968a). Personality and attitude change: An information-processing theory. *Psychological Foundations of Attitudes, 171*, 196.

McGuire, W. J. (1968b). Theory of the structure of human thought. In *Theories of cognitive consistency: A sourcebook* (pp. 140–162). Chicago, IL: Rand-McNally.

McGuire, W. J. (1972). Attitude change: The information-processing paradigm. In C. G. McClintock (Ed.), *Experimental social psychology* (pp. 108–141). New York, NY: Holt, Rinehart, and Winston.

McGuire, W. J. (1985). Attitudes and attitude change. In *The handbook of social psychology* (pp. 233–346). New York, NY: Random House.

McGuire, W. J., & McGuire, C. V. (1991). The affirmational versus negational self-concepts. In *The self: Interdisciplinary approaches* (pp. 107–120). New York, NY: Springer.

McGuire, W. J., & Papageorgis, D. (1961). The relative efficacy of various types of prior belief-defense in producing immunity against persuasion. *Journal of Abnormal and Social Psychology, 62*, 327–337. https://doi.org/10.1037/h0042026

McHale, S. M., Dariotis, J. K., & Kauh, T. J. (2003). Social development and social relationships in middle childhood. *Handbook of Psychology, 6*, 241–265. https://doi.org/10.1002/0471264385.wei0610

McKenzie, C. R. M., Liersch, M. J., & Finkelstein, S. R. (2006). Recommendations implicit in policy defaults. *Psychological Science, 17*(5), 414–420.

Medin, D. L., & Coley, J. D. (1998). Concepts and categorization. In *Perception and cognition at century's end: Handbook of perception and cognition* (pp. 403–439). San Diego, CA: Academic Press.

Meier, B. P., Schnall, S., Schwarz, N., & Bargh, J. A. (2012). Embodiment in social psychology. *Topics in Cognitive Science, 4*(4), 705–716. https://doi.org/10.1111/j.1756-8765.2012.01212.x

Mellers, B. A., Schwartz, A., Ho, K., & Ritov, I. (1997). Decision affect theory: Emotional reactions to the outcomes of risky options. *Psychological Science, 8*(6), 423–429.

Mellott, D. S., & Greenwald, A. G. (2000). But I don't feel old! Implicit self-esteem, age identity, and ageism in the elderly. Unpublished manuscript.

Melnyk, D., & Shepperd, J. A. (2012). Avoiding risk information about breast cancer. *Annals of Behavioral Medicine, 44,* 216–224. https://doi.org/10.1007/s12160-012-9382-5

Meslot, C., Gauchet, A., Allenet, B., François, O., & Hagger, M. S. (2016). Theory-based interventions combining mental simulation and planning techniques to improve physical activity: Null results from two randomized controlled trials. *Frontiers in Psychology, 7,* 1–16. https://doi.org/10.3389/fpsyg.2016.01789

Meugnot, A., Almecija, Y., & Toussaint, L. (2014). The embodied nature of motor imagery processes highlighted by short-term limb immobilization. *Experimental Psychology, 61*(3), 180–186. https://doi.org/10.1027/1618-3169/a000237

Meyers, R. J., & Smith, J. E. (1995). *Clinical guide to alcohol treatment: The community reinforcement approach.* New York, NY: Guilford Press.

Meyers-Levy, J., & Maheswaran, D. (2004). Exploring message framing outcomes when systematic, heuristic, or both types of processing occur. *Journal of Consumer Psychology, 14*(1–2), 159–167.

Miles, E., Miles, E., & Crisp, R. J. (2013). A meta-analytic test of the imagined contact hypothesis. *Group Processes and Intergroup Relations, 17*(1), 3–26. https://doi.org/10.1177/1368430213510573

Milfont, T. L., & Schultz, P. W. (2019). The role of attitudes in environmental issues. In B. T. Albarracín & D. Johnson (Eds.), *Handbook of attitudes: Vol. 2. Applications* (2nd ed., pp. 337–363). Hoboken, NJ: John Wiley.

Miller, N. E. (1944). Experimental studies of conflict. In J. M. Hunt (Ed.), *Personality and the behavior disorders* (pp. 431–465). N.p.: Ronald Press.

Monin, B., & Norton, M. I. (2003). Perceptions of a fluid consensus: Uniqueness bias, false consensus, false polarization, and pluralistic ignorance in a water conservation crisis. *Personality and Social Psychology Bulletin, 29*(5), 559–567.

Monroe, A. E., Dillon, K. D., Guglielmo, S., & Baumeister, R. F. (2018). It's not what you do, but what everyone else does: On the role of descriptive norms and subjectivism in moral judgment. *Journal of Experimental Social Psychology, 77,* 1–10. https://doi.org/10.1016/j.jesp.2018.03.010

Montoya, R. M., Horton, R. S., Vevea, J. L., Citkowicz, M., & Lauber, E. A. (2017). A re-examination of the mere exposure effect: The influence of repeated exposure on recognition, familiarity, and liking. *Psychological Bulletin, 143*(5), 459–498. https://doi.org/10.1037/bul0000085

Morales, A., Gandhi, N., Chan, M.-P. S., Lohmann, S., Sanchez, T., Brady, K. A., . . . Zhai, C. (2019). *Multi-attribute topic feature construction for social media-based prediction.* Paper presented at the IEEE International Conference on Big Data, Big Data 2018. https://doi.org/10.1109/BigData.2018.8622347

Moreland, R. L., & Levine, J. M. (1988). Group dynamics over time: Development and socialization in small groups. In J. E. McGrath (Ed.), *The *social psychology of time: New perspectives* (pp. 151–181). Thousand Oaks, CA: Sage.

Moscovici, S., & Zavalloni, M. (1969). The group as a polarizer of attitudes. *Journal of Personality and Social Psychology, 12*(2), 125.

Mostafa, M. M. (2013). More than words: Social networks' text mining for consumer brand sentiments. *Expert Systems with Applications, 40*(10), 4241–4251. https://doi.org/10.1016/j.eswa.2013.01.019

Müller, B. C. N., Ritter, S. M., Glock, S., Dijksterhuis, A., Engels, R. C. M. E., & van Baaren, R. B. (2016). Smoking-related warning messages formulated as questions positively influence short-term smoking behaviour. *Journal of Health Psychology, 21*(1), 60–68. https://doi.org/10.1177/1359105314522083

Mussweiler, T., Rüter, K., & Epstude, K. (2004). The ups and downs of social comparison: Mechanisms of assimilation and contrast. *Journal of Personality and Social Psychology, 87*, 832–844. https://doi.org/10.1037/0022-3514.87.6.832

Muthukrishnan, A. V. (2003). *Changing positive and negative attitudes.* Unpublished manuscript.

Muthukrishnan, A. V., Pham, M. T., & Mungalé, A. (1999). Comparison opportunity and judgment revision. *Organizational Behavior and Human Decision Processes, 80*, 228–251. https://doi.org/10.1006/obhd.1999.2859

Muthukrishnan, A. V., Pham, M. T., & Mungalé, A. (2001). Does greater amount of information always bolster attitudinal resistance? *Marketing Letters, 12*, 131–144. https://doi.org/10.1023/A:1011113002473

Nagy, E., & Molnar, P. (2004). Homo imitans or homo provocans? Human imprinting model of neonatal imitation. *Infant Behavior and Development, 27*(1), 54–63. https://doi.org/10.1016/j.infbeh.2003.06.004

Napolitano, M. A., Hayes, S., Bennett, G. G., Ives, A. K., & Foster, G. D. (2012). Using Facebook and text messaging to deliver a weight loss program to college students. *Obesity, 21*, 25–31.

Newby-Clark, I. R., McGregor, I., & Zanna, M. P. (2002). Thinking and caring about cognitive inconsistency: When and for whom does attitudinal ambivalence feel uncomfortable? *Journal of Personality and Social Psychology, 82*(2), 157.

Newcomb, T. M. (1943). *Personality and social change: Attitude formation in a student community.* Fort Worth, TX: Dryden Press.

Niederdeppe, J., Heley, K., & Barry, C. L. (2015). Inoculation and narrative strategies in competitive framing of three health policy issues. *Journal of Communication, 65*(5), 838–862. https://doi.org/10.1111/jcom.12162

Nisson, C., & Earl, A. (2016). Regulating food consumption: Action messages can help or hurt. *Appetite, 107*, 280–284. https://doi.org/10.1016/j.appet.2016.08.100

Noguchi, K., Albarracín, D., & Durantini, M. (2007). Non random attrition in health prevention programs: A meta-analysis of retention in HIV prevention interventions. *ACR North American Advances, 34*, 444–445.

Noguchi, K., Albarracín, D., Durantini, M. R., & Glasman, L. R. (2007). Who participates in which health promotion programs? A meta-analysis of motivations underlying enrollment and retention in HIV-prevention interventions. *Psychological Bulletin, 133*(6),955. https://doi.org/10.1037/0033-2909.133.6.955

Noguchi, K., Handley, I. M. I. M., & Albarracín, D. (2011). Participating in politics resembles physical activity: General action patterns in international archives, United States archives, and experiments. *Psychological Science, 22*(2), 235–242. https://doi.org/10.1177/0956797610393746

Nolder, C. J., & Blankenship, K. L. (2019). Application of attitudes research across domains. current state of knowledge and future directions. In B. T. Albarracín & D. Johnson (Eds.), *Handbook of attitudes: Vol. 2. Applications* (2nd ed., pp. 589–602). Hoboken, NJ: John Wiley.

NORC Center for Public Affairs. (2015). American attitudes toward substance use in the United States. Retrieved from www.apnorc.org/projects/Pages/HTML Repor ts/american-attitudes-toward-substance-use-in-the-united-states.aspx

Norman, D. A. (1983). Some observations on mental models. In *Mental models* (pp. 7–14).

Norman, K. L. (1976). A solution for weights and scale values in functional measurement. *Psychological Review, 83*, 80–84.

Nosek, B. A., Aarts, A. A., Anderson, J. E., Kappes, H. B., & Open Science Collaboration. (2015). Estimating the reproducibility of psychological science. *Science, 349*(6251), aac4716.

Nyhuis, M. (2012). The reduction problem of priming: An analysis of potential solutions. MS thesis, University of Twente. Retrieved from http://essay .utwente.nl/62293/

Nyhuis, M., Gosselt, J. F., & Rosema, M. (2016). The psychology of electoral mobilization: a subtle priming experiment. *Journal of Elections, Public Opinion and Parties, 26*(3), 293–311. https://doi.org/10.1080/17457289.2016.1160909

Ohira, H., Winton, W. M., & Oyama, M. (1998). Effects of stimulus valence on recognition memory and endogenous eyeblinks: Further evidence for positive-negative asymmetry. *Personality and Social Psychology Bulletin, 24*(9), 986–993.

Oliver, R. L. (1977). Effect of expectation and disconfirmation on postexposure product evaluations: An alternative interpretation. *Journal of Applied Psychology, 62*(4), 480.

Olson, J. C., & Dover, P. A. (1979). Disconfirmation of consumer expectations through product trial. *Journal of Applied Psychology, 64*(2), 179.

Olson, J. M., & Zanna, M. P. (1982). Repression-sensitization differences in responses to a decision. *Journal of Personality, 50*(1), 46–57. https://doi.org/10 .1111/j.1467-6494.1982.tb00744.x

Olson, M. A., & Fazio, R. H. (2004). Reducing the influence of extrapersonal associations on the Implicit Association Test: personalizing the IAT. *Journal of Personality and Social Psychology, 86*(5), 653.

Orbell, S., & Verplanken, B. (2015). The strength of habit. *Health Psychology Review, 9*, 311–317. https://doi.org/10.1080/17437199.2014.992031

Orehek, E., Mauro, R., Kruglanski, A. W., & van der Bles, A. M. (2012). Prioritizing association strength versus value: The influence of self-regulatory modes on means evaluation in single goal and multigoal contexts. *Journal of Personality and Social Psychology, 102*(1), 22–31. https://doi.org/10.1037/a0025881

Osgood, C. E. (1962). Studies on the generality of affective meaning systems. *American Psychologist, 17*(1), 10–28. https://doi.org/10.1037/h0045146

Ostafin, B. D., Bauer, C., & Myxter, P. (2012). Mindfulness decouples the relation between automatic alcohol motivation and heavy drinking. *Journal of Social and Clinical Psychology, 31*(7), 729–745. https://doi.org/10.1521/jscp.2012.31.7.729

Ostafin, B. D., & Marlatt, G. A. (2008). Surfing the urge: Experiential acceptance moderates the relation between automatic alcohol motivation and hazardous drinking. *Journal of Social and Clinical Psychology, 27*(4), 404–418. https://doi .org/10.1521/jscp.2008.27.4.404

Osterhouse, R. A., & Brock, T. C. (1970). Distraction increases yielding to propaganda by inhibiting counterarguing. *Journal of Personality and Social Psychology, 15*(4), 344+. https://doi.org/10.1037/h0029598

Oswald, F. L., Mitchell, G., Blanton, H., Jaccard, J., & Tetlock, P. E. (2013). Predicting ethnic and racial discrimination: A meta-analysis of IAT criterion studies. *Journal of Personality and Social Psychology, 105*(2), 171.

Ottati, V. C., & Wyer, R. S., Jr. (1993). Affect and political judgment. In S. Iyengar & W. J. McGuire (Eds.), *Duke studies in political psychology: Explorations in political psychology* (pp. 296–315). Durham, NC: Duke University Press.

Ottati, V., Edwards, J. R., & Krumdick, N. D. (2005). Attitude theory and research: intradisciplinary and interdisciplinary connections. In D. Albarracín, B. T. Johnson, & M. P. Zanna (Eds.), *The handbook of attitudes* (pp. 707–742). New York, NY: Psychology Press.

Ouellette, J. A., & Wood, W. (1998). Habit and intention in everyday life: The multiple processes by which past behavior predicts future behavior. *Psychological Bulletin, 124*, 54–74. https://doi.org/10.1037/0033-2909.124.1.54

Pacherie, E. (2008). The phenomenology of action: A conceptual framework. *Cognition, 107*(1), 179–217. https://doi.org/10.1016/j.cognition.2007.09.003

Paek, H. J., Kim, S., Hove, T., & Huh, J. Y. (2014). Reduced harm or another gateway to smoking Source, message, and information characteristics of E-cigarette videos on YouTube. *Journal of Health Communication, 19*, 545–560. https://doi.org/10.1080/10810730.2013.821560

Paluck, E. L., & Shepherd, H. (2012). The salience of social referents: A field experiment on collective norms and harassment behavior in a school social network. *Journal of Personality and Social Psychology, 103*(6), 899–915. https://doi .org/http://dx.doi.org/10.1037/a0030015

Papageorgis, D., & McGuire, W. J. (1961). The generality of immunity to persuasion produced by pre-exposure to weakened counterarguments. *Journal of Abnormal and Social Psychology, 62*, 475–481. https://doi.org/10.1037 /h0048430

Patry, A. L., & Pelletier, L. G. (2001). Extraterrestrial beliefs and experiences: An application of the theory of reasoned action. *Journal of Social Psychology, 141*(2), 199–217. https://doi.org/10.1080/00224540109600547

Payne, B. K., Cheng, C. M., Govorun, O., & Stewart, B. D. (2005). An inkblot for attitudes: Affect misattribution as implicit measurement. *Journal of Personality*

and Social Psychology, *89*(3), 277–293. https://doi.org/10.1037/0022-3514
.89.3.277

Peck, J., & Childers, T. L. (2003). Individual differences in haptic information
processing: The "Need for Touch{"} scale. *Journal of Consumer Research, 30*(3),
430–442. https://doi.org/10.1086/378619

Perkins, M. B., Jensen, P. S., Jaccard, J., Gollwitzer, P., Oettingen, G.,
Pappadopulos, E., & Hoagwood, K. E. (2007). Applying theory-driven approaches
to understanding and modifying clinicians' behavior: What do we know?
Psychiatric Services, 58(3), 342–348. https://doi.org/10.1176/appi.ps.58.3.342

Peters, E., Dieckmann, N., Dixon, A., Hibbard, J. H., & Mertz, C. K. (2007).
Less is more in presenting quality information to consumers. *Medical Care
Research and Review, 64*(2), 169–190. https://doi.org/10.1177
/1077558707064002030I

Peters, K., & Kashima, Y. (2015). A multimodal theory of affect diffusion. *Psychological
Bulletin, 141*(5), 966–992. https://doi.org/10.1037/bul0000020

Petty, R. E., Brinol, P., & DeMarree, K. G. (2007). The meta-cognitive model
(MCM) of attitudes: Implications for attitude measurement, change, and
strength. *Social Cognition, 25*(5), 657–686. https://doi.org/10.1521/soco
.2007.25.5.657

Petty, R. E., Tormala, Z. L., Briñol, P., & Jarvis, W. B. G. (2006). Implicit ambivalence from attitude change: An exploration of the PAST model. Journal of
Personality and Social Psychology, 90(1), 21–41. https://doi.org/10.1037/0022-
3514.90.1.21

Petty, R. E., Brinol, P., & Tormala, Z. L. (2002). Thought confidence as
a determinant of persuasion: The self-validation hypothesis. *Journal of Personality
and Social Psychology, 82*(5), 722–741. https://doi.org/10.1037//0022-3514.82.5.722

Petty, R. E., & Cacioppo, J. T. (1986a). *Communication and persuasion: Central
and peripheral routes to attitude change*. New York, NY: Springer.

Petty, R. E., & Cacioppo, J. T. (1986b). The elaboration likelihood model of
persuasion. *Advances in Experimental Social Psychology, 19*, 124–192. https://doi
.org/10.1016/S0065-2601(08)60214-2

Petty, R. E., & Cacioppo, J. T. (1990). Involvement and persuasion: Tradition
versus integration. *Psychological Bulletin, 107*, 367–374. https://doi.org/10.1037
/0033-2909.107.3.367

Petty, R. E., Wells, G. L., & Brock, T. C. (1976). Distraction can enhance or
reduce yielding to propaganda: Thought disruption versus effort justification.
Journal of Personality and Social Psychology, 34, 874–884. https://doi.org/10.1037
/0022-3514.34.5.874

Pfister, R., Janczyk, M., & Kunde, W. (2013). Editorial: Action effects in perception and action. *Frontiers in Psychology, 4*. https://doi.org/10.3389/fpsyg
.2013.00223

Pham, M. T. (1998). Representativeness, relevance, and the use of feelings in
decision making. *Journal of Consumer Research, 25*(2), 144–159. https://doi.org
/10.1086/209532

Pham, M. T., & Muthukrishnan, A. V. (2002). Search and alignment in judgment revision: Implications for brand positioning. *Journal of Marketing Research, 39* (1), 18–30. https://doi.org/10.1509/jmkr.39.1.18.18929

Pierro, A., Mannetti, L., Erb, H. P., Spiegel, S., & Kruglanski, A. W. (2005). Informational length and order of presentation as determinants of persuasion. *Journal of Experimental Social Psychology, 41*(5), 458–469. https://doi.org/10.1016 /j.jesp.2004.09.003

Pierro, A., Mannetti, L., Kruglanski, A. W., Klein, K., & Orehek, E. (2012). Persistence of attitude change and attitude-behavior correspondence based on extensive processing of source information. *European Journal of Social Psychology, 42*(1), 103–111. https://doi.org/10.1002/ejsp.853

Pierro, A., Mannetti, L., Kruglanski, A. W., & Sleeth-Keppler, D. (2004). Relevance override: On the reduced impact of "cues{"} under high-motivation conditions of persuasion studies. *Journal of Personality and Social Psychology, 86*(2), 251–264. https://doi.org/10.1037/0022-3514 .86.2.251

Pratkanis, A. R., Greenwald, A. G., Leippe, M. R., & Baumgardner, M. H. (1988). In search of reliable persuasion effects: III. The sleeper effect is dead: Long live the sleeper effect. *Journal of Personality and Social Psychology, 54*(2), 203.

Praxmarer, S. (2011). Message strength and persuasion when consumers imagine product usage. *Journal of Consumer Behavior, 231,* 225–231. https://doi.org/10 .1002/cb

Prentice, D. A., & Miller, D. T. (1993). Pluralistic ignorance and alcohol use on campus. Some consequences of misperceiving the social norm. *Journal of Personality and Social Psychology, 64*(2), 243–256. https://doi.org/10.1037/0022- 3514.64.2.243

Prislin, R., & Wood, W. (2005). Social influence in attitudes and attitude change. In D. Albarracín, B. T. Johnson, & M. P. Zanna (Eds.), *The handbook of attitudes* (pp. 671–705). Mahwah, NJ: Erlbaum.

Prochaska, J. O., DiClemente, C. C., & Norcross, J. C. (1992). In search of the structure of change. In *Self change* (pp. 87–114). Berlin, Germany: Springer.

Prochaska, J. O., Redding, C. A., Harlow, L. L., Rossi, J. S., & Velicer, W. F. (1994). The transtheoretical model of change and HIV prevention: A review. *Health Education Quarterly, 21*(4), 471–486.

Putnam, R. (1993). The prosperous community: Social capital and public life. *The American Prospect, 13*(4). Retrieved from www.prospect.org/print/vol/13

Rampell, C. (2011, September 1). Do parents put too much pressure on students? *New York Times.*

Reddit. (n.d.). In *Wikipedia.* Retrieved from http://en.wikipedia.org/wiki/Reddit

Regan, D. T., & Fazio, R. H. (1977). Consistency between attitudes and behavior: Look to method of attitude formation. *Journal of Experimental Social Psychology, 13*(1), 28–45. https://doi.org/10.1016/0022-1031(77)90011-7

Reid, A. E., Cialdini, R. B., & Aiken, L. S. (2010). Social norms and health behavior. In *Handbook of behavioral medicine* (pp. 263–274). New York, NY: Springer. https://doi.org/10.1007/978-0-387-09488-5_19

Remington, N. A., Fabrigar, L. R., & Visser, P. S. (2000). Reexamining the circumplex model of affect. *Journal of Personality and Social Psychology, 79*(2), 286.

Rice, T. W., & Pepper, M. L. (1997). Region migration, and attitudes in the United States. *Social Science Quarterly, 78*(1), 83–95.

Richardson, A., & Vallone, D. M. (2014). YouTube: A promotional vehicle for little cigars and cigarillos? *Tobacco Control, 23*, 21–26. https://doi.org/10.1136/tobaccocontrol-2012-050562

Richardson-Klavehn, A., & Bjork, R. A. (1988). Measures of memory. *Annual Review of Psychology, 39*(1), 475–543.

Rinck, M., & Becker, E. S. (2007). Approach and avoidance in fear of spiders. *Journal of Behaviour Therapy and Experimental Psychiatry, 38*, 105–120. https://doi.org/10.1016/j.jbtep.2006.10.001

Robinson, J. P., Shaver, P. R., & Wrightsman, L. S. (1999). *Measures of political attitudes*. New York, NY: Academic Press.

Roese, N. J. (2004). Twisted pair: Counterfactual thinking and the hindsight bias. In *Blackwell handbook of judgment and decision making* (pp. 258–273). Malden, MA: Blackwell.

Roese, N. J., Hur, T., & Pennington, G. L. (1999). Counterfactual thinking and regulatory focus: Implications for action versus inaction and sufficiency versus necessity. *Journal of Personality and Social Psychology, 77*(6), 1109–1120. https://doi.org/10.1037/0022-3514.77.6.1109

Roese, N. J., & Olson, J. M. (1997). Counterfactual thinking: The intersection of affect and function. *Advances in Experimental Social Psychology, 29*, 1–59. https://doi.org/10.1016/S0065-2601(08)60015-5

Ronis, D. L., Yates, J. F., & Kirscht, J. P. (1989). Attitudes, decisions, and habits as determinants of repeated behavior. In A. R. Pratkanis, S. J. Breckler, & A. G. Greenwald (Eds.), *Attitude structure and function* (pp. 213–239). Hillsdale, NJ, Lawrence Erlbaum.

Rosario, A. B., Sotgiu, F., De Valck, K., & Bijmolt, T. H. A. (2016). The effect of electronic word of mouth on sales: A meta-analytic review of platform, product, and metric factors. *Journal of Marketing Research, 53*(3), 297–318. https://doi.org/10.1509/jmr.14.0380

Rosenberg, M. J. (1960a). Cognitive reorganization in response to the hypnotic reversal of attitudinal affect. *Journal of Personality, 28*, 39–63.

Rosenberg, M. J. (1960b). Inconsistency arousal and reduction in attitude change. *Public Opinion Quarterly, 24*, 319–340.

Rossano, M. J., & Reardon, W. P. (1999). Goal specificity and the acquisition of survey knowledge. *Environment and Behavior, 31*(3), 395–412. https://doi.org/10.1177/00139169921972164

Rucker, D. D., & Petty, R. E. (2004). When resistance is futile: Consequences of failed counterarguing for attitude certainty. *Journal of Personality and Social Psychology, 86*(2), 219–235. https://doi.org/10.1037/0022-3514.86.2.219

Rumelhart, D. (1994). Schemata and the cognitive system. In R. S. Wyer (Ed.), *Handbook of social cognition* (pp. 1–40). Mahwah, NJ: Erlbaum.

Rumelhart, D. E. (2018). Schemata: The building blocks of cognition. *Theoretical issues in Reading Comprehension*, *11*, 33–58. https://doi.org/10.4324/9781315107493-4

Rumelhart, D. E., & McClelland, J. L. (1986). On learning the past tenses of English verbs.

Russell, J. A. (2003). Core affect and the psychological construction of emotion. *Psychological Review*, *110*(1), 145.

Sanbonmatsu, D. M., Kardes, F. R., & Gibson, B. D. (1991). The role of attribute knowledge and overall evaluations in comparative judgment. *Organizational Behavior and Human Decision Processes*, *48*(1), 131–146. https://doi.org/10.1016/0749-5978(91)90009-I

Schachter, S. (1951). Deviation, rejection, and communication. *Journal of Abnormal and Social Psychology*, *46*(2), 190–207. https://doi.org/10.1037/h0062326

Schifter, D. E., & Ajzen, I. (1985). Intention, perceived control, and weight loss: An application of the theory of planned behavior. *Journal of Personality and Social Psychology*, *49*(3), 843–851. https://doi.org/10.1037/0022-3514.49.3.843

Schimmack, U., & Crites, S. L. (2005). The structure of affect. In D. Albarracín, B. T. Johnson, & M. P. Zanna (Eds.), *The handbook of attitudes* (pp. 397–435). New York, NY: Psychology Press.

Schmidt, M. F. H., Butler, L. P., Heinz, J., & Tomasello, M. (2016). Young children see a single action and infer a social norm: Promiscuous normativity in 3-year-olds. *Psychological Science*, *27*(10), 1360–1370. https://doi.org/10.1177/0956797616661182

Schroeder, C. M., & Prentice, D. A. (1998). Exposing pluralistic ignorance to reduce alcohol use among college students. *Journal of Applied Social Psychology*, *28*(23), 2150–2180. https://doi.org/10.1111/j.1559-1816.1998.tb01365.x

Schultz, P. W., Nolan, J. M., Cialdini, R. B., Goldstein, N. J., Schultz, P. W., Nolan, J. M., . . . Griskevicius, V. (2019). The constructive, destructive, and reconstructive power of social norms. *Psychological Sciences*, *18*(5), 429–434.

Schwartz, H. A. (2016). Predicting well-being through the language of social media. In *Pacific Symposium on Biocomputing* (pp. 516–527). Retrieved from http://psb.stanford.edu/psb-online/proceedings/psb16/schwartz.pdf

Schwartz, H. A., Eichstaedt, J. C., Kern, M. L., Dziurzynski, L., Ramones, S. M., Agrawal, M., . . . Ungar, L. H. (2013). Personality, gender, and age in the language of social media: The open-vocabulary approach. *PloS ONE*, *8*(9), e73791. https://doi.org/10.1371/journal.pone.0073791

Schwarz, N. (1999). Self-reports: How the questions shape the answers. *American Psychologist*, *54*(2), 93.

Schwarz, N., & Bless, H. (1992). Assimilation and contrast effects in attitude measurement: An inclusion/exclusion model. *ACR North American Advances*, *19*, 72–77.

Schwarz, N., Bless, H., Strack, F., Klumpp, G., Rittenauer-Schatka, H., & Simons, A. (1991). Ease of retrieval as information: Another look at the availability heuristic. *Journal of Personality and Social Psychology, 61*, 195–202. https://doi.org/10.1037/0022-3514.61.2.195

Schwarz, N., & Bohner, G. (2001). The construction of attitudes. In *Blackwell handbook of social psychology: Intraindividual processes* (Vol. 1, pp. 436–457). Malden, MA: Blackwell.

Schwarz, N., & Clore, G. L. (1983). Mood, misattribution, and judgments of well-being: Informative and directive functions of affective states. *Journal of Personality and Social Psychology, 45*(3), 513–523. https://doi.org/10.1037/0022-3514 .45.3.513

Schwarz, N., & Clore, G. L. (2007). Feelings and phenomenal experiences. In *Social psychology: Handbook of basic principles* (pp. 385–407). New York, NY: Guilford Press. https://doi.org/10.1023/A:1021223113233

Schwarz, N., & Oyserman, D. (2001). Asking questions about behavior: Cognition, communication, and questionnaire construction. *The American Journal of Evaluation, 22*(2), 127–160.

Schwarz, N., & Scheuring, B. (1992). Frequency-reports of psychosomatic symptoms: What respondents learn from response alternatives. *Zeitschrift für Klinische Psychologie, 22*, 197–208.

Seidenberg, A. B., Rodgers, E. J., Rees, V. W., & Connolly, G. N. (2012). Youth access, creation, and content of smokeless tobacco ("dip") videos in social media. *Journal of Adolescent Health, 50*, 334–338. https://doi.org/10.1016/j .jadohealth.2011.09.003

Seligman, M. (2018). PERMA and the building blocks of well-being. *Journal of Positive Psychology, 13*, 333–335. https://doi.org/10.1080/17439760.2018.1437466

Senay, I., Albarracín, D., & Noguchi, K. (2010). Motivating goal-directed behavior through introspective self-talk: The role of the interrogative form of simple future tense. *Psychological Science, 21*, 499–504. https://doi.org/10.1177 /0956797610364751

Seske, K. (2012). Type 1 diabetes and its effects on active/inactive goal priming for exercise. John Wesley Powell Student Research Conference 2. http://digitalcom mons.iwu.edu/jwprc/2012/oralpres3/2

Sevincer, A. T., & Oettingen, G. (2009). Alcohol breeds empty goal commitments. *Journal of Abnormal Psychology, 118*(3), 623–633. https://doi.org /10.1037/a0016199

Shah, J. Y., Fishbach, A., Friedman, R., Chun, W. Y., & Sleeth-Keppler, D. (2002). A Theory of goal systems. *Advances in Experimental Social Psychology, 34*, 331–378. https://doi.org/10.2307/2092805

Shah, J. Y., Friedman, R., & Kruglanski, A. W. (2002). Forgetting all else: On the antecedents and consequences of goal shielding. *Journal of Personality and Social Psychology, 83*, 1261–1280. https://doi.org/10.1037/0022-3514.83.6.1261

Shah, J. Y., & Kruglanski, A. W. (2000). Aspects of goal networks. In *Handbook of self-regulation* (pp. 85–110). San Diego, CA: Academic Press. https://doi.org/10 .1016/B978-012109890-2/50033-0

Shah, J. Y., & Kruglanski, A. W. (2002). Priming against your will: How accessible alternatives affect goal pursuit. *Journal of Experimental Social Psychology, 38*(4), 368–383. https://doi.org/10.1016/S0022-1031(02)00005-7

Shah, J. Y., Kruglanski, A. W., & Friedman, R. (2003). Goal systems theory: Integrating the cognitive and motivational aspects of self-regulation. In S. J. Spencer, S. Fein, M. P. Zanna, & J. Olson (Eds.), *Motivated social perception: Ontario symposium* (Vol. 9, pp. 247–275). Mahwah, NJ: Erlbaum.

Shank, D. B., Peters, K., Li, Y., Robins, G., & Kirley, M. (2019). Norm talk and human cooperation: Can we talk ourselves into cooperation? *Journal of Personality and Social Psychology, 117*(1), 99–123.

Shavitt, S. (1989). Operationalizing functional theories of attitude. In A. R. Pratkanis, S. J. Breckler, & A. G. Greenwald (Eds.), *Attitude structure and function* (pp. 311–337). Hillsdale, NJ, Lawrence Erlbaum.

Shavitt, S., Lalwani, A. K., Zhang, J., & Torelli, C. J. (2006). The horizontal/vertical distinction in cross-cultural consumer research. *Journal of Consumer Psychology, 16*(4), 325–342. https://doi.org/10.1207/s15327663jcp1604_3

Sheeran, P., Godin, G., Conner, M., & Germain, M. (2017). Paradoxical effects of experience: Past behavior both strengthens and weakens the intention-behavior relationship. *Journal of the Association for Consumer Research, 2*(3), 309–318. https://doi.org/10.1086/691216

Sheridan, S. L., Halpern, D. J., Viera, A. J., Berkman, N. D., Donahue, K. E., & Crotty, K. (2011). Interventions for individuals with low health literacy: A systematic review. *Journal of Health Communication, 16*, 30–54. https://doi.org/10.1080/10810730.2011.604391

Sherif, M., & Hovland, C. (1961). *Social judgment: Assimilation and contrast effects in communication and attitude change.* New Haven, CT: Yale University Press.

Sherif, M., & Sherif, C. (1936). The psychology of social norms. *Journal for the Theory of Social Behaviour.* https://doi.org/10.1111/j.1468-5914.2011.00472.x

Sherman, D. K., Gangi, C., & White, M. L. (2010). Embodied cognition and health persuasion: Facilitating intention – behavior consistency via motor manipulations. *Journal of Experimental Social Psychology, 46*(2), 461–464. https://doi.org/10.1016/j.jesp.2009.12.008

Shigehisa, T., & Symons, J. R. (1973). Effect of intensity of visual stimulation on auditory sensitivity in relation to personality. *British Journal of Psychology, 64*(2), 205–213.

Silvestrini, N., & Gendolla, G. H. E. (2013). Automatic effort mobilization and the principle of resource conservation: One can only prime the possible and justified. *Journal of Personality and Social Psychology, 104*(5), 803.

Simmons, J. P., & Nelson, L. D. (2006). Intuitive confidence: Choosing between intuitive and nonintuitive alternatives. *Journal of Experimental Psychology: General, 135*(3), 409.

Simons-Morton, B. (2004). Prospective association of peer influence, school engagement, drinking expectancies, and parent expectations with drinking initiation among sixth graders. *Addictive Behaviors, 29*(2), 299–309. https://doi.org/10.1016/j.addbeh.2003.08.005

Singelis, T. M., Triandis, H. C., Bhawuk, D. P. S., & Gelfand, M. J. (1995). Horizontal and vertical dimensions of individualism and collectivism: A theoretical and measurement refinement. *Cross-Cultural Research*, *29*(3), 240–275. https://doi.org/10.1177/106939719502900302

Sivacek, J., & Crano, W. D. (1982). Vested interest as a moderator of attitude-behavior consistency. *Journal of Personality and Social Psychology*, *43*(2), 210–221. https://doi.org/10.1037//0022-3514.43.2.210

Skurka, C., Niederdeppe, J., & Romero-Canyas, R. (2018). Pathways of influence in emotional appeals: Benefits and tradeoffs of using fear or humor to promote climate change-related intentions and risk perceptions. *Journal of Communication*, *68*, 169–193. https://doi.org/10.1093/joc/jqx008

Slater, M. D., & Rouner, D. (2002). Entertainment education and elaboration likelihood: Understanding the processing of narrative persuasion. *Communication Theory*, *12*(2), 173–191.

Slater, M., Sadagic, A., Usoh, M., & Schroeder, R. (2000). Small-group behavior in a virtual and real environment: A comparative study. *Presence: Teleoperators and Virtual Environments*, *9*, 37–51. https://doi.org/10.1162/105474600566600

Smith, E. R. (1989). Procedural efficiency: General and specific components and effects on social judgment. *Journal of Experimental Social Psychology*, *25*(6), 500–523. https://doi.org/10.1016/0022-1031(89)90003-6

Smith, E. R. (1994). Procedural knowledge and processing strategies in social cognition. *Handbook of Social Cognition*, *1*, 99–151.

Smith, E. R., Branscombe, N. R., & Bormann, C. (1988). Generality of the effects of practice on social judgment tasks. *Journal of Personality and Social Psychology*, *54*(3), 385.

Smith, E. R., Fazio, R. H., & Cejka, M. A. (1996). Accessible attitudes influence categorization of multiply categorizable objects. *Journal of Personality and Social Psychology*, *71*(5), 888.

Smith, R. E., & Swinyard, W. R. (1988). Cognitive response to advertising and trial: Belief strength, belief confidence and product curiosity. *Journal of Advertising*, *17*(3), 3–14. https://doi.org/10.1080/00913367.1988.10673118

Smith, S. M., Haugtvedt, C. P., & Petty, R. E. (1994). Need for cognition and the effects of repeated expression on attitude accessibility and extremity. In D. Allen & C. T. John (Eds.), *Advances in consumer research* (Vol. 21, pp. 234–237). Provo, UT: Association for Consumer Research.

Snyder, M. (1974). Self-monitoring of expressive behavior. *Journal of Personality and Social Psychology*, *30*, 526–537. https://doi.org/10.1037/h0037039

Soussignan, R. (2002). Duchenne smile, emotional experience, and autonomic reactivity: A test of the facial feedback hypothesis. *Emotion*, *2*(1), 52–74. https://doi.org/10.1037/1528-3542.2.1.52

Sparkman, G., & Walton, G. M. (2019). Witnessing change: Dynamic norms help resolve diverse barriers to personal. *Journal of Experimental Social Psychology*, *82*, 238–252. https://doi.org/10.1016/j.jesp.2019.01.007

Spencer-Rodgers, J., Boucher, H. C., Mori, S. C., Wang, L., & Peng, K. (2009). The dialectical self-concept: Contradiction, change, and holism in East Asian cultures. *Personality and Social Psychology Bulletin*, *35*(1), 29–44. https://doi.org/10.1177/0146167208325772

Spencer-Rodgers, J., Peng, K., & Wang, L. (2010). Dialecticism and the co-occurrence of positive and negative emotions across cultures. *Journal of Cross-Cultural Psychology*, *41*(1), 109–115. https://doi.org/10.1177/0022022109349508

Spencer-Rodgers, J., Williams, M. J., & Peng, K. (2010). Cultural differences in expectations of change and tolerance for contradiction: A decade of empirical research. *Personality and Social Psychology Review*, *14*(3), 296–312. https://doi.org/10.1177/1088868310362982

Staats, C. K., & Staats, A. W. (1957). Meaning established by classical conditioning. *Journal of Experimental Psychology*, *54*(1), 74.

Stecker, T., Fortney, J., Hamilton, F., Sherbourne, C. D., & Ajzen, I. (2010). Engagement in mental health treatment among veterans returning from Iraq. *Patient Preference and Adherence*, *4*, 45–49.

Stecula, D., Kuru, O., Albarracín, D., & Jamieson, K. H. (in press). Policy views and negative beliefs about vaccines in the United States, 2019. *American Journal of Public Health*.

Steele, C. M., & Liu, T. J. (1981). Making the dissonant act unreflective of self: Dissonance avoidance and the expectancy of a value-affirming response. *Personality and Social Psychology Bulletin*, *7*(3), 393–397.

Steinmetz, H., Knappstein, M., Ajzen, I., Schmidt, P., & Kabst, R. R. (2016). How effective are behavior change interventions based on the theory of planned behavior? A three-level meta-analysis. *Zeitschrift für Psychologie*, *224*(3), 216–233. https://doi.org/10.1027/2151-2604/a000255

Stern, C., & Ondish, P. (2019). Political attitudes. In B. T. Albarracín & D. Johnson (Eds.), *Handbook of attitudes: Vol. 2. Applications* (2nd ed., pp. 488–523). Hoboken, NJ: John Wiley.

Stone, J., & Cooper, J. (2001). A self-standards model of cognitive dissonance. *Journal of Experimental Social Psychology*, *37*, 228–243. https://doi.org/10.1006/jesp.2000.1446

Strahan, E. J., Spencer, S. J., & Zanna, M. P. (2002). Subliminal priming and persuasion: Striking while the iron is hot. *Journal of Experimental Social Psychology*, *38*(6), 556–568. https://doi.org/10.1016/S0022-1031(02)00502-4

Streicher, M. C., & Estes, Z. (2016). ScienceDirect Shopping to and fro: Ideomotor compatibility of arm posture and product choice. *Journal of Consumer Psychology*, *26*(3), 325–336. https://doi.org/10.1016/j.jcps.2015.12.001

Suitner, C., Giacomantonio, M., & Maass, A. (2015). Embodied social cognition. In *International encyclopedia of the social and behavioral sciences* (2nd ed., Vol. 7). Oxford, England: Elsevier. https://doi.org/10.1016/B978-0-08-097086-8.24056-7

Sunderrajan, A., & Albarracín, D. (2017). How to initiate adoption of healthy behaviors: Action, inaction, and intentionality. Unpublished manuscript.

Suri, G., Sheppes, G., Leslie, S., & Gross, J. J. (2014). Stairs or escalator? Using theories of persuasion and motivation to facilitate healthy decision making.

Journal of Experimental Psychology: Applied, 20(4), 295–302. https://doi.org/10.1037/xap0000026

Swann, W. B., Pelham, B. W., & Chidester, T. R. (1988). Change through paradox: Using self-verification to alter beliefs. *Journal of Personality and Social Psychology, 54*(2), 268.

Sweeny, K., Melnyk, D., Miller, W., & Shepperd, J. A. (2010). Information avoidance: Who, what, when, and why. *Review of General Psychology, 14,* 340–353. https://doi.org/10.1037/a0021288

Sweeny, K., & Rankin, K. (2019). The role of attitudes in cancer. In B. T. Albarracín & D. Johnson (Eds.), *Handbook of attitudes: Vol. 2. Applications* (2nd ed., pp. 3–30). Hoboken, NJ: John Wiley.

Symbaluk, D. G., Heth, C. D., Cameron, J., & Pierce, W. D. (1997). Social modeling, monetary incentives, and pain endurance: The role of self-efficacy and pain perception. *Personality and Social Psychology Bulletin, 23,* 258–269. https://doi.org/10.1177/0146167297233005

Tait, A. R., Voepel-Lewis, T., Zikmund-Fisher, B. J., & Fagerlin, A. (2010). Presenting research risks and benefits to parents: Does format matter? *Anesthesia and Analgesia, 111*(3), 718–723. https://doi.org/10.1213/ANE.0b013e3181e8570a

Tait, R. J., Hulse, G. K., Waterreus, A., Flicker, L., Lautenschlager, N. T., Jamrozik, K., & Almeida, O. P. (2007). Effectiveness of a smoking cessation intervention in older adults. *Addiction (Abingdon, England), 102,* 148–155. https://doi.org/10.1111/j.1360-0443.2006.01647.x

Takahashi, K. J., & Earl, A. (2019). Effect of extraneous affect on health message reception. *Personality and Social Psychology Bulletin, 46,* 270–284. https://doi.org/10.1177/0146167219855042

Takarada, Y., & Nozaki, D. (2014). Maximal voluntary force strengthened by the enhancement of motor system state through barely visible priming words with reward. *PLoS ONE, 9*(10). https://doi.org/10.1371/journal.pone.0109422

Tannenbaum, M. B., Hepler, J., Zimmerman, R. S. R. S., Saul, L., Jacobs, S., Wilson, K., & Albarracín, D. (2015). Appealing to fear: A meta-analysis of fear appeal effectiveness and theories. *Psychological Bulletin, 141*(6), 1178–1204. https://doi.org/10.1037/a0039729

Taub, J. M. (1998). Eysenck's descriptive and biological theory of personality: a review of construct validity. *International Journal of Neuroscience, 94*(3–4), 145–197.

Tausczik, Y. R., & Pennebaker, J. W. (2010). The psychological meaning of words: LIWC and computerized text analysis methods. *Journal of Language and Social Psychology, 29,* 24–54. https://doi.org/10.1177/0261927X09351676

Taylor, S. E., & Schneider, S. K. (1989). Coping and the simulation of events. *Social Cognition, 7*(2), 174–194. https://doi.org/10.1521/soco.1989.7.2.174

Technology Review. (2019, January 23). *The average American spends 24 hours a week online.* Retrieved from www.technologyreview.com/f/610045/the-average-american-spends-24-hours-a-week-online/

Terry, D. J., Hogg, M. A., & White, K. M. (1999). The theory of planned behaviour: Self-identity, social identity and group norms. *British Journal of Social Psychology, 38*, 225–244. https://doi.org/10.1348/014466699164149

Tesser, A. (1978). Self-generated attitude change. *Advances in Experimental Social Psychology, 11*, 289–338. https://doi.org/10.1016/S0065-2601(08)60010-6

Tesser, A., & Leone, C. (1977). Cognitive schemas and thought as determinants of attitude change. *Journal of Experimental Social Psychology, 13*, 340–356. https://doi.org/10.1016/0022-1031(77)90004-X

Tesser, A., Whitaker, D., Martin, L., & Ward, D. (1998). Attitude heritability, attitude change and physiological responsivity. *Personality and Individual Differences, 24*(1), 89–96.

Time. (2018). Donald Trump approval rating graph. Retrieved from https://time.com/5103776/donald-trump-approval-rating-graph/

Tom, G., Pettersen, P., Lau, T., Burton, T., & Cook, J. (1991). The role of overt head movement in the formation of affect. *Basic and Applied Social Psychology, 12*, 281–289. https://doi.org/10.1207/s15324834basp1203_3

Tormala, Z. L., Brinol, P., Petty, R. E., Horcajo, J., Petty, R. E., & Brinol, P. (2007). Changing beliefs and behavior through experience-taking. *Journal of Personality and Social Psychology, 99*(3), 562–572.

Tormala, Z. L., & Petty, R. E. (2002). What doesn't kill me makes me stronger: The effects of resisting persuasion on attitude certainty. *Journal of Personality and Social Psychology, 83*(6), 1298–1313. https://doi.org/10.1037//0022-3514.83.6.1298

Tormala, Z. L., & Petty, R. E. (2004). Resisting persuasion and attitude certainty: A meta-cognitive analysis. In J. Knowles & E. S. Linn (Eds.), *Resistance and persuasion* (pp. 65–82). Mahwah, NJ: Erlbaum.

Treadwell, J. R., & Nelson, T. O. (1996). Availability of information and the aggregation of confidence in prior decisions. *Organizational Behavior and Human Decision Processes, 68*(1), 13–27. https://doi.org/10.1006/obhd.1996.0086

Triandis, H. C. (2005). Issues in individualism and collectivism research. In *Cultural and social behavior: The Ontario symposium* (Vol. 10, pp. 207–225). Mahwah, NJ: Erlbaum.

Triandis, H. C., & Gelfand, M. J. (1998). Converging measurement of horizontal and vertical individualism and collectivism. *Journal of Personality and Social Psychology, 74*(1), 118–128. https://doi.org/10.1037/0022-3514.74.1.118

Triandis, H. C., & Suh, E. M. (2002). Cultural influences on personality. *Annual Review of Psychology, 53*, 133–160. https://doi.org/10.1146/annurev.psych.53.100901.135200

Trope, Y., & Liberman, N. (2010). Construal-level theory of psychological distance. *Psychological Review, 117*(2), 440.

Tsakiris, M., & Haggard, P. (2005). Experimenting with the acting self. *Cognitive Neuropsychology, 22*(3–4), 387–407. https://doi.org/10.1080/02643290442000158

Tuk, M. A., Zhang, K., & Sweldens, S. (2015). The propagation of self-control: Self-control in one domain simultaneously improves self-control in other domains. *Journal of Experimental Psychology: General, 144*(3), 639–654. https://doi.org/10.1037/xge0000065

Turney, P. D. (2002). Thumbs up or thumbs down? Semantic orientation applied to unsupervised classification of reviews. In *Proceedings of the 40th annual meeting of the Association for Computational Linguistics* (pp. 417–424).

Turner, J. C. (1985). Social categorization and the self concept: A social cognitive theory of group behavior. *Advances in Group Process*, pp. 243–272.

Turner-McGrievy, G., & Tate, D. (2011). Tweets, apps, and pods: Results of the 6-month Mobile Pounds Off Digitally (Mobile POD) randomized weight-loss intervention among adults. *Journal of Medical Internet Research, 13*(4), e120–e120. https://doi.org/10.2196/jmir.1841

Tversky, A., & Kahneman, D. (1973). Availability: A heuristic for judging frequency and probability. *Cognitive Psychology, 5*, 207–232. https://doi.org/10.1016/0010-0285(73)90033-9

Tyson, M., Covey, J., & Rosenthal, H. E. S. (2014). Theory of planned behavior interventions for reducing heterosexual risk behaviors: A meta-analysis. *Health Psychology, 33*, 1454–1467. https://doi.org/10.1037/hea0000047

Valins, S. (1966). Cognitive effects of false heart-rate feedback. *Journal of Personality and Social Psychology, 4*(4), 400.

Vallacher, R. R. (2014). *A theory of action identification.* New York, NY: Taylor and Francis. https://doi.org/10.4324/9781315802213

Vallacher, R. R., & Wegner, D. M. (2012). Action identification theory. In *Handbook of theories of social psychology* (Vol. 1, pp. 327–348). London, England: Sage. https://doi.org/10.4135/9781446249215.n17

Valle, C. G., Tate, D. F., Mayer, D. K., Allicock, M., & Cai, J. (2013). A randomized trial of a Facebook-based physical activity intervention for young adult cancer survivors. *Journal of Cancer Survivorship: Research and Practice, 7*(3), 355–368. https://doi.org/10.1007/s11764-013-0279-5

Vallerand, R. J. (1997). Toward a hierarchical model of intrinsic and extrinsic motivation. *Advances in Experimental Social Psychology, 29*, 271–360.

van Baaren, R. B., Holland, R. W., Steenaert, B., & van Knippenberg, A. (2003). Mimicry for money: Behavioral consequences of imitation. *Journal of Experimental Social Psychology, 39*(4), 393–398. https://doi.org/10.1016/S0022-1031(03)00014-3

van Baaren, R. B., Maddux, W. W., Chartrand, T. L., de Bouter, C., & van Knippenberg, A. (2003). It takes two to mimic: Behavioral consequences of self-construals. *Journal of Personality and Social Psychology, 84*(5), 1093–1102. https://doi.org/10.1037/0022-3514.84.5.1093

Van Harreveld, F., der Pligt, J., de Vries, N. K., Wenneker, C., & Verhue, D. (2004). Ambivalence and information integration in attitudinal judgment. *British Journal of Social Psychology, 43*(3), 431–447.

van Kleef, E., Shimizu, M., & Wansink, B. (2011). Food compensation: Do exercise ads change food intake? *International Journal of Behavioral Nutrition and Physical Activity, 8*(1), 6. https://doi.org/10.1186/1479-5868-8-6

van Laer, T., de Ruyter, K., Visconti, L. M., & Wetzels, M. (2014). The extended transportation-imagery model: A meta-analysis of the antecedents and consequences of consumers' narrative transportation. *Journal of Consumer Research*, *40*, 797–817. https://doi.org/10.1086/673383

Vreeman, R. C., Scanlon, M. L., Tu, W., Slaven, J. E., McAteer, C. I., Kerr, S. J., . . . Nyandiko, W. M. (2019). Validation of a self-report adherence measurement tool among a multinational cohort of children living with HIV in Kenya, South Africa and Thailand. *Journal of the International AIDS Society*, *22* (5), e25304. https://doi.org/10.1002/jia2.25304

Wallace, D. S., Paulson, R. M., Lord, C. G., & Bond, C. F., Jr. (2005). Which behaviors do attitudes predict? Meta-analyzing the effects of social pressure and perceived difficulty. *Review of General Psychology*, *9*(3), 214–227.

Walton, D., Reed, C., & Macagno, F. (2008). *Argumentation schemes*. Cambridge, England: Cambridge University Press. https://doi.org/10.1017 /CBO9780511802034

Wanke, M., Bless, H., & Biller, B. (1996). Subjective experience versus content of information in the construction of attitude judgments. *Personality and Social Psychology Bulletin*, *22*(11), 1105–1113.

Wasserman, T. (2013). *Exclusive: Report says YouTube overtakes Facebook among teens*. Retrieved from http://Mashable.Com/2013/11/05/Teens-Facebook-y Outube-Most-Popular/#qCZoq_GYXakL. Nov. 5, 2013.

Watson, D., & Tellegen, A. (1985). Toward a consensual structure of mood. *Psychological Bulletin*, *98*(2), 219.

Watson, D., & Tellegen, A. (1999). Issues in dimensional structure of affect effects of descriptors, measurement error, and response formats: Comment on Russell and Carroll (1999). *Psychological Bulletin*, *125*, 601–610.

Wegener, D. T., Clark, J. K., & Petty, R. E. (2019). Cognitive and meta-cognitive processes in attitude formation and change. In B. T. Albarracín & D. Johnson (Eds.), *Handbook of attitudes: Vol. 1. Basic principles* (2nd ed., pp. 291–331). Hoboken, NJ: John Wiley.

Wegener, D. T., Petty, R. E., Blankenship, K. L., & Detweiler-Bedell, B. (2010). Elaboration and numerical anchoring: Breadth, depth, and the role of (non-) thoughtful processes in anchoring theories. *Journal of Consumer Psychology*, *20* (1), 28–32. https://doi.org/10.1016/j.jcps.2009.12.007

Wegner, D. M., Fuller, V. A., & Sparrow, B. (2003). Clever hands: Uncontrolled intelligence in facilitated communication. *Journal of Personality and Social Psychology*, *85*, 5–19. https://doi.org/10.1037/0022-3514.85.1.5

Wegner, D. M., & Sparrow, B. (2004). Authorship processing. In M. S. Gazzaniga (Ed.), *The cognitive neurosciences* (pp. 1201–1209). Boston, MA: Boston Review.

Wegner, D. M., Sparrow, B., & Winerman, L. (2004). Vicarious agency: Experiencing control over the movements of others. *Journal of Personality and Social Psychology*, *86*, 838–848. https://doi.org/10.1037/0022-3514.86.6.838

Weingarten, E., Chen, Q., McAdams, M., Yi, J., Hepler, J., & Albarracín, D. (2016a). From primed concepts to action: A meta-analysis of the behavioral effects of incidentally presented words. *Psychological Bulletin, 142*(5), 472–497. https://doi.org/10.1037/bul0000030

Weingarten, E., Chen, Q., McAdams, M., Yi, J., Hepler, J., & Albarracín, D. (2016b). On priming action: Conclusions from a meta-analysis of the behavioral effects of incidentally-presented words. *Current Opinion in Psychology, 12,* 53–57. https://doi.org/10.1016/j.copsyc.2016.04.015

Wells, G. L., & Petty, R. E. (1980). The effects of overt head movements on persuasion: Compatibility and incompatibility of responses. *Basic and Applied Social Psychology, 1*(3), 219–230. https://doi.org/10.1207/s15324834basp0103_2

White, B. X., & Albarracín, D. (2018). Investigating belief falsehood. Fear appeals do change behaviour in experimental laboratory studies: A commentary on Kok et al. (2018). *Health Psychology Review, 12*(2), 147–150. https://doi.org/10.1080/17437199.2018.1448292

White, B. X., Chan, M. S., Repetto, A., Gratale, S., Cappella, J. N., & Albarracín, D. (2019). The role of attitudes in the use of tobacco, alcohol, and cannabis. In B. T. Albarracín & D. Johnson (Eds.), *Handbook of attitudes: Vol. 2. Applications* (2nd ed., pp. 31–66). Hoboken, NJ: John Wiley.

White, B. X., Jiang, D., & Albarracín, D. (2019). *The impact of choice time on the in by default advantage.* Unpublished manuscript.

Wiebe, J. (2000). *Learning subjective adjectives from corpora.* Paper presented at the 17th National Conference on Artificial Intelligence (AAAI-2000), Austin, TX.

Wiener, N. (2011). *Cybernetics, or control and communication in the animal and the machine* (2nd ed.). Washington, DC: American Psychological Association. https://doi.org/10.1037/13140-000

Wigboldus, D. H. J., Holland, R. W., & van Knippenberg, A. (2004). Single target implicit associations. Unpublished manuscript.

Wiggins, N., Hoffman, P. J., & Taber, T. (1969). Types of judges and cue utilization in judgments of intelligence. *Journal of Personality and Social Psychology, 12*(1), 52.

Wilder, D. A. (1977). Perception of groups, size of opposition, and social influence. *Journal of Experimental Social Psychology, 13,* 253–268. https://doi.org/10.1016/0022-1031(77)90047-6

Wilson, K., & Albarracín, D. (2015). Barriers to accessing HIV-prevention in clinic settings: Higher alcohol use and more sex partners predict decreased exposure to HIV-prevention counseling. *Psychology, Health, and Medicine, 20* (1), 87–96. https://doi.org/10.1080/13548506.2014.902484

Wilson, K., Durantini, M. R., Albarracín, J., Crause, C., Albarracín, D., Albarracín, J., ... Albarracín, D. (2013). Reducing cultural and psychological barriers to Latino enrollment in HIV-prevention counseling: Initial data on an enrollment meta-intervention. *AIDS Care, 25*(7), 881–887. https://doi.org/10.1080/09540121.2012.729803

Wilson, K., Senay, I., Durantini, M., Sánchez, F., Hennessy, M., Spring, B., & Albarracín, D. (2015). When it comes to lifestyle recommendations, more is sometimes less: A meta-analysis of theoretical assumptions underlying the effectiveness of interventions promoting multiple behavior domain change. *Psychological Bulletin, 141*(2), 474–509. https://doi.org/10.1037/a0038295

Wilson, T. D., Gilbert, G. T., & Wheathey, T. P. (1998). Protecting our minds: The role of lay beliefs. In V. Y. Yzerbyt, & G. Lories (Eds.), *Metacognition: Cognitive and social dimensions* (pp. 171–201). Thousand Oaks, CA: Sage Publications.

Wood, W., Lundgren, S., Ouellette, J. A., Busceme, S., & Blackstone, T. (1994). Minority influence. A meta-analytic review of social-influence processes. *Psychological Bulletin, 115*(3), 323–345. https://doi.org/10.1037/0033-2909 .115.3.323

Wood, W., Pool, G. J., Leck, K., & Purvis, D. (1996). Self-definition, defensive processing, and influence: The normative impact of majority and minority groups. *Journal of Personality and Social Psychology, 71*, 1181–1193. https://doi .org/10.1037/0022-3514.71.6.1181

Wood, W., Quinn, J. M., & Kashy, D. A. (2002). Habits in everyday life: Thought, emotion, and action. *Journal of Personality and Social Psychology, 83* (6), 1281–1297. https://doi.org/10.1037//0022-3514.83.6.1281

Wood, W., Tam, L., & Witt, M. G. (2005). Changing circumstances, disrupting habits. *Journal of Personality and Social Psychology, 88*(6), 918.

Wright, A. A., & Lynch, J. G. (1995). Communication effects of advertising versus direct experience when both search and experience attributes and present. *Journal of Consumer Research, 21*(4), 708–718. https://doi.org/10.1086/209429

Wyer, R. S., Jr. (1974a). *Cognitive organization and change: An information-processing approach.* Hillsdale, NJ: Erlbaum.

Wyer, R. S. (1974b). Some implications of Socratic effect for alternative models of cognitive consistency. *Journal of Personality, 42*(3), 399–419. https://doi.org/10 .1111/j.1467-6494.1974.tb00683.x

Wyer, R. S., Jr. (2015). The mental representation of persons, events, and behavioral mindsets. In J. Stroessner & S. J. Sherman (Eds.), *Social perception from individuals to groups* (pp. 29–51). New York, NY: Psychology Press.

Wyer, R. S., Jr. (2016). Priming decisions and motor behavior. *Current Opinion in Psychology, 12*, 76–79.

Wyer, R. S., Jr. (2019). Some determinants and consequences of beliefs: Cognitive, social, and motivational. In B. T. Albarracín & D. Johnson (Eds.), *Handbook of attitudes: Vol. 1. Basic principles* (2nd ed., pp. 332–376). Hoboken, NJ: John Wiley.

Wyer, R. S., & Albarracín, D. (2005). Belief formation, organization, and change: Cognitive and motivational influences. In D. Albarracín, B. T. Johnson, & M. P. Zanna (Eds.), *The handbook of attitudes* (pp. 273–322). New York, NY: Psychology Press.

Wyer, R. S., Budesheim, T. L., & Lambert, A. J. (1990). Cognitive representations of conversations about persons. *Journal of Personality and Social Psychology, 58* (2), 218–238. https://doi.org/10.1037/0022-3514.58.2.218

Wyer, R. S., Budesheim, T. L., Lambert, A. J., & Swan, S. (1994). Person memory and judgment. Pragmatic influences on impressions formed in a social context.

Journal of Personality and Social Psychology, 66(2), 254–267. https://doi.org/10.1037/0022-3514.66.2.254

Wyer, R. S., Jr., Clore, G. L., & Isbell, L. M. (1999). Affect and information processing. *Advances in Experimental Social Psychology, 31*, 1–77. https://doi.org/10.1016/S0065-2601(08)60271-3

Wyer, R. S., & Goldberg, L. (1970). Probabilistic analysis of relationships among beliefs and attitudes. *Psychological Review, 77*(2), 100–120. https://doi.org/10.1037/h0028769

Wyer, R. S., Jr., & Srull, T. K. (1989). *Memory and cognition in its social context.* New York, NY: Psychology Press.

Xu, A. J., & Wyer, R. S., Jr. (2009). The comparative mindset: From animal comparisons to increased purchase intentions. *Advances in Consumer Research, 36*, 594.

Xu, X., Leung, D. Y. P., Li, B., Wang, P., & Zhao, Y. (2015). Smoking-related knowledge, attitude, social pressure, and environmental constraints among new undergraduates in Chongqing, China. *International Journal of Environmental Research and Public Health, 12*(1), 895–909. https://doi.org/10.3390/ijerph120100895

Yan, C., Dillard, J. P., & Shen, F. (2010). The effects of mood, message framing, and behavioral advocacy on persuasion. *Journal of Communication, 60*, 344–363. https://doi.org/10.1111/j.1460-2466.2010.01485.x

Ybarra, O., & Trafimow, D. (1998). How priming the private self or collective self affects the relative weights of attitudes and subjective norms. *Personality and Social Psychology Bulletin, 24*(4), 362–370. https://doi.org/10.1177/0146167298244003

YouTube. (n.d.) Press [Web page]. Retrieved from www.youtube.com/yt/press/

Youyou, W., Kosinski, M., & Stillwell, D. (2015). Computer-based personality judgments are more accurate than those made by humans. *Proceedings of the National Academy of Sciences, 112*(4), 1036–1040. https://doi.org/10.1073/pnas.1418680112

Zajonc, R. B. (1968). Attitudinal effects of mere exposure. *Journal of Personality and Social Psychology, 9*(2, Pt. 2), 1.

Zanna, M. P., & Cooper, J. (1974). Dissonance and pill: Attribution approach to studying arousal properties of dissonance. *Journal of Personality and Social Psychology, 29*(5), 703–709. https://doi.org/10.1037/h0036651

Zell, E., Su, R., Li, H., Ho, M. H. R., Hong, S., Kumkale, T., . . . Albarracín, D. (2013). Cultural differences in attitudes toward action and inaction: The role of dialecticism. *Social Psychological and Personality Science, 4*(5), 521–528. https://doi.org/10.1177/1948550612468774

Zell, E., Warriner, A. B., & Albarracín, D. (2012). Splitting of the mind: When the You I talk to is Me and needs commands. *Social Psychological and Personality Science, 3*, 549–555. https://doi.org/10.1177/1948550611430164

Zemore, S. E., & Ajzen, I. (2014). Predicting substance abuse treatment completion using a new scale based on the theory of planned behavior. *Journal of*

Substance Abuse Treatment, 46(2), 174–182. https://doi.org/10.1016/j .jsat.2013.06.011

Zgierska, A., Rabago, D., Chawla, N., Kushner, K., Koehler, R., & Marlatt, A. (2009). Mindfulness meditation for substance use disorders: A systematic review. *Substance Abuse, 30*(4), 266–294. https://doi.org/10.1080 /08897070903250019

Zhang, S., & Markman, A. B. (2001). Processing product unique features: Alignability and involvement in preference construction. *Journal of Consumer Psychology, 11*(1), 13–27. https://doi.org/10.1207/S15327663JCP1101_2

Zhou, Z., Yu, R., & Zhou, X. (2010). To do or not to do? Action enlarges the FRN and P300 effects in outcome evaluation. *Neuropsychologia, 48*, 3606–3613. https://doi.org/10.1016/j.neuropsychologia.2010.08.010

Ziegler, R., & Diehl, M. (2011). Mood and multiple source characteristics: Mood congruency of source consensus status and source trustworthiness as determinants of message scrutiny. *Personality and Social Psychology Bulletin, 37*(8), 1016–1030. https://doi.org/10.1177/0146167211410438

Index

CPSIA information can be obtained
at www.ICGtesting.com
Printed in the USA
BVHW091953071222
653680BV00008B/90